ECONOMIC ANALYSIS OF LAW

RICHARD A. POSNER

PROFESSOR OF LAW, UNIVERSITY OF CHICAGO

Little, Brown and Company

Boston　　1972　　Toronto

*Published simultaneously in Canada
by Little, Brown & Company (Canada) Limited*

PRINTED IN THE UNITED STATES OF AMERICA

TABLE OF CONTENTS

PART II
PUBLIC REGULATION OF THE MARKET

PART III
THE REGULATION OF BUSINESS ORGANIZATIONS AND FINANCIAL MARKETS

PART IV
LAW AND THE DISTRIBUTION OF INCOME AND WEALTH

PART V
THE CONSTITUTION AND THE FEDERAL SYSTEM

PART VI
THE LEGAL PROCESS

PREFACE

In recent years economists, and academic lawyers with a bent for economic analysis, have used the theoretical and empirical methods of economics to illuminate a variety of issues and problems in the law. Formerly law and economics intersected only in the fields of antitrust and public utility regulation; today the diligent reader of scholarly journals can also find economic analyses of crime control, accident law, contract damages, race relations, judicial administration, corporations and securities regulation, environmental problems, and other areas of central concern in the contemporary legal system. The growing importance of economics in legal education is indicated by the appointment of economists to the faculties of many law schools and by the gradual suffusion of law school courses with economic reasoning and evidence.

Because economics is a technical discipline (and becoming more so all the time), the introduction of economics into legal education and scholarship has created difficulties for those law students and teachers — the majority — who do not have a good grounding in the subject. Their difficulties are compounded by the absence of any textbook addressed to them. There are two obvious possibilities for filling the gap. The first would be another elementary economics text — but one that emphasized those areas of economics having particular relevance to the law and that contained legal illustrations. The second would be a book of excerpts from the law-economics literature. This book, however, adopts a third approach, although one that attempts to combine the strengths of the other two. It weaves exposition of the relevant economic principles into a systematic (although necessarily incomplete) survey of the rules and institutions of the legal system. This procedure enables the principal findings of the scholarly literature on the application of economics to law to be summarized and in places extended, free from forbidding technical jargon or inappropriate detail; and it forces the reader to confront economics not as a body of abstract theory but as a practical tool of analysis with a remarkably broad application to the varied problems of the legal system. The emphasis on concrete application rather than abstract theory should be congenial to the law student trained by the case method. The relentless if not complete suppression in the book of the jargon of modern welfare economics ("Pareto optimality" and the like) is designed to prevent the student from confusing economic analysis with the mastery of a vocabulary.

The book is mainly designed for use either as a textbook in a law school course in economic analysis of law[1] or as supplementary reading for law students who are interested in finding out what economics may have to add to their understanding of the legal process. Law students who wish to study economics more systematically may find the book a suitable introduction to two excellent but difficult textbooks on price theory.[2] While I have written primarily with the law student (and teacher) in mind, little prior knowledge of law is presupposed, and so the book may be of some interest to economics and business students interested in exploring the relevance of economics to law. Finally, I should like to think that the book might attract an audience of lawyers and economists professionally interested in the relevance of economics to law, since, as mentioned, the book not only summarizes the literature of economic analysis of law, but also adds to it in some areas.

Since many law teachers are not accustomed to teaching from textbooks, a word on methods of using this book in a classroom may be in order. The text is, I hope, sufficiently clear in most places that the instructor will not be obligated to translate it into still simpler terms for his students. He should be able to use class time to probe the depths of the students' understanding, both by putting questions to them based on the text and by working through with them the problems that appear in footnotes and at the end of chapters; many of the problems carry the analysis

1. Many law schools now have optional courses for first-year students in their last semester or quarter. A course on economic analysis of law might be an appropriate candidate for the optional first-year course. Part II of the book (Public Regulation of the Market) should probably be omitted in such a course. However, the remaining parts would be suitable, with Parts III (The Regulation of Business Organizations and Financial Markets), IV (Law and the Distribution of Income and Wealth), and V (The Constitution and the Federal System) serving as introductions to second- and third-year courses in corporations, securities regulation, federal income taxation, law and poverty, and constitutional law.

2. Gary S. Becker, Economic Theory (1971); George J. Stigler, The Theory of Price (3d ed. 1966).

into areas not covered by the text. The instructor will also want to use class time to explore the limitations of economic analysis, as both an interpretive and a normative tool. I have not emphasized these limitations in the text, in part to provoke student and instructor to challenge it by formulating and arguing those limitations. I predict that students will undertake the task with relish.

The bibliographical references in the footnotes and at the end of the chapters will help the reader who wishes to explore the literature of law and economics more deeply to do so.[3]

I am grateful to Fischer Black, Walter J. Blum, Ronald H. Coase, Harold Demsetz, Richard A. Epstein, Owen M. Fiss, Stanley A. Kaplan, Hein D. Kötz, Henry G. Manne, Bernard D. Meltzer, and George J. Stigler for their helpful comments on portions of earlier drafts. My other debts are acknowledged in the bibliographical references, with some important exceptions. Harold Demsetz, in conversation and in a seminar on property rights that he gave at the University of Chicago Law School in 1970, made a significant contribution to the view of the common law developed in Part I of the book. The analysis of antitrust law presented in Chapter 7 has been influenced by the work, mostly unpublished (under his own name), of Aaron Director. My greatest debt is to those who through their writings and conversation have enriched my general understanding of economic theory and of the relationship of economics to law: Gary S. Becker, Ronald H. Coase, Aaron Director, and George J. Stigler.

Richard A. Posner

March 1973

---

3. Besides these references, mention should be made of Gordon Tullock, The Logic of the Law (1971), which discusses a number of legal topics, including contracts, crime, and evidence, mainly from an economic viewpoint.

ECONOMIC ANALYSIS OF LAW

CHAPTER 1

THE ECONOMIC APPROACH TO LAW

This book is written in the conviction that economics is a powerful tool for analyzing a broad range of questions of legal interpretation and policy but that most lawyers — even very bright lawyers — and most law students — even very bright ones — have difficulty connecting economic precepts to concrete legal problems. A student takes a course in price theory and learns what happens to the price of wheat when the price of corn falls and to the price of grazing land when the price of beef rises; but he does not understand what these things have to do with free speech or accidents or crime or the Rule Against Perpetuities or corporate indentures. The design of this book is to anchor discussion of economic theory in concrete, numerous, and varied legal questions; the discussion of economic theory in the abstract is confined to this chapter.

§1.1. *The nature of economic reasoning.* Economics is the science of human choice in a world in which resources are limited in relation to human wants. It explores and tests the implications of the assumption that man is a rational maximizer of his ends in life, his satisfactions — what we shall call his "self-interest." (Self-interest should not be confused with selfishness: the welfare of other people may be a part of one's satisfactions.)

It is implicit in the definition of man as a rational maximizer of his self-interest that people respond to incentives — that if you change a person's surroundings so that he could increase his satisfactions by altering his behavior, most of the time he will do so. From the proposition that people's behavior can be altered by changing their incentives we derive three fundamental economic concepts. The first is that of the inverse relation between price charged and quantity demanded.[1] Let the price of steak

§1.1. 1. Actually, it has been shown that the law of demand can be deduced from the fact of scarcity of goods; consumer rationality is not a necessary as-

rise by ten cents a pound. If other prices remain unchanged, a steak will now cost the consumer more, relatively, than it did before. How will he, being rational and self-interested, react? By investigating the possibility of substituting goods that he preferred less when steak was at its old price but that are more attractive now because they are cheaper relative to steak. Many consumers will continue to buy as much steak as before; for them, other goods are not good substitutes even at somewhat lower relative prices. But some purchasers will reduce their purchases of steak and substitute other meats (or other foods, or different products altogether).

In general, then, if the price of one product rises and all other prices remain unchanged, the quantity of the product demanded by purchasers, and hence the amount produced, will decline.[2] This is one of the fundamental predictions of economic theory and it has many applications to the legal system. The convicted criminal who has served his sentence is said to have "paid his debt to society." An economist would find the metaphor apt. Punishment is the price that society charges for a criminal offense. The economist is led to predict that an increase in either the severity of the punishment or the likelihood of its being imposed will raise the price of crime and therefore reduce its incidence. The criminal will be encouraged to substitute other activity.[3]

The consumers in our beef example — and the criminal — were assumed to be trying to maximize their utility (satisfactions). The same is presumably true of the producers of beef, although in the case of sellers one usually speaks of profit maximization rather than utility maximization. Sellers seek to maximize the difference between their costs and their sales revenues, but for the moment we are interested only in the lowest price that a rational self-interested seller would charge. That minimum is the price that the resources consumed in making (and selling) the seller's product would command in their next best

---

sumption. Gary S. Becker, Economic Theory 19–23 (1971). This is one of many refinements that we will ignore in order to simplify exposition.

For a graphic presentation of the law of demand see Figure 1, §6.1 infra.

2. As with many propositions in economics, this one must be qualified in order to be completely accurate. For example, if the demand for the product were increasing (meaning what?) at the same time that its price was rising, the quantity demanded might not decline, and might even increase. Demonstrate this result graphically. (Hint: cf. Figure 1, §6.1 infra.)

3. A fuller discussion of the economic theory of punishment may be found infra Chapter 25.

use — the alternative price. It is what the economist means by the "cost" of a good, and suggests why a rational seller (subject to some exceptions that need not trouble us here) will not sell below cost.

Let us explore the concept of cost equal to alternative price — our second basic concept — a little more deeply. The cost of making a lawn mower is the price the manufacturer must pay for the labor, materials, and other resources consumed in making it. That price must equal or exceed the price at which the resources could have been sold to the next highest bidder for them: had our manufacturer not been willing to meet or beat that price, he would not have been the high bidder and would not have obtained the resources. (We postpone the complication that is introduced when the sellers of the resources price them higher than *their* alternative prices.)

A corollary of the notion of cost as alternative price is that a cost is incurred only when someone is denied the use of a resource. Since I can breathe as much air as I want without depriving anyone of all the air he wants to breathe, no one will pay me to relinquish my air to him. Therefore, air is costless.[4] So is a good with only one use. (Can you see why?) Cost to the economist is "opportunity cost" — the benefit forgone by employing a resource in a way that denies its use to someone else.

Our discussion of cost should help dispel one of the most tenacious fallacies about economics — that it is about money. On the contrary, it is about resource use, money being merely a claim on resources.[5] The economist distinguishes between transactions that affect the use of resources, whether or not money changes hands, and purely pecuniary transactions — "transfer payments." Housework is an economic activity, even if the houseworker is a wife who does not receive pecuniary compensation. It involves cost — primarily the opportunity cost of the housewife's time. In contrast, the transfer by taxation of $1000 from me to a poor (or to a rich) family *may* be a pure money transaction that does not affect the use of resources, although this is unlikely. The transfer diminishes my purchasing power but increases the recipient's by the same amount. If we have the same spending pattern and it is unaffected by the transfer, if the

---

4. That is not to say that *clean* air is costless. Cf. §2.6 *infra*.

5. Laymen attach more significance to money than economists. One of Adam Smith's great achievements was to demonstrate that mercantilism, the policy of trying to maximize a country's gold reserves, would impoverish rather than enrich the country that followed it.

transfer has no effects on our incentives to work, and if no administrative costs are involved in effecting the transfer, then resource use will not be affected. The transfer is in fact quite likely to have economic effects: it may deter me from working as hard, or, if the recipient has different tastes in spending or saving, it may alter the demands for various goods. But a money transfer per se is not a social cost.[6] (When might it affect resource use but still be costless?)

The third basic concept, which is also derived from reflection on how self-interested people react to a change in their surroundings, is the tendency of resources to gravitate toward their highest valued uses if exchange is permitted. Why did the manufacturer of lawn mowers pay more for labor and materials than competing users of these resources? Assuming he is rational, it must be because he thought he could use them to obtain a higher price for his finished good than could competing demanders. They were worth more to him. Why does farmer A offer to buy farmer B's farm at a price higher than B's minimum price for the property? Because the property is worth more to A than to B: meaning, A can use it to produce a more valuable output as measured by the prices that consumers are willing to pay. By a process of voluntary exchange, resources are shifted to those uses in which the value to the consumer, as measured by the consumer's willingness to pay, is highest. When resources are being used where their value is greatest, we may say that they are being employed efficiently.

Despite the use of terms like "value" and "efficiency," economics cannot tell us how society should be managed. Efficiency is a technical term: it means exploiting economic resources in such a way that human satisfaction as measured by aggregate consumer willingness to pay for goods and services is maximized. Value too is defined by willingness to pay. Willingness to pay is in turn a function of the existing distribution of income and wealth in the society. Were income and wealth distributed in a different pattern, the pattern of demands might also be different and efficiency would require a different deployment of our economic resources. The economist cannot tell us whether the existing distribution of income and wealth is just,[7] although he may be able to tell us something about the costs of altering it as well as about the distributive consequences of various policies. Nor

---

6. It does, of course, represent a cost to the individual — a "private cost."
7. A question we reconsider, however, in Chapter 15.

can he tell us whether, assuming the existing distribution is just, consumer satisfaction should be the dominant value of society. The economist's competence in a discussion of the legal system is limited to predicting the effect of legal rules and arrangements on value and efficiency, in their strict technical senses, and on the existing distribution of income and wealth.

The reader may be troubled by what may appear to him to be the severely unrealistic assumptions that underlie economic theory. The notion of a rational self-interested man conjures up the image of an utterly selfish, ruthlessly calculating individual unlike anyone encountered in real life. Economic theory is quite flexible enough to allow for, and to analyze the effects of, altruism.[8] Its normal assumption is no stronger than that most people in most affairs of life are guided by what they conceive to be their self-interest and that they choose means reasonably (not perfectly) designed to promote it. Although the assumptions of economic theory are to some extent, certainly, oversimplified and unrealistic as descriptions of human behavior, there is abundant evidence that theories derived from those assumptions have considerable power in predicting how people in fact behave.

In one important respect, moreover, the economist admits, indeed asserts, a considerable variety in human response. If the noneconomist is asked what people will do if the price of pork doubles he is apt to reply either that no one will buy pork anymore or that no one will stop buying pork. The economist thinks in terms of continuous functions: he expects some people to stop buying pork altogether; some to buy much less; some to buy slightly less; some to buy as much. Criminologists often classify people in just two groups: law abiding and criminal. The economist's presumption is that some people are law abiding in the sense that they would not commit crimes even if the penalties were much milder than they are; others would continue to commit as many crimes even if the penalties were a good deal stronger; and still others, perhaps a majority, would commit more or fewer crimes as the severity of the penalty changed.

The reader who understands the three fundamental concepts introduced in this section — the inverse relationship between price and output, alternative or opportunity cost, and the tendency of resources to gravitate from lower valued to higher valued uses if voluntary exchange is permitted — is prepared to deal with a surprising variety of economic questions. Subsequent

8. See §18.2 *infra.*

chapters will present additional concepts deduced from the assumption of man as rational maximizer, but they will pose few difficulties to the reader who has conscientiously mastered the three fundamental concepts.

§*1.2.   The relevance of economics to law.*   Economics turns out to be a powerful tool of normative analysis of law and legal institutions — a source of criticism and reform. This statement is not inconsistent with the point stressed in the previous section that the economist is not the ultimate arbiter of social choice. He cannot tell society whether it should seek to limit theft, but he can show that it would be inefficient to allow unlimited theft. Or, taking a goal of limiting theft as a given, the economist may be able to show that the means by which society has attempted to attain that goal are inefficient — that society could obtain more prevention, at lower cost, using different methods. Since efficiency is a widely regarded value in our world of limited resources, a persuasive showing that one course of action is more efficient than the alternatives may be an important factor in shaping public choice.

The normative role of economic analysis in the law is fairly obvious. The positive role — that of explaining the rules and outcomes in the legal system as they are — is less obvious, but not less important. As we shall see, many areas of the law, especially the great common law fields of property, torts, and contracts, bear the stamp of economic reasoning. Few legal opinions, to be sure, contain explicit references to economic concepts and few judges have a substantial background in economics. But the true grounds of decision are often concealed rather than illuminated by the characteristic rhetoric of judicial opinions. Indeed, legal education consists primarily of learning to dig beneath the rhetorical surface to find those grounds. It is an advantage of economic analysis rather than a drawback that it does not analyze cases in the conceptual modes employed in the opinions themselves.

Nor is it correct that only a trained economist can behave in accordance with the predictions of economic theory. Economic theory is designed to predict the behavior not of economists but of businessmen, consumers, and others who generally know little of economics. Since judges are frequently called upon to decide cases in which economic factors are inescapable, it is not surprising that they should frequently decide in accordance with an intuitive perception of cost and efficiency.

But do not the lawyer and the economist approach the same case in such different ways as to suggest a basic incompatibility between law and economics? X is shot by a careless hunter, Y. The only question in which the parties and their lawyers are interested, the only question tendered to the judge and jury, is whether the cost of the injury should be shifted from X to Y — whether it is "just" or "fair" that X should receive compensation. X's lawyer will argue that it is just that X be compensated since Y was at fault and X blameless. Y's lawyer may argue that X was also careless and hence that it would be just for the loss to remain on X. Not only are justice and fairness not economic concepts, but the economist is not interested in the one question that concerns the victim and his lawyer: who should bear the costs of *this* accident? To the economist, the accident is a closed chapter. The costs that it inflicted are "sunk" costs that cannot be retrieved by a transfer payment from the injurer to the victim (why?). The economist is interested in methods of preventing future accidents and thus reducing accident costs but the parties to the litigation have no interest in the future. Their concern is limited to the financial consequences of a past accident.

The dichotomy is overstated. The decision in the case will affect the future, and so should interest the economist, because it will confirm or establish a rule for the guidance of people engaged in dangerous activities. The decision is a warning that if one behaves in a certain way and an accident results, he will have to pay a judgment (or will be unable to obtain a judgment, if the victim). By thus altering the prices that confront people, the warning may affect their behavior and therefore accident costs.

Conversely, the judge (and hence the lawyer) in the case cannot ignore the future. Since any ruling of law will constitute a precedent, the judge must consider the probable impact of alternative rulings on the future behavior of people engaged in activities that give rise to the kind of accident involved in the case before him. If, for example, judgment were awarded to the defendant on the ground that he was a "deserving," albeit careless, fellow, the decision would encourage similar people to be careless, a type of costly behavior.

Once the frame of reference is expanded beyond the immediate parties to the case, justice and fairness assume broader meanings than what is just or fair as between this plaintiff and this defendant. The issue becomes what is a just and fair result for a *class* of activities, and cannot be resolved without at least some consideration of the impact of alternative rulings on the frequency of accidents and the cost of accident precautions. The legal and economic approaches are not so divergent after all.

SUGGESTED READINGS

1. Jack Hirshleifer, James C. De Haven & Jerome W. Milliman, Water Supply: Economics, Technology, and Policy 36–42, 74–82 (1960).
2. Frank H. Knight, The Economic Organization (1933).
3. George J. Stigler, The Theory of Price, Ch. 2 (2d ed. 1966).

PROBLEMS

1. We said that the measure of value, in economic terms, is willingness to pay. Can you think of instances where unwillingness to accept payment would describe the economic measure of value more accurately?

2. Would economics be worth studying if resources were not scarce? Can contemporary American society be described as one of scarcity? It is said from time to time that there is a scarcity of doctors, or fuel oil, or something else. How do these episodes differ from the scarcity of all valuable goods?

3. What determines human wants? Is that an economic question? Are human wants insatiable? How is this question relevant?

4. The market is only one possible method of directing the allocation of resources to various uses. Another might be administrative decision by a governmental body. How would these methods differ?

PART I

THE COMMON LAW

CHAPTER 2

PROPERTY

§2.1. The economic theory of property rights. Imagine a society in which all property rights have been abolished. A farmer plants corn, fertilizes it, and erects scarecrows, but when the corn is ripe his neighbor reaps and sells it.[1] The farmer has no legal remedy against his neighbor's conduct since he owns neither the land that he sowed nor the crop. After a few such incidents the cultivation of land will be abandoned and the society will shift to methods of subsistence (such as hunting) that involve less preparatory investment.[2]

This example suggests that the legal protection of property rights has an important economic function: to create incentives to use resources efficiently. Although the value of the crop in our example, as measured by consumer willingness to pay, may have greatly exceeded the cost in labor, materials, and forgone alternative uses of the land, without property rights there is no incentive to incur these costs because there is no reasonably assured reward for incurring them. The proper incentives are created by the parceling out among the members of society of mutually exclusive rights to the use of particular resources. If every piece of land is owned by someone, in the sense that there is always an individual who can exclude all others from access to any given area, then individuals will endeavor by cultivation or other improvements to maximize the value of land.

The creation of exclusive rights is a necessary rather than sufficient condition for the efficient use of resources. The rights

§2.1. 1. The example is somewhat artificial: presumably the "buyer" could simply grab the corn and would be under no obligation to pay for it.

2. Some interesting anthropological evidence relevant to this point may be found in Harold Demsetz, Toward a Theory of Property Rights, 57 Am. Econ. Rev. Papers & Proceedings 347 (1967).

must be transferable. Suppose the farmer in our example owns the land that he sows but is a bad farmer; his land would be more productive in someone else's hands. The maximization of value requires a mechanism by which the farmer can be induced to transfer rights in the property to someone who can work it more productively. A transferable property right is such a mechanism.

An example will illustrate. Farmer A owns a piece of land that he anticipates will yield him $100 a year, in excess of labor and other costs, indefinitely. The value of the right to a stream of future earnings can be expressed as a present sum. Just as the price of a share of common stock expresses the present value of the anticipated earnings to which the shareholder will be entitled,[3] so the present value of a parcel of land that yields an annual net income of $100 can be calculated and is the minimum price that A will accept in exchange for his property right.[4] Farmer B believes that he can use A's land more productively than A. Stated another way, B thinks he could net more than $100 a year from working A's land.[5] The present value of B's higher expected earnings stream will, of course, exceed the present value calculated by A. Assume the present value calculated by A is $1000 and by B $1500. Then sale of the property right by A to B will yield benefits to both parties if the price is anywhere between $1000 and $1500. At a price of $1250, for example, A receives $250 more than the land is worth to him and B pays $250 less than the land is worth to *him*. Thus, there are strong incentives for the parties voluntarily to exchange A's land for B's money, and if B is as he believes a better farmer than A, the transfer will result in an increase in the productivity of the land. Through a succession of such transfers, resources are shifted to their highest valued, most productive uses and efficiency in the use of economic resources is maximized.

The foregoing discussion suggests three criteria of an efficient system of property rights. The first is *universality*. Ideally, all resources should be owned, or ownable, by someone, except resources so plentiful that everybody can consume as much of them

3. Discounting to present value is discussed in §4.10 *infra*.
4. The certainty with which A anticipates continuing to receive this return, the prevailing interest rate, his preference for or aversion to risk, and other factors will enter into his valuation of the property. Cf. §13.1 *infra*. We can disregard these refinements here; they do not affect the analysis.
5. We again disregard the factors mentioned *supra* note 4.

as he wants without reducing consumption by anyone else (sunlight is a good, but not perfect, example — why?). No issue of efficient use arises in such a case.

The second criterion — but one that requires, as we shall see, careful qualification — is *exclusivity*. We have assumed so far that either the farmer can exclude no one or he can exclude everyone, but of course there are intermediate stages: the farmer may be entitled to exclude private individuals from reaping his crop, but not the government in time of war. It might appear that the more exclusive the property right, the greater the incentive to invest the right amount of resources in the development of the property. Suppose our farmer estimates that he can raise a hog with a market value of $100 at a cost of only $50 in labor and materials. Suppose further that there is no alternative combination of resources and land use that would yield a greater excess of value over cost: in the next best use his net income from the land would be only $20. He will raise the hog. But now suppose his property right is less than exclusive in two respects. First, he has no right to prevent an adjacent railroad from accidentally emitting engine sparks that may set fire to the hog's pen, killing it prematurely. Second, he has no right to prevent the local government from rezoning his land from agricultural to residential use and compelling him to sell the hog at disadvantageous terms before it is grown. In light of these contingencies he must reevaluate the yield of his land: he must discount the $100 to reflect the probability that the yield may be much less, perhaps zero. Suppose, after discounting, the expected revenue from raising the hog (market value times the probability that it will reach the market) is only $60. He will not raise the hog. He will shift to the next best use of the land, which we said was less valuable.[6]

The analysis, however, is incomplete. While the farmer will be induced, as a consequence of no longer enjoying an exclusive property right, to shift to an alternative land use that *seems* less efficient, overall efficiency may be increased. The removal of the hog may result in an increase in the value of surrounding residential land greater than the reduction in the value of the farmer's parcel. The cost of preventing the emission of engine sparks may be larger than the reduction in the value of the farmer's land when he switches from hog raising to, say, growing

6. The profit from raising the hog is now only $10, since his costs are $50. The next best use, we said, yields a profit of $20.

radishes. To this, the very alert reader may be tempted to reply that if the increase in value to others from a different use of the farmer's land exceeds the decrease to him, they can buy his right: the railroad can purchase an easement to emit sparks; the surrounding homeowners can purchase a covenant from the farmer not to raise hogs. Often, however, the costs of effecting a transfer of rights — transaction costs — are prohibitive; but more on this shortly.[7]

The third criterion of an efficient system of property rights is *transferability*. If a property right cannot be transferred,[8] there is no way of shifting a resource from a less productive to a more productive use through voluntary exchange. The costs of transfer may be high to begin with; a legal prohibition against transferring may, depending on the penalties for violation, make the costs utterly prohibitive. We shall see that when the costs of transferring property rights are high, the attempt to achieve our second criterion, exclusivity, may actually reduce the efficiency of the property rights system.

§2.2. *Property rights in law and economics: The case of broadcast frequencies.*   Property rights in our society are not in fact universal, exclusive, or freely transferable. For example, the law has purported not to recognize property rights in broadcasting at all. This is a good place at which to begin our discussion of the property rights system because it illustrates the difference between the legal conception of property right and the broader economic conception.[1]

In the early days of radio, before comprehensive federal regulation was imposed, there was some judicial support for the proposition that the right to broadcast on a particular frequency in a particular area without interference from other users was a property right that could be protected by injunction. With the creation in 1928 of the Federal Radio Commission (forerunner of the Federal Communications Commission) Congress determined upon a different approach. Licenses authorizing the use of particular frequencies in particular areas were to be granted at nominal charge for renewable three-year terms to applicants who persuaded the commission that licensing them would promote

7. See §2.6 *infra*.

8. We use transfer in a broad sense: if sales in fee simple were forbidden, but leases allowed, A could lease his farm to B in our example and the objective of shifting it to its highest valued use would be achieved.

§2.2. 1. The classic study of public regulation of the broadcasting industry, on which this section draws heavily, is Ronald H. Coase, The Federal Communications Commission, 2 J. Law & Econ. 1 (1959).

the public interest. Congress expressly provided that licensees were to have no property rights in the use of the frequencies assigned them; the purpose of this provision was to foreclose any claim to compensation by a licensee whose license was withdrawn at the end of the three-year term.

Some of the objections that were advanced to the recognition of private property rights in the use of radio frequencies have an odd ring, at least in an economist's ear. For example, it was said that if broadcasting rights could be bought and sold like other property, the broadcast media would come under the control of the wealthy. This confuses willingness to pay with ability to pay. The possession of money does not dictate the objects that will be purchased. The poor frequently bid goods away from the rich by being willing to pay more. To be sure, willingness to pay presupposes ability to pay, but a group of poor people may have much greater financial resources in the aggregate than one wealthy person or a small group of wealthy people.

In the actual administration of the federal regulatory scheme for broadcasting, willingness to pay has played a decisive role and a system of de facto property rights has emerged. The desirable radio and television licenses have been awarded in comparative proceedings in which, much as in a system of property rights, willingness to pay — not for the license as such but for the legal representation and political influence that typically determine the outcome — has probably decided in most cases who would control the resource at stake.[2] However, this method of initially assigning broadcast rights is less efficient than an auction or other conventional private sale. First, since there is a good deal of uncertainty in the political regulatory process, the applicant who pays his lawyers, lobbyists, etc., the most money — thereby indicating that he attaches the greatest value to obtaining the right — will often not receive it. Second, the costs of this method of allocation are much greater than the cost of allocation through

2. This is not to say that the successful applicant will have expended on obtaining the license an amount anywhere near as great as the value of the license. Since there is a high risk of his failing to obtain the license, he will stop spending at the point where, if he prevails, the difference between his expenditures and the value of the license will be large enough to compensate him for the risk. If he were risk neutral (see §4.5 *infra*), if the value of the license if he were to receive it were $1 million, and if the probability of his receiving it were ten percent, he would expend no more than $100,000 in seeking to obtain the license. The amount of money he spent would influence the likelihood of his success; we ignore this point here (but cf. §§24.4, 26.2 *infra*).

the market: participation in an auction of broadcast frequencies would not necessitate costly legal services.

The first source of inefficiency is transitory, for once broadcast rights have been obtained by the method just outlined they are thereafter salable as an incident to the sale of the physical assets of a radio or television station. When a television station having a transmitter and other physical properties worth only a few hundred thousand dollars is sold for $10 million, one can be confident that the major part of the purchase price is payment for the right to use the frequency. Given such transfers, we may presume that, as with land, broadcast rights end up in the hands of those who value them most highly (and are therefore willing to pay the most money for them), even if the initial "auction" may not have allocated the rights very efficiently. The willingness of broadcasters to pay tens of millions of dollars for a right terminable after three years may seem peculiar. In fact, broadcast licenses have been terminated only for misconduct, in much the same way that one can lose one's land for nonpayment of real estate taxes.

In economic if not in formal legal terms, then, there are property rights in broadcast frequencies. The right is obtained initially in a competition in which willingness to pay plays an influential, and quite possibly decisive, role. Once obtained the right is transferable. It is exclusive: interference with a licensee's use of his frequency will be enjoined. And it is for all practical purposes perpetual. The right holder is subject to various regulatory constraints, but less so than a public utility, the principal assets of which are private property in the formal legal sense.

§2.3. *Future rights.*   The rights system in broadcasting is not only costly and sub rosa but also incomplete in important respects. One we discuss later under transferability. Another, which has an interesting parallel in the law of water rights, is the difficulty of obtaining rights for future use. To purchase vacant land with the intention of holding it for future development is a common type of transaction, while to disclose in a broadcast license application an intention to defer indefinitely the commencement of broadcast operations would guarantee denial. So also in the case of water rights under the appropriation system that prevails in the western states: one acquires property rights in water by the actual diversion and use of a stream and the right embraces only the amount of water actually used; one cannot obtain a right for exercise at some future date. Both the broadcast and water limitations are circumvented to some extent, in the case of broadcasting by deferring actual construction after the license has been obtained, in the case of water by obtaining a preliminary permit that establishes the applicant's prior right even though the construction of diversion works and use of the water diverted are postponed.

The hostility to recognizing rights for future use may be related to the apparent "windfall" element that is present in both the broadcasting and water contexts. In both cases the right is awarded without charge — although the applicant may have gone to considerable expense to obtain it — and often can be immediately resold at a considerable profit. This need not be evidence of a true windfall.[1] The "windfall," however, would appear even larger if the profit were obtained by one who appeared not to be providing any service.

The objection is bound up with a general hostility, reflected in many corners of the law, to speculation. Speculation is the purchase of a good not to use but to hold in the hope that it will appreciate in value.[2] The speculator performs a valuable economic function in the adjustment of prices to changing values. In the case of land, water, or broadcast frequencies he can (if permitted) perform the additional function of preventing the premature commitment of resources. Moreover, the principal effect of forbidding speculative purchases of water or broadcast frequencies is not to prevent speculation but to encourage uneconomical resource uses — uses not to meet a demand but to stake a claim.

§2.4. *Incompatible uses.*   Property rights are never exclusive, if only because exclusive property rights would so often be incompatible. If a railroad is to enjoy the exclusive use of its right of way it must be permitted to emit engine sparks without legal limitation. The value of its property will be impaired otherwise. But if it is permitted to emit engine sparks the value of adjacent farmland will be impaired because of the fire hazard created by the sparks. Is the emission of sparks an incident of the railroad's property right or an invasion of the farmer's? Does anything turn on the answer? Suppose that the right to emit

§2.3. 1. Observe that while the successful applicant in §2.2, note 2 *supra*, will obtain a large return on his investment, broadcast license applicants as a class will obtain no more than a normal return, at least if there are no limitations on who may compete for a broadcast license.

2. Or the sale of a good in the expectation that its value will decline, as in short selling of stocks. On the economic utility of speculation see also §13.4 *infra*.

sparks, by enabling the railroad to dispense with costly spark-arresting equipment, would increase the value of its property by $100 but reduce the value of the farmer's property by $50 because it would prevent him from growing crops close to the tracks. If the farmer has a legal right to be free from engine sparks, the railroad presumably will offer to pay and the farmer will accept compensation for the surrender of his right. Since the right to prevent spark emissions is worth only $50 to the farmer but imposes costs on the railroad of $100, a sale of the farmer's right at any price between $50 and $100 will make both parties better off. If instead of the farmer's having a right to be free from sparks the railroad has a legal right to emit sparks, no transaction will occur. The farmer will not pay more than $50 for the railroad's right and the railroad will not accept less than $100. Thus, whichever way the legal right is assigned, the result, in terms of resource use, is the same: the railroad emits sparks and the farmer moves his crop.

The principle is not affected by reversing the numbers. Assume that the right to emit sparks would increase the value of the railroad's property by only $50, but would reduce the value of the farmer's property by $100. If the railroad has a right to emit sparks, the farmer will offer to pay and the railroad will accept some price between $50 and $100 for the surrender of the railroad's right. If instead the farmer has a right to be free from emissions, there will be no transaction since the farmer would insist on a minimum payment of $100 and the railroad will pay no more than $50.

Whatever the relative values of the competing uses, it seems that the initial assignment of legal rights does not affect which use ultimately prevails. The efficient, or value-maximizing, accommodation of the conflict will be chosen whichever party is granted the legal right to exclude interference by the other.[1]

§2.4. 1. This was demonstrated in Ronald Coase's important article, The Problem of Social Cost, 3 J. Law & Econ. 1 (1960). The article makes three other important points which are sometimes overlooked, relating to the case in which the costs of transferring the property right are so high that transfer is not feasible. (a) Placing liability on the party who causes the damage (the railroad in our example) may not produce the efficient solution to the conflict. (The reader can verify this by referring to our first example and assuming that the farmer has the property right and cannot, due to heavy transaction costs, transfer it to the railroad.) (b) The common law of nuisance can be understood as an attempt to increase the value of resource use by assigning property rights to those parties to conflicting land uses in whose hands the rights are most valuable. (c) In deciding whether governmental intervention in the economic system is appropriate, it is never sufficient to demonstrate that, without intervention, the market

But it does not follow that the initial assignment of rights is immaterial from an economic standpoint. Since transactions are not costless, efficiency is promoted by assigning the legal right to the party who would buy it — the railroad in our first hypothetical and the farmer in the second — were it assigned initially to the other party. Moreover, as we shall see, transaction costs are sometimes so high as to make transactions impracticable. In such a case the initial assignment of rights is final.

These observations suggest an economic principle for deciding, in cases of conflicting land (or other property) uses, which party shall have the right to exclude the other. The right should be assigned to the party whose use is the more valuable — the party, stated otherwise, for whom discontinuance of the interference would be most costly. By assigning rights in accordance with this principle the law can anticipate and thus obviate the necessity for a market transaction. Transaction costs are minimized *when the law (1) assigns the right to the party who would buy it from the other party if it were assigned to the other party instead and if transaction costs were zero, or (2) alternatively, places liability on the party who, if he had the right and transaction costs were zero, would sell it to the other party.*

It is easier to state than to apply the criterion. Our engine-spark example was grossly oversimplified in that it permitted only two property right assignments, a right to emit sparks and a right to be free from sparks. The combined value of the farmer's and the railroad's property might actually be maximized by a more complex definition of property rights, such as one that permitted the farmer to grow one kind of crop but not another, to plant nothing within 200 feet of the tracks, and to have no

---

would operate imperfectly; government also operates imperfectly so what is necessary is a comparison between the actual workings of market and government in the particular setting.

A qualification of the Coasian analysis should be mentioned here. The initial assignment of rights, even where transaction costs are zero so that efficiency is not affected, may affect the relative wealth of the parties and this may affect the use of resources in two ways. First, if the parties do not spend their money in identical ways, a shift of wealth between them will alter demand for the various goods and services that they buy, however slightly. Second, where the right ends up may depend on how the initial assignment is made, if the value of the right represents a large fraction of the wealth of either party. The extreme example is the right to a barrel of water as between two dying men in a desert. This point is developed in E. J. Mishan, Pareto Optimality and the Law, 19 Oxford Econ. Papers (n.s.) 255 (1967). Neither point undermines Coase's conclusion that efficiency is unaffected by the rule of liability if transaction costs are zero; do you think either point has much practical significance?

wooden buildings within 250 feet of the tracks, while permitting the railroad to emit sparks only up to a specified level. The possible combinations are endless, and it is unrealistic to expect courts always to discover the optimum one. They may, however, in most cases and without excessive cost, be able to come up with at least a crude approximation of the optimum definition of property rights and this, however imperfect, is a more efficient method of guiding resource use than a random assignment of property rights would be.

Some examples may help clarify the fundamental point that is involved. At common law, if a landowner built in such a way as to block his neighbor's windows he was considered to have infringed the neighbor's property rights. Observe the consequences if the property right had been given to the other party. Ordinarily the cost to the person whose windows were blocked would exceed the cost to the other person of setting back his wall slightly, so the former would buy the right. The assignment of the right to him in the first instance avoids the transaction and its attendant costs.[2] But the courts did not extend the rule to protect distant views. If I had a house on a hill with a beautiful prospect, and someone else built a house that ruined it, I would not be able to establish an invasion of my property rights even though the value of my property had diminished. Here the presumption of relative values is reversed. A house with a view commands a large land area. The values that would be created by development of such an area are likely to exceed the loss of value to the one household whose view is impaired.

Another common law rule was that a railroad owed no duty of care to people using the tracks as paths (except at crossings). The cost to these "trespassers" of using alternative paths would generally be small in comparison with the cost to the railroad of making the tracks safe for them. The railroad's right, however, was a qualified one: it was required to keep a careful lookout for trespassing cattle. It would be very costly for farmers to erect fences that absolutely prevented cattle from straying, so we would expect that, if transactions between farmers and railroads were feasible, farmers would frequently pay railroads to keep a careful lookout for animals on the track.

As with cattle, the burden of preventing accidents to child trespassers in the absence of a duty in the landowner would fall

2. This rule of the English common law was rejected in America. Can you think of an economic reason why?

on an adult custodian and would be costly: children are difficult to pen. Even young children, however, have more sense than cattle or sheep. The doctrine of attractive nuisance provides an ingenious solution to the conflicting interests of parents and landowners. The doctrine provides that the landowner must fence or otherwise secure against child trespassers those artificial land conditions (classically, railroad turntables) that young children mistake for playthings and misperceive the dangers of. It would be impracticable to expect either the child or his parents to protect effectively against this type of hazard, but the landowner can do so at relatively small cost. The cost of fencing these hazardous places is much less than the cost of fencing an entire right of way. Observe that this is another area in which the initial assignment of rights is also the final assignment: it would be impracticable for landowners to negotiate in advance with all the parents whose children might stray onto their property.

The economic theory of property rights implies that rights will be redefined from time to time as the relative values of different resource uses change. It is possible to object, however, that a process of continuously redefining property rights to secure efficiency under changing conditions is bound to create instability and discourage investment. X buys a farm long before there is a railroad in his area. The price he pays is not discounted to reflect future crop damage from sparks because the construction of a railroad line is not foreseen. But eventually a line is built and is sufficiently near X's farm to inflict spark damage on his crops. He sues the railroad but the court holds that the level of spark emission is reasonable because it would be more costly for the railroad than for the farmer to prevent the crop loss. With property values thus exposed to uncompensated depreciation by virtue of unforeseen changes in neighboring land uses, the incentive to invest optimally in farming will be impaired.[3] The problem is easily exaggerated. If a harmful neighboring land use is foreseen at the time of sale, the price of land will be reduced accordingly and the buyer will have no disappointed expectations. If the use is unforeseen, chances are that it lies well in the future, and a cost to be incurred in the far future will have relatively little impact on present decisions.[4] The alternative — always to award the property right to the prior of two conflicting land uses —

3. Cf. Leroy Fibre Co. v. Chicago, M. & St. P.R.R., 232 U.S. 340 (1914). The example in the text is not a realistic one since the coming of the railroad usually increased the agricultural value of the land proximate to it.

4. Cf. §4.10 infra.

would be highly inefficient, for the later use will often be the more valuable. Moreover, the uncertainty created by the comparative-value approach is mitigated by the special treatment of an important class of intrusions, discussed in the next section.

The law can resolve incompatible uses either by recognizing a property right in the party whose use is the more valuable or by imposing liability on the other party. The first is the method of the law of property, the second of tort law. The difference in approach is primarily terminological and historical rather than analytical. The most distinctive class of interferences governed by tort law comprises accidents that cause personal injury. They involve problems of uncertainty and of damage valuation not ordinarily involved in the interferences discussed in this chapter, and are the particular subject of Chapter 4.

§2.5. *Trespass and eminent domain.*   The landowner's right to repel a physical intrusion in the form of engine sparks is only a qualified right. The intruder can defeat it by showing that his land use, which is incompatible with the injured landowner's, is more valuable. But if my neighbor parks his car in my garage I have a right to eject him as a trespasser no matter how convincingly he can demonstrate to a court that the use of my garage to park his car is more valuable than my use of it.

The different treatment of the cases has an economic justification. The market is a more efficient method of determining the optimum use of land than legal proceedings.[1] If my neighbor thinks his use of my garage would be more productive than mine, he should have no trouble persuading me to rent it to him. But if he merely *claims* that he can use my garage more productively, he thrusts on the courts a difficult evidentiary question: which of us would really be willing to pay more for the use of the garage? In the spark case, negotiation in advance may be infeasible due to the number of landowners potentially affected, so if the courts want to encourage highest valued land use they cannot avoid comparing the values of the competing uses.

If the *government* wants land, it can seize it under the eminent domain power. It need not come to terms with the owner. This result is seemingly inconsistent with the distinction just suggested. It is sometimes argued that the eminent domain power is necessary to overcome the stubbornness of people who refuse to sell at a "reasonable" (that is, the market) price. This is not

§2.5. 1. This is a point that recurs repeatedly in this book. See, e.g., §§23.1, 25.1 *infra.*

an economic argument. If I refuse to sell for less than $25,000 a house that no one else would pay more than $15,000 for, it does not follow that I am irrational, even if no "objective" factors such as moving expenses justify my insisting on such a premium. It follows only that I value the house more than other people. The extra value I place on the property has the same status in economic analysis as any other value.

An economic reason for eminent domain, although one applicable primarily to its use by railroads and other right-of-way companies rather than by government, is that it is necessary to prevent monopoly. Once the railroad or pipeline has begun to build its line, the cost of abandoning it for an alternative route becomes very high. Knowing this, people owning land in the path of the advancing line will be tempted to hold out for a very high price — a price in excess of the actual opportunity cost of the land. The high cost of acquiring land will, by increasing the costs of right-of-way companies, induce them to raise the prices of their services; the higher prices will induce some consumers to shift to substitute services; the companies will therefore have a smaller output; and as a result the companies will need, and will purchase, less land than they would have purchased at prices equal to (or slightly above) the opportunity costs of the land. Furthermore, higher land prices will give the companies an incentive to substitute other inputs for some of the land that they would ordinarily purchase. As a result of these factors land that would have been more valuable to a right-of-way company than to its present owners remains in its existing, lower valued uses, and this is inefficient.

In an eminent domain taking, the condemnor must compensate the owner for the value of the land taken. The requirement of compensation operates to limit takings to circumstances where the value of the land to the condemnor is in fact greater than the value to its present owner; to require the government merely to prove to a court's satisfaction that the land was more valuable to it than to the condemnee would be a less efficient alternative.[2]

2. This analysis supplies a straightforward economic justification of the compensation requirement. Frank I. Michelman, in Property, Utility, and Fairness: Comments on the Ethical Foundations of "Just Compensation" Law, 80 Harv. L. Rev. 1165 (1967), suggests an alternative economic justification: that failure to compensate would often impose "demoralization costs" on the condemnees, leading them to use resources less efficiently in the future. This approach is questionable (and unnecessary to establish an economic justification for the requirement of just compensation). So long as the practice of not compensating were clearly understood, the risk of a government taking would be reflected in

The requirement of compensation has the additional virtue of increasing the security of the owner's property rights and hence the incentive to improve land. Why then is not the compensation principle applied when the railroad "takes" the farmer's land through spark damage? The economic answer is that where, as in the spark case, the "taking" is the result of one landowner's using his land at the expense of another landowner's enjoyment of *his* land, it is not clear who should be asked to compensate whom. If the railroad is recognized to have the right to emit sparks, the farmer's land will be less valuable, so perhaps the railroad should be required to pay the farmer; but if the farmer is recognized to have the right to grow crops free from spark damage, the railroad's right-of-way is now less valuable, so perhaps the farmer should be required to compensate the railroad. We return to this point in the next section.

The fact that the condemnor in an eminent domain proceeding is not required to show that his use of the land will be more valuable than the present owner's, but only to render compensation, will result in inefficient land uses if the required compensation is not equal to the opportunity costs of the land seized. And it commonly is not. The disregard of nonmarket values mentioned earlier creates a systematic downward bias in the prices paid in eminent domain proceedings. Where land is worth more to the owner in its present use than fair market value, the effect of eminent domain is to transfer land at a lower price than the market. And since land worth *less* to the owner than fair market value is not likely to be involved in an eminent domain proceeding at all — he would have sold it already — there is little offsetting tendency to overcompensate some owners. The standard of fair market value also ignores the owner's moving and transaction costs (including the legal costs of establishing fair market value). If the condemnor bought in the market, the existence of such expenses would frequently force him to pay higher prices in order to obtain the land that he wanted.

Another problem with the just-compensation principle is its extremely limited scope. Although a person's labor is ordinarily his most valuable property, the government may take it without compensation for military service or jury duty. The government is also substantially free to destroy the value of property rights

the price of property (or in the cost of insurance against such takings), and there would be no occasion for anyone to be surprised or demoralized by such a taking, any more than if his building had been destroyed by lightning.

through taxation and regulation, forms of invasion for which compensation is not required. Incidentally, this makes the government a rather undependable contracting partner, as the companies that leased oil drilling rights from the State of Alaska are finding out.[3]

§2.6. *Pollution: Nuisance and easement approaches.*   A factory belches smoke from its smokestacks. The smoke blackens laundry and drapes in a nearby residential area and increases the incidence of respiratory diseases. Analytically the problem is much the same as in our spark example: to allocate rights and liabilities in such a way as to minimize the sum of the costs of smoke damage and of avoiding smoke damage. There are many possible adjustments. The factory could install smoke-suppression equipment; as an extreme measure it could shut down. The affected homeowners could install air-cleaning equipment, or move away from the vicinity of the factory. The question of which of these or other methods of resolving the conflicting land uses is cheapest is even more difficult than in the engine-spark problem primarily because the effects of pollution on human health are not as yet clearly understood and because the aesthetic costs of pollution are difficult to measure. The choice of the correct initial assignment of rights is likely to be critical: high transaction costs may make it impossible to rectify a mistaken initial assignment through subsequent market transactions.

It is time we inquired more closely into the sources of high transaction costs. Uncertainty as to whom to transact with is one: it is likely to be important in the factory example. In addition, if homeowners have a right to be free from pollution, the factory that wishes to acquire the right to pollute must acquire it from every homeowner. If only one out of a thousand refuses to come to terms, the rights that the factory has purchased from the other 999 are worth nothing (why?). The hold-out can extract an exorbitant price as in our right-of-way example. Each homeowner will therefore have an incentive to delay in coming to terms with the factory, and the process of negotiation may become endlessly protracted.

There is also the sheer cost of dealing separately with a multitude of rights holders. The cost of an individual transaction rises with the size of the transaction but probably at a diminishing

3. See Amerada Hess Corp. v. State, No. 72-2719 (Ala. Super. Ct., Sept. 12, 1972), in which the oil companies have challenged a series of taxes placed by the state on their activities, claiming that the state is in effect unilaterally revising the terms of the leases.

rate. The cost of a set of transactions, in contrast, is probably a linear function of the number of transactions. If the value to each homeowner of the right to be free from pollution is relatively small and the aggregate value of these rights is substantial only because many people are affected, the transaction costs involved in the factory's acquisition of the rights, when added to the total purchase price, may well exceed the value of the rights to the factory — even if there are no hold-outs and the value of the rights to the factory, ignoring transaction costs, is greater than their value to the homeowners.

If instead of the homeowners' having the right to be free from pollution, the factory has the right to pollute, the homeowners must get together and purchase the factory's right if they wish to be free from pollution. Transaction costs will again be high. Each homeowner will again have an incentive to drag his feet in coming to terms with the factory. He will think: "If I refuse to contribute my fair share of the purchase price, others, who care more deeply about pollution than I do, will make up the difference. The factory will be induced to stop polluting. I will benefit along with the others but at zero cost." The costs of overcoming this foot dragging by negotiations among the affected homeowners will be high if there are many of them, so again a transaction may be infeasible.

In the presence of heavy transaction costs, exclusive rights, whether to pollute or to be free from pollution, are likely to promote inefficiency. If the factory has the absolute right to pollute, and transaction costs are prohibitive, the factory will have no incentive to reduce or stop pollution even if the costs of stopping would be much less than the costs of pollution to the homeowners. Conversely, if homeowners have an absolute right to be free from pollution and transaction costs are again prohibitive, the homeowners will have no incentive to take steps of their own to minimize the effects of pollution or tolerate some pollution, even if the costs of avoidance or acceptance are much lower than the costs to the factory of not polluting.

The common law recognized the danger of assigning exclusive rights either to polluters or to their victims. Under the doctrine of nuisance and cognate doctrines applicable to special areas such as water rights, courts followed a standard of reasonable use. Pollution was lawful if reasonable in the circumstances, which meant (but only approximately) if the benefit from continuing to pollute exceeded the cost to the victims of pollution of either tolerating or eliminating it, whichever was cheaper. This is the same standard we suggested earlier for arbitrating conflicts in land use, as in the spark example. But while correct in principle, the approach had little bite in practice, due primarily to the lack of a procedural device for aggregating small claims. If no single victim of a polluter suffered damage as great as the cost of bringing a lawsuit, no suit would be brought even if the aggregate harm to all of the victims exceeded the benefits of continued pollution. Recent developments in the class action, discussed in a subsequent chapter, may help to overcome this procedural shortcoming.[1]

Another possible solution is suggested by the law's treatment of airplane noise damage. Owners of airplanes that fly directly over a person's property at very low altitudes are liable to the property owner for the diminution in the market value of his property brought about by the airplane's noise, whether or not the costs to the owner exceed the benefits of flight. The property owner cannot enjoin the invasion as a trespass. He cannot, therefore, compel the airline to negotiate with him. But he can compel the airline to condemn an easement to continue its overflights. Where the cost of noise-abatement procedures is greater than the noise damage suffered by the subjacent property owners, the airline will presumably purchase flight easements. If the noise damage is greater than the cost of the noise-abatement procedures, the airline will adopt the procedures. Conceivably, if the cheapest method of noise abatement happens to be soundproofing the subjacent houses, the airline will pay the subjacent owners to soundproof, since by hypothesis the payment will be less than the airline's liability; but transaction costs may be so heavy as to preclude this result; and if so the eminent domain approach may produce less efficient consequences than a nuisance approach (why?). It is, however, superior to a trespass approach. If the subjacent owners had property rights against airplane noise that they could not be forced to sell (i.e., if they could enjoin the overflight) then in cases where the efficient solution was for the airline to continue to make noise and for the subjacent owners either to suffer the noise or to soundproof their houses, the market would often fail to produce efficient results. The airline, at the mercy of the few owners in the path of flight who demanded an exorbitant price to surrender their right to prevent overflights, would find it difficult to purchase all of the rights of subjacent owners to be free from noise, so it would have either to discon-

§2.6. 1. See §24.5 *infra.*

tinue its flights or to adopt sound-abatement procedures — by hypothesis inefficient solutions.

A problem with the eminent domain approach is that once the airline, having found that the costs of noise-abatement procedures are greater than the benefits to it in reduced liability to the subjacent owners, acquires easements from them that authorize it to maintain a high level of noise, it has no incentive to reconsider the adoption of such procedures in the future, when and if their cost falls or their effectiveness increases: the benefit of a lower noise level would inure entirely to the subjacent owners. This problem could be solved by creating time-limited noise easements,[2] but the solution would create a fresh problem. With perpetual easements, the subjacent owners, after receiving payment from the airline, have every incentive to adopt their own noise-reduction measures if the cost of such measures is less than the increment in the value of their property that results. The incentive to take such measures is impaired under a system of time-limited easements, because any measure that reduces noise damage will result in an equal reduction in the easement price in the next period.

§2.7. *Other solutions to the problem of incompatible land uses.* The achievement of an efficient solution in the spark case, the factory smoke case, and our other examples of conflicting land uses would have been much simpler if a single individual or firm had owned all of the land involved in the conflict. A single owner of the factory and the residential property affected by its smoke would want to maximize the combined value of both properties. This is the correct economic goal and his effort to reach it would not be burdened by the costs of obtaining the agreement of many separate owners. Yet such mergers appear to be infrequent. Why? First, the costs of buying up all of the affected property may be considerable since there are many individual rights holders to be transacted with. Second, it may be difficult for a single firm to operate in unrelated markets — factory production and residential real estate, railroading and farming, airport management and real estate. The firm may have

---

2. As proposed in William F. Baxter & Lillian R. Altree, Legal Aspects of Airport Noise, 15 J. Law & Econ. 1 (1972), a highly recommended study of the problem. If the easement is limited (say) to ten years, the airline will periodically review the state of the art in noise abatement in order to determine whether the adoption of noise-abatement procedures would save it money by reducing its expected easement costs by more than the noise-abatement procedures would add to its capital and operating costs.

higher costs in both markets than firms specializing in either one. The extra costs may offset the savings resulting from solving the incompatible-uses problem effectively.[1]

An alternative method that has some of the strengths of the single-ownership approach but avoids the problem of underspecialization is the use of restrictive covenants. The developer of a tract will want to maximize the value of the entire property; but he may not want to administer it. One possibility is to include in each deed of sale restrictions against land uses that would reduce the net value of the property as a whole. The restrictions "run with the land" and so assure the purchaser permanent protection, especially since any owner of property in the tract can bring suit to enforce them. The value of the property is maximized without common ownership.

As a method of maximizing land values, restrictive covenants suffer from two limitations. First, generally they are feasible only in the rather limited situation of (initial) single ownership of a large tract of land. They provide no solution to the typical pollution problem, for it is rare that an area large enough to encompass the factory and all of the residences affected by its smoke will be under common ownership.[2] Second, the system is inflexible in the face of changes that may alter the comparative values of conflicting land uses. The owner who desires to put his land to a use forbidden by a restrictive covenant must obtain the consent of all the property owners in whose favor the covenant runs; if there are many of them, the costs of transacting may be prohibitive. Some covenants, however, provide that they will expire after a certain number of years unless renewed by majority vote of the affected landowners.[3] And courts will sometimes refuse to enforce a restrictive covenant on the ground that the covenant is obsolete — i.e., that the forbidden use is now clearly more valuable than the conflicting use protected by the covenant.

There would be another safety valve if courts refused to enjoin violations of restrictive covenants, instead limiting plaintiffs to the recovery of damages. Damages liability would not deter a

§2.7. 1. It may be possible to offset some of the costs of underspecialization by leasing, but the coordination of the lessees may in practice be almost as costly as the operation of the market. On this point, cf. §12.1 *infra*.

2. Moreover, within a limited area, a good deal of voluntary segregation of conflicting uses can be expected, quite apart from legal or contractual restrictions. Factories are not found in residential areas primarily because residential real estate commands a much higher price than industrial.

3. Bernard A. Siegan, Non-zoning in Houston, 13 J. Law & Econ. 71, 79–83 (1970).

breach of the covenant that increased the value of the breaching owner's property by more than it diminished the value of the other properties in the tract, since, by hypothesis, his total liability in damages would be smaller than his gain from the breach. In contrast, the injunctive remedy places the prospective violator in the same position as the airline that is enjoinable by subjacent property owners or the railroad that is enjoinable from trespassing on property that it requires to complete its right of way: he must negotiate with every right holder, may have to pay an exorbitant price to a few hold-outs, and — the most important economic point — may fail to complete the transaction.

The discussion of remedies in this and the preceding section may be generalized as follows: In conflicting-use situations where transaction costs are high, the allocation of resources to their highest valued uses is facilitated by denying property right holders an injunctive remedy against invasions of their rights and instead limiting them to a remedy in damages (why?).[4] Where transaction costs are low, injunctive relief should be allowed as a matter of course (why?).

The inflexibility of restrictive covenants has led increasing numbers of developers to establish homeowners' associations empowered to modify the restrictions on the uses to which they may put their property. This method of coping with the problem of heavy transactions costs resembles another method, the business firm, which we discuss in a later chapter.[5]

An interesting device is used to deal with a problem of conflicting resource uses peculiar to common-pool resources, such as oil. The separate owners of drilling rights in an oil field will usually be drawing oil from the same underground pool. Each has an incentive to remove as much oil as rapidly as he can, and the common law entitled him to do this. The result, however, is inefficient. More oil in the aggregate can be obtained if the rate of withdrawal is slower.[6] But if a large number of separate owners are involved, the working out of an agreement limiting the rate of withdrawal of each, although to the mutual benefit of all, may be prohibitively expensive. The answer of most oil states is "compulsory unitization," whereby the vote of a major-

---

4. This problem is discussed in Frank I. Michelman, Book Review, 80 Yale L.J. 647, 670–672 (1971), and in Guido Calabresi & A. Douglas Melamed, Property Rules, Liability Rules, and Inalienability: One View of the Cathedral, 85 Harv. L. Rev. 1089 (1972).

5. See Chapter 12.

6. More precisely, the present value of the pool is maximized by slower withdrawal.

ity (usually a two-thirds majority) of the owners of a field is sufficient to constitute the field a unit to be operated as under common ownership. Dispensing with unanimity reduces the power of the hold-out. Perhaps this approach should be emulated in other areas where transaction costs are high.

The recording system for real property, although much maligned, may be viewed as a method for reducing the costs of transacting in land, as we shall see when we discuss water sales.[7] In sum, the law and the market have not been indifferent to the problem of transaction costs and the opportunities for overcoming it.[8]

Economists often describe the problem of incompatible land uses as one of "externalities." The damage to the farmer's crops caused by engine sparks is said to be a cost of railroading that the railroad, unless forced by law or unless it is the owner of the farmland, will not take into account in making its decisions; the cost is external to its decision-making processes. (What would be an "external benefit"?) We have avoided the term because it is misleading. It suggests that the correct solution in the spark case is to impose liability on the railroad for spark damage, whereas in fact there is no presumption in economic theory that the railroad rather than the farmer should be made to bear the cost of spark damage. If the joint value of railroading and farming would be maximized by the discontinuance of crop production, the substitution of a more fire-resistant crop, or the removal of the crop to some distance from the railroad right-of-way, then imposition of liability on the railroad would produce an inefficient result (assuming, of course, prohibitive transaction costs). Moreover, even if externality is defined as external to market processes of decision rather than to the injurer, it is misleading since if transaction costs are low, the market may operate efficiently despite the presence of externalities.

§2.8. *Estates in land.*   It is common for more than one person to have a property right in the same thing. Our common-pool resource was an example of this; a more traditional example is the different "estates" in land. Property rights in real estate

---

7. See §2.11 *infra.*

8. Problems of conflicting land use are frequently dealt with by public regulation, such as zoning and the burgeoning direct regulation of pollution. We discuss public regulation later (see in particular §10.3 *infra*). Land-use controls are analyzed from an economic standpoint in Robert Ellickson, An Alternative to Zoning: Covenants, Nuisance Rules and Fines as Land Use Controls, forthcoming in U. Chi. L. Rev. (1973).

may be divided between a life tenant and a remainderman, be-tween joint tenants (a special type of co-ownership), between a tenant and a landlord, and in other ways. Such divisions create incentives for inefficient use similar to those created by the sepa-rate ownership of the railroad right-of-way and the adjacent farmland, or the airport and the adjacent residential community. Indeed, it used to be thought that the poverty of Ireland was due to tenant farming: the tenant had little incentive to improve the land because any improvement that outlasted the period of the lease would confer an uncompensated benefit on the landlord. The example is an odd one. Since there are only two parties to a lease, it should not be insuperably difficult to draft a provision that would encourage the tenant to make lasting improvements by compensating him for them. The obverse problem — damage to the property by the tenant that reduces the value of the prop-erty to the landlord — is commonly solved by the device of a security deposit.[1]

The owner of a property may want to convey the life estate to one person and the remainder to another. The life tenant, who will be in immediate control of the property, will have an incen-tive to maximize, not the value of the property, i.e., the present value of the entire future earnings obtainable from the property, but only the present value of the future earnings obtainable dur-ing his lifetime. He will want to cut timber before it has attained its mature growth, even though the present value of the timber would be maximized by postponing the cutting,[2] if the increment in value produced by waiting would be received by the remain-derman rather than by him. One might have thought this prob-lem could be taken care of easily by a rule requiring the life ten-ant to obtain the remainderman's agreement to any substantial alteration of the property: a simple two-party transaction. But remaindermen are often numerous, infants, legally incapable of contracting, or even unborn, so an elaborate law of "waste" had to be developed to limit the life tenant's power over the property.

§2.8. 1. But it should not be thought that two-party transaction costs are al-ways low. If they were, the United States and the Soviet Union would long ago have divided the world between them. A more mundane example is provided by automobile rentals. The driver of a rental car tends to drive the car very hard because he bears very little of the cost of wear and tear. The rental company could negotiate with the driver for a provision requiring him to take good care of the car. But it would be very costly to enforce, which is perhaps why it is not found in auto-rental contracts.

2. The extra value from waiting might exceed the interest obtainable from the reinvestment of the proceeds of an immediate sale.

Observe that from an economic standpoint this body of law is aptly named.

The law of waste has largely been supplanted by a more efficient method of administering property divided among different generations so as to maximize its value: the trust. By placing property in trust, the donor or testator can split up the beneficial interest as many ways as he pleases while assuring that the property will be managed as a unit, and hence its value maximized.

Common ownership (whether a tenancy in common, a tenancy by the entirety, or a joint tenancy) will be our final example. A leaves a plot of land to B and C, his children. B and C are in much the same position as the inhabitants of a society in which there are no property rights. If B spends his money to improve the property, C will share equally in the improvement, and vice versa, so neither party will have an incentive to invest in improvements. With only two parties, and a system of enforceable contracts, the absence of initial property rights is not very important: B and C can enter into a binding agreement allocating the costs and benefits of improvements. Nonetheless, the law, perhaps sensitive to the inefficiency of communal rights, permits any party to a tenancy in common or joint tenancy to obtain a partition of the property into separate, individually owned parcels.

§2.9.   *Time-limited rights: Patents and copyrights.*   An interesting class of property rights consists of those that, while otherwise exclusive, are limited in duration. Patents and copyrights are the usual examples. Useful ideas, like crops, are generally the product of hard work, which must be rewarded in order to be encouraged. This is the rationale for recognizing property rights in useful ideas. There is nonetheless a certain arbitrariness to the ownership of ideas. Suppose two companies are working independently to develop a new type of television receiver. One firm completes development first and obtains a patent. The other firm is now excluded from making or selling the new receiver, even though it would have developed the same product on its own within, let us assume, a month of its rival. The reward, a monopoly of the product, seems incommensurate with the patentee's actual achievement — the completion of its developmental work a few weeks ahead of its rivals. The reward is excessive in another respect. It consists of the right to obtain monopoly profits from the sale of the product embodying the patented idea and since this is a larger reward than most producers are able to obtain, resources may be diverted from the production of equally or more valuable goods to the production of ideas.[1]

These considerations support some limitation on the duration of a patent. But even if they were entitled to no weight, the recording problems that would be entailed by a system of perpetual patent rights would compel a time limit. How many current products and processes might plausibly be said to embody ideas first disseminated centuries ago? Were patents perpetual, how many contemporary manufacturers would owe royalties to the descendants of Leonardo? [2]

§2.10. *The right of privacy.* The emergence of a right of privacy further illustrates the utility of a conception of property broader than land and other tangibles. An individual's photograph may have value as advertising, but its use for that purpose may also reduce his satisfactions. Since a market transaction is feasible, by giving the individual the right to exclude the use of his picture for advertising purposes we can assure that the photograph will be used in advertising only when the value of such use exceeds the cost.

The principle is not limited to people who are shy. A celebrity might not want his picture used in certain advertising not because he was averse to publicity but because he could obtain a higher price from another advertiser. By recognizing his "right of privacy" we assure that his picture will be used in its highest valued advertising use.

Where transaction costs are high, the assignment of an exclusive right, to privacy as to other goods, becomes problematical. Suppose the rule were that a magazine could not sell the list of its subscribers to another company for purposes of soliciting unless the subscribers consented. It would be costly to obtain such consent, so if we are reasonably confident that the value of the list to the purchaser ordinarily is greater than the cost to the subscribers of the slight impairment of their interest in being let alone by direct-mail advertisers, we would want to assign the property right to the magazine.

Another example where transaction costs are usually prohibitive is that of news photographs. It would be costly for news-

§2.9. 1. For good discussions see Arnold Plant, The Economic Theory concerning Patents for Invention, 1 Economica (n.s.) 30 (1934); George J. Stigler, The Organization of Industry 124 (1968).

2. This does not complete our discussion of property rights in ideas. See especially §22.2 *infra*.

paper photographers, before photographing an accident or a demonstration or a political rally, to negotiate with each participant for the right to publish his picture. The high value that society attaches to the dissemination of news, including photographs, presumably exceeds the cost of the invasion of privacy that results.

A difficult case is presented when the information desired to be withheld is deservedly discrediting — information, for example, about criminal proclivities that bear on a job applicant's fitness for the job. One solution is to consider the cost of disclosure to the applicant as part of the price of his criminal conduct.[1]

§2.11. *Problems in the transfer of property rights.* In order to facilitate the reallocation of resources from lower valued to higher valued uses, property rights should, ideally, be freely transferable. But sometimes a transfer may injure third parties more than it benefits the parties to the transfer. Water rights provide a good example of this point.[1] As mentioned earlier, in the western states a property right in water is obtained by diverting water from a natural stream and using it for irrigation or other purposes. Over the course of time a stream will become completely appropriated in the sense that the total volume of the stream is owned in varying amounts by various users. Thus, A will have a right to take ten cubic feet per second during the months of July to December from a ditch at a specified location, B a right to take a certain quantity at another location during a specified period, and so forth. In addition, water rights are labeled by the date acquired (i.e., the date of the first diversion, or appropriation). In times of drought the available supply is rationed in accordance with priority of appropriation.

If A wants to sell his right to X, and X plans to use the water in the same place and manner as A, the transfer has no impact on the water rights of the other users of the stream. But suppose that A and all of the other present users are farmers who use the water they divert for irrigation, while X, the prospective purchaser of A's right, is a municipality. Then the transfer will affect rights holders downstream from the point of diversion.

---

§2.10. 1. See §22.2 *infra*.

§2.11. 1. The problem is discussed in Charles J. Meyers & Richard A. Posner, Market Transfers of Water Rights: Toward an Improved Market in Water Resources (National Water Commission report, July 1, 1972, pub. Natl. Tech. Info. Serv.).

About one half of the water that a farmer diverts for irrigation seeps back into the stream. This return flow can be and is appropriated by other farmers. A municipality may consume a much higher percentage of the water it diverts and what it does not consume may be returned to the stream at a different point. It may flow into a different stream altogether if the municipality is located in a different watershed from the farmer whose water right it has bought.

If the return-flow problem were ignored, water transfers would frequently reduce overall value. Suppose A's water right is worth $100 to him and $125 to the municipality; a sale will occur. But suppose further that whereas A returns one half of the water he diverted to the stream, where it is used by B, the municipality will return only one fourth of the water it obtains from A, and at a point far below B, where it will be appropriated by D. B would not sell his right to A's return flow for less than $50, while D would sell his right to the municipality's return flow for $10. Under these facts, the value of the water in its new uses (X and D's) — $135 — is less than in its old uses (A and B's) — $150.

The law deals with this problem by requiring the parties to the transfer to establish that it will not injure other users of the stream. In practice, this means that A and X, in order to complete their transaction, would be required to compensate B for the loss of A's return flow; they would not do so; and the transaction would fall through, as under our assumptions it should.

But there is a weakness in this solution: any new return flow that the purchaser generates will not be his property. Let the values to A, X, and B remain $100, $125, and $50 respectively but now let the value of X's return flow to D be $60. The value of the water in its new uses now exceeds its value in the old uses, but the law compels X to pay at least $150 for water that is worth only $125 to it. X is not compensated for the $60 in new value that its use will create, so it will refuse to complete the sale unless it can induce D to ante up the difference between $125 and what it owes to A and B. To do this it must convince D that it will not complete the purchase without such a contribution, for D knows that it will be able to appropriate X's return flow, should it materialize, without any charge. A more efficient solution, especially where more than one user may be benefited by the newly created return flow, would be to deem the transferee the owner of any new return flow that the transfer creates.

The absence of explicit property rights in broadcast frequen-

cies, a resource that has many of the same economic characteristics as water, may be responsible for the lack of any mechanism for permitting the sale of a frequency for a different use.
The broadcaster can sell to another broadcaster:[2] this is like the
sale by one farmer to another. But he cannot sell to a nonbroadcast
user, for example, a municipal police department that wants another frequency for its patrol cars. Such a sale would create much
the same problems as our example of the sale of water by a farmer
to a municipality. The mobile radio user, unlike the broadcaster
with his fixed transmitter, will be transmitting part of the time
from the former periphery of the broadcaster's broadcast radius,
and this will interfere with stations broadcasting on the same frequency in adjacent areas. Such problems could be solved by
judicial procedures similar to those employed in the transfer of
water rights, but this has not been the approach followed. The
only machinery that the law provides for the transfer of a frequency to a new use is a petition to the Federal Communications
Commission requesting a change in the allocation of frequencies
as between classes of use. Willingness to pay for the expenses involved in influencing the commission is substituted for willingness to pay a present owner of the resource.[3]

A serious problem in the transfer of water rights is the absence
of an adequate recording system. As mentioned earlier, the ownership of water rights is dependent on use. Not only can water
rights not be acquired save by actually using the amount of
water claimed, but disuse will lead, after a period of years, to a
forfeiture of the rights. A "deed" to water rights, stating that A
has the right to take ten cubic feet per second during a specified
period at a specified point, is but evidence of what A's legal right
is, and of what, therefore, he has the power to convey to a purchaser. An on-the-site investigation is necessary to verify that A
in fact owns (i.e., uses) what the paper record shows him to own.
And, in order to determine the significance of A's priority for
times of drought, the actual uses of other users of the stream and
the history of A's and other users' uses must also be investigated.

§2.12. *The effect of property right assignments on income*

2. See §2.2 *supra*.
3. The feasibility of instituting an explicit property rights system in frequencies
is explored in Arthur S. De Vaney, et al., A Property System for Market Allocation of the Electromagnetic Spectrum: A Legal-Economic-Engineering Study,
21 Stan. L. Rev. 1499 (1969).

distribution. The economist can assist the policy-maker not only by explaining the effects of an actual or proposed policy on the efficiency with which resources are used, but also by tracing the effects of the policy on the distribution of income and wealth. Consider, for example, a proposal to make a factory liable for the smoke damage to residential property owners. On a superficial analysis it might seem that the only wealth effect is to make the homeowners better off and the factory owner — surely a rich man — worse off. But the matter is more complicated. If the amount of smoke damage (and the cost of various measures to reduce it) increases as output increases, the new liability will increase the factory's production costs. If the firm was previously selling its product at a price just equal to its cost, either it must raise its price to cover the new cost or it must curtail its output (perhaps to zero) for, as we saw in Chapter 1, a firm will not sell below cost. Suppose, however, that the firm is in competition with other factories that also sell at a price equal to cost, and their costs are identical to its costs except that they are not liable for smoke damage (or perhaps have newer machinery that does not produce smoke). Then the firm cannot raise its price: consumers would immediately switch to its competitors, which sell the identical product at a price equal to the firm's old cost. If its cost of production is lower with a smaller output, it may be able to cover the new cost by contracting its output; otherwise it must close down. In either case there will be a reduction not only in profits but in the number of people the factory employs, in the amount of supplies it purchases, and in the amount of rent that it can afford to pay for the land on which the factory is located. If the employees have equally good employment opportunities elsewhere, and zero relocation costs, they will not be injured by the layoffs; otherwise they will be.

Now suppose that all of the competing factories are subjected to smoke liability and all experience, as a result, an increase in their production costs. A price increase is now feasible. Sales will not drop to zero: the product is identical for all of the firms but it is not identical to other products, so consumers may pay more rather than do without. But we know from Chapter 1 that there will be *some* substitution effects; the output of the industry will decline. The only difference between this and the previous case is that the consumers now share the burden of the liability, for some of them substitute other products when they would have preferred to continue to buy the industry's product at its former price, while others continue to buy and pay higher prices for the product.[1]

The workers and consumers who pay a part of the cost of compliance with a measure to reduce pollution may be a less affluent group than those who benefit from the reduction in pollution. A major cost of pollution is aesthetic and this is a cost primarily to well-educated, leisured, and well-to-do people. (Stated otherwise, the well to do are the principal consumers of aesthetic amenities.) And if the properties whose value is enhanced by a reduction in pollution are rental properties, the primary beneficiaries will be not the tenants but the owners (who may be wealthy): they will demand a higher rent for what is now more valuable property.

Observe that whether the creation of new (and therefore the alteration of existing) property rights will have significant wealth effects depends on whether the resources affected by the change are specialized, in the sense that they cannot command so high a price in an alternative use. If the land on which the factory is located is just as valuable for some other purpose not involving production of smoke, the imposition of liability will not affect the value of the land. If the workers have equally good alternative employment opportunities, they will suffer only to the extent of relocation costs from the reduction in the factory's demand for their services. Only if the land and their skills are more valuable in their present use than in any other use will the contraction or disappearance of the factory affect the landowner's and the workers' wealth.

The incidence of the wealth effects may depend on contract. If the employees have long-term employment contracts with the factory owner, he will be forced to absorb a portion of the costs that otherwise would have fallen on them. If the renters have long-term leases, a part of the benefit of reduced pollution will inure to them rather than to the owners. Although it is thus possible to protect by contract against the wealth effects of a change in property rights, the party desiring protection may have to compensate the other party for the risk.

When contracting is not feasible, due to high transaction costs, the wealth effects may be cushioned by anticipation. Suppose the traditional rule is that farmers have the right to be free from spark damage but there is some expectation that the rule might

§2.12. 1. A graphic presentation of the economic effects of changes in a firm or industry's costs may be found *infra* §20.1.

be changed. Then purchasers of farmland will pay less, and if the change materializes their loss will be smaller. The element of windfall gain and loss is thus largest when the change in property rights is completely unanticipated. Stability of property rights reduces the windfall gains and losses of the holders of the rights.[2]

SUGGESTED READINGS

1. Ronald H. Coase, The Problem of Social Cost, 3 J. Law & Econ. 1 (1960).

2. Harold Demsetz, Toward a Theory of Property Rights, 57 Am. Econ. Rev. Papers & Proceedings 347 (1967).

3. ————, When Does the Rule of Liability Matter? 1 J. Leg. Studies 13 (1972).

PROBLEMS

1. Suppose that it is possible to ascertain whether there is a deposit of oil under someone's land by directing a radio wave under the surface of his land. Moreover, to do this one need not be directly over the deposit, i.e., within his boundary lines; the beam can be directed obliquely. Should the owner of the land have the right to enjoin such electronic penetration as a trespass? Is the owner's possible aversion to gambling relevant here?

2. If the government auctioned off rights to use broadcast frequencies, would the amount bid by the high bidder be equal to the expected value of the use? Why not?

3. Should the government be required to pay for the information that it collects from individuals and firms for census purposes?

4. Would it make any difference from an economic standpoint if, instead of granting the individual the right to withhold his photograph for use in advertising, the law granted the advertiser the right to use an individual's photograph in advertising without his consent?

5. A beautiful waterfall runs by A's house. Should A be permitted to appropriate a right to the waterfall as against other users of the stream (assuming he is the prior claimant)? Are there any technical difficulties in recognizing such a right?

6. If there were no right to prevent a man from building so as to block a neighbor's windows, would the man be able to practice extor-

---

2. The wealth effects of property rights assignments are discussed in Harold Demsetz, Wealth Distribution and the Ownership of Rights, 1 J. Leg. Studies 223 (1972).

Topics sometimes discussed in property law courses appear later in this book. See §§16.5 (real estate taxes), 18.6 (housing policy) *infra;* cf. §20.2 *infra.*

tion? Is the possibility of extortion reduced by recognizing such a right? How does the law deal with this kind of extortion?

7. Are the following formulations of an economic test for which party to assign the property right to equivalent? If not, which is best? (a) Assign the right so as to minimize transaction costs. (b) Assign the right so as to maximize the probability that, if the right is more valuable to someone else than to the right holder, a transaction will occur. (c) Assign the right so as to make a transaction unnecessary to achieve efficiency.

8. What is the fallacy in the following statement? "Efficiency does not require that the government pay just compensation in an eminent domain proceeding, since if the property is worth more to the condemnee than to the government, he can pay the government not to exercise its eminent domain power."

9. A tuberculosis sanatorium is built in a residential area. Property values decline because the residents of the area fear contagion from the patients in the sanatorium. Their fear has no scientific basis. Should the sanatorium nonetheless be deemed a nuisance if the fall in residential property values is greater than the increase in the value of the parcel used for the sanatorium? See Everett v. Paschall, 61 Wash. 47, 111 Pac. 879 (1910); cf. §22.2 infra.

CHAPTER 3

CONTRACTS

§*3.1.* *The process of exchange and the roles of contract law.*
The last chapter emphasized the importance of voluntary exchange as a method of moving resources from lower valued to
higher valued uses. The process of exchange was assumed to be
dependable and uncomplicated, but this is true only in rather
artificial cases. I go to a store to buy a pound of rock salt. The
storekeeper and I negotiate a price. He inspects my money and
ascertains that it is legal tender. I examine the rock salt, taste it,
sift it, weigh it (on a scale that I carry with me), and so satisfy
myself that it is in fact a pound of rock salt of acceptable quality.
The inspections completed, the storekeeper and I simultaneously
exchange the money for the salt. One can be reasonably confident
that the salt was worth more to me than the money and the
money worth more to the storekeeper than the salt; otherwise
the exchange would not have taken place. But it is easy to alter
the facts so as to cast doubt on the proposition that exchange
always produces a movement to a higher plateau of value. The
salt is worth less to me than the storekeeper's minimum price
but I "buy" it anyway, not with cash but with a promise to pay
later that I intend to break. A pound of rock salt is worth $.50
to me and that is the price I pay, but the storekeeper short-
weights me. Or, perhaps through no fault of his, the bag he gives
me contains iron filings instead of rock salt. Another example: I
pay him $1 to deliver the bag of rock salt to me next Tuesday.
He pockets my money but fails to deliver on the agreed date,
perhaps because his delivery men go out on strike.

There are many contingencies that may prevent the process
of exchange from operating to reallocate resources to higher valued uses, especially when the exchange is carried out over a
period of time rather than simultaneously or when the performance of one or both parties involves a complicated undertaking.

To minimize breakdowns in the process of exchange is the basic function of the law of contracts.

Although the law has a useful role to play in assuring that exchanges in fact increase value, it would be a mistake to think that without a law of contracts the system of voluntary exchange would no longer function. The individual who regularly failed to perform his side of bargains would eventually find it difficult to find anyone willing to enter into exchanges with him — a costly penalty — except perhaps upon deposit of adequate security — also a costly penalty. Although contracts in the legal sense would not exist in our hypothetical world, we would expect at least as much explicit definition, either in writing or by reference to custom, of the undertakings of the parties to an exchange. They would be eager to minimize misunderstandings that might engender charges of bad faith, since someone against whom such charges were lodged might find it difficult to induce people to enter into exchanges with him in the future.

The alternative (or supplement) to reliance on mutual advantage, backed up by extensive use of credit bureaus, security deposits, and other means of self-protection, is to impose legal sanctions on the party to an exchange who fails to carry out his end of the bargain. Suppose I hire a contractor to build me a house. When the house is completed I refuse to pay him the agreed-upon price, solely in order to increase my wealth at his expense. To impose legal sanctions on such conduct is an appropriate method of facilitating voluntary exchange by protecting parties who perform in good faith against the bad faith of other contracting parties. Without such protection, exchanges would be more risky and therefore costlier undertakings. The provision of remedies for bad-faith breach of contract reduces transaction costs.

But this does not exhaust the function of contract law in promoting the efficient use of resources, as some examples will illustrate. A wealthy man in an expansive moment promises to pay my way through college. I give up my part-time job. He breaks his promise. I am unable to get a new job. A promises to deliver goods to B "on the twelfth." B thinks he means the twelfth of this month, but in fact A means the twelfth of next month — he could not possibly deliver so soon as B (unbeknownst to him) expects. A steel company agrees to deliver steel to a bridge-building company within sixty days, but the steel company has a wildcat strike and cannot make delivery. In none of these cases is the issue whether a party to an exchange has refused to carry out his end of the bargain. There is no exchange in the first case: my giving up my part-time job confers no advantage on the wealthy promisor. Indeed, he may not even have known that I gave it up. In the second case there is no voluntary exchange because the parties intended different transactions. In the third case performance was prevented by circumstances beyond the promisor's control. Yet in all three cases there is an economic argument for imposing sanctions on the party who fails to perform. The wealthy man's idle promise induced reliance that cost the promisee heavily when the promise was broken. Such a cost can be avoided for the future by holding such a promisor liable for the promisee's reliance costs. Of course it is necessary to distinguish the sort of donative promise that is likely to induce reliance from the sort that is not. I promise you a trivial gift and the next day withdraw my promise. I had no reason to expect you to rely, so whether or not you do rely the law will not hold me to my promise.

Suppose, in the case where the buyer and seller confuse the date, that there is a custom in the industry that a delivery date without specification of the month refers to the current month. A is new to the industry and ignorant of the custom. To hold A to the promise understood by B will have the salutary effect of inducing newcomers to master the language of the trade promptly. As for the third case, the steel company is probably in a better position to anticipate and take appropriate safeguards against an interruption of production due to a wildcat strike. If so, placing the risk of such an interruption on the steel company, by making it liable for damages to the purchaser from delay, may be the cheapest way of minimizing the costs of such delays in the future.

As these examples suggest, the question whether to treat a failure to carry through an undertaking as a breach of contract is in economic analysis similar to the question whether to treat an interference with a neighbor's land use as an invasion of the neighbor's property rights. The economic test in either case is whether the imposition of liability will create incentives for value-maximizing conduct in the future. Suppose I sell wool to a garment manufacturer, neither of us inspects, the wool turns out to have a latent defect, and the suits he makes out of the wool I sold him are ruined. Assume that the cost of inspection by either of us would be lower than the cost of the damage, discounted by the probability that the wool would have a defect. The manufacturer sues me for breach of contract. The central legal issue in the case is which of us had a duty to inspect. The answer depends, as to an economist it should depend, on the relative costs of inspection. If it is cheaper for him to inspect, his suit will fail in order to encourage him in his future dealings and others in similar situations to inspect; that is the solution that minimizes the sum of inspection and damage costs.

Does it make any difference to the future conduct of the parties which way the court decides? If it is really cheaper for me to inspect but the court, ignoring or mistaking the point, holds that I did not breach the contract, in subsequent contracts the buyer will pay me to include a clause in which I promise to compensate him for any latent defects. A corrective transaction is more likely than in a pollution or a chance-encounter accident case, where transaction costs are normally prohibitive. If there is already a contract, the cost of negotiating another clause should not be great. But this point only underscores the futility of a contract-law ruling that ignores the economics of the case. The ruling will not affect future conduct; it will be reversed by the parties in their subsequent dealings. But it will impose additional transaction costs, and these will be a pure waste of resources.

We have thus far emphasized the role of contract law in furnishing incentives to efficient conduct in exchange situations, a role that underscores the essential continuity among the law of property, of contracts, and (as we shall see in the next chapter) of torts. But the law of contracts has two other economic functions besides the maintenance of appropriate incentives. The first is to reduce the complexity and hence cost of transactions by supplying a set of normal terms which, in the absence of a law of contracts, the parties would have to negotiate expressly. The second is to furnish prospective transacting parties with information concerning the many contingencies that may defeat an exchange, and hence to assist them in planning their exchange sensibly. The parties, through their lawyers, are guided around the pitfalls in the process of exchange revealed by the opinions in decided contract cases.

§3.2. *Consideration.*   Let us examine some of the specific doctrines of the law of contracts. We begin with the principle that a promise, to be enforceable, must be supported by "consideration." The principle is used to deny liability for breach of a promise mainly in two types of cases. The first is where there is no exchange and where, therefore, enforcement of the promise would not advance the economic purpose of the law of contracts, which is to facilitate exchange. A truly gratuitous, nonreciprocal promise to confer a benefit is not a part of the process by which resources are moved, through a series of exchanges, into successively more valuable uses. This justification of the doctrine of consideration has been obscured by the characterization of "detrimental reliance" (my giving up my part-time job, in the first example of the preceding section) as consideration sufficient to support a wholly one-sided promise. There is, as we have seen, a good economic reason for awarding damages to one who has reasonably relied, to his detriment, on another's promise; but it obscures analysis to equate reliance with consideration in circumstances where no exchange is contemplated. A better approach would be to treat the breach of a promise likely to induce reliance as a form of negligence actionable under tort law.[1]

If gratuitous promises were generally enforced, however, people would be very cautious about making any statement that could possibly be construed as promissory; they might go to considerable lengths to disclaim promissory intentions whenever there was the slightest ambiguity. Such elaborate forbearance would involve costs not offset by benefits in the form of a more efficient system of exchange. It is uneconomical to require people to be too careful. By the same token it is uneconomical to encourage people to be too careless, which is why promises that can reasonably be expected to induce reliance give rise to liability despite the absence of consideration.

The second major type of case in which the doctrine of consideration renders promises unenforceable is one where, although the context is one of exchange, the undertaking of one or both of the parties to the exchange is left entirely vague. For example, the parties may not have specified a price or any method or formula for computing a price. To enforce the parties' agreement in such a case, a court would have to determine a reasonable price. But courts have no comparative advantage in determining at what price goods should be sold. On the contrary, in all but very exceptional cases negotiation between buyer and seller is the more reliable method of determining a reasonable price, i.e.,

---

§3.2. 1. See §4.2 *infra*. The detrimental reliance of the promisee may be likened to an accident that could have been prevented by an inexpensive precaution of the injurer — i.e., refraining from making a promise likely to be acted upon. The reader may wish to consider, after reading Chapter 4 (Crimes and Torts), the question whether the tort remedy would yield a different result from the contract remedy in the case where the promisor was prevented by circumstances beyond his control from fulfilling his promise.

one at which exchange is mutually beneficial. Whether the parties were simply incompetent in failing to specify a price, or were attempting to shift some of the costs of transacting to the taxpayers who pay for the judicial system, voluntary exchange is fostered by refusing to enforce the contract and thereby compelling the parties to complete their negotiations.[2]

Courts inquire only as to the existence, and not as to the adequacy, of the consideration for a contract. The distinction is important and economically sound. To ask whether there is consideration is simply to inquire whether the situation is one of exchange and a bargain has been struck. To go further and ask whether the consideration is adequate would require the court to do what we have just said it is less well equipped to do than the parties — decide whether the price (and other essential terms) specified in the contract are reasonable. It does not follow that a court is bound to enforce every contract. We shall see that there are cases where the presumption that the contemplated exchange increases value can be rebutted without inquiry into the reasonableness of particular terms and where, therefore, it is appropriate to refuse enforcement even though the promise sought to be enforced is supported by consideration.

§3.3. *Mutual assent.*   The presumption mentioned above is valid only when the parties in fact agree upon the terms of the exchange. If you offer to buy something from me for $10, but the telegraph company makes a mistake in transmission and the telegram as I receive it says "$20," the fact that I accept the offer as I understand it is no evidence that the sale will increase value: the good might be worth $14 to me, and only $12 to you. The "subjective" theory of contract, which holds that there must be an actual meeting of the minds of the contracting parties for an enforceable contract to arise, thus makes economic sense. But it does not follow that damages should never be assessed against one who refuses to carry out a promise that he would not have made but for a failure of communication — the "objective" theory of contract, too, has a core of economic justification — although it would promote clarity to classify such a refusal as a tort rather than a breach of contract.

In the telegraph case, the question that principally interests

2. Recall the discussion in the last chapter of the desirability of compelling market rather than legal exchanges where the costs of the market exchange are reasonably low (§2.5 *supra*).

the economist is which party[1] is in a better position to prevent misunderstandings as a result of garbled transmission. Possibly it is the party who selects the method of communication; he could send a confirmatory letter, or use the telephone or a messenger. If he could have avoided the misunderstanding at least cost, then placing liability on him may lead to a reduction in future such mishaps. Even if liability is imposed, however, it is misleading to speak of the defective communication as having created an enforceable contract; the defect makes it impossible to say whether an exchange was intended. Contract law treats conduct that imports acceptance of an offer as if it were subjective acceptance not because it wants to encourage exchanges that do not reflect the actual desires of the parties but because it wants to discourage misleading conduct. The analysis is identical to that of promises that induce reliance, where the fact that no exchange was intended does not defeat liability either.

The law's handling of the question whether to rescind a contract where the party seeking rescission made a mistake is generally consistent with the approach just suggested. If the contract is still executory, that is, if performance has not begun, the party will be permitted to rescind even though the mistake was the product of his own carelessness. The mistake destroys the presumption that an exchange pursuant to the terms of the contract would increase value, and, since the performance of the contract has not begun, is unlikely to have imposed costs on the other party. If the careless mistake is not discovered until after performance has begun, rescission is refused, because it would probably impose costs on the other party.

In the famous case of the sale of the cow "Rose 2d of Aberlone," [2] both seller and buyer believed that the cow was barren, and the price was set accordingly. In fact the cow was pregnant and worth about ten times as much as the selling price. The mistake was discovered before the cow was delivered to the buyer, and the seller promptly cancelled the sale. The court upheld the cancellation. If we accept the version of the facts presented in the majority opinion, the result appears consistent with efficiency. There could be no presumption that the cow was more valuable in the buyer's possession than in the seller's, its true

§3.3. 1. We ignore for purposes of this discussion the possible liability of the telegraph company. The reader can if he wishes assume that the telegraph company could not have prevented the error in transmission at a reasonable cost.

2. Sherwood v. Walker, 66 Mich. 568, 33 N.W. 919 (1887).

worth being an order of magnitude different from what the parties had thought. Neither party had been careless in thinking the cow barren. The cancellation imposed no cost on the buyer (other than the loss of a windfall gain). The only consequence of enforcement of the contract, in fact, would have been to confer a windfall gain on the buyer. No economic purpose would have been served by a finding of liability.

Suppose the cow is delivered before the mistake is discovered: should the courts intervene on behalf of the seller? Probably not. No economic purpose would be served by 'imposing liability on the buyer. Indeed, once the buyer has taken possession, there is an additional reason to cut off the seller's right to reopen the sale: in order to facilitate subsequent exchanges of the animal.

Sometimes a case of mutual mistake can be resolved by decomposing the contract into two distinct agreements: an agreement respecting the basic performance (the transfer of the cow) and an agreement respecting a risk associated with the transfer (that the cow will turn out to be different from what the parties believed). Had there been evidence[3] that the sale price of Rose 2d of Aberlone included her value if pregnant, discounted (very drastically of course) by the probability of that happy eventuality, the court would have been entitled to conclude that the parties had intended to transfer the risk of the cow's turning out to be pregnant to the buyer, in which event delivery should have been enforced.[4]

§3.4. *Fraud, incapacity, and duress.*   There are other situations in which the presumption that a contract, if carried out, will produce a value-increasing exchange fails. An example is where one party has induced a mistake by the other. The case for nonenforcement is very clear where the promisee induced the promise by an outright and calculated lie: not only would enforcement not facilitate voluntary exchange, but nonenforcement may discourage such conduct in the future. The case is less clear where the promisee failed to disclose a material fact to the promisor, who would not have made the promise had he known the fact. Information is costly to acquire, to disseminate, and to absorb. It would be inefficient to require the seller of a house to obtain and disclose every fact that might be material to a purchaser; it would be particularly inefficient to require the seller

---

3. As perhaps there was. See id. at 580, 33 N.W. at 924–925 (dissenting opinion).
4. Cf. §3.5 *infra.*

to obtain and disclose information that the buyer could obtain at lower cost.[1]

The case for nonenforcement of contracts against people deemed incapable of judging their self-interest, such as children and insane people, is also clear. If someone cannot judge what is in his self-interest, there is no presumption that the contracts he makes increase value. The defense of duress involves greater difficulty. The term is used in four distinct senses. It is frequently a synonym for fraud, as where an illiterate is induced to sign a contract that contains unfavorable terms which are not explained to him. Most cases involving the abuse of a confidential relationship, although grouped with duress cases, are at bottom cases of fraud. Duress in its original sense implies a threat of violence. B gives a promissory note to A who is holding a knife at B's throat. A court will not compel B to make good on his note to A, not because B did not act of his own free will — on the contrary, he was probably extremely eager to exchange the note for A's forbearance to kill him — but because A's behavior retards rather than advances the movement of resources to successively more valuable uses.[2] Duress is used in a third sense as a synonym for monopoly. A finds B wandering lost in a snowstorm and refuses to help him until B promises all his wealth to A. Perhaps here too B should be excused from having to make good on the promise; if we permit monopoly profits in rescue operations, an excessive amount of resources will be attracted to the rescue business.[3] In its fourth and vaguest sense, duress is used to refer to situations where, due to circumstances beyond the control of either party, the price of a good or service is much higher, or the terms of the sale much less favorable, to some people than to others. We offer examples of this fourth sense when we discuss consumer sales.[4]

§3.5. *Frustration and impossibility.* We have observed the confusion engendered by stating the issue in a contract case as whether to enforce the contract rather than whether to impose liability. The first formulation implies that if performance of a contract becomes impossible, it will be excused since the contract cannot be enforced. But whether the contract can actually be carried out is not the issue. Suppose I agree to supply someone

§3.4. 1. See further §3.6 *infra.*
2. See §4.1 *infra.*
3. Cf. §2.9 *supra;* but cf. §4.8 *infra.*
4. See §3.7 *infra.*

with 1000 widgets by July 1; my factory burns to the ground; and I cannot procure widgets from anyone else in time to fulfill the contract. Suppose, further, that there was no way in which I could have anticipated or prevented the fire, so that fulfillment of the contract was genuinely impossible. It does not follow that I should not be liable for the buyer's losses that resulted from my failure to perform. My undertaking may have implicitly included a promise to insure him in the event of my inability to deliver the promised goods on time. If such a contract of insurance was implicit in the transaction, it should be enforced.

A related case is where completion of performance by one of the parties is prevented, again by circumstances beyond his control, and that party wants to be excused from further performance or even wants to be paid for what he has done although it is not what the contract called for him to do. I hire a contractor to build me a house and midway through construction the building burns down. The contractor demands to be paid for the material and labor that he expended on the construction or, alternatively, refuses to rebuild the house without a new contract. The fact that he was prevented through no fault of his own from performing as contemplated by the contract should not automatically entitle him to cancel the contract (or be paid as if the burned-down building had been what I contracted for). The issue should be which of the parties was intended to bear the risk of fire. In the absence of evidence of the parties' actual intentions, the question can be answered by comparing the relative costs to the parties of insuring. Presumably in the case just put the contractor would be the cheaper insurer since he is in a better position than the owner to assess and to minimize fire hazards during construction.

§3.6.   *Consumer transactions: Fraud.*   Concern about fraud in the contracting process is most often expressed with respect to consumer sales, on the assumption that consumers are more easily gulled than business purchasers. The assumption is no more than plausible. If the business purchaser is deemed especially competent because he specializes in the purchase of goods that he uses in his business, why is it not possible to view the housewife as a specialist in the purchase of consumer goods? Indeed, the gain from specialization in purchasing consumer goods is presumably one reason why many women are full-time housewives.

We have suggested a criterion for allocating liability for ignorance between seller and buyer: according to who can obtain the relevant information at lower cost. If a consumer product is simple, any defects in it are patent, and it is the type of product that the consumer buys frequently (so that he has ample opportunity to become acquainted with its qualities), then a rule of caveat emptor makes good economic sense. If, however, the product is complex and any defects latent, and if it is purchased infrequently, the cost of obtaining relevant information may be much higher to the consumer than to the seller and the seller should be liable for nondisclosure of information important to a sensible choice by the consumer.

As products become more complex, the costs of consumers' obtaining necessary product information increase relative to those of sellers. The consumer can examine a horse's teeth as readily as the seller, but inspecting a brake assembly is another matter. It is no surprise that there has been a gradual expansion, through the doctrine of implied warranties, in sellers' duties of disclosure. But it is easy to exaggerate the importance of law in regulating the flow of information in markets. There are powerful private forces for generating product information. Competition among sellers is one. A seller whose product is superior in one respect or another to a rival's product has an incentive to inform consumers of this fact. By doing so he gives them information not only about his product but implicitly about rival products. If a firm is gaining sales away from his rivals by making false claims about his (or about their) products, they have an incentive to expose the false claims to the consumer. The efforts of firms to correct misleading advertising by rivals are commonly centralized in trade associations, which establish standards of quality and quantity upon which consumers can rely. With the increasing complexity of products and services, a variety of businesses have come into being whose function is to inform consumers with respect to the merits of particular goods. The department store is an important example. An expert purchaser of the goods of many competing manufacturers, it helps the consumer choose sensibly among competitive products.

But these arguments are not altogether compelling. The cost of the consumer's obtaining information on his own or through consumer intermediaries such as the department store or drugstore may in some cases be very high. And there can be no assurance that sellers' markets, left to themselves, will produce as much and as accurate information as consumers want (and would be willing to pay for). First of all, the process by which competitors correct misleading impressions created by one of their number does not work instantaneously, and the interim profits obtainable by the fraudulent seller may exceed any long-term costs in loss of reputation; this is especially likely if the seller can leave the market at low cost. Second, if a fraudulent seller is diverting only a small amount of business from any one of his rivals, none of them will have an incentive to take costly measures to correct that seller's misrepresentations, although the aggregate number of sales diverted by him may be very large. Perhaps this is why disparagement of competitors is relatively infrequent. The trade association is only a partial answer, for members of an industry do not have strong incentives to support trade association activity on a generous scale. Indeed, the seller who contributed nothing to the trade association's campaign against fraud would derive the same benefits from the campaign as the other sellers, and at no cost.

Third, not all industries are competitive. A monopolist (or cartel) may have a greater incentive to misrepresent the qualities of his product in order to increase the demand for it than a competitive seller. The fact of being a monopolist implies that the effect of his larger output will be diffused among a large number of substitute goods, none of which will be greatly affected, so there is even less likelihood than in the competitive case that any seller will have a strong incentive to combat the misrepresentation. A related point is that where information about a product pertains equally to all brands of the product, no producer will have a strong incentive to disclose it. For example, no cigarette manufacturer can profit from advertising that cigarettes are unhealthful, and since there are no close nontobacco substitutes whose producers could anticipate a marked increase in sales by convincing consumers of the hazards of smoking, no other type of manufacturer has a strong incentive to disseminate such information either. Observe that a cigarette manufacturer would also have a relatively weak incentive to advertise that cigarettes are good for you, even if it were true, because the gains from increasing the demand for cigarettes would be divided among the different cigarette manufacturers, even though none of the others had contributed to the cost of the advertisement.

Although the market may not produce as much consumer product information as consumers would be willing to pay for,[1] the role of contract law in protecting consumers against fraud or

---

§3.6. 1. To what extent is this a problem of an inadequate property rights system in information?

nondisclosure will remain a limited one so long as there is no effective device for aggregating many small claims into a single claim large enough to justify the expense of litigation; we discuss the possibility of such devices in a later chapter.[2] The limitations of contract law in this regard provide the conventional justification for public regulations, such as those administered by the Federal Trade Commission, of advertising and sales materials.[3] But contract law may provide a quite adequate remedy to the defrauded consumer when his performance under the contract follows the seller's in time, as in the typical installment contract. In such a case the consumer can rescind without instituting a lawsuit.

§3.7. *Consumer transactions: The question of equality of bargaining power.* We noted earlier the elastic character of the concept of duress as a defense to a suit to enforce a contract. Where a transaction is between a large corporation and an ordinary individual, it is tempting to compare the individual to the helpless fellow forced to sign a promissory note with a knife at his throat, especially if his contract with the corporation is a standard contract, or the consumer is a poor person. But is the analogy sound?

Many contracts (insurance contracts are a good example) are offered on a take-it-or-leave-it basis. The seller hands the purchaser a standard printed contract that sets forth in detail the respective obligations of the parties. The purchaser can sign it or not as he pleases, but there is no negotiation over terms. It is an easy step from the premise that there is no negotiation to the conclusion that the purchaser lacked a free choice and therefore should not be bound by onerous terms. However, there are two possible explanations, only one of them sinister, for why a seller might adopt a take-it-or-leave-it policy. The innocent explanation is that he wishes to avoid the costs involved in negotiating and drafting a separate agreement with each purchaser. These costs are likely to be especially high for a large organization that engages in so many transactions that it must adopt routine procedures for the guidance of its line personnel. The sinister explanation is that the seller refuses to negotiate terms with each purchaser because the purchaser has no choice but to accept his terms.

The sinister explanation is in general implausible because it

---

2. See §24.5 *infra.*
3. We discuss such regulation later. See §10.2 *infra.*

implicitly assumes the absence of competition. If one seller offers unattractive terms to a purchaser, a competing seller, desiring to obtain the sale for himself, will offer more attractive terms. The process should continue until the terms are optimal from the purchaser's standpoint. Thus, the purchaser who is offered a printed contract on a take-it-or-leave-it basis does have a real choice: he can refuse to sign, knowing that if better terms are possible another seller will offer them to him. All of the firms in the industry may find it economical to use standard contracts and to refuse to negotiate with purchasers. But what is important is not whether there is haggling in every transaction but whether competition forces sellers to incorporate in their standard contracts terms that maximize the purchaser's benefits from transacting.

Under monopoly, by definition, the purchaser has no good alternatives to dealing with the seller and the seller is therefore in a position, within limits, to compel the purchaser to agree to terms that in a competitive market would be bettered by another seller. Generally, however, the terms — all but one — will be the same whether under competition or under monopoly. The only difference will be that the monopolist's price is higher. But in any event the objection is to monopoly rather than to printed contracts.

An occasional feature of printed contracts that is objectionable but is not a problem of unequal bargaining power is the use of fine print to slip an onerous provision past an unwary customer. This may well amount to fraud. The economic test is whether the wording, placement, or format of the clause is such as to impose excessive search costs on prospective customers. But it is a problem of fraud rather than of bargaining power.

Contracts are sometimes said to involve duress if the terms seem disadvantageous to purchasers and the purchasers are poor people. An example is a sale on credit where the purchaser agrees that the seller may discount the purchaser's note to a finance company. The finance company can enforce the note free from any defense that the purchaser might have interposed in a collection suit brought by the seller. Suppose the purchaser buys a chest of drawers from a furniture store and the chest is delivered badly damaged. Meanwhile the store has discounted the purchaser's note to a finance company and the purchaser must therefore pay the full amount of the note. He has legal remedies against the furniture company if it refuses to replace the damaged chest but these may be costly to pursue.

It would be incorrect, however, to draw from the correct observation that such a contractual provision operates in favor of the seller the conclusion that the purchaser must have been coerced into agreeing to it. The provision reduces the cost of financing installment purchases by making collection suits cheaper and more certain.[1] In its absence the finance cost — a cost borne mainly by the consumer[2] — would be higher. Is it obviously wiser for a consumer to decide to pay more for a product than to decide to surrender one of his legal remedies against the seller? Of course, if the purchaser does not understand the effect of such provisions, he does not have a meaningful choice. This may be a problem but again it is one of fraud rather than of inequality of bargaining power.

§3.8. *Fundamental principles of contract damages.* When a breach of contract is established the issue becomes one of the proper remedy.[1] A starting point for analysis is Holmes' view that it is not the policy of the law to compel adherence to contracts, but only to require each party to choose between performing in accordance with the contract and compensating the other party for any injury resulting from a failure to perform.[2] This view contains an important economic insight. In many cases it is uneconomical to induce the completion of a contract after it has been breached. I agree to purchase 100,000 widgets custom-ground for use as components in a machine that I manufacture. After I have taken delivery of 10,000, the market for my machine collapses. I promptly notify my supplier that I am terminating the contract. I admit that my termination is a breach of the contract. When notified of the termination he has not yet begun the custom grinding of the other 90,000 widgets, but he informs me that he intends to complete his performance under the contract and bill me accordingly. The custom-ground widgets have no use other than in my machine, and a negligible scrap value.

In such a case, to grant the supplier any remedy that induced

§3.7. 1. Suppose abrogation of such provisions led finance companies to extract from sellers promises to indemnify them for any losses suffered as a result of inability to collect their notes due to the purchaser's having a good defense against the seller. Would this alter the conclusion that abrogation would result in a higher price to consumers?

2. The circumstances under which costs are passed on to buyers are considered in some detail *infra* §20.1.

§3.8. 1. A recent discussion of contract remedies from the standpoint of economics is John H. Barton, The Economic Basis of Damages for Breach of Contract, 1 J. Leg. Studies 277 (1972).

2. See, e.g., Oliver Wendell Holmes, The Path of the Law, in Collected Legal Papers 167, 175 (1902).

him to complete the contract after the breach would result in a waste of resources. The law is alert to this danger and, under the doctrine of mitigation of damages, would refuse to permit the supplier to recover any costs he incurred in continuing production after my notice of termination.

Let us change the facts. I need 100,000 custom-ground widgets for my machine but my supplier, after producing 50,000, is forced to suspend production because of a mechanical failure. Other suppliers are in a position to supply the remaining widgets that I need but I insist that the original supplier complete his performance of the contract. If the law compels completion, the supplier will probably have to make arrangements with other widget producers to complete his contract with me. It may be more costly for him to procure an alternative supplier than for me to do so directly. Indeed, were it cheaper for him than for me, he would do it voluntarily in order to minimize his liability for breach of contract. To compel completion of the contract would again result in a waste of resources and again the law does not compel completion but remits the victim to a simple damages remedy.

The problem exposed in the foregoing examples is a quite general one due to the fact, remarked earlier, that contract remedies are frequently invoked in cases where there is no presumption that an exchange pursuant to the contract would in fact increase value — such as cases of defective communication. Here we clearly do not want a remedy that will induce the party made liable to complete the exchange.

A system of contract remedies should, in short, give the party to a contract an incentive to fulfill his promise unless the result would be an inefficient use of resources — the production of the unwanted widgets in the first example, the roundabout procurement of a substitute supplier in the second. The dual objective can usually be achieved by allowing the victim of a breach to recover his expected profit on the transaction. If the supplier in the first example receives his expected profit from completing the 100,000 widgets, he will have no incentive to produce the remaining 90,000. We do not want him to produce them; no one wants them. In the second example, if I receive my expected profit from dealing with the original supplier, I become indifferent to whether he completes his performance.

In these examples the breach was in a sense involuntary. It was committed only to avert a larger loss. The breaching party would have been happier had there been no occasion to commit a breach. But in some cases a party would be tempted to breach the contract simply because his profit from breach would exceed his expected profit from completion of the contract. If his profit from breach would also exceed the expected profit to the other party from completion of the contract, and if damages are limited to loss of expected profit, there will be an incentive to commit a breach. There should be. Recall that cost, to an economist, is benefit forgone. The cost of completion to the breaching party is the profit that he would make from a breach and if it is greater than his profit from completion, then completion will involve a loss to him. If that loss is greater than the gain to the other party from completion, it is clear that commission of the breach would be value maximizing and should be encouraged. And because the victim of the breach is made whole for his loss, he is indifferent; hence encouraging breaches in these circumstances will not deter people from entering into contracts in the future.

An arithmetical illustration may be helpful here. I sign a contract to deliver 100,000 custom-ground widgets at $.10 apiece to A, for use in his boiler factory. After I have delivered 10,000, B comes to me, explains that he desperately needs 25,000 custom-ground widgets at once since otherwise he will be forced to close his pianola factory at great cost, and offers me $.15 apiece for 25,000 widgets. I sell him the widgets and as a result do not complete timely delivery to A, who sustains $1000 in damages from my breach. Having obtained an additional profit of $1250 on the sale to B, I am better off even after reimbursing A for his loss. Society is also better off. Since B was willing to pay me $.15 per widget, it must mean that each widget was worth at least $.15 to him. But it was worth only $.14 to A — $.10, what he paid, plus $.04 ($1000 divided by 25,000), his expected profit. Thus the breach resulted in a transfer of the 25,000 widgets from a lower valued to a higher valued use. To be sure, had I refused to sell to B, he could have gone to A and presumably negotiated an assignment of part of A's contract with me to him. But this would have introduced an additional step and so imposed additional transaction costs.

The rule that contract damages are measured by the loss of expected profit to the victim of the breach thus promotes efficiency. But the courts do not always follow this rule. An interesting case of deviation is *Groves v. John Wunder Co.*[3] The defendant, as part of a larger deal, had agreed to level some land

3. 205 Minn. 163, 286 N.W. 235 (1939).

owned by the plaintiff, but wilfully failed to carry out his agreement, and the plaintiff sued. The cost of levelling would have been $60,000 and the value of the land, after levelling, no more than $12,000. The court held that the plaintiff's damages were $60,000, reasoning that he was entitled to get the performance he had contracted for and that it was no business of the defendant whether or how much his performance enhanced the market value of the plaintiff's property.

The decision appears to be incorrect from an economic standpoint. It was not a case, familiar to us from our discussion, in the last chapter, of just compensation,[4] where value and market price were different. The land in question was a commercial parcel. If the plaintiff had wanted the performance rather than the $60,000, he would probably have brought an action for specific performance. He did not bring such an action and, even more telling, he did not use the money he won from the defendant to level the land.[5] The measure of damages was incorrect from an economic standpoint because, had it been known to the defendant from the outset, it would have made him indifferent as between breaching his agreement to level the land and performing it, whereas efficiency dictated breach: the $60,000 worth of labor and materials that would have been consumed in levelling the land would have purchased something less than a $12,000 increase in value.

The court never alluded to the real economic issue in the case, which was how the contract allocated the risk of a fall in the market for real estate, the 1930s depression having occurred after the contract was signed. Since the plaintiff as owner of the land would have enjoyed the benefit of any general increase in real estate values, the parties probably contemplated that he would also bear the cost of a general decline in those values. The effect of the court's judgment was to give the plaintiff a cushion, for which he had not contracted, against the impact of the depression on land values.

The application of the expected-profit rule presents many interesting questions. We discuss one more here. Compare the following cases. (1) A tenant defaults and the landlord promptly rents the property to another tenant at a rental only slightly be-

4. See §2.5 *supra*.
5. See John P. Dawson & William Burnett Harvey, Cases on Contracts and Contract Remedies 12 (2d ed. 1969).

low the rental of the defaulting tenant. In a suit against the defaulting tenant for the rental due on the balance of the tenant's lease, should the landlord be required to deduct the rental of the substitute tenant? (2) A manufacturer of widgets receives an order for 1000 widgets from X, but X refuses to accept delivery and the manufacturer resells the widgets he tried to deliver to X to Y at a price only slightly lower than the price X had agreed to pay. In a suit against X for the lost profits on the sale, should the manufacturer be required to deduct the profits he received on the substitute sale to Y?

The law answers yes in the first case and no in the second, and these answers are correct from an economic standpoint. The good supplied by the landlord is fixed in the short run: he cannot add a room because one more family wants to lease from him. The rental that he receives from the substitute tenant in our first case is a gain *enabled* by the breach of contract by the first tenant.[6] His true loss is, therefore, the difference between the two rentals. But a manufacturer can usually vary his output, at least somewhat, in the short run. X's default did not enable the manufacturer to obtain a profit from selling to Y: if X had not defaulted, the manufacturer could still have supplied Y with 1000 widgets. The profit on the sale to Y is a gain that the manufacturer would have obtained regardless of the default, so his true loss is the entire expected profit from the sale to X.[7]

§3.9. *Penalties and liquidated damages.* The law permits parties to a contract to specify in advance the damages to be assessed in the event of a breach. Their specification will be enforced unless the court finds that the parties' intention was to impose a penalty rather than to estimate the actual damages caused by the breach. If a contract makes a breaching party liable for substantially more than the actual damages that the vic-

6. Must mitigation of damages be required for this damage rule to be efficient?

7. A related question is whether overhead expense allocated to a sale should be deducted from damages for breach of contract, on the theory that if the sale falls through, the seller has saved the overhead as well as the direct expense of the sale. As most courts hold, it should not be deducted because it is not in fact saved. Overhead expenses (rent, interest, insurance, etc.) are by definition expenses that do not vary with short-run changes in output. Therefore a reduction in output due to the buyer's breach will not produce a savings in overhead expenses to the seller: his rent, etc., will not be lower because of his not making the particular sale. The question is incorrectly analyzed in Richard E. Speidel & Kendall O. Clay, Seller's Recovery of Overhead Under UCC Section 2-708(2): Economic Cost Theory and Contract Remedial Policy, 57 Cornell L. Rev. 681 (1972).

tim of the breach might suffer — which is the essence of a penal sanction[1] — the party will have an incentive to complete the contract even though, as in our last example, efficiency would be maximized by a breach.

One may wonder why parties to a contract would ever want to impose penalties for a breach. The answer is that a true penalty clause, as distinct from a liquidated-damages clause that seems very stiff only because actual damages would be hard to assess or would exclude certain elements of real loss (such as attorneys' fees), is in the nature of a wager on the likelihood of a breach. The party who insists on a penalty clause must pay the other party to accept the higher potential liability that it involves. What the first party gets for the payment is a windfall return in the event of a breach. The breach will make him better off than if it had not been committed. Why are such wagers not enforced? Perhaps as an aspect of a general hostility to the enforcement of gambling contracts; perhaps because the acceptance of a penalty clause is thought strong evidence of duress.

§3.10. *Foreseeability of damage.*   The economic rationale of contract damages is nicely illustrated by the famous rule of *Hadley v. Baxendale*[1] that the breaching party is liable only for the foreseeable consequences of the breach. Consider this variant of the facts in that case: A commercial photographer purchases a roll of film to take pictures of the Himalayas for a magazine. The cost of development of the film by the manufacturer is included in the purchase price. The photographer incurs heavy expenses (including the hire of an airplane) to complete the assignment. He mails the film to the manufacturer but it is mislaid in the developing room and never found.

Compare the incentive effects of allowing the photographer to recover his full losses and of limiting him to recovery of the price of the film. The first alternative creates little incentive to avoid similar losses in the future. The photographer will take no precautions. He is indifferent as between successful completion of his assignment and the receipt of adequate compensation for its failure. The manufacturer of the film will probably not take additional precautions either; the aggregate costs of such freak losses are probably too small to justify substantial efforts to prevent them. The second alternative, in contrast, should induce the

§3.9. 1. See §§4.7 and 25.1 *infra.*
§3.10. 1. 9 Ex. 341, 156 Eng. Rep. 145 (1854).

photographer to take precautions that turn out to be at once inexpensive and effective: using two rolls of film or requesting special handling when he sends the roll in for development.

The general principle illustrated by this example is that where a risk of loss is known to only one party to the contract, the other party is not liable for the loss if it occurs. This principle induces the party with knowledge of the risk either to take any appropriate precautions himself or, if he believes that the other party might be the more efficient loss avoider, to disclose the risk to that party. In this way incentives are generated to deal with the risk in the most efficient fashion.

§3.11. *Specific performance.* The existence of a variety of equitable remedies, such as specific performance, for breach of contract may seem inconsistent with our proposition that expected profit should be the measure of contract damages. But it is not clear that this is so, at least where equitable relief is decreed because damages would be difficult to quantify. Consider a typical real estate case (where specific performance is allowed as a matter of course): I have a contract to buy a house and the seller defaults. The estimation of damages may be very difficult, since, as we have seen, I may value the house a good deal more than the market does.[1] To remit a purchaser to damages in such cases might result in a systematic undervaluation of the costs of breach, since a court will perforce be guided by market price and be skeptical of a buyer's claim that the house is worth more to him. This problem can be solved by decreeing specific performance; but another economic problem is created. The fact that the seller defaulted may indicate that there is another transaction that increases value by even more than would completion of the sale to me; if so we want to encourage the breach. The results of decreeing specific performance are not catastrophic, since the seller can always pay me to surrender my right of specific performance and presumably will do so if a substitute transfer would yield him a higher price. But to require the seller to conduct this additional negotiation does impose additional transaction costs.

§3.12. *Marriage contracts and family law.* The law frequently imposes special rules on particular types of contract. One example is contracts in restraint of trade, discussed in Chapter 7. Another is the marriage contract. In formation much like other

§3.11. 1. See §2.5 *supra.*

contracts — a voluntary arrangement in which services are exchanged presumably to the mutual benefit of the parties — it is unusual in that, in theory anyway, it cannot be terminated unilaterally or even by mutual agreement. It is terminable only by the victim of a serious breach of the contract.

The policy of the law is thus to discourage agreements to dissolve marriage contracts. To describe it this way is to suggest why the policy is so widely flouted. An agreement to dissolve a marriage involves only two people. Transaction costs should therefore be low. And once the parties have arrived at mutually agreeable terms they need only manufacture evidence of a breach that provides legal grounds for divorce. Since the manufacture of evidence is not costless, a stringent divorce law will preserve some marriages by increasing the costs of dissolution. But most of those will be "preserved" in only a formal sense; the parties, although "married," will live apart. Were society more determined to preserve marriages it would, at the very least, prevent the parties from controlling the evidence. It would authorize divorce only when the public prosecutor, or some other third party, had established the commission of a breach of the marriage contract. The present system is tantamount to confiding the enforcement of laws punishing such "victimless" crimes as bribery and dope peddling to the bribed official and the narcotics purchaser.

A different economic issue is presented by recent proposals to permit unilateral divorce. If "unilateral divorce" connoted no more than that one party could dissolve the marriage subject to the payment of appropriate compensation to the other, it would mean simply that the marriage contract was now to be treated like other contracts, which either party can terminate at will if prepared to pay the damages of the other. But the proposals are not so straightforward as this. For example, under the proposal of the Uniform State Commissioners, in community property states the spouse who decided unilaterally to breach the marriage contract would be automatically entitled to receive one half of any property accumulated during the marriage.[1] This approach creates incentives for divorce and for marriages designed from the outset to end in divorce. A poor young woman marries a rich old man, knowing that every year his income exceeds his expenses and produces substantial savings. At the end of five years, pursuant to her original intention, she dissolves the mar-

§3.12. 1. National Conference of Commissioners on Uniform State Laws, Uniform Marriage and Divorce Act 35 (1971).

riage and claims one half of the savings built up during it. The sexes can be reversed in the example.

The unilateral divorce proposals complete a circle from the pre-Victorian era, when upon marriage the wife's property became the property of her husband. That rule, properly repudiated as part of the movement for women's emancipation in the latter part of the nineteenth century,[2] encouraged bounders to marry wealthy women. Unilateral divorce in the form proposed by the Uniform State Commissioners resurrects that incentive plus the symmetrical incentive for unscrupulous poor women to marry rich men.

The household is an important unit of production (child care, food, etc.) in the economy. Marriages not undertaken for mutual advantage create inefficiency, just as in the market sector. This argues for treating marriage contracts like other contracts, albeit there would be some practical problems in doing so. It would frequently be difficult to determine whether a breach had occurred, because the parties' mutual obligations were not well-defined. Damages for breach would often be difficult to measure. And while the agreement to marry and the exchange of vows could be treated as just another contract, the marriage relationship itself is in the nature of a partnership. Upon dissolution it becomes necessary to divide up the partnership assets. But the wife's share is difficult to determine because her contribution to the assets of the partnership is frequently nonpecuniary, although substantial.[3] The 50-50 rule of the community property states is probably reasonable, given the difficulty of monetizing the wife's contribution.

An efficient rule governing the dissolution of marriage might have the following elements:

1. Either party can terminate the marriage at will.

2. Upon termination either party may show (a) that the termination was the consequence of a breach of the marital undertaking by the other and (b) that he or she suffered damages as a result of the breach.

3. The breaching party's normal share of the partnership assets (property owned at the time of marriage plus 50 percent of the property accumulated during marriage) would be reduced by the amount of the damages.

2. For a good discussion see A. V. Dicey, Lectures on the Relation Between Law and Public Opinion in England During the Nineteenth Century 371–395 (2d ed. 1914).
3. See further *infra* §17.6.

4. As with other contracts, parties would be free to provide by express agreement for different terms and conditions of dissolution.

A major objection to treating marriage contracts like other contracts, and therefore within the power of the parties to shape and alter at will, may be anticipated: that dissolution of the marriage contract affects third parties, namely the children of the marriage. The costs to the children from the dissolution may exceed the costs to the parents of continuing the marriage. One reply is that the parents can be depended on to represent faithfully the interest of the children, which is manifestly false in many cases; another, that children should be regarded as the property of their parents, and thus as having no interests of their own worthy of legal protection. Since the economic interests of parents and children are frequently in conflict, and since the view of children as chattels does not accord with modern sensibilities, legal protection of the welfare of children, not only within the family but with respect to school attendance, safety, and the like, are distinguishable from other interventions in market processes. But the state lacks the will to prevent easy divorce, and the chief effect of the remaining legal barriers is to waste legal resources.[4]

SUGGESTED READINGS

1. George J. Stigler, The Economics of Information, in The Organization of Industry 171 (1968).

2. John H. Barton, The Economic Basis of Damages for Breach of Contract, 1 J. Leg. Studies 277 (1972).

PROBLEMS

1. Suppose courts, in determining the rights and duties of parties to a contract, do not use the criterion of efficiency to guide their decision but instead use a noneconomic criterion of fairness: what effect would their decisions have on the exchange process? Why is contract law in general an inappropriate area in which to enforce moral (insofar as they may be distinct from economic) principles?

2. Suppose A posts a reward of ten dollars for the return of his cat. B finds the cat and returns it to A without having known of the reward. He later finds out about it and claims the reward. From an economic standpoint, should B be entitled to claim the reward? (Hint: cf. §4.6

---

4. On the economics of marriage see Gary S. Becker, A Theory of Marriage: Part I, forthcoming in J. Pol. Econ. (1973).

infra.) *Should it make a difference whether A had disseminated notice of the reward widely?*

3. *Under the doctrine of "past" or "moral" consideration, a promise to repay a debt discharged in bankruptcy or otherwise uncollectible will be enforced. Can this result be justified on economic grounds?*

4. *What would be the economic effects of making breaches of contract enjoinable? In cases of frustration or impossibility?*

5. *To what extent could society use the law of contracts to alter the existing distribution of income and wealth?*

6. Paradine v. Jane, *Alleyn 26, 82 Eng. Rep. 897 (K.B. 1647), was an action for rent by a landlord. The lessee's defense was that he had been dispossessed by the army of Prince Rupert, a foreign invader. On economic grounds, should the court have accepted this defense?*

7. *From the standpoint of economic efficiency, should the law recognize and uphold homosexual marriages?*

CHAPTER 4

CRIMES AND TORTS

§4.1. *Crime as a distinct category of conduct.* Theft and the negligent running down of a pedestrian are both torts, and both crimes as well. Yet, intuitively, there is a difference between the character of the acts. We shall attempt to explain the difference on economic grounds, after first arguing that they cannot usefully be distinguished on the ground that one is intentional and the other unintentional.

Most accidental injuries are intentional in the sense that the injurer knew that he could have reduced the probability of the accident by taking additional precautions. The element of intention is unmistakable when the tortfeasor is an enterprise which can predict from past experience that it will inflict a certain number of accidental injuries every year. Conversely, in many intentional torts the element of intention is attenuated, as when a surgeon who unwittingly exceeds the limits of the patient's express or implied consent to surgical procedures is guilty of a battery.

Not only are unintentional torts such as negligent running down frequently crimes but, as the last example shows, intentional torts are often not criminal. In the usual medical battery case the issue is whether there was a sufficient emergency to justify a procedure to which the patient's consent had not been obtained in advance. This in turn depends on whether the costs of delay (such as the risk that the patient's condition might deteriorate and the added danger of subjecting him a second time to a general anesthetic) exceed the value to the patient of an opportunity to consider whether to undergo the procedure; if so, implied consent to the procedure will be found. The case is like the property and contract cases that we discussed in previous chapters. It does not isolate a qualitatively distinct form of conduct.

Another example of how intentional tort cases may dissolve into a dispute over the efficient solution to a conflict between legitimate activities is provided by the spring-gun cases, such as *Bird v. Holbrook*.[1] The defendant in that case owned a valuable tulip garden located about a mile from his home. Although the garden was walled, some tulips had been stolen. The defendant therefore rigged a spring gun. A neighbor's peahen escaped and strayed into the garden. A young man (the plaintiff in the case) followed the peahen into the garden in an attempt to recapture it for its owner, tripped the spring gun, and was injured. The court held that the defendant was liable for the plaintiff's injury because of his failure to post notices that a spring gun had been set (the incident occurred during the daytime).

The issue in the case, at least as an economist would frame it, was the proper accommodation of two legitimate activities, growing tulips and raising peacocks. The defendant had a substantial investment in the tulip garden; he lived at a distance; and the wall had not proved effective against thieves. In an era of negligible police protection, perhaps a spring gun was the most "cost effective" means of protection for the tulips. But since spring guns do not discriminate between the thief and the innocent trespasser, they deter owners of domestic animals from pursuing their animals onto other people's property, and so increase the costs (enclosure costs or straying losses) of keeping animals. The court in the *Bird* case implied an ingenious, but perhaps fragile, accommodation: one who sets a spring gun must post notices that he has done so. Then animal owners will not be reluctant to pursue their animals onto property not so posted. A notice will be of no avail at night, but animals are more likely to be secured then and in any event few owners would chase their straying animals after dark.

Observe that the analysis is ultimately the same as in the engine-spark case discussed in the chapter on property rights. The peahen is the counterpart of the sparks and the tulips of the farmer's crop.

What distinguishes common law crimes, such as murder, theft,

§4.1. 1. 4 Bing. 628, 130 Eng. Rep. 911 (C.P. 1828). For a more extended economic analysis of the case, see Richard A. Posner, Killing or Wounding to Protect a Property Interest, 14 J. Law & Econ. 201, 209–211 (1971).

and rape, from the conduct heretofore discussed is that the courts do not compare the values to the contestants of the right in question (to life, an automobile, a woman's body).[2] The theft of an automobile may increase the value of resource use: the automobile may be worth more to the thief than to the owner in the sense that the thief, if unable to steal it, would have bought it. Theft is punished because it is inefficient to permit the market to be bypassed in this way. Only two parties are involved; if the automobile is really worth more to the thief, a sale can readily be arranged.[3] We prefer this to his taking the car without the owner's consent. The taking substitutes for an inexpensive market transaction a costly legal transaction, in which a court must measure the relative values of the automobile to the parties. The objection to theft is thus similar to the objection to trespass.[4]

Observe the consequences if theft were freely permitted. Property owners would spend a great deal of money on devices for the protection of property and would substitute otherwise less valuable goods that happened to be less easy to steal.[5] Thieves would spend large sums to neutralize the owners' protective measures. The costs involved in allocating resources by these means would surely exceed those of voluntary exchange. Theft would be a somewhat more efficient method of resource allocation if the thief, like the railroad when it "takes" the farmer's crops through spark damage, were required to prove that the value to him of the object taken was greater than its value to the previous owner. But this is still a less efficient method of resource allocation than the market, so it is forbidden too. We tolerate it in the engine-spark case only because there the cost of market transactions is higher than the cost of legal transactions.

Theft and trespass are torts as well as crimes, not because they are like negligence and nuisance and medical battery, but because tort law provides distinctive remedies that are appropriate

2. See Guido Calabresi & A. Douglas Melamed, Property Rules, Liability Rules, and Inalienability: One View of the Cathedral, 85 Harv. L. Rev. 1089, 1125–1127 (1972).

3. What if the thief has no money (or borrowing ability)? Might not the auto still be worth more to him than to the owner? As the reader will recall from Chapter 1, "value" has a special meaning to the economist: it is willingness to pay. If the thief will not, because he cannot, pay the price that the owner would charge, then it cannot be said that the transfer of the automobile to him would increase value.

4. See §2.5 supra. A more complete discussion of the point may be found infra §25.1.

5. Do you see a parallel to the use of trade secrets as a method of securing property rights when patent protection is unavailable?

substitutes for or supplements to criminal remedies in many cases. Similarly, much conduct has been made criminal solely because the criminal law provides appropriate sanctions for it. Criminal sanctions are the subject of a later chapter. The important point here is the identification of a class of conduct that is distinctively criminal in the sense that the scope of appropriate justification is much narrower than in the ordinary property, contract, or tort dispute.

§4.2. *Negligence under the Hand formula.* The legal standard applicable to most unintentional tort cases is that of negligence, defined by Judge Learned Hand as follows: the defendant is guilty of negligence if the loss caused by the accident, multiplied by the probability of the accident's occurring, exceeds the burden of the precautions that the defendant might have taken to avert it.[1] This is an economic test. The burden of precautions is the cost of avoiding the accident. The loss multiplied by the probability of the accident is the cost that the precautions would have averted. If a larger cost could have been avoided by incurring a smaller cost, efficiency requires that the smaller cost be incurred.[2]

Why must the accident cost be discounted (that is, multiplied) by the probability of the accident? Compare two equal costs, one of which is incurred every year and the other every other year. If the second cost is averaged over the same period as the first, the second cost is found to be exactly one half of the first. Suppose that for every hour a railroad runs its trains at a speed of 50 rather than 60 miles per hour it incurs costs (in delay) of $1000 and reduces the chances of an accident (involving an average loss of $100,000) from one in 1000 to one in 2000. The average hourly savings in accident costs is $50 and this is the

§4.2. 1. United States v. Carroll Towing Co., 159 F.2d 169 (2d Cir. 1947). The economic interpretation of the Hand formula is elaborated in Richard A. Posner, A Theory of Negligence, 1 J. Leg. Studies 29 (1972).

2. A more precise formulation of the Learned Hand test — and one also more descriptive of how the courts in fact apply the test — would emphasize the difference between total and marginal loss avoidance (cf §6.1 *infra*). Suppose the accident cost is $1000 and the probability of its occurring, if no precautions are taken, is 100 percent. If precaution A, which costs $100, is taken, the probability will be reduced to 10 percent, involving a net savings in expected costs of $800 ($1000 × .90 — $100). If precaution B is also taken, the probability of the accident will fall to zero. But B costs $200. While the costs of A and B — $300 — are less than the accident costs avoided by taking them — $1000 — the marginal benefit of B — $100 — is less that the marginal cost — $200 — and clearly value would be maximized by taking only precaution A and devoting the resources consumed in B to an alternative use. See John P. Brown, Toward an Economic Theory of Liability, forthcoming in J. Leg. Studies (1973).

proper amount to compare with the $1000 accident prevention cost.

§4.3.   Contributory and comparative negligence.   Applied only to the defendant, the Hand formula would not always produce the efficient solution. Suppose that an accident cost (after discounting) of $1000 could be prevented by the defendant at a cost of $100, but by the plaintiff at a cost of only $50. The efficient solution is to make the plaintiff liable by refusing to allow him to recover damages from the defendant. If the defendant is liable, the plaintiff will have no incentive to take preventive measures (unless the damages to which he would be entitled would not fully compensate him for his injury), and the value-maximizing solution to the accident problem will not be obtained.

The doctrine of contributory negligence is the law's answer to this problem. If the plaintiff could have prevented the accident at a cost lower than the discounted accident cost, he cannot recover. This takes care of the previous example. But suppose it is the plaintiff who can prevent the $1000 accident at a cost of $100, and the defendant at a cost of $50. If the plaintiff is barred from recovery by the doctrine of contributory negligence, as the Hand formula, applied literally to the plaintiff, would require, the defendant will have no incentive to take what turns out to be the more efficient preventive measure.[1]

Several states have replaced contributory negligence with a comparative negligence standard, whereby the plaintiff's damages are reduced by the percentage by which his own negligence contributed to the accident. This is not the correct economic standard either, because in a case like the last put, for example, it would result in the parties' spending more than the efficient amount on accident prevention. If the defendant in the last example is fully liable for the accident, he will spend $50 to prevent it and the plaintiff nothing, so the accident will be prevented at a cost of only $50. Suppose the defendant is liable for only, say, two thirds of the accident cost, because the plaintiff was also negligent (i.e., could also have prevented the accident at a cost, $100, less than the accident cost). Being liable for a judgment of $666.67, the defendant will still have an incentive to spend $50 on accident prevention, while the plaintiff, since he must bear a cost of $333.33 if an accident occurs, will have an incentive to spend $100 to prevent the accident. The parties may invest a

---

§4.3. 1. Do you think courts in fact apply the Hand formula literally in such cases?

total of $150 in accident prevention, resulting in a $100 increase in the cost of preventing the same accident, or may invest nothing (either party, knowing that the other party had an incentive to prevent the accident, might, in reliance thereon, make no attempt to prevent it himself), resulting in an avoidable cost of $950.[2]

Having sketched the basic test of negligence liability, we turn to some specific applications. We begin with the defense of custom.

§4.4. *Custom as a defense.*   Should the defendant's compliance with the standard of safety that is customary in its industry be recognized as a defense to a negligence action? If the answer is yes, only firms that lag behind the average firm in their industry in adopting safety precautions will be held liable. This is a satisfactory result if there is reason to expect the average firm to take all cost-justified precautions without the coercion of law. However, no firm will have an incentive to take precautions against accidents that are dangerous only to people with whom the firm does not, and due to high transaction costs cannot, deal. The potential victims will not pay the firm to take precautions; nor will its customers since they do not benefit from the precautions. If the firm tried to pass on to them, in the form of higher prices, the added costs of the precautions, it would be undercut by a competitor.

In these circumstances there is no presumption that the industry average safety level is optimum and the law properly rejects compliance with custom as a defense. Where, however, the accident in question is dangerous only to the industry's customers, the level of precautions taken by the industry's firms is more likely to be efficient. The industry's customers will pay extra money for the industry's product or service until the last dollar spent buys just one dollar in accident cost reduction.[1] Moreover, firms will have an incentive to discover and introduce new safety improvements that bring about a reduction in accident costs greater than the costs of the improvements, for the firm that first introduces such an improvement will be able to increase prices by the amount of the accident cost reduction, and thereby increase its profits.[2] It is thus ironic that the classic statement of

2. How would you reformulate the defense of contributory or comparative negligence to avoid inefficient results?

§4.4. 1. The example assumes that the customers are risk neutral. The significance of the assumption is discussed in the next section.

2. But cf. §4.14 *infra.*

the principle that compliance with custom is not a defense to a negligence action should have been made in a case in which the plaintiff was the defendant's customer.[3]

In one area of negligence, that of medical malpractice, the courts, consistent with the distinction just suggested, have allowed the defense of custom. The duty of care of a physician toward his patient is to comply with the customary standards of the medical profession in the area in which the physician is practicing. Because victim and injurer are in ,a buyer-seller relationship, the potential injurers (doctors) have an incentive independent of the law to provide the level of care for which potential victims are willing to pay. Observe the overlap here between tort and contract rights. The physician implicitly promises to treat the patient with the care customary among physicians in the area. If he does not use that much care he is guilty of malpractice, a tort, but he has also and by the identical conduct violated his contract with the patient.[4]

§4.5. *Attitudes toward risk and the assumption of risk defense.* Our earlier statement that the customer would presumably pay for safety until the last dollar he paid was just equal to the reduction in the discounted accident cost facing him implicitly assumed that he was risk neutral rather than risk preferring or risk averse. What do we mean? Let us first define "expected gain" (or loss) as the amount of a gain (or loss), if it materializes, discounted by the probability that it will materialize. The expected gain of a 100 percent chance of obtaining $100 is $100. This is identical to the expected gain of a one percent chance of obtaining $10,000. Yet one observes that people are not indifferent among transactions in which the expected gains are identical but the risks different. Many people would sell a one percent chance of obtaining $10,000 for $99, or indeed for a good deal less; they are risk averse. Many other people would buy the same chance for $101, or a good deal more; they like risk. A risk averter always prefers the certain value of an expected gain to the expected gain; a risk preferrer, the opposite. One who is risk neutral is indifferent between the expected gain and its certain value.

Taste for risk is relevant in the accident field because the failure to take safety precautions normally creates a risk rather than a certainty of an accident. People who are risk preferrers will

3. The T. J. Hooper, 60 F.2d 737 (2d Cir. 1932).
4. For a further discussion of the defense of custom see §23.1 *infra.*

often refuse to pay for what to the risk neutral would be a cost-justified precaution. Suppose that manufacturers of soft drinks could, at a cost of 10¢ per bottle, reduce the probability of the bottle's exploding and injuring the customer (average injury: $10,000) from one in 20,000 to one in 40,000. A risk-neutral customer would be happy to pay 10¢ more per bottle, since the expected gain is 25¢. A risk-averse customer would pay more than 25¢ more per bottle. But the risk preferrer is a gambler: he may not be willing to pay even 10¢. Depending on the distribution of attitudes toward risk among their customers, and the costs of making some but not all bottles safer, bottle manufacturers may not be able to recoup the cost of the improvement, albeit it would reduce accident costs by a greater amount.

To apply the Hand formula, which assumes risk neutrality, in such a case would reduce efficiency. The economist is no more disposed to look behind the taste for risk than the taste for pickled beets. If the opportunity cost of the bottle safety improvement is 10¢ but it is worth less than 10¢ to the purchasers of the improvement because they like risk, then value would be increased by diverting the resources used to make the improvement to their next best (10¢) use. A rule of law that induces bottle manufacturers to adopt the improvement will reduce the value of those resources. The assumption of risk doctrine is thus in accord with economic theory. Nor is it equivalent to saying that the defendant was not negligent or the plaintiff contributorily negligent. To be sure, no one who is not a risk preferrer would knowingly assume a risk that he could avert at a price lower than the expected accident loss. In a world without risk preferrers, an assumption of risk defense would have no applications. The function of the defense is to permit those who like risk to trade on their taste. The defense of contributory negligence is unrelated. Plaintiff's willingness to waive cost-justified precautions by the defendant does not imply that the plaintiff could have prevented the accident by cost-justified precautions of his own.

The converse of the assumption of risk doctrine is not found in tort law. This would be a rule that required potential injurers to take precautions beyond those justified by the discounted accident cost, to protect potential victims who were risk averse.[1]

§4.5. 1. Would this rule be necessary in cases where there was, or at reasonable cost could be created, a seller-buyer relationship between the parties to the accident?

§4.6. *Duties toward trespassers.*   As a general rule, a land-owner is not liable for negligent injuries to trespassers. This seems to contradict the Hand formula, but can be reconciled with it by assuming that in the usual case the accident could have been prevented at lower cost by the trespasser, simply by not trespassing, than by the landowner. Although there are cases where the cost of avoidance by the trespasser is larger than the cost of avoidance by the landowner, normally the trespasser can purchase the land (or an easement in it) and so cease to be a trespasser. The principle that there is no duty of care to tres-passers may thus be viewed as serving the function — by now familiar to the reader — of encouraging market rather than legal transactions where feasible. Occasionally, however, a transaction between landowner and trespasser will not be feasible, as in the famous case of *Ploof v. Putnam.*[1] The plaintiff, caught in a storm, attempted to moor his boat at the defendant's dock. An employee of the defendant shoved the boat away and it was later wrecked by the storm. The plaintiff sued for the damage. The value to the plaintiff of being able to trespass on the defendant's property during the storm was great and the cost to the defen-dant of preventing the wreck of plaintiff's boat small. But nego-tiations for landing rights were, in the circumstances, hardly feasible. The court properly held the defendant liable for the wreck.

Two additional points about the case are worth noting. (1) The plaintiff would probably have been liable to the defendant for any damage caused his dock.[2] This liability is appropriate to encourage dock owners to cooperate with boats in distress.[3] (2) It is by no means clear that defendant would have been adjudged negligent had there been no effort to shove off plaintiff's boat but the dock had been in bad repair and had collapsed when the plaintiff attempted to moor his boat. The probability of a boaṫ's being in distress in the vicinity of the dock may have been so slight that, under the Hand formula, proper maintenance of the dock would not have been a cost-justified precaution. But at the point in time when plaintiff's boat attempted to land, the probability of a serious accident was high, the expected accident loss great, and the cost of avoidance small.

Ploof may be viewed as a special application of the "last clear

§4.6. 1. 51 Vt. 471, 71 A. 188 (1908).
2. See Vincent v. Lake Erie Transp. Co., 109 Minn. 456, 124 N.W. 221 (1910).
3. The need for encouraging rescues is discussed in the next section.

chance" doctrine. A man is using the railroad track as a path. Since he is a trespasser, the railroad has no duty to keep a careful lookout for him. But if in fact the crew sees him it must blow the train's whistle and take any other necessary and feasible precautions to avoid running the trespasser down. The economic rationale of this rule is that, even though the accident might have been prevented at very low cost had the trespasser simply had sense enough to stay off the track, at the moment when the train is bearing down upon him it is the engineer who can avoid an accident at least cost and this cost is substantially less than the expected accident cost. Alternatively, the case may be viewed as one where, although the cost to the victim of preventing the accident is less than the accident cost, the cost to the injurer of preventing the accident is lower than the victim's accident prevention cost.[4]

§4.7. *Foreseeability.* In several cases landowners have been held liable for simple negligence to trespassers where the negligent injury could not have been foreseen by the trespasser. A trespasser beds down for the night in a newly constructed but unoccupied house in a real estate development and is asphyxiated because the developer had accidentally spliced a gas main and a water pipe to the house.[1] There is a sound economic basis for refusing to permit the developer to interpose the defense of no duty to trespassers. In some cases the value of trespassing to the trespasser will be greater than the expected accident cost (plus any damage to the owner), and transaction costs will be prohibitively high. In these cases trespassing will increase value. Therefore, we want prospective trespassers to weigh the relevant values and costs. But they cannot weigh accident costs that are unforeseeable. A newly constructed residential building is normally a safe place. The trespasser has no reason to foresee being asphyxiated. He may have made a perfectly rational judgment that the value of his trespass exceeded all expected costs, including accident costs.[2]

If the trespasser should not be liable for failing to take precautions the utility of which he had no reason to foresee, neither should defendants be liable for unforeseeable accidents. This is the principle of the *Palsgraf* decision.[3] The probability of a freak accident is by definition very low; therefore the expected acci-

4. See §4.3 *supra.*
§4.7. 1. Ehret v. Village of Scarsdale, 269 N.Y. 198, 199 N.E. 56 (1935).
2. Is Bird v. Holbrook, §4.1 *supra,* a similar case?
3. Palsgraf v. Long Island R.R., 248 N.Y. 339, 162 N.E. 99 (1928).

dent cost will usually be low. In a truly freak accident the expected accident cost may approach zero, and was surely little more than that in *Palsgraf*. Not preventing a negligible expected accident cost is consistent with the Hand formula.

Observe the symmetry between torts and contracts in the treatment of foreseeability. The asphyxiated trespasser is like the contract breaker in *Hadley v. Baxendale*: neither could foresee the consequences of his conduct, and neither was held liable for those consequences. The developer is like the commercial photographer in our variant of *Hadley v. Baxendale*: each could foresee the consequences of a failure to take precautions and should either have taken precautions himself or, if the other party could do so more cheaply, communicated the danger to the other party.

§4.8.   *The duty of rescue.*   In both *Ploof* and the conventional last clear chance case, the courts in effect require defendants to warn or rescue someone who is in danger through no fault of theirs — they did not endanger him by failure to take cost-justified precautions. In some cases, however, courts take the inconsistent position that there is no duty to help people in distress, even when assistance can be rendered at trivial cost. Walking down the street I see a flower pot fall out of a window, threatening another pedestrian. I could save him simply by shouting a warning but I keep silent. The expected accident cost is high; the cost of my taking the precaution that will avert it would be trivial. Nonetheless I am not liable for failing to do so. The result is irreconcilable with the economic standard implicit in the Hand formula. Had transaction costs not been prohibitive the endangered pedestrian would surely have paid me enough to overcome my reluctance to utter a warning cry. To make me liable, therefore, would increase value. Nor would there be a difference in principle if the attempt to warn or rescue might endanger the rescuer, as in many drowning cases. If the danger to the rescuer (and hence expected cost of precautions) is less than the danger to the person in distress (and hence expected accident cost), then the rescue will increase value, at least if the lives of the two parties are equally valuable or the life of the victim more valuable.

There is an alternative approach, which the law has adopted in a few cases (notably that of physicians who render aid under emergency conditions): to grant the rescuer a legal right to be compensated for his costs of rescue. If these costs are correctly computed, so that the rescuer is fully compensated for the time and any risk involved in the rescue as well as for his out-of-pocket expenses, rescuers will no longer be reluctant to rescue. Unfortunately they may be indifferent as between rescuing and not rescuing. The liability approach is more effective in inducing rescue. Under that approach the cost to the putative rescuer of not rescuing is the value of the rescue to the victim minus the costs of the rescue to the rescuer; this difference will often exceed the costs of the rescue. To award the rescuer the value of the rescue would not be an appropriate solution since if the value exceeded the costs of the rescue, the rescuer would obtain an excessive return and this might induce overinvestment of resources in rescue operations.[1]

§4.9. *Compensatory vs. punitive damages.* The general rule is that a negligence victim is entitled only to compensatory damages, while the victim of an intentional tort may sometimes obtain punitive damages as well. The limitation to compensatory damages in negligence cases is consistent with the economic criterion implicit in the Hand formula. If the defendant's liability exceeded the expected accident cost he would have an incentive to incur prevention costs in excess of the accident cost and this would be uneconomical. The reasons for sometimes allowing punitive damages in intentional tort cases are various. In some areas where punitive damages are allowed, notably defamation, the injury to the plaintiff is exceedingly difficult to quantify. In cases of conduct that is "criminal" in the limited sense discussed at the beginning of this chapter, punitive damages are necessary in order to prevent people from substituting legal for market transactions. Where a tort is concealable, there is an additional reason for awarding punitive damages. Suppose that a professional thief can expect to be caught only one time in ten. If the judgment in the one case in which he is caught is limited to the damages of that particular victim, it will be the equivalent of imposing a 10 percent licensing tax on thievery, and will fail as a deterrent. Damages should be determined by dividing the victim's loss in the particular case by the percentage of cases in which tortfeasors of this type are brought to bar. Since not all negligent injurers are apprehended, some punitive damages should probably be allowed in negligence cases. But the problem of

§4.8. 1. Again compare §2.9 *supra.*
Is the law's (vanishing) distinction, illustrated by this section, between misfeasance and nonfeasance as bases of liability equivalent to the economist's distinction between "external costs" and "external benefits?" From an economic standpoint, should the distinction lead to a difference in liability?

apprehension is especially acute with regard to the intentional torts that overlap with common law crimes, such as theft and battery, and it is here that punitive damages are commonly allowed.[1]

The association of negligence with purely compensatory damages has promoted the erroneous impression that liability for negligence is intended solely as a device for compensation. Its economic function is different: it is to deter uneconomical accidents. As it happens, the right amount of deterrence is produced by compelling negligent injurers to make good the victim's losses. Were they forced to pay more (punitive damages), some economical accidents would also be deterred; were they permitted to pay less than compensation, some uneconomical accidents would not be deterred. It is thus essential that the defendant be made to pay damages and that they be equal to the plaintiff's loss. But that the damages are paid *to the plaintiff* is, from an economic standpoint, a detail.[2] It is payment *by the defendant* that creates incentives for more efficient resource use. The transfer of the money to the plaintiff affects his wealth but does not affect efficiency or value.[3]

§4.10. *Damages for loss of earning capacity.* A nonfatal accident may have three economic consequences for the victim. It may compel him to make outlays for medical and related expenses, impair his earning capacity, and cause pain and suffering. All three kinds of loss are economic (the first obviously so) in

§4.9. 1. The nature of punitive sanctions is explored at greater length in Chapter 25.

2. But a very important detail: it is necessary to the private enforcement of tort law, as explained *infra* §23.1.

3. This conclusion may be somewhat overstated, apart from the important qualification pointed out in note 2 *supra*. If victims of negligent accidents are not compensated, they will take some precautions for they know that the law of negligence will not be administered so perfectly that all negligent accidents are in fact deterred. This seems at first glance a desirable result since, if the victim's precaution costs less than the expected negligent-accident cost (and this is the only circumstance in which the victim will take precautions), value is maximized if the precaution is taken and the accident prevented. However, the knowledge that victims will take precautions against negligent accidents will reduce the incentive of potential injurers to avoid inflicting such accidents. Suppose, for example, that the expected accident cost is $1000, the cost of prevention to the injurer is $100, and the cost of prevention to the victim is $200. Under a proper rule of negligence–contributory negligence the injurer in this case would be fully liable if an accident occurs, and let us suppose he is. But if the victim is not entitled to compensation, the injurer may take no precautions, confident that the potential victims (once they get wind of his decision, perhaps after similar accidents have occurred) will take precautions. The accident will be prevented, and the injurer will have saved $100. But society will have incurred an unnecessary expense of $100 to prevent the accident.

that they impose opportunity costs. A victim no longer able to work sustains a cost equal to the net income that he would have received for his labor. A victim who loses a finger sustains a cost that can be conceived of in various ways, including as the price he would have demanded from someone who made a credible offer to purchase the finger.

Where an accident disables the victim from working for some period into the future, courts, rather than ordering the defendant to make periodic payments during the period of disability (analogous to alimony payments), order him to pay the victim a lump sum equal in value to the expected future stream of earnings. They do not make the mistake of computing the lump sum by simply multiplying the amount of the periodic payment by the number of periods during which the victim is expected to remain disabled. This method of computation would overcompensate the victim, because at the end of the period he would have received not only an amount equal to the sum of the periodic payments, but interest on that sum, which he would not have received had payment been made periodically rather than in a lump at the outset. The lump sum should be equal to the price that the victim would have had to pay in order to purchase an annuity calculated to yield the periodic payment for the expected duration of the disability, and no more.

The payment of a lump sum is preferable to periodic payment on two economic grounds. First, it economizes on administrative expenses. Second, it avoids the disincentive effects of tying continued receipt of money to continued disability. Having received the lump sum, the victim has every incentive to overcome his disability sooner than had been estimated. A system of periodic disability payments, in contrast, would be the equivalent of a 100 percent tax on earned income. For example, suppose the victim had an earning capacity of $5000 per annum and is believed to have been totally disabled. He receives a periodic payment of $5000. If he recovers, returns to work, and earns $5000, his disability payment of $5000 will cease. The cost of returning to work thus equals $5000, the benefit, so he has nothing to gain from returning to work.[1]

Courts have had some trouble with the proper criterion of

§4.10. 1. Actually, he will lose money by returning to work, since working involves costs (income tax, commuting, work clothes, etc.) that are avoided by staying home and collecting disability payments. Of course, work might yield nonpecuniary income that would offset these expenses (or, for that matter, might impose nonpecuniary costs).

damages in cases involving disabled housewives. To value a housewife's services by adding up the amounts that would be required to hire the various components of these services (cleaning, child care, cooking, etc.) has troubled the courts, and rightly so; it would violate the opportunity cost concept. The value of a housewife's services, and hence the cost to the family if those services are eliminated, is the price that her time would have commanded in an alternative use. Suppose she had been trained as a lawyer and could have earned $15,000 working for a law firm but chose instead to be a housewife. Suppose further that the various functions she performed as a housewife could have been hired in the market for $8000. Since she chose to stay at home, presumably her services in the home were considered by the family to be worth at least $15,000;[2] if not, the family could have increased its real income by having her work as a lawyer and by hiring others to perform her household functions. The decision that she remain at home may have been quite rational, for her skills as a housewife, particularly in child care, may have exceeded what could be obtained in the market at the same price. Therefore, the loss when she was disabled was at least $15,000. Courts do not use the opportunity cost concept in determining damages in such cases, but they approximate it by allowing testimony of the quality of the housewife's household services. This is an oblique method of avoiding the pitfall of valuing such services at the cost of domestic servants.

Where the earnings lost as a result of a disabling injury would have been obtained over a long period of time into the future, the choice of the interest rate to use to discount those earnings to present value greatly affects the size of the award. The higher the interest rate, the smaller the award since it will earn more interest. At 8 percent, the present value of $1.00 received every year for 25 years is $10.67; at 5 percent, it would be

2. This ignores, however, the incentive that the income tax system gives a woman to remain at home even if the value of her services outside of the home would be greater than the value of her services as a housewife. See §16.8 *infra*. An additional possibility is that the woman derives nonpecuniary income, perhaps in the form of leisure, from remaining at home. This income may be unaffected by the disability. Suppose, in the example in the text, that the value of the wife's services in the home, $15,000, is composed of $10,000 in services rendered and $5000 in leisure produced. If the value of her leisure time is unaffected by the disability (it could, however, be reduced by the disability), then the cost of the disability is $10,000 rather than $15,000 a year. It is also possible, however, that the job outside the home would have yielded additional nonpecuniary income above the $15,000, in which event that figure might well be too low an estimate of the cost of the accident.

$14.09, almost one third greater. It is intuitively appealing but, if there is inflation,[3] incorrect to use the current market rate of interest for this purpose.

The market rate of interest has two components: the opportunity cost of money, or true interest rate, and the rate of inflation. Suppose the opportunity cost of money is 4 percent a year but the value of the dollar is falling at a rate of 3 percent a year. If I lend $100 for one year at 4 percent, at the end of the year I will receive $104 but it will be worth only $100.88. In order to be compensated for the loan I must receive $107 at the end of the year — the amount I loaned plus its opportunity cost plus the amount lost during the year through inflation. Therefore, I will charge 7 percent interest, and this is the market rate. Were the market rate used in discounting lost earnings, the victim of the accident would receive a lump sum that, invested at that rate, would yield him each year the same number of dollars he would have earned had the value of the dollar remained constant throughout the period. Since, however, the value of the dollar declines in an inflation, he would in fact, if working, have received higher (nominal) wages in order to offset the effects of inflation. To place him in the same position that he would have occupied had he not been injured, the award must enable him to obtain the same number of dollars, over the period of lost earnings, that he *would have received* had he continued to work.

This objective can be achieved by use of the true interest rate (the market rate minus the rate of inflation) in discounting to present value. If there is no inflation, the true rate will equal the market rate and the victim will receive the same number of dollars that he would have received had he not been injured. If there is inflation, then by investing the lump sum at the market rate, which exceeds the true interest rate by the rate of inflation, he obtains a sufficiently larger number of dollars to offset the decline in the value of each one. A numerical illustration may be helpful. An accident occurs, and the award is made, in January of this year; the period of disability is January of next year. The victim's earnings at the time of the accident were $1000 a month, the market rate of interest is 7 percent, and the expected rate of inflation is 3 percent. If the market rate of interest is used in discounting the $1000 of lost

3. Or deflation, although that seems a rather remote possibility at the present time. The analysis for deflation is the same as that presented in the text for inflation, but with a minus rather than a plus sign in front of the change in the value of the dollar.

earnings to present value, the victim will receive $935. This is the amount that invested at 7 percent interest will be worth $1000 in one year. But in one year today's $1000 will be worth only $970. The victim's employer would presumably have increased his salary to $1031 — the equivalent, in inflated dollars, of $1000 today — in order to prevent his real income from declining. Now assume the true interest rate (i.e., net of inflation) — 4 percent — is used to discount the $1000 of lost earnings to present value. So computed, the award to the victim is $962, which, invested at 7 percent, will grow to $1029 at the end of one year.[4]

§4.11. *Damages for pain and suffering, and the problem of valuing human life.*[1] The layman's confusion, remarked in the first chapter of this book, between pecuniary loss and economic loss is at the bottom of most criticisms of the practice of awarding damages (frequently quite substantial) for pain, disfigurement, loss of mobility, and other forms of suffering inflicted by accidents. It is true that such losses, if they do not impair earning capacity, have no pecuniary dimension. But this is not because they are not true economic losses; it is because of the absence of markets in mutilation. A cannot buy B's ears and tongue to gratify his taste for mutilating people and therefore these things do not have prices. But they have opportunity costs: B would not part from them for nothing. The attempt to affix a money value to human suffering is disagreeable. But arguably it is even more disagreeable to increase that suffering by reducing the incentives to avoid inflicting it.

If anything, awards for pain and suffering probably undercompensate victims seriously crippled by accidents. Since the loss of vision or limbs reduces the amount of pleasure that can be purchased with a dollar, a very large amount of money will frequently be necessary to place the victim in the same position of relative satisfaction that he occupied before the accident. This factor is most pronounced in a death case. Most people would not exchange their life for anything less than an infinite sum of money, if the exchange were to take place immediately, since

4. An alternative, and even better, approach would be to use the market rate of interest but estimate the lost earnings in future (inflated) rather than present dollars. This would result in an award of $964 in our example, which invested at 7 percent would grow to $1031 in a year's time.

§4.11. 1. A useful discussion of the subject of this section is E. J. Mishan, Evaluation of Life and Limb: A Theoretical Approach, 79 J. Pol. Econ. **687** (1971).

they would have so little time in which to enjoy the proceeds of the sale. Yet it cannot be correct that the proper award of damages in a death case is infinity. This would imply that the optimum rate of fatal accidents was zero, or very close to it, and it is plain that people are unwilling individually or collectively to incur the costs necessary to reduce the rate of fatal accidents so drastically.

The courts have resolved the vexing problem of the proper valuation of life by ignoring it. Damages in a death case are generally limited to the pecuniary loss to survivors (in some states, to the deceased victim's estate), plus any medical expenses and pain and suffering sustained by the victim before death. The loss-to-survivors measure is lost earnings, net of the victim's living expenses. The test is thus the same as in disability cases with the single difference that since the personal expenses of the victim (his food, etc.) are eliminated by death but not by disability, they are subtracted from the amount awarded in a death case but not in a disability case.

A frequent loser when a person is killed or disabled, besides his survivors, is the person's employer. Employers invest money in training their employees. They hope to recoup the investment in the higher productivity that the training will generate. The human capital thus created is as real an asset of the employer as his machinery and its destruction as real a cost — as some courts have (implicitly) recognized in awarding damages to the employer for an injury to an employee.[2]

§4.12. *The collateral benefits rule.* Should the tort victim's damages be reduced by the amount of any compensation that he receives from a collateral source, such as accident insurance? The law's answer is no. If I have an accident insurance policy that entitles me to $10,000 for a certain kind of accidental injury, and I sustain that injury in an accident in which the injurer is negligent, I can both claim the $10,000 from the insurance company and obtain full damages (which, let us assume, are $10,000) from the injurer. This result is economically correct. To permit the defendant to set up my insurance policy as a bar to the action would result in underdeterrence. The economic cost of the accident, however defrayed, is $10,000 and if the judgment against him is zero his incentive to spend up to $10,000 (dis-

---

2. See Football Club de Metz *C*. Wiroth, 1456 Recueil Dalloz 723 (Cour d'Appel de Colmar); Camerlo *C*. Dassary et Demeyère, 1958 Recueil Dalloz 253 (Cour d'Appel de Lyon).

counted by the probability of occurrence) to prevent a similar accident in the future will be reduced. It may be less obvious that the double recovery is not a windfall to me. I purchased the insurance policy at a price presumably equal to the discounted cost of my injury plus the cost of writing the policy. The company could if it wished have excepted from the coverage of the policy accidents in which the injurer was liable to me for the cost of the injury, or it could have required me to assign to it any legal rights that I might have arising from an accident. In either case my premium would have been less. I am entitled to receive what I paid for.

Some courts have had trouble when the collateral benefit was not rendered pursuant to a contract but was "gratuitous." However, almost all gratuitous benefits turn out to be ones for which the beneficiary has paid indirectly. If an employer renders medical treatment to his injured employees "free of charge," this means only that the employer pays for their labor partly in money and partly in kind, so that the money wage would be higher if the "gratuitous" benefits were lower.

§4.13.   *No-fault automobile compensation plans.*   The negligence system has had a bad press for many years.[1] The principal criticism is that it is an expensive and inadequate compensation system. Attention naturally focuses on automobile accident cases, the most frequent type of negligence case today. Studies show that administrative costs, mainly legal expenses, are a very substantial fraction of the total amounts paid victims in settlements and lawsuits and that many people injured in automobile accidents receive little or no compensation — sometimes because the victim himself was negligent, sometimes because the defendant was uninsured and insolvent or was a hit-and-run driver and unknown.[2]

If compensation is the only purpose of the negligence system, it is a poor system, being both costly and incomplete. Its economic function, however, is not compensation, but deterrence of noncost-justified accidents. If the system yields substantial savings in accident costs, the heavy administrative costs of the system, which relate primarily to the determination of liability — the determination whether the accident was uneconomical — may well be justified. As for coverage, the deficiencies of the

§4.13. 1. For a forceful attack, primarily economic, on the negligence system, see Guido Calabresi, The Costs of Accidents (1970), especially pts. 4–5.

2. Alfred F. Conard, et al., Automobile Accident Costs and Payments (1964), is a massive empirical study of the compensation of automobile accident victims.

system could be remedied by wider purchase of accident insurance.

The most telling criticism of the negligence system from an economic standpoint is that it is a bad system of accident control. The deterrent impact of automobile damage awards is impaired by liability insurance, now almost universal. With insurance, the cost of an accident to the negligent injurer is no longer the victim's loss, but is rather the present value of any premium increases that the injurer may incur as a result of being found negligent. Partly because of administrative expense, partly because of regulatory hostility toward "discriminatory" premium rate structures, partly because of assigned-risk pools that enable the most dangerous drivers to purchase liability insurance at rates only slightly higher than normal, liability insurance premiums seem not to be tailored with any precision to the expected accident costs of particular drivers. Although the premiums are not uniform, the differences frequently reflect criteria, such as accident involvement (whether or not the insured was negligent) or what age group the insured belongs to, that are only loosely related to negligence. The variance in expected accident costs within the classes is probably very high, in which event the method of calculating liability insurance rates may overdeter some drivers and underdeter others.

An even more fundamental criticism of the behavioral effects of negligence law is that it is unrealistic to expect people who are not deterred from careless conduct by fear of bodily injury to be deterred by fear of a money judgment, or, in the case where the negligence of the victim is a bar to recovery, by inability to obtain compensation for the injury from the injurer. Several observations on this point are in order. First, the argument is inapplicable to injurers not themselves in any personal jeopardy, to employers of injurers (such as a truck or taxi company), and to accidents where the only significant danger is to property. Second, the argument ignores the accident prevention effect of liability insurance premium rates that are so high, reflecting the expected liability of the insured, that they discourage him from attempting to drive. Third, the proposition that the prospective victim of an accident will not be deterred from behaving carelessly by fear of not being compensated implies that tort compensation is never full compensation. If so, this would reinforce our earlier point that the tendency of tort damages, although so often criticized as excessive, is in fact to undercompensate the victims of serious accidents. If damages fully compensated the victim, he would be indifferent as between being injured and not being injured and a rule of contributory negligence would be indispensable to the creation of incentives for careful behavior.

Since tort compensation is often not fully adequate, it is a fair question whether the additional deterrence created by a rule such as one of contributory negligence is worth the costs involved in its administration. On the other hand, a frequent criticism of the present system is that it overcompensates minor injuries.[3] If true, this would indicate that the rule of contributory negligence may be necessary to deter careless behavior by some victims.

Criticisms of the operation of the negligence system in the automobile field have led to a number of proposals for no-fault automobile accident compensation, and to some enactments incorporating portions of the proposals. A surprising feature of these proposals, at least from an economic standpoint, is that they are not concerned with creating better incentives for accident avoidance. They do not seek to make the tort system a better deterrent of unsafe conduct. They seek to increase the coverage of the system and to reduce the cost of insurance. These goals are inconsistent with each other as well as with the goal of reducing the number of accidents.

The Keeton-O'Connell plan[4] illustrates the dilemma. Under the plan, every motorist is required to carry basic protection insurance that entitles him in the event of an accident to recover his medical expenses plus lost earnings, regardless of the injurer's negligence or his own freedom from negligence. Pain and suffering are not compensated, and any collateral benefits are deducted. The victim may waive basic protection and sue in tort in the usual way if he sustains more than $10,000 in damages other than pain and suffering. Basic protection is first-party (accident) rather than third-party (liability) insurance. The motorist pays premiums to and collects damages from his own insurer. The injurer and his insurance company are liable only if the victim waives basic protection and sues in tort.

Why does the plan exclude damages for pain and suffering and require deduction of collateral benefits for accidents within its scope? Apparently not because the authors do not consider pain and suffering to be real losses, or consider collateral benefits to

---

3. Robert E. Keeton & Jeffrey O'Connell, Basic Protection for the Traffic Victim, A Blueprint for Reforming Automobile Insurance 2 (1965).
4. See id.

be pure windfalls, for they do not exclude these items in serious accidents. The explanation may be that they had somehow to reduce the average damage award in order to prevent the plan from increasing the cost of insurance. Because the plan permits victims of faultless drivers and victims themselves at fault to recover, its coverage is broader than that of the tort system. Hence if the average claim were no smaller under the plan than under the existing tort system, the total amount paid out in claims, and therefore insurance premium costs, would probably be greater (even assuming lower administrative costs) than under the present system. The savings from the deduction of collateral benefits may prove transitory: people may reduce their existing accident insurance to offset the accident insurance that they are forced to buy under basic protection. The strategy of the plan, however, is clear: to increase the number of accident victims who are compensated but to reduce the average compensation. Many victims who are fully compensated under the present system would be undercompensated under the Keeton-O'Connell plan.

The economic criticism of the plan is that it may have undesirable effects on safety incentives. Companies writing basic protection insurance will want to charge relatively low premiums to drivers, including careless drivers, of large, heavy automobiles who have no dependents, since they are less likely to sustain heavy accident costs than drivers — even careful ones — of small, vulnerable cars who have large families. The result will be to increase the incentive of the second group to take precautions but reduce the incentive of the first group. Yet the cost of accident avoidance may be larger for members of the second group than for members of the first, many of whom could reduce expected accident costs at relatively low cost to themselves either by driving more carefully or by substituting a lighter car.

The proponents of automobile compensation plans often take the position that deterrence is the province of the criminal law. Since it is generally unlawful to insure against criminal punishment, the effect of liability insurance in sapping the deterrent efficacy of negligence liability is eliminated. At the same time, a greater emphasis on criminal punishment of negligent participants in automobile accidents would undermine the compensatory purpose of the plans. If the negligent victim of an accident is fined, his compensation is in effect reduced by the amount of the fine and, so reduced, is no longer equal to his injuries. In addition, the burden and hence costs of proving negligent conduct would be higher in a proceeding to impose a noninsurable penalty, since the court would naturally be sensitive to the quandary of the mistakenly accused defendant unable by virtue of the noninsurability rule to protect himself against the consequences of an erroneous punishment. Indeed, the fact that it is normally impossible to insure against criminal penalties may be one reason why the requirements of proof are more exacting in a criminal than in a civil case.

The objections to the no-fault auto compensation plans need not be decisive. Their costs may be outweighed by the administrative cost savings which proponents of such plans anticipate.[5]

An alternative approach altogether would be to change those public policies that aggravate the impairment through liability insurance of the deterrent effects of tort liability. One of these policies is that against insurance companies' "discriminating" in their premium rates. There is no discrimination in the economic sense when premiums are differentiated according to propensity to impose liability on the company. Another such policy is the implicit policy, reflected in many assigned-risk plans, against pricing dangerous drivers off the road. A change in these policies might lead to better control of accident rates.

§4.14. *Products liability.*   We conclude this chapter with brief discussions of, first, the special rules that have evolved to govern liability for injuries caused by defective products,[1] and, second, the broader debate over negligence versus strict liability that has been stimulated, in part, by the evolution of doctrine in products cases.

The products liability rules involve an interesting amalgam of tort and contract doctrine. Traditionally, a manufacturer's liability in tort to people injured by a defect in his product was narrowly circumscribed by the doctrine of privity of contract, under which the manufacturer was liable for negligence only to his immediate purchaser — usually a dealer — and not to the ultimate consumer, who purchased from the dealer. From an economic standpoint the privity limitation is arbitrary but relatively inconsequential. The cost of a product to the consumer is the (nominal) price plus the expected accident cost. Let the cost of a widget to the consumer be $1, composed of $.60, wholesale price, $.20, dealer's mark-up, and $.20, expected accident cost due

5. For a good discussion of the problems of various no-fault proposals see Guido Calabresi, note 1 *supra,* at 3–16.

§4.14. 1. The economics of products liability is debated in Symposium: Products Liability: Economic Analysis and the Law, 38 U. Chi. L. Rev. 1 (1970).

to a defect. Assume that the cost to the manufacturer of eliminating the defect is $.10 and is less than the cost of doing so by either dealer or consumer. If the manufacturer eliminates the defect, he should be able to increase his wholesale price from $.60 to $.80, for the consumer should be willing to pay him $1 for the safer widget. (Think of the expected accident cost as an insurance premium. The consumer was willing to pay a total of $1 to dealer and insurance company; he should be willing to pay the same dollar to the dealer if the risk against which he insured is eliminated.) The result is an increase in the manufacturer's profit per widget of $.10.[2]

The reason that the privity limitation does not eliminate the manufacturer's incentive to achieve an efficient level of safety is that he has a preexisting (albeit indirect) trading relationship with the consumer. He will sell him cost-justified precautions just as he will sell any other product improvement that the consumer values more than the cost to him of making it. He is not like the driver prevented by high transaction costs from attempting to sell pedestrians a reduction in their expected accidents brought about by his installing a rubber bumper or watching the road more carefully or driving more slowly.

The privity of contract limitation of negligence liability was first riddled with exceptions, and then, following the *MacPherson* decision in 1928,[3] repudiated. But it was still necessary for the plaintiff to prove negligence. An alternative theory of liability developed out of implied-warranty law. A warranty is a promise with respect to the characteristics or quality of a product and is a very common term in a sales contract. We would expect courts to imply a warranty, in order to reduce transaction costs, whenever it appeared likely to allocate risks in such a way as to minimize losses. If the cost of inspecting canned fish for wholesomeness is lower for the manufacturer than for the consumer, and lower than the expected illness costs from not inspecting, then efficiency requires that the manufacturer inspect. But privity is still a problem, since the manufacturer does not contract directly with the consumer and a warranty is a term in a contract.

Gradually, courts extended the implied warranty of fitness to

2. The manufacturer may be able to increase his total profits even more by selling each widget at a lower price and profit margin; or he may find that his advantage is short-lived because other widget manufacturers duplicate his safety improvement and compete away the additional profits that the improvement makes possible. See §6.1 *infra*. But these details do not affect the analysis.
3. MacPherson v. Buick Motor Co., 217 N.Y. 382, 111 N.E. 1050 (1916).

include freedom from hazardous defects, and so far discarded the privity requirement that not only may the ultimate consumer now enforce the warranty but so may members of his family and, increasingly, even bystanders. In effect (and in many states explicitly), manufacturers have become strictly liable for injuries resulting from defective products — subject, however, to the interesting defense of "mishandling." This defense may approximate more closely than contributory negligence the economically correct criterion for barring victims of negligent injurers from recovery: when the victim could have prevented the accident at lower cost than the defendant.

Strict liability is sometimes defended on the ground that it results in safer products. Against this view it can be argued that the manufacturer would have an incentive to take all cost-justified precautions (as well as to conduct research on new safety improvements) even if he were not liable to the consumer for negligently inflicted injuries. To be sure, subjecting him to strict liability requires that he elect in all instances between paying the accident cost, in the form of a legal judgment, and paying the cost of precautions that would avert the accident, but where the accident cost is lower than the avoidance cost he will prefer the judgment. He will invest in avoidance only when it costs less than the accident cost, and he would do the same under a negligence standard, or under no standard.

But the argument is incomplete. Strict liability and no liability do not result in an identical safety level if many or most of the customers for the manufacturer's product are risk preferrers, if there is no assumption of risk defense, and if the manufacturer is not permitted to disclaim liability. A risk preferrer is not always willing to pay for a safety precaution that costs him less than the expected cost of the accident that it prevents, and under a rule of no liability the manufacturer of a product will not supply a safety precaution for which the customer is unwilling to pay. Under strict liability, assuming liability cannot be waived, the only question that interests the manufacturer is whether the cost of a safety precaution is less than the expected accident cost,[4] for the latter is the measure of his liability and if he can reduce his net liability costs he will do so. The same result follows with a negligence standard, again assuming that no waivers of liability are permitted; indeed courts are more reluctant to honor disclaimers of negligence liability than of strict liability.

4. What if the manufacturer is a risk preferrer? Why is this unlikely?

The effect of strict (or negligence) liability where disclaimers are barred in increasing the safety of a product sold mainly to risk preferrers is to reduce rather than increase efficiency: it makes people pay for something that they would rather do without. But there is an argument that strict or negligence liability may bring about not only a higher, but a more efficient, level of product safety than no liability. Most product hazards are very small, and the consumer will have no personal knowledge of their magnitude. He needs to be supplied with information about relative product hazards. The natural source of such information, producers who think their products are safer than their competitors', may be reluctant to supply it. Advertising a product as safer is a double-edged sword, because it necessarily implies that the product is relatively unsafe; otherwise it would be meaningless to speak of its having been made safer. If everybody knows that the product is unsafe, the producer has nothing to lose by raising the question of safety. But with many products, consumers are not aware, or only dimly aware, of any hazards. In these cases the manufacturer who advertises that his product is safer than his competitors' product runs the risk of planting fears where none existed which may lead consumers to substitute other products that they believe to be safer.

The problem is especially acute if a safety hazard affects all manufacturers of a product equally for then no one in the industry has an incentive to draw the consumer's attention to it. Producers in other industries have little incentive to do so, since their sales would increase only slightly if demand for the product declined.[5] And because the system of property rights in information is highly incomplete, we find few private firms engaged in selling product information directly to consumers.

The problem of consumer safety information is solved by a rule of strict — or negligence — liability, for then the only relevant knowledge is that of the manufacturers. They adopt safety improvements not to impress consumers but to reduce their net liability costs.

Even if strict liability has no effect whatever on the safety level or accident rate, it does have an economic effect: it compels the manufacturer to insure consumers against accidents resulting from nonnegligent defects in his product. This will increase efficiency if the manufacturer can insure at lower cost than accident insurance companies and if the consumer wants to buy insur-

5. Cf. §7.4 *infra*.

ance at all rather than to take his chances (self-insure). One might argue that if the manufacturer is the better insurer, then even without strict liability he will insure consumers; but this would not follow if transaction costs were high in relation to the size of the insurance premium, and they may be. Observe that even if strict liability can be justified by reference to relative insurance costs, this would not justify an interpretation of strict liability under which the manufacturer was forbidden to disclaim — however unmistakably — liability for some or all injuries resulting from defects in his product. Such a prohibition prevents the manufacturer from shifting the cost of insurance to the consumer in cases where the consumer is the cheaper insurer and prevents the consumer who is a risk preferrer from trading on his taste.

§*4.15.   Strict liability vs. negligence.*   It is with respect to problems such as railroad crossing accidents, where high transaction costs preclude negotiated determination of the accident level, that the issue of the relative efficiency of strict liability and of negligence as liability standards is most sharply joined.[1]

If there exists a safety precaution that costs less than the expected cost of the accidents it would prevent, the railroad will adopt the precaution whether it is subject to a negligence or to a strict liability standard. In either case the railroad will be liable if it fails to adopt the precaution and liability will be more costly than prevention. If no such safety precaution is available, the railroad will not adopt it — again under either standard. Under a negligence standard it will not be liable for the accidents that occur and under a strict liability standard, while it will be liable, liability will be cheaper than prevention. As a first approximation, then, the choice of standards does not affect the level of safety.

It may seem that strict liability might increase the level of safety in the long run, however. The Learned Hand formula imposes liability on the railroad if it fails to take cost-justified precautions. While in principle the benefits from safety research could and should be taken into account in determining whether a precaution is cost justified, in practice the question whether a precaution is cost justified is determined solely with reference to the existing technology of accident prevention. Consequently, the law gives the railroad no incentive to advance the state of

§4.15. 1. A recent economic analysis of strict liability is Richard A. Posner, Strict Liability: A Comment, 2 J. Leg. Studies 205 (1973).

safety technology by investing in the development of new and better safety appliances to protect travelers at crossings. Nor does the market supply an incentive. The railroad could sell new crossing safety appliances neither to its customers (for whom they have no value) nor to people who might be injured in crossing accidents (because of transaction costs). If, however, the railroad were liable for all accidents, or at least all those that could not be prevented at lower cost by the victim or by someone else, it would compare the liability that it could not avoid by means of existing safety precautions with the feasibility of developing new precautions that would reduce that liability. If safety research and development seemed likely to reduce accident costs by more than the cost of research and development, the railroad would undertake it, and efficiency would be increased.

This analysis, however, ignores the fact that a change from negligence to strict liability, while increasing the railroad's incentive to conduct safety research and development, reduces the potential victims' willingness to finance such activity. Under the negligence standard, victims of "unavoidable" (under the existing state of the art of safety protection) accidents must bear the full costs of those accidents. To the extent that their accident costs are thus greater than they would be under strict liability, there is extra incentive for research into and development of new safety devices to protect potential victims against what, in the existing state of the art, is unavoidable. The victims themselves will not do the inventing but in all probability neither would the railroad under the contrary rule. The railroad under one rule and the potential victims under the other provide the market for inventors of new safety appliances. To decide which rule would induce the more fruitful research and development entails a judgment of the relative value of alternative paths of technical improvement with respect to the prevention of particular accident types. One would have to answer the question whether research and development on crossing signals was likely to be more fruitful than research and development on warning buzzers in cars — an intractable question, in most cases.

Two additional arguments for strict liability deserve attention. The first is that by placing liability for unavoidable accidents on enterprises rather than individuals,[2] it enables losses to be spread further, since the enterprise will distribute the cost of the acci-

2. Of course, enterprises are sometimes victims rather than injurers, as when a privately owned automobile crashes into a company-owned automobile.

dent judgment among its customers, shareholders, etc. Even if spreading were considered an economic objective,[3] the argument would be incorrect because the prospective victim of an accident is almost always able to insure, thereby spreading the loss among the customers (and sometimes shareholders) of the insurance company.

The second argument is that only a rule of strict liability compels a firm to "internalize" all of its accident costs. The argument illustrates the confusion that the concept of externalities so frequently engenders. The question *whose* cost is not a profitable one in economic analysis. The crop damage in our engine-spark case was the result both of farming and of railroading. It could be prevented either by the farmer's changing his behavior or by the railroad's changing its behavior. The relevant question from the standpoint of economic analysis is who could prevent the loss at lower cost, not whose cost the damage "really" is. Indeed, the externality approach obscures an essential point — that a pure rule of strict liability would frequently result in inefficient solutions to conflicting resource use problems because it would give the victim of the accident no incentive to take steps to prevent it even if those steps cost less than prevention by the injurer. In fact, pure strict liability is in principle no more efficient than no liability, even though transaction costs are assumed to be prohibitive. Strict liability imparts the correct incentive to the injurer; it induces him to adopt safety precautions if they cost less than the expected cost of the accidents they prevent and not to otherwise. But it eliminates the incentive of the victim to take cost-justified precautions. No liability imparts the correct incentive to the victim, who will adopt safety precautions if they cost less than the accident cost that they avert, but eliminates the incentive of the injurer to take cost-justified precautions.

If we add to strict liability a defense of contributory negligence, we eliminate the objection to it on efficiency grounds.[4] We do not thereby establish its superiority to negligence. The difference becomes that under strict liability the cost of accidents that can be prevented only at a cost greater than the expected accident

3. The idea that shifting a large loss from one individual to a group of individuals, each of whom is made to bear a small loss, increases welfare is a misapplication of the concept of diminishing marginal utility of money. See §15.2 *infra*.

4. Assuming contributory negligence is not determined by literal application of the Hand formula. See *supra* §4.3.

cost is shifted to the injurer, whereas under negligence it is left on the victim. One consequence of not imposing unavoidable accident costs on the injurer is to understate the social costs of dangerous activities relative to those of safer activities. Suppose the only difference between canals and railroads were that railroads created safety hazards that could not be prevented at reasonable cost, so that the railroads were not liable for them under a negligence standard. The private costs of railroads would be no higher than those of canals but the social costs would be higher. In principle the Hand formula prevents this divergence because if canals are a perfectly good substitute for railroads the cost of avoiding the "unavoidable" accidents is zero: discontinuance of railroading would be costless in view of the adequacy of the canal substitute. We may assume that in practice the Hand formula does not enable interindustry comparisons. But the problem is not solved, only changed, by a rule of strict liability. Strict liability facilitates comparison of the social costs of railroads and of canals, but it obscures comparison of the social costs of activities endangered by railroad accidents and of substitute activities. Suppose that neither the farmer nor the railroad in our engine-spark example can prevent crop damage from sparks. Under a rule of strict liability the damage cost would be borne by the railroad. But what if the same crop could be grown at the same (or only slightly higher) cost in an area remote from the railroad, the only difference being that crop damage would be zero in the new location? A rule of negligence liability would facilitate the transfer of the crop to the better location, just as in the earlier example a rule of strict liability would have facilitated a shift to a better method of transportation.

There are a number of traditional pockets of strict liability in the law, including such areas as liability for injuries resulting from vicious animals, from blasting, and from the torts of an employee (respondeat superior); it is left as an exercise for the reader to consider whether these examples of strict liability can be explained as special applications of the economic theory of negligence. The benefits of a general rule of strict liability are problematical.[5]

We discuss the question of strict liability versus negligence further in the next chapter.

---

5. An arguable advantage in terms of lower costs of legal administration is discussed *infra* §24.3.

SUGGESTED READINGS

1. John P. Brown, Toward an Economic Theory of Liability, forthcoming in J. Leg. Studies (1973).
2. Guido Calabresi, Some Thoughts on Risk Distribution and the Law of Torts, 70 Yale L.J. 499 (1961).
3. ――――, The Costs of Accidents (1970).
4. Richard A. Posner, A Theory of Negligence, 1 J. Leg. Studies 29 (1972).
5. ――――, Strict Liability: A Comment, 2 J. Leg. Studies 205 (1973).
6. Symposium, Products Liability: Economic Analysis and the Law, 38 U. Chi. L. Rev. 1 (1970).

PROBLEMS

1. If most victims of accidents are risk averse, will the Hand formula produce the right amount of investment, from an economic standpoint, in accident prevention? Does your answer depend on the availability of accident insurance?

2. Consider the following hypothetical situation. The expected cost of a certain kind of accident is $1000. The potential injurer could prevent the accident at a cost of $100, the potential victim at a cost of $50. Alternatively, if each party spends $20 in a certain way the accident will not occur. In these circumstances, will the negligence–contributory negligence standard produce the efficient solution?

3. Melvin M. Belli has challenged the practice of discounting future earnings to present value: (The Use of Demonstrative Evidence 33 (1951).) He argues that the plaintiff's earnings should be multiplied by the period of the plaintiff's disability and then multiplied again to reflect the estimated increase in the cost of living during the period of disability. Is this the correct economic approach? How would you argue to a judge or jury that it is not?

4. Suppose that a nuclear power plant is strictly liable for radiation injuries and emits radiation that increases the probability of contracting cancer from one in 10,000 to one in 1000. X is exposed to the radiation and contracts cancer. As a matter of economic theory, should the plant be liable for all or any part of the cost of his illness? Is your answer consistent with the result in the Palsgraf case?

5. Were there no liability for medical malpractice, would there be too much malpractice, too little, or the right amount, from an economic standpoint?

6. Suppose that on average one out of every million bottles of a certain soft drink is found to contain mouse parts. And suppose that the bottling company could not improve this record at a cost equal to or lower than the cost (in shock, distaste, etc.) incurred by the consumer unlucky enough to purchase one of the defective bottles. Would or should the factory nonetheless be liable in negligence to these consumers? Would strict liability make a difference in such a case? Would it make a difference in a case where the defect was in the bottle when received by the bottling company, and the company could not have discovered the defect by a reasonable inspection? Can it be argued that the primary significance of strict products liability is to increase the plaintiff's litigating alternatives?

7. *An airplane crashes as the result of a nonnegligent defect in an instrument supplied by A. The airplane was manufactured by B from various components, including the instrument supplied by A, and is operated by C, an airline. What economic difference does it make, if any, whether A is liable for the damages resulting from the crash, or B, or C? (Cf. Goldberg v. Kollsman Instrument Corp., 12 N.Y.2d 432, 191 N.E.2d 81 (1963).)*

8. *Suppose there is a class of automobile accidents in which the injurers are all very wealthy men. The opportunity costs of their time are so great that the expected accident costs are lower than the costs to them of preventing the accidents by driving more slowly, slower driving being the only method by which the accidents might be prevented. In these circumstances, which rule of liability would be more efficient: strict liability with no contributory negligence defense; or no liability at all?*

CHAPTER 5

THE UNITY OF THE COMMON LAW

§5.1. *The implicit economic logic of the common law.* Our survey of the major common law fields suggests that the common law exhibits a deep unity that is economic in character. The differences among the law of property, the law of contracts, and the law of torts are primarily differences in vocabulary, detail, and specific subject matter rather than in method or policy. The common law method is to allocate responsibilities between people engaged in interacting activities in such a way as to maximize the joint value, or, what amounts to the same thing, minimize the joint cost of the activities. It may do this by redefining a property right, by devising a new rule of liability, or by recognizing a contract right, but nothing fundamental turns on which device is used. The engine-spark example that we discussed in the chapter on property rights could just as easily have been framed as a tort case. Breaches of contract would look much the same if treated as torts. The Hand formula expresses a general test of liability at common law.

There are important distinctions to be made in the economic analysis of the common law, but they cut across conventional subject-matter divisions. One is between cases in which compensation is required only if there has been a failure to take some cost-minimizing loss-avoidance measure and cases in which compensation is required regardless. A contract breaker is required to pay damages even if the breach of contract leads to a more valuable use of resources. Likewise a trespasser. But one who accidentally inflicts a personal injury, in circumstances where no cost-justified precaution could have prevented the accident, normally is not liable. There are economic reasons for these differences. If parties to contracts have no protection in the event of a breach, they will be reluctant to enter into contracts. This will increase the costs of voluntary exchange. If people who have invested money in property have no protection against forced redistribution of their wealth, the incentives to invest will be impaired. But these considerations are absent from most accident cases, where a requirement of payment of compensation to victims of nonnegligent (that is, economical) injuries would impose transaction costs without conferring offsetting economic benefits.

A second distinction, which again cuts across conventional subject-matter lines, is between cases in which transaction costs are very high and cases in which, because there is either an actual or a realistically potential buyer-seller relationship between the parties to the interaction, transaction costs are relatively low. This distinction does not imply that in the latter cases the law's assignment of rights or liabilities is economically unimportant. It is important in order to minimize transaction costs and to avoid futility. If the law fails to allocate responsibilities between the parties in such a way as to maximize value, the parties will, by an additional and not costless transaction, nullify the legal allocation. This is the economic reason why the common law does not recognize a right to be free from competition. It is a right that the successful competitor would always buy (why?), so its only economic effect would be to increase the number of transactions, and so transaction costs.

Clearly, however, the economic function of the common law is smaller in the areas where transaction costs are low. The presumption in such areas is that existing customs and practices are efficient and rules intended to alter them are inefficient as well as futile.

The reader may wonder whether it is plausible to attribute economic insight to common law judges, especially since litigants rarely couch their arguments in economic terms. However, the character of common law litigation forces a confrontation with economic issues.[1] The typical common law case involves a dispute between two parties over which one should bear a loss. In searching for a reasonably objective and impartial standard, as the traditions of the bench require him to do, the judge can hardly fail to consider whether the loss was the product of wasteful, uneconomical resource use. In a culture of scarcity, this is an urgent, an inescapable question. And at least an approximation to the answer is in most cases reasonably accessible to intuition and common sense.

§5.1. 1. On this point see §23.1 *infra*.

The economic theory of liability at common law does not require rejection of the traditional approach in the legal literature, which emphasizes issues of morality, fairness, and justice. The traditional view of negligence liability, for example, as requiring a demonstration that the defendant was "at fault" and the plaintiff free from fault is compatible with (or even identical to) the economic approach if it is assumed that a society's moral ideas are strongly influenced by the scarcity of resources and the consequent necessity of economizing on their use. This seems a reasonable assumption, especially as applied to the conditions of scarcity that characterized society in the formative years of the principal common law doctrines.

§5.2. The common law and economic growth.   Economic analysis can help to clarify the controversial role of the common law in the economic growth of this country. The usual view is that the common law, by the permissiveness toward economic activity that it displayed during the nineteenth century, helped to foster rapid economic development. A variant is that the common law subsidized growth by failing to make industry bear all of the costs that an efficiency standard would have required that it bear. The permissiveness of the common law in the nineteenth century is contrasted with the many restrictions imposed on economic activity by the law in both the preceding and following periods.

It is necessary to clarify the concepts of growth and of subsidy. The rate of economic growth is the rate at which the output (or output per capita) of a society increases. Since growth is fostered by efficient resource use, there is a sense, but a rather uncontroversial one, in which the common law, insofar as it has been shaped by a concern with efficiency, may be said to have fostered growth. Society can force the pace of growth by compelling people to consume less and save more and by increasing the returns to capital investment. If the common law played any role in accelerating economic growth, it must have been by making capital investment more profitable.

In this vein, it has been argued that nineteenth century contract law consistently favored the performing over the paying party in order to encourage entrepreneurship.[1] But every business firm is simultaneously, and more or less equally, performer and payor: it is the performer with respect to contracts for the

§5.2. 1. Grant Gilmore, Products Liability: A Commentary, 38 U. Chi. L. Rev. 103 (1970).

sale of its output; it is payor with respect to contracts for the purchase of its inputs. It derives no clear gain from having the law tilted in favor of performers. It has been suggested that the common law of industrial accidents favored industry. But we have seen that, as between parties already in a contractual relationship, the efficient level of safety would be achieved (or approximated) even if the law imposed *no* liability for accidental injury.[2]

The area in which the argument that the law favored growth seems most plausible is that of accidents to strangers. Consider two alternative rules of law, one that a railroad is liable to travelers injured at railroad crossings only if the railroad was negligent, and the other that the railroad is strictly liable to them (unless, perhaps, they were contributorily negligent). The accident rate will be similar under both rules, but the railroad's costs will be higher under the second, and this will lead to an increase in its prices and a fall in its output and profits. The first rule encourages, and the second rule discourages, railroading, although perhaps trivially.[3]

It does not follow, however, that the first rule constitutes a subsidy to railroading in any useful sense of that term. As we saw in the last chapter, probably both rules are efficient.[4] Either, properly implemented, would bring about a cost-justified level of railroad crossing accidents. The level would be different. It would be lower under the second rule, because the scale of railroading and hence number of accidents would be smaller (the accident *rate* might be the same, however). But the first rule is not less efficient unless railroads could insure the victims of crossing accidents at lower cost than the victims could insure themselves. One can if one wishes refer to the choice of the first rule as a decision to "subsidize" the railroad — but not in any invidious sense of that term.

Given two possible liability standards for railroads, both reasonably efficient but under one of which the railroad's costs are lower and under the other higher, it is possible to argue that the first should be preferred as a method of partially compensating railroads for their inability to capture in the rates they charge their customers the full social benefits of railroading. The construction of a railroad line (in the nineteenth century, not today)

2. See §4.14 *supra*. For a discussion of the common law of industrial accidents see Richard A. Posner, A Theory of Negligence, 1 J. Leg. Studies 29, 67–72 (1972).
3. See id. at 76, n.42.
4. See §4.15 *supra*.

increased the value of land up and down the line by giving the owners better access to markets. Unless the railroad owned the affected land, however, or could negotiate in advance of construction with every landowner, it would not be able to capture the entire increase in value and hence would not invest in new construction up to the point where the last dollar spent increased land values[5] by just one dollar. If the courts chose the less costly (to railroads) of the two efficient liability rules because they sensed that railroad revenues were less than they should be to stimulate an appropriate level of investment in the railroad industry, it does not necessarily mean that they were forcing the pace of economic growth or subsidizing (in an invidious sense) the railroad industry. They may simply have been nudging the economy a bit closer to the most efficient employment of its resources.

PROBLEMS

1. *Assess the argument that employers had such great bargaining power vis-à-vis employees in the nineteenth century that the employees were in no position to bargain for cost-justified safety precautions. (Cf. §3.7 supra.)*

2. *What would be the effects on the distribution of income and wealth of a judicial ruling that shifted from farmers to railroads the cost of injuries to cattle resulting from failure to fence the railroad's right of way? Assume farmers are the principal customers of railroads.*

3. *Should accident cases arising out of a contractual relationship (e.g., between a railroad and its passengers) be treated as breach of contract rather than as tort cases? Is there any utility to maintaining the distinction between tort and contract in such cases?*

---

5. *Net* values: any reductions in land value due to the construction of the line (the line might, for example, reduce the locational advantage of land closer to markets) would have to be offset against the increases. For an attempt to estimate the social benefits from railroading in nineteenth century America, see Robert William Fogel, Railroads and American Economic Growth, in The Reinterpretation of American History 187 (Robert William Fogel & Stanley L. Engerman eds. 1971).

PART II

PUBLIC REGULATION OF THE MARKET

Chapter 6

THE THEORY OF MONOPOLY

§6.1. Output under monopoly. We observed in Chapter 1 that a seller would not knowingly sell below his opportunity cost, for that would mean forgoing a higher for a lower price. But what determines the upper bound of his price? He would like to maximize profits, defined as the difference between total revenues and total costs. With profit maximization his goal, his choice of price is constrained by the demand for his product and by the cost of production. From Chapter 1 the reader will recall the basic economic law that people buy more of a product when the price of the product falls and less of it when it rises. This relationship is portrayed by the line labeled "demand" in Figure 1.

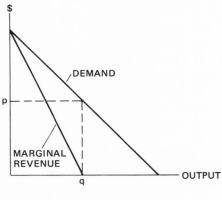

Figure 1

Dollars are plotted on the vertical axis and quantity of output on the horizontal. To every price at which the product might be sold there corresponds a quantity that consumers in the aggregate would purchase. The quantity is larger the lower the price, and smaller the higher the price.

The seller is interested in price only insofar as it affects his revenue (price times quantity). The price that maximizes his revenue can be found with the aid of the concept of "marginal revenue," the contribution to total revenue of selling one additional unit. So long as marginal revenue is positive, total revenue is growing. When marginal revenue falls to zero, it means that total revenue will not grow with additional output. If the demand schedule is known, the marginal revenue schedule can be derived mathematically from it; this has been done in Figure 1.[1] The point at which the marginal revenue curve crosses the horizontal axis marks the level of output at which total revenue is maximized. That point is q in Figure ·1. The price corresponding to that level of output is p. If the seller sold a smaller quantity, he would be to the left of the marginal revenue curve and additional output would increase his total revenues. If he sold a larger quantity, his revenue would be in the negative region of the marginal revenue curve, signifying that a *reduction* in output would increase his total revenue.

But the seller does not want to maximize total revenue. He wants to maximize the excess of total revenue over total cost. To show how this is done, we add two cost schedules to Figure 1: an average cost schedule corresponding to the demand schedule (the schedule of average revenue) and a marginal cost schedule corresponding to the marginal revenue schedule. The marginal cost schedule reveals the addition to total costs of selling one more unit of output. The cost curves are drawn sloping upward because as a firm purchases more and more inputs it usually finds itself forced to pay higher prices in order to bid the inputs away from users who lack good substitutes. But cost curves need not always slope upward, as we shall see.[2] Figure 2 depicts our four curves.

§6.1. 1. Marginal revenue is simply the rate of change, or in mathematical terms the first derivative, of total revenue. And demand is simply the schedule of average revenue (total revenue divided by quantity), or price, at various levels of output. In the special case where the demand schedule for a product can be approximated by a straight line, as in Figure 1, the marginal revenue curve can be plotted very easily by drawing a straight line from the intersection of the demand curve with the vertical axis to the point on the horizontal axis that is midway between the origin and the intersection of the demand curve with the horizontal axis.

2. See §9.1 *infra*. The cost functions for most products are U-shaped rather than continuously rising or continuously falling as output rises. At low levels of output, average costs are likely to fall as increased production enables more

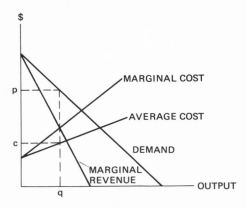

Figure 2

The seller will want to expand output so long as an additional unit sold adds more to his total revenues than to his total costs, and to stop when the sale of an additional unit would increase his total costs by more than his total revenues. The profit-maximizing output is therefore the quantity at which marginal revenue and marginal cost are equated, q in Figure 2. At this level of output, total revenue equals pq and total cost cq. Observe that if output were smaller, profits would be smaller too, since one would be at the left of the intersection, where additional output would add more to total revenues than to total costs. With a larger quantity, profits would also be smaller, since the seller would be at the right of the intersection, which is a region where each unit sold adds more to his total costs than to his total revenues.

Another name for p in Figure 2 is the monopoly price, because it is the price that a firm having no competitors would charge. Competition would make the price untenable. Let A be the only seller of the product (widgets) whose cost and demand curves are shown in Figures 1 and 2. He establishes a price of p and sells q widgets. Assume other sellers can produce and sell widgets at the same cost as A. One of these sellers, B, attracted by A's large profits $(pq - cq)$, decides to sell some widgets, also at price p. Figure 3 shows the result. With B selling one fourth as

efficient utilization of plant, while at higher levels the producer runs into the problem, mentioned in the text, of having to bid away inputs from users lacking good substitutes. These refinements are not necessary to the present analysis.

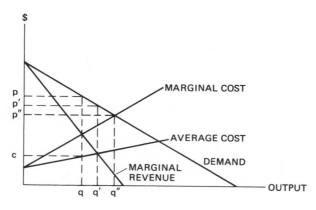

Figure 3

many widgets as A (B's output is $q' - q$ in Figure 3), the total
quantity of widgets on the market (q') is one fourth again as
large as before. Consumers will not pay p for the larger quantity
of widgets, but only p'. Perhaps A and B will now cut their outputs — but C, D, E, and others are waiting to enter the market
in order to capture a share of the profits that enticed B. Entry
will continue to be attractive until price is bid down to p'', where
it is just equal to the opportunity costs of producing additional
widgets. Entry is attractive until that point is reached because
resources devoted to manufacturing widgets earn more than their
opportunity costs, and hence more than they could earn in competitive markets. The output of widgets will not be expanded beyond q'' (corresponding to p'') because then those resources
would be earning less than their opportunity costs.

Figure 3 indicates that, under monopoly, output is smaller —
q instead of q''. The higher, monopoly price induces some consumers to substitute other products. The substitution involves a
loss in value. Consumers must value the substituted products
less than they did widgets at the old price or else they would
have made the substitution before the price of widgets was
raised. Stated differently, monopoly confronts consumers with
false alternatives. By increasing price above opportunity cost, the
monopolist makes substitute products the opportunity costs of
which are actually higher than those of his product look cheaper
to the consumer. He thus encourages the consumer to satisfy his
demands at a greater cost than necessary.

§*6.2.   Other effects of monopoly.*   Another effect of monopoly is to transfer wealth from those consumers who continue to buy the monopolized product to the monopolist. The transfer does not diminish value directly. The added cost to the consumers ($pq - p''q$ in Figure 3) is fully captured by the monopolist, so while they are worse off he is better off by the same amount. But the existence of opportunities to effect such transfers will attract resources into the business of monopolizing, just as the existence of lucrative opportunities for theft attracts resources into thieving. In both cases the resources are wasted because they are used in an unproductive activity — an activity that does not increase value.

The monopolist may be able to shift the demand curve for his product outward — leading to overproduction rather than underproduction. He may be able to misrepresent the price or quality of his product.[1] Or he may be able to prevail upon government to reduce the supply of competitive products or increase the demand for complementary ones.[2]

Some economists believe that monopoly reduces the incentive of the firm to innovate and to use its inputs efficiently. The theoretical basis for this view is obscure, the evidence mixed. On the one hand, it has been argued that a monopolist is not penalized as heavily as a competitive firm for failure to innovate and to minimize costs vigorously; but it can be shown that the penalty is identical, at least where the monopolist's common stock is publicly traded.[3] On the other hand, it would seem that the reward for successful innovation and cost minimization is often greater for the monopolist, since the competitive seller's success may be promptly duplicated by his rivals. It is concern about prompt duplication that has led to the grant of patent protection; but patents are limited in time and scope.[4]

§6.2. 1. See §3.6 *supra.*

2. Two products are complementary when an increase in the demand for one will lead to an increase in the demand for the other. The ability of firms to obtain governmental assistance in suppressing competition is discussed later. See especially Chapter 23. Observe that a competitive industry acting through a trade association may be able to obtain the same kind of governmental protection as a monopolist. This is an instance of the more general proposition that independent firms can often by coordination achieve the same results as monopoly. See §7.1 *infra.*

3. See §13.2 *infra.*

4. See §2.9 *supra.* Could it be argued that monopoly may create *excessive* incentives to invent new products? For a discussion of the question of innovation by monopolists, and a review of the literature, see Richard A. Posner, Natural Monopoly and Its Regulation, 21 Stan. L. Rev. 548, 577–584 (1969). For another possible effect of monopoly, see §6.5 *infra,* note 2.

§6.3. *Price discrimination.* The theory of monopoly developed in the preceding sections rests on a number of assumptions that need to be examined. The first is that the monopolist sells his product at a single price. Ordinarily the assumption is justified. If he sold at two different prices purchasers charged the lower price would resell to purchasers charged the higher price. Such resale activity (known as arbitrage) would make it impossible for the seller to maintain different prices. But arbitrage is sometimes difficult or impossible. The product may be difficult to resell (as in the case of some services) or there may be contractual restrictions on resale. If the monopolist can prevent arbitrage, he is likely to fix different prices to different purchasers depending not on the costs of selling to them — which are the same — but on the intensity of their demands for his product. This is price discrimination.

The downward slope of the demand curve implies that consumers would be willing to pay prices well in excess of cost for some units of the monopolist's output, but prices only slightly higher than cost for others, and nothing at all for still others. There is no single price that extracts the full value which consumers attach to being able to purchase some units of the good that does not sacrifice the smaller but still positive profits at which additional units could be sold. Ideally the monopolist would like to negotiate separately with each consumer over each unit. One result would be that he would never turn away a customer willing to pay a price equal to cost, so his output would be identical to that under competition. But the transaction costs of perfect price discrimination are prohibitive. Usually the best the discriminating monopolist can do is to divide his customers into a few groups and set a different price for each group. The effect on output of this kind of crude price discrimination is indeterminate. Suppose, for example, that the single monopoly price is $10 but rather than charging that price the monopolist classifies his customers into two groups and charges $5 to members of one class and $20 to members of the other. He gains sales — to those who will not pay $10 but are willing to pay $5. But he also loses sales — to those who are willing to pay $10 but refuse to pay $20. The lost sales may outnumber the sales gained. His output may be lower although his profits will be higher.

Even perfect price discrimination would not eliminate the economic objection to monopoly. Competitive and monopoly outputs would be the same, to be sure; but the availability of monopoly profits would draw away from competitive markets resources that were more productive in those markets but earned a lower return there due to the absence of monopoly pricing.

We discuss the efficiency effects of price discrimination further in the next chapter.[1]

§6.4. *Competition for the market.*[1]   A second assumption of the theory of monopoly is that there is no competition to be a monopolist. If I agree to take all my requirements of a particular good from a single seller, I grant that seller a monopoly over that supply to me. But it does not follow that I will pay him a monopoly price. I will not have to pay more than the competitive price if two conditions are satisfied: that there be more than one seller in a position to supply me and that the cost of making an effective contract for the period of the monopoly not be prohibitive. If there is competition to serve me, sellers will vie with one another to offer me an attractive contract and the price fixed in the contract will be bid down to the competitive level. Suppose, however, that once the seller with whom I have signed a contract begins to perform, it will take a long time for any other seller to step into his place as my supplier. In such a situation, I will need a long-term contract in order to protect me against monopoly pricing and long-term contracts may involve costly inflexibilities.

§6.5. *Durability.*   Ronald H. Coase has pointed out in a recent article that there is a special difficulty in monopolizing durable goods.[1] He uses the example of land. If one person owned all of the land in the United States and wanted to sell it at a price that maximized his profits, like any other monopolist he would fix a price at which only a portion of the land would be bought. Once the sale was completed, however, he would have an incentive to begin selling off the remaining portions of land at a lower price, until eventually all of the land was sold. Knowing this, people would not pay his initial price and his attempt to monopolize would fail.

Land may be a somewhat misleading example because it is not continuously produced. Diamonds are a durable good too, yet the

§6.3. 1. See §7.8 *infra.* See also §9.4 *infra.*

§6.4. 1. See Harold Demsetz, Why Regulate Utilities? 11 J. Law & Econ. 55 (1968); Richard A. Posner, The Appropriate Scope of Regulation in the Cable Television Industry, 3 Bell J. Econ. & Management Sci. 98, 110–116 (1972); cf. United States v. El Paso Natural Gas Co., 376 U.S. 651 (1964).

§6.5. 1. Ronald H. Coase, Durability and Monopoly, 15 J. Law & Econ. 143 (1972).

production of diamonds is said to be controlled by a cartel that limits output and charges monopoly prices. The reason may have to do with the fact that diamonds are continuously produced. If the cartel one year stepped up production and slashed prices in order to reach a segment of the community that could not ordinarily afford diamonds, the value of every diamond in existence would fall. Having thus once demonstrated its unreliability, the cartel would never again be able to charge so high a price as it had before it went on its spree.

The land monopolist could credibly limit his output if he leased rather than sold land. If, after having leased a limited portion of his land, he began leasing or selling additional parcels at lower prices, his ability to continue to charge a monopoly price when the lease came up for renewal, like the diamond cartel's ability to continue to sell diamonds at the monopoly price, would be impaired. Knowing that he had an incentive to abide by his initial limitation of output, purchasers would be less afraid to pay the monopoly price.[2]

§6.6. *Entry.*   The theory of monopoly does not explain how a monopolist maintains a monopoly price, in view of the attraction that such a price must hold for sellers in other markets. Since a monopoly return is larger than a competitive return, sellers in competitive markets will be attracted to a market in which a monopoly price is being charged. To obtain monopoly profits the new entrant must sell. His sales increase the output of the market, causing price to fall. Entry will continue until price has fallen back to a competitive level, for until that point is reached sellers will be attracted to the market by the hope of above-normal returns. Monopolies thus contain the seeds of their own destruction.

The *rate* at which new firms enter a market in which a monopoly price is being charged is critical. Where the monopolist has a patent or other legal monopoly, that rate may be zero and the monopoly price will persist until the termination of the legal monopoly. Sometimes monopoly will persist because the costs of the monopolist are lower than those of any new entrant, so that even though the monopolist charges a monopoly price, it is lower

---

2. Assurance would be greatest if the monopolist's revenue from the leases were a percentage of the lessees' revenues. Then any action by the monopolist that reduced their revenues would reduce his own revenues directly.

Question: might the monopolist try to solve the problem discussed in this section by reducing the durability of his product?

than the price that a new entrant would have to charge in order to cover his costs.[1] Monopoly may also be a durable condition of the market because there is room for only one seller.[2]

The existence of an entry time lag is a necessary rather than sufficient condition of substantial monopoly effects. If the monopoly is anticipated sufficiently far in advance and efforts to enter begun immediately, the period of actual monopolization may be very short.

§6.7. *The problem of second best.* Discussions of monopoly usually assume that substitutes for the monopolist's product are not themselves sold at monopoly prices. If they are, it ceases to be certain that the monopoly will result in the substitution of products that have higher opportunity costs than the monopolized product. Consider: leather buttons are monopolized and sell at a price of 10¢, even though the cost of production is only 6¢. The nearest substitute for leather buttons, plastic buttons, sell for 8¢ each. As a result of the monopolization of leather buttons, some people substitute plastic buttons for them but if the price of a plastic button is equal to its cost this substitution is inefficient. A product that costs 8¢ to produce is being purchased in place of one that costs only 6¢ to produce. Resources are being diverted from the production of a less costly method of satisfying consumer wants to the production of a more costly one. But suppose now that plastic buttons are not being sold at a price equal to cost. They are being sold at 8¢, a monopoly price, but cost only 5¢ to produce. With leather buttons being sold at the monopoly price of 10¢, people will buy more plastic buttons despite their monopoly price, and this is efficient since plastic buttons cost less to produce. If the monopoly of leather buttons is terminated, price will decline to the competitive level, 6¢, and people will begin to substitute leather for plastic buttons. Termination of the leather button monopoly confronts the consumer with a false alternative. Given the monopoly of plastic buttons, the "second best" solution to the problem of economizing on resource use is a monopoly of leather buttons; first best, of course, would be no monopolies.

Even if the output effects of monopolizing were completely indeterminate (a rather extreme inference to draw from the existence of second-best problems), there would still be at least one good reason for prohibiting monopolies — to prevent re-

---

§6.6. 1. This is the problem of barriers to entry, discussed *infra* §7.7.
2. See §§7.10, 9.1 *infra*.

sources from being attracted to an activity (monopolizing) that is socially unproductive.

We have not discussed the most interesting question in the theory of monopoly: how monopolies come into being. The next three chapters deal in part with this question.

SUGGESTED READING

George J. Stigler, The Theory of Price, ch. 11 (3d ed. 1966).

CHAPTER 7

THE ANTITRUST LAWS

§7.1. *Cartels and the Sherman Act.* A contract among competing sellers to fix the price of the product they sell is like any other contract in the sense that the parties would not sign it unless it made them all better off than before. But it injures others, consumers, who are not parties to the contract; and as we learned in the last chapter, when substitution effects are taken into account the costs to consumers exceed the cartelists' gains. It is not surprising that by the latter part of the nineteenth century, courts were refusing to enforce such contracts on the ground that they were against public policy.

From our earlier discussion of contracts, it might appear that nonenforcement would be a patently inadequate remedy, for we said that even without legal sanctions for breach of contract, people would ordinarily be led by considerations of reciprocal advantage to adhere to their contracts. But a price-fixing agreement is less stable than most contracts. The party to such an agreement "buys" the agreement of the other parties not to sell below a certain price. However, the "product" (forbearance to compete in price) is difficult to inspect. I lose sales. There are any number of reasons why this might have happened. One is that a competitor undercut me. But how am I to find out? I could ask the purchasers whom I have lost, but I could not trust their answers. They might tell me my competitor was underselling me, even if he was not, in order to induce me to grant a price reduction. Moreover, my competitor might have adhered to the cartel price but improved his product — a subtle method of cheating.[1] Yet, despite the instability of cartels, nonenforcement

§7.1. 1. On the problems of enforcing cartels, see George J. Stigler, A Theory of Oligopoly, in The Organization of Industry 39 (1968); John S. McGee, Ocean Freight Rate Conferences and the American Merchant Marine, 27 U. Chi. L. Rev.

of cartel agreements is unlikely to be an adequate remedy. By reducing the efficacy of price fixing by contract, it creates an incentive for the members of the cartel to consolidate into a single firm.[2] The monopoly price can then be enforced without reliance on contracts.

The Sherman Act, which was passed in 1890, attempted to deal with the monopoly problem by imposing criminal and civil sanctions on contracts and other combinations "in restraint of trade" and on "monopolization" and conspiracies and attempts to monopolize. Early decisions interpreted the act as forbidding cartels. Although the sanctions for violation were weak,[3] it appears that the act was effective in preventing cartelists from employing certain highly effective, but also highly visible, devices for eliminating cheating by cartel members.

To explain why this is so, we must consider more closely the problems of cartel enforcement. The temptation of members to cheat is strong, not only because, as mentioned above, it is difficult to catch the cheater, but also because the returns from cheating are substantial if the cheater can avoid, at least for some period, getting caught. If the expansion of the market's output brought about by his cheating is small, the resulting fall in his profits due to the decline in market price caused by the larger output may be outweighed by the increase in his profits due to the sale of additional units, each at a monopoly profit. To illustrate, suppose the output of the market, before cheating, is 100 units, and each seller's quota is 10. The unit price is $2 and the cost of production $1, so each seller has a monopoly profit of $1 per unit and $10 overall. One seller decides to cheat. He increases his output to 15 units. The market's output is now 105 and so price will fall — say to $1.80. The cheater sells 15 units at $1.80 and obtains a profit of $.80 per unit. His total profit is thus $12. He has increased his profits by 20 percent.

One way a cartel may be able to reduce the likelihood of cheating is by organizing a common sales agency. All sales of the cartel's product are channeled through the agency, which sets a uniform price. This is the kind of cartelizing device that the Sherman Act suppressed [4] (but when faith in competition wav-

---

191 (1960); Richard A. Posner, Oligopoly and the Antitrust Laws: A Suggested Approach, 21 Stan. L. Rev. 1562, 1569–1575 (1969).

2. Cf. §12.1 *infra*.

3. Cf. §25.3 *infra*.

4. See George J. Stigler, The Economic Effects of the Antitrust Laws, in The Organization of Industry 259 (1968).

ered during the Depression, the Supreme Court upheld one cartel's use of a common sales agency).[5]

By preventing the most effective methods of cartelization, the Sherman Act reduced the effectiveness and the returns of cartelizing. This presumably increased efficiency. But it had another effect that was inefficient. The output of a monopolized market is smaller than that of a competitive market. Upon formation of a cartel, therefore, much of the productive capacity of the market becomes excess, and it should be retired in order to economize on resources. But if the members are worried that the cartel may be unstable and short-lived, they will be reluctant to retire capacity lest they find themselves unable to expand output if and when the cartel weakens or collapses and price falls. The common sales agency and other "efficient" methods of cartelizing suppressed by the Sherman Act facilitate the withdrawal of excess capacity by increasing the stability and longevity of the cartel that employs them, and in this respect are less wasteful of resources than the underground cartel that has replaced it.

In the enforcement of the Sherman Act against cartels, emphasis has been placed upon establishing the fact of an agreement pertaining to price — a legal issue — rather than upon establishing the effects of the sellers' conduct on price and output — the economic issue. A presumably unintended consequence of such an emphasis is that the cartels most likely to be discovered and prosecuted are those in which the price and output effects are small. These are the cartels that have many members, so there is a better chance that one will become disgruntled and inform on the others; that depend on explicit and reiterated negotiation and agreement, which provide the essential evidence of violation; and that are likely to be riddled with cheating and collapse shortly amidst mutual recrimination — circumstances that create opportunities to obtain evidence of agreement and willing witnesses to offer it. The smoothly functioning cartel is less likely to generate evidence of actual agreement. What the law mainly punishes is the attempt to fix prices. The completed conspiracy often escapes attention.

Could criteria be developed for identifying industries in which effective conspiracies are likely, and for detecting and proving conspiracies by their economic effects? [6] Perhaps. Economic anal-

---

5. Appalachian Coals, Inc. v. United States, 288 U.S. 344 (1933).

6. The discussion that follows draws heavily on Richard A. Posner, A Program for the Antitrust Division, 38 U. Chi. L. Rev. 500 (1970).

ysis could be used, first, to identify the characteristics which indicate a market's predisposition to effective price fixing. One such characteristic is the number of sellers: the fewer the number, the lower the costs of coordinating their activities — a point that will be recalled from our discussion of transaction costs in Chapter 2. Another predisposing characteristic is the homogeneity of the product: the more homogeneous a product is, the more difficult it will be to cheat by altering product quality.

Another — but one especially difficult to measure — is the elasticity of demand with respect to price. Demand is elastic at any point in a demand schedule where a small change in price would cause a proportionately greater change in quantity demanded. It is inelastic at any point where a small price change would cause a proportionately smaller change in quantity demanded.[7] Other things being equal, the less elastic demand is, the larger are the profits that a monopoly price will generate and hence the greater the incentive to monopolize. Intuitively, the further quantity demanded declines in response to price increases, the less freedom the monopolist has to raise price. Another important predisposing characteristic to cartelization, but again one difficult to measure, is the condition of entry. If entry can be effected rapidly and entrants have no higher long-run costs than the members of the cartel, the profits of cartelization will be small, and so also the incentive to cartelize.

The predisposing characteristics are neither well understood nor readily measurable. They could, however, provide some guidance to enforcement agencies as to which industries to concentrate their investigative resources in.

The economist can also suggest the kinds of evidence that indicate whether a market is being successfully cartelized. One kind of evidence is the existence of price discrimination, a method, as we have seen, of exploiting a monopoly position. Another is an unexplained decline over time in the market share of the largest firms in the market, which may indicate that they have been charging a monopoly price that has attracted new entrants who have bid business away from them by charging lower prices. A third is industry-wide resale price maintenance, which, unless justifiable on grounds to be discussed shortly,[8] may have been adopted to prevent cheating in the form of selling at a reduced mark-up to dealers. (If a dealer cuts his price, competitors of the

7. Elasticity is thus a measure of the responsiveness of one variable (such as quantity demanded) to a change in another variable (such as price charged).
8. See §7.9 *infra*.

dealer's supplier may be uncertain whether the price cut reflects a change in the retailer's operating costs or a price cut by the supplier; resale price maintenance eliminates this uncertainty.) A fourth kind of evidence is market shares too stable to be a product of normal competitive activity among the sellers. A fifth is regional price variations that cannot be explained by inter-regional differences in cost or demand. A sixth is a price rise, coupled with a reduction in output, that cannot be explained other than by a hypothesis of cartelization.

Unfortunately, these and other economic criteria of effective collusion are difficult to apply in practice,[9] so even if greater reliance were placed on economic analysis many cartels would go undetected. Moreover, the courts in the past have often mis-handled economic evidence in antitrust cases. Two examples will illustrate this point.

In the *United States Steel Corporation* monopoly case, the Supreme Court, in dismissing the complaint, was impressed by the fact that U.S. Steel's market share had declined steadily after the combination of competing steel manufacturers to form the corporation.[10] The Court failed to recognize in this predictable monopoly behavior. The establishment of a monopoly price creates incentives for new sellers to come into the industry. The monopolist has three choices. He can cease charging a monopoly price, in order to discourage entry; he can do nothing; or he can reduce his output in an effort to offset the price effects of the new entrants' output. The first course of action utterly defeats the purpose of the monopoly. Under the second or third, the monopolist obtains some monopoly profits, at least temporarily, so we would expect him to follow either of these. Both result in a decline in his market share.[11]

In the second *American Tobacco* case, the Court, in holding that the major cigarette manufacturers had conspired to eliminate competition, attached significance to the fact that the manufacturers had raised their prices during the Depression

9. Among other problems, it may sometimes be difficult to distinguish between evidence of monopolizing by a single firm and evidence of monopolizing by a cartel — an important distinction from the standpoint of appropriate remedy (see §7.10 *infra*). This problem could perhaps be solved by placing the burden of proof on the firm to establish that the evidence of monopolization presented by the government actually described a single-firm monopoly rather than a cartel.

10. United States v. United States Steel Corp., 251 U.S. 417 (1920).

11. This analysis was applied to the U.S. Steel case in George J. Stigler, The Dominant Firm and the Inverted Umbrella, in The Organization of Industry 108 (1968).

despite the fact that it was a period of declining demand.[12] However, it is in general incorrect that a monopolist will raise prices
in the face of declining demand; he will reduce them. This is
shown in Figure 4, where D' depicts the effect of a fall in demand: the price that consumers are willing to pay at any level
of output is lower by a uniform percentage. The new profit-
maximizing price is lower than the old. One can vary the assumptions. If, for example, demand were also becoming less
elastic, this would, as noted earlier, encourage the monopolist to
raise price, and this effect might dominate his incentive to reduce
price because demand was declining. But demands probably be-

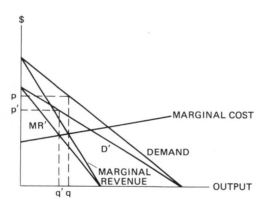

Figure 4

come more rather than less elastic during depressions because
people shop more carefully. This prediction is supported by the
competitive inroads made by the minor tobacco brands when the
major tobacco companies made their price increase.[13]

§7.2. *Mergers to monopoly.*   A law that punished only
monopolies effected by cartelization could be evaded by consolidation of the cartel members into one firm. Since cartelists would
merge if the gains to them from monopoly pricing exceeded the
costs involved in replacing several firms with one even if those

12. American Tobacco Co. v. United States, 328 U.S. 781 (1946), discussed in
Richard A. Posner, *supra* note 6, at 521–523.
13. The tobacco companies may have raised their prices because they perceived
(perhaps mistakenly) an upward shift in the industry demand curve. See Richard
A. Posner, *supra* note 1, at 1586–1587.

costs (which we discuss in a subsequent chapter) [1] were substantial, an anticartel law might encourage a continuation of cartel pricing in another and more costly form. This is the economic justification for the refusal of a majority of the Supreme Court in the *Northern Securities* case[2] to adopt Justice Holmes' position that the Sherman Act was inapplicable to mergers. But Holmes was right to be troubled about the implications of the law's reaching beyond cartels to mergers. The conditions of supply and demand in a market may be such that one firm can supply, at lower average cost than two or more firms, the entire output demanded; or one firm may have a superior management, in whose hands the assets of all the other firms would be more valuable. Either situation could lead to a monopoly through merger that might generate cost savings greater than the costs of the monopoly pricing that would result.[3] Unfortunately it is exceedingly difficult to distinguish situations of this kind from the case of a merger to create a monopoly that involves no cost savings.

§7.3. *Mergers and oligopoly.*   Monopolies, despite their analytical interest, are rare. Oligopolies — markets in which a few firms account for most sales — are quite common and the question of their competitive significance is a controversial one. The 1950 amendment of section 7 of the Clayton Act,.which has been interpreted as placing exceedingly stringent limitations on mergers between competitors, is frequently defended as necessary to prevent further increases in oligopoly. As mentioned earlier, the number of firms in a market is relevant to a concern with cartels because the fewer the firms, the lower the costs of coordinating their policies. However, there are so many other factors relating to the propensity to cartelize that it is doubtful whether this point alone would justify a draconian antimerger law. It is rather the view of some economists that oligopoly leads to supracompetitive prices even when each firm's pricing decisions are independent that provides the intellectual basis of the antimerger law.

The reasoning is that each firm will be reluctant to cut prices, knowing that its price cut will have so immediate and substantial an effect on the market shares of its rivals that they will quickly match the price cut, thus wiping out the first firm's gains. On the other hand, if the firm raises its price, its competitors will be in-

§7.2. 1. See §12.1 *infra.*
2. United States v. Northern Securities Co., 193 U.S. 197 (1904).
3. How effective would be a decree dissolving the merger in such a case? Cf. §7.10 *infra.*

clined to raise their prices too, knowing that all will make higher profits at the higher price. However, this "interdependence" theory[1] has serious weaknesses. It is true that in a market of two firms of equal size, an increase in one firm's output of 50 percent will cause so sharp a drop in the output of the other firm[2] that the other firm is quite likely to make a prompt matching price reduction, whereas in a 100-firm market an increase in one firm's output of 50 percent would reduce the other firms' output by no more than one half of one percent. But is this the correct comparison? If in our second market fifty firms each raised their output by 50 percent, the effect on the remaining firms would be identical to that of a 50 percent increase in the output of one firm in a two-firm market.

Moreover, the interdependence theory does not explain very well how oligopolists establish a price higher than the competitive price in the first place. If, as the theory posits, oligopolists are very wary of each other's reactions to any price change, a firm contemplating a price increase would worry that its competitors would delay in matching the increase, since by lagging behind him they would gain sales at his expense.

Still another difficulty of the theory is that the optimum pricing strategy of a firm that takes account of the reactions of its rivals to its pricing moves is indeterminate. The firm must figure out not only how the competitor will react to a given price move but how the competitor will react to its reaction to the competitor's reaction, and so on ad infinitum.

An alternative approach is to view anticompetitive pricing in oligopolistic markets as a special form of collusion in which the necessity for overt communication is minimized by the fewness of the sellers. The theory of oligopoly becomes a special case of the theory of cartels.[3]

§7.4.   *The definition of market.*   With antitrust legality for good or ill so dependent on ascertaining the number of rivals, the definition of the market — the set of sellers that will be included in the count — becomes crucial. Market has two dimensions, product and geographical. The first is illustrated by the celebrated cellophane monopolization case, in which the Supreme Court held that cellophane was not a relevant market because

---

§7.3. 1. See, e.g., Edward Hastings Chamberlin, The Theory of Monopolistic Competition 30–55 (8th ed. 1962).

2. But not a 50 percent drop. Why not?

3. See George J. Stigler, *supra* §7.1, note 1.

there was a high "cross-elasticity of demand" between cellophane and other flexible packaging materials.[1]

Glance back at Figure 2[2] and place an imaginary point on the demand curve directly above the intersection of the marginal revenue curve and the horizontal axis. At every point to the left of this imaginary point demand is elastic with respect to price; at every point to the right it is inelastic. In the elastic region a price reduction will increase the firm's total revenues because the resulting increase in quantity demanded generates more additional revenue than is lost by virtue of the lower price. In the inelastic region an increase in quantity demanded as a result of a price reduction does not generate sufficient additional revenue to offset the revenue loss from the price reduction. The point at which marginal revenue falls to zero marks the border between the two regions.[3]

A monopolist always sells in the elastic region of his demand schedule. He would never make an additional sale that reduced his total revenues: since the cost of the additional unit sold would be positive, his total profits (revenues minus costs) would fall. (The members of a competitive industry, in contrast, often sell in the region of inelastic demand.) One reason that most demand schedules have an elastic region is that the higher the price of a product, the more attractive substitute products become to the consumer. Hence it is not surprising to find a high cross-elasticity of demand between a monopolized product and other products at the monopoly price-output level, meaning that at that level, the demand for the substitute products is highly responsive to a change in the price of the monopolized product. The cross-elasticity of demand of the same product sold at the competitive price might be a good deal less.

Thus the high cross-elasticity of demand for cellophane may have signified no more than that duPont could not have increased the price of cellophane further without losing a great deal of business to substitute products. This would be completely consistent with the existing price being the monopoly price. The Court's use of evidence of high cross-elasticity of demand would have made more sense had the case involved a challenge to a consolidation of the producers of cellophane, where the issue was whether the consolidation would create monopoly power. If the

§7.4. 1. United States v. E. I. duPont de Nemours, 351 U.S. 377 (1956).
2. In §6.1 *supra.*
3. To the right of this point, the marginal revenue produced by an additional sale is negative — i.e., total revenue is lower than if the sale had not been made.

cross-elasticity of demand between cellophane and substitute packaging materials was high before the consolidation, when a competitive price was being charged for cellophane, then it would follow that the consolidated firm would have but little ability to obtain monopoly profits by raising price. (But the assumption that the price was competitive before the consolidation would have to be examined.) The converse does not follow. If, in our hypothetical cellophane merger case, the cross-elasticity of demand between cellophane and various other packaging materials was low, we would not be entitled to conclude that demand for cellophane was price inelastic. The fact that a product has no close substitutes does not imply a willingness on the part of consumers to pay higher prices rather than do without. All that is necessary to assure that demand for a product is price elastic is that consumers have alternative uses for their money to which they will turn in the event of an increase in the relative price of the product.

Manufacturers of a product frequently do not sell outside of limited geographic areas. Which sellers are to be included in deciding whether monopoly or potential monopoly conditions exist with respect to some group of consumers? The courts' tendency has been to include those sellers who actually sell to the group in question and exclude those who do not. This is at once too many and too few. If the market is monopolized, the monopoly price will attract sellers from distant markets who could not have covered their transportation and other selling costs if the competitive price had been charged. If the market is not monopolized, there may be a group of distant sellers who at the moment do not ship into the market but who could and would do so if the price rose even slightly. Perhaps the outside sellers would have two percent higher costs than the inside sellers due to transportation expense. This would imply that if, as a result of monopolization, the market price rose by two percent, the outside sellers would begin to ship into the market and price could not rise any further.

The existence of even heavy freight costs may not assure monopoly opportunities to the proximate sellers. Suppose that southeastern producers selling in the northeast incur transport costs (that northeastern producers do not have) equal to six percent of their total costs but that their nontransport costs are four percent below the costs of the northeastern sellers; the potential monopoly power of the northeastern sellers would be no greater than in our previous example.

§7.5. *Predation.*   Our emphasis thus far has been on the acquisition of monopoly power by consolidation or other forms of cooperation among competitors. An important question is whether such power can be obtained or enlarged through the efforts of one firm. We may put aside the case where it obtains a monopoly or a large market share by superior efficiency or a government license and confine our attention to tactics that are thought to be abuses of the competitive process. One is "predatory price discrimination": a firm sells below cost in some markets; after its competitors are driven out, it sets a monopoly price.[1] Confirmed instances of predatory price discrimination were rare even before the practice was clearly illegal. The reason is that the practice is very costly to the predator. He incurs a present and substantial loss for gains that are not only deferred, but that may be temporary since once the existing competitors are driven out of the market and a monopoly price is established new competitors will be attracted to the market by that price; the tactic may have to be repeated. Ordinarily it is cheaper to buy off a competitor than to destroy him by selling below cost.

If the threat to engage in predatory price discrimination were sufficient to bring competitors into line, it would be employed often since it costs little to make a threat (excluding legal punishment costs). But a threat, to be effective, must be credible. A threat to sell below cost would ordinarily not be credible since the victim of the threat would know that the threatener would be restrained by his self-interest from carrying it out. The threat may be credible, however, where the threatener has a monopoly position in a number of different markets while each of his competitors sells in only one of these markets. The monopolist may be able to convince each competitor that he will carry out a threat to sell below cost in particular markets in order to make his threats in other markets more credible. The cost of one or two episodes of below-cost selling may be small relative to the benefits that he derives from having established his credibility.

§7.6.   Foreclosure.   A number of other practices that are claimed to create monopoly power also have the property of imposing on the monopolist costs that are usually at least as high as those the intended victims must bear. Suppose a manufacturer were to buy up all of the retail outlets for the product of his industry in order to foreclose his competitors from access to the

§7.5. 1. For interesting discussions of predatory pricing see John S. McGee, Predatory Price Cutting: The Standard Oil (N.J.) Case, 1 J. Law & Econ. 137 (1958); L. G. Telser, Cutthroat Competition and the Long Purse, 9 J. Law & Econ. 259 (1966).

market. They would react by building their own outlets. This would involve costs to them, but no more (and probably less) than the cost to the would-be monopolist of purchasing a chain of retail outlets that turned out to have a great deal of excess capacity after his rivals built their own outlets.

Foreclosure has often been considered an effective method of obtaining monopoly power for a firm that already has a monopoly in a related market. Suppose a firm has a patent for one product, say computers, and refuses to sell or lease its product unless the purchaser or lessee agrees to obtain its supplies of some other product, say computer punchcards, from it. The firm thereby obtains a monopoly of punchcards (the "tied" product) used with its computers (the "tying" product). But — and this is the fatal flaw in the "leverage" theory — the firm obtains no monopoly profits from the second monopoly. If it charges its computer lessees a price higher than the competitive price for the cards, they will treat this as an indirect increase in the computer rental; but if they are willing to pay a higher computer rental, it means that the computer company could have exploited their willingness directly, by charging a higher rental.

A possible advantage to a monopolist of imposing a tie-in is that it may enable him to discriminate effectively. If the computer company in our example collects its monopoly revenues through the price that it fixes for each card, in effect the computer rental rate varies from customer to customer according to the intensity of each customer's use.[1] We consider the appropriate policy toward price discrimination in a subsequent section.[2] Here we emphasize that it is not a method by which a firm can use a monopoly in one market to obtain monopoly profits in a second market as well, nor is it likely in fact to foreclose access to the market to competing manufacturers of the tied product (punchcards, in our example). Since the monopolist of the tying product cannot extract monopoly profits from the sale of the tied product, he has no interest in controlling its manufacture. His interest is only in having sales of the tied product funneled through him. Thus, tying agreements do not disturb the existing structure of the market for the tied product.

A practice analytically similar to the tie-in is reciprocal buying: I buy from you on condition that you buy something from

§7.6. 1. This theory of tie-in arrangements is elaborated in Ward Bowman, Tying Arrangements and the Leverage Problem, 67 Yale L.J. 19 (1967). How convincing is it? Would other metering devices be as cheap or cheaper?
2. See §7.8 infra.

me. This condition cannot increase monopoly power. The only way that I can induce you to pay a monopoly price for the good that you buy from me is to pay you a higher price for the good that you sell to me; I gain nothing. Reciprocal buying is primarily a device for granting price concessions indirectly: I pay you your regular price but you agree to buy something from me at higher than my regular price, in effect granting me a discount on your sale to me. Reciprocal buying is thus likely to be employed where there are legal or cartel restrictions on overt discounts.[3]

§7.7. *Barriers to entry.*   A subtler version of the foreclosure theory holds that foreclosure increases monopoly power indirectly by creating a "barrier to entry," a concept we must pause to define. Strictly speaking, a barrier to entry is a condition that makes the long-run costs of a new entrant into a market higher than the long-run costs of the existing firms in the market; a good example is a regulatory limitation on entry. The term is also used, more questionably, as a synonym for heavy start-up costs. Thus, a market in which the capital or advertising expenditures necessary to obtain a foothold are large is frequently described as one in which there are barriers to entry, and it is in the latter sense of the term that foreclosure may create a barrier to entry. If the existing firms in the market owned all of the retail outlets and were determined to deny them to new entrants, a new entrant would have to open his own retail outlets, and this would increase his capital requirements. So also, if punchcards were tied to computer rentals, a new entrant into the computer business would have to arrange to supply his customers with punchcards as well. But the capital costs of the existing firms are also higher as a result of vertical integration, so it is unclear what advantage these firms derive.[1] Likewise with advertising. A market in which firms advertise heavily may be difficult to enter without heavy advertising, but the entrant can take comfort in the fact that the firms in the market must incur heavy advertising costs themselves in order to maintain their positions. Advertising is a poor example of a barrier to entry for two additional reasons. The new entrant obtains something of a "free ride" on

---

3. An example is discussed in Chapter 11.
§7.7. 1. Might the new entrant, however, have to pay a higher interest rate for capital to establish a position in the market than firms already in the market had to pay for capital to replace their plants and other assets as they wore out? Might this depend on whether the new entrant was a new firm, or an established firm going into a new market?

the advertising of the original firms in the market, which has created public acceptance for the product; and he always has the option of advertising less and underpricing the existing firms, relying on the large retail chains to publicize the availability of a new low-price substitute.

§7.8. *Price discrimination again.* Many of the practices forbidden by the antitrust laws, such as patent tie-ins, are designed not to create a monopoly but to enable a seller to maximize his profits from an existing monopoly by practicing price discrimination. If there is an economic justification for forbidding such practices, therefore, it must be that price discrimination has worse consequences for efficiency than single-price monopoly. Arguably it does. To be sure, as pointed out earlier,[1] the output effects of price discrimination (unless perfect, which it never is) are indeterminate. It may result in a larger output than if a single price is involved, a smaller output, or the same output, and it will usually be impossible in a particular case to say which. However, by increasing the profits of monopoly, price discrimination has two related effects that are clearly undesirable. By making monopoly more profitable, it (1) attracts greater resources into the socially unproductive activity of monopolizing, and these resources are wasted; (2) increases the amount of monopoly. Since the output effects of price-discriminating monopolies are probably on average the same as those of single-price monopolies, the aggregate output effects of monopoly will be greater, because monopoly is more common, if price discrimination is permitted.

Price discrimination is more costly than nondiscriminating monopoly in another sense. The monopolist must incur costs in attempting to prevent low-price purchasers from reselling to high-price purchasers. These costs, on average, have no social product. Finally, price discrimination may create inefficiencies in the markets of the purchasers subject to discrimination. Suppose two competing firms both purchase from the monopolist but one is classified with a high-price group and the other with a low-price group. The second will have a competitive advantage unrelated to superior efficiency. A similar result could occur under a single monopoly price if a purchaser of the monopolized product was in competition with a firm that used a nonmonopolized substitute. But in that case the disadvantaged competitor could presumably switch to the nonmonopolized substitute too. In the

---

§7.8. 1. See §6.3 *supra.*

first case, the disadvantaged competitor has no recourse if the price discrimination is enforced.

The case against price discrimination is weakest in the particular case with which we began — the patent tie-in. A patent is a "good" monopoly. There is no presumption that a method by which a patentee maximizes his profits creates inefficiency. Indeed, by increasing the rewards to patent ownership, price discrimination increases the incentive to channel resources into the acquisition of patents, a type of activity that the patent laws, on plausible if not necessarily compelling efficiency grounds, seeks to encourage. However, as pointed out in Chapter 2, the effects of the patent system on efficiency are in fact mixed.[2] There is no presumption that the patent system provides inadequate incentives to innovation unless price discrimination is permitted. Discrimination might — or might not — result in overcompensation of patentees.

Even if price discrimination is inefficient, it does not follow that it should be prohibited. The administrative costs of enforcing a general prohibition against price discrimination would probably be high, due to the difficulty of distinguishing between price discrimination as a strategy of monopolistic profit maximization and the sporadic discriminations that are incidental to the movement from one equilibrium to another, for example, from a cartel to a competitive price. A prohibition of sporadic discriminations would promote monopoly by making it more costly for members of a cartel to cheat. They could cut price only by a general price reduction, which would be likely to be detected by the other members of the cartel.

§7.9.   Resale price maintenance.   An interesting intermediate case between horizontal combinations and single-firm abuses is resale price maintenance, the practice by which a manufacturer fixes a minimum retail price and requires its retail dealers to adhere to it. Sometimes the manufacturer is merely a cat's paw of the dealers, who are using him to police a cartel among themselves. The antitrust laws, in treating all resale price maintenance as illegal per se, assume that all resale price maintenance is of this type. But a manufacturer may sometimes impose resale price maintenance for reasons unrelated to monopoly.[1] Suppose the product is an automobile and the manufacturer wants the

2. See §2.9 supra.
§7.9. 1. See Lester G. Telser, Why Should Manufacturers Want Fair Trade? 3 J. Law & Econ. 86 (1960).

retail dealer to provide costly display and repair services and carry a large inventory in order to market the product most effectively. Some dealers will be tempted to curtail these ancillary services in order to be able to undercut other dealers. They will say to the customer: "go to Dealer A's showroom, talk to the salesman, pick out a model, tell me what it is, and I will get it from the factory for you at a discount." If enough dealers do this, A will find himself unable to sell many cars; he too will curtail his services; and the manufacturer will be unable to obtain the optimum mixture of price and service to customers. One way of preventing freeloading of the sort practiced on A is to fix a minimum retail price to which all of the manufacturer's dealers must adhere; then none of them has an incentive to curtail services because none can offer a compensating discount to the customer.

§7.10. *The deconcentration controversy.*   The idea that monopoly pricing is likely to arise in an oligopolistic market without any cooperative action by the sellers has led to proposals that leading firms in such markets be broken up into smaller units. And dissolution is now considered the standard remedy in a single-firm monopoly case. Economic analysis suggests, however, that even where oligopolists or monopolists are charging monopoly prices, the dismemberment of the firms may be an uneconomical remedy. The process of remaking one firm into two or more firms takes a long time[1] and costs a great deal. It is justified only when there is evidence that monopoly pricing has persisted for a reasonably long period of time. How might a monopoly price be maintained for a substantial period of time without attracting new entry that would erode it? There are five possibilities, and none justifies taking apart the firms. First, the firms in the market may be protected from new entry by valid, unexpired patents or other government licenses. These are largely outside the scope of the antitrust laws. Second, the sellers may be fending off new entry by means of predatory or abusive practices; if so they can be enjoined from or punished for committing these practices at lower cost than a dissolution proceeding would entail. Third, the existing firms may have better management than the new entrants, so that even though the market price is higher than the costs of the existing firms it is no higher than a new entrant's costs would be. Dissolution in this case would penalize superior

---

§7.10. 1. Eight years, on average. See Richard A. Posner, A Statistical Study of Antitrust Enforcement, 13 J. Law & Econ. 365, 417 n.50 (1970).

management. And the threat of dissolution might result in still higher prices and still lower output. As a firm's market share approached the level that would subject it to a dissolution order, it would have an incentive to limit further growth by increasing its price. If the other leading firms in the market followed the same policy, the result would be a price level higher than the previous monopoly level, and with worse output effects, especially since inefficient entrants would be attracted to the market by the price umbrella held over their heads by the existing firms.

Fourth, monopoly pricing may persist because there is room in the market for only one or a few firms (which collude), in the sense that if there were more firms each would have higher costs than the present firm or firms. After deconcentration, either some of the firms would expand to take advantage of the opportunity for lower costs with larger output until the market was again concentrated or the market would operate permanently at an unnecessarily high level of costs. And as in the previous case the threat of dissolution would create an incentive for the existing firms to raise prices to a level at which inefficient new entrants would be attracted.

Fifth, the existing firms may be shielded by barriers to entry, but, as we have seen,[2] apart from patents and other government grants, most so-called barriers to entry turn out to be conditions equally costly to both the sellers in the market and the new entrants. A price that exceeds the long-run costs of the existing sellers will therefore exceed the long-run costs of the new entrants as well, and they will have an incentive to enter the market.

Deconcentration is sometimes defended on grounds other than efficiency. The Alcoa case[3] is an important example. The outcome of the case — that Alcoa was guilty of unlawful monopolization — is difficult to understand if the purpose of the antitrust laws is to promote efficiency. Alcoa's monopoly of aluminum production had persisted for many years. It was not protected by patents, and it had not been defended against new entrants by means of predatory tactics. Judge Hand criticized Alcoa's action in adding new capacity in anticipation of new demands for its product, but this was perfectly normal, efficient business be-

2. In §7.7 *supra.*
3. United States v. Aluminum Co. of America, 148 F.2d 416 (2d Cir. 1945).

havior. That leaves three plausible explanations for the persistence of Alcoa's monopoly. First, it may not have had a real monopoly. Aluminum was still a new product in the late 1930s when the case was tried and the users may not yet have been convinced that it had substantial advantages over substitutes. Also, aluminum is a highly durable good with an active secondary (i.e., scrap) market that may have constrained Alcoa's pricing behavior.[4] Second, Alcoa may have had superior management. Third, Alcoa's market share may have enabled it to operate at lower cost than smaller firms.

Judge Hand had the last point in mind when he stated that Congress in passing the Sherman Act was motivated by a desire to preserve a system of small competitive units, even if that meant higher costs. This may or may not have been a motivation for the Sherman Act but economic analysis suggests that, if it was, Congress misconceived the means appropriate to achieve such an end. Suppose that the aluminum industry could support only one firm economically, which the court ordered split into ten units. Since their costs would by hypothesis be higher than the costs of one firm producing the same output, each firm would try to expand its output in order to reduce its costs. But they could not all expand equally. The most efficient firm would expand most rapidly until eventually it was the only firm left in the market. The judicial decree would not have accomplished the supposed congressional purpose of maintaining an organization of industry in inefficiently small units.[5]

SUGGESTED READINGS

1. George J. Stigler, The Theory of Price, chs. 12–13 (3d ed. 1966).
2. ———, The Organization of Industry, chs. 5–10, 21 (1968).
3. Aaron Director & Edward H. Levi, Law and the Future: Trade Regulation, 51 Nw. U.L. Rev. 281 (1956).
4. Richard A. Posner, A Program for the Antitrust Division, 38 U. Chi. L. Rev. 500 (1971).

---

4. Cf. §6.5 *supra*.

5. Alcoa was never broken up. The tremendous increase in the demand for aluminum, which was engendered by the requirements of the armed forces in World War II but persisted in the post-war period, made it possible to create new competitors for Alcoa.

A further discussion of antitrust policy may be found *infra* §14.4, and of antitrust remedies *infra* §25.3.

PROBLEMS

1. The following are some leading antitrust cases decided by the Supreme Court. Read each decision. Then answer the following questions: Why did the defendant or defendants in fact adopt the challenged practice — to monopolize, or for some other purpose? To what extent does the decision of the Court rest on a judgment of the economic consequences of the challenged practice? Does the Court use economic analysis correctly?

United States v. Reading Co., 253 U.S. 26 (1920).

Board of Trade v. United States, 246 U.S. 231 (1918).

United States v. Container Corp. of America, 393 U.S. 333 (1969).

United States v. Sealy, Inc., 388 U.S. 350 (1967).

United States v. Continental Can Co., 378 U.S. 441 (1964).

Eastern States Retail Lumber Dealers' Assn. v. United States, 234 U.S. 600 (1914).

Fortner Enterprises, Inc. v. United States Steel Corp., 394 U.S. 495 (1969).

Standard Fashion Co. v. Magrane-Houston Co., 258 U.S. 346 (1922).

United States v. Arnold, Schwinn & Co., 388 U.S. 365 (1967).

United States v. Singer Mfg. Co., 374 U.S. 174 (1963).

2. Analyze the following proposition: antitrust policy is profoundly antipathetic to the achievement of economically optimum amounts of (a) environmental protection and (b) consumer product information and safety. (Cf. §§2.6, 3.6, and 4.14 supra.)

3. What do you think "cross-elasticity of supply" means? How might it be relevant to the proper definition of the market in an antitrust case?

CHAPTER 8

A NOTE ON LABOR LAW

§8.1. The special treatment of labor monopolies.   In the
nineteenth century, the main question of antitrust policy was
whether unions should be suppressed as unlawful combinations
in restraint of trade. The classical economists thought not,[1] but
neither did they believe that workers' combination could be
distinguished from combinations of employers to lower wages or
of sellers to raise prices.[2] The equivalence is correct, at least as a
matter of economic logic. The primary purpose of a union is to
control the supply of labor so that the employer cannot depend
on competition among individual laborers to keep down the price
of labor. It used to be thought that competition in labor markets
would result in depressing wages to the subsistence level — the
cost of keeping the worker alive and just healthy enough to work
efficiently — but economists no longer hold this view. The worker
has a valuable asset to sell — his productivity (the result of his
training, skill, energy) — and there is no reason to believe that he
could not sell it at a good price without collusion, just as there is
no reason to believe that landowners could not rent land for a
good price without colluding. But neither should we expect the
worker to be content with the competitive price for his services
if he can get more.

As the classical economists might have predicted, the Sherman
Act was applied to labor union activities, notably in the Pullman
strike of 1894.[3] But even after the Clayton Act in 1914 exempted
labor from the antitrust laws, some state courts continued to im-

§8.1. 1. See, e.g., John Stuart Mill, Principles of Political Economy, bk. 5, ch.
10, §5 (1848).
2. See, e.g., The Combination Act, 1824, 5 Geo. 4, c. 95; A. V. Dicey, Lectures
on the Relation Between Law and Public Opinion in England During the
Nineteenth Century 190–201 (2d ed. 1914).
3. See Almont Lindsey, The Pullman Strike chs. 8, 12 (1942). See also Anderson
v. Shipowners Assn. of Pacific Coast, 272 U.S. 359 (1926).

pede monopolization of the labor supply by enjoining concerted activity. The strike is the primary method by which workers who have a monopoly position enforce it. Prohibiting striking is analogous to prohibiting a monopolistic seller from refusing to sell his product to a customer who refuses to pay the monopoly price; the requirement that a franchised monopolist serve all comers has an analogous purpose to a no-strike rule.

The Wagner Act, which placed most nonviolent union activity, including strikes, beyond the reach of injunctions or other legal remedies, was the decisive step in the emergence of a national labor relations policy favorable toward labor monopolizing. The implementation of this policy was in fact followed by a dramatic rise in wage rates in a number of industries.[4] Recall, however, that an increase in price brought about by monopolization is likely to have substitution as well as wealth effects. Employers attempt to substitute cheaper for costlier labor (for instance, by relocating their activities to regions where unions are weak), capital for labor, and white-collar for blue-collar workers. The ultimate effects of unionization on welfare are thus complex. Some workers benefit — those who are paid higher wages in the unionized industries and those who are newly employed by employers seeking substitutes for union labor. So do some shareholders: of firms whose competitors formerly paid lower wages than they did but are compelled as a result of unionization to pay the same wage. The losers are the consumers who buy from unionized industries (for those industries will pass along to their consumers a portion, at least, of their higher labor costs),[5] some stockholders and suppliers in those industries, and workers who cannot find employment due to the reduction in the demand for labor brought about by union wage scales.[6]

Many government policies serve to reinforce the monopoly power of unions. Minimum wage laws make nonunion labor less attractive (more costly) to employers. Building-code restrictions on the use of prefabricated building methods limit substitution for the costly labor supplied by the building-trades unions. In both cases demand for union labor is increased by raising the price of substitute goods. Not all worker protection legislation is of this type, however. Child labor laws, while they have the

4. On the effect of unionism on wage rates, see H. Gregg Lewis, Unionism and Relative Wages in the United States: An Empirical Inquiry (1963).

5. Cf. §§2.12 *supra* and 20.1 *infra*.

6. Minority workers may be most adversely affected in this regard. See §21.3 *infra*.

effect of reducing competition in the labor market, may be justifiable as necessary to prevent parents from exploiting their children.[7]

Some readers may take umbrage at the use of the term "monopoly" to characterize the aim and method of the union movement. The term is exact, and no pejorative connotation is intended. Since economics is a positive rather than a normative science, the economist steps out of his professional role when he condemns monopoly, in any context, as evil. Indeed, economic analysis may help one to sympathize with the conditions of the American worker in the latter part of the nineteenth century that fostered the union movement. Because most labor was unskilled, it commanded a low price compared to the modern worker, whose high wages include a return on a capital investment represented by his education and training, for which he normally does not pay in full.[8] With immigration unrestricted, large numbers of foreign workers entered the American labor market. The resulting increase in the supply of labor prevented wages from rising as rapidly as they otherwise would have.

§8.2. *Countervailing power and monopsony.* Occasionally, unionization is defended on economic rather than on broader normative grounds. The notion of "countervailing power" holds that union monopolizing is necessary to offset the effect of product monopolies — but ignores the fact that if a monopolist is forced as a result of unionization to pay a higher price for labor he will be led to increase his price to the consumer, and curtail his supply, still further.[1] The analysis, however, is slightly more complex when the employer is a monopsonist in the labor market.

Monopsony is to a buyer what monopoly is to a seller: the ability to increase profits by curtailing purchases. The analysis of monopsony is similar to that of monopoly. In Figure 5, the supply price is the average price that the purchaser (the employer in this context) must pay for various quantities of labor purchased and *dd* is the schedule of prices that the employer is willing to pay for various quantities. The employer would prefer not to purchase labor beyond the point (the intersection of mar-

---

7. Observe, however, that such laws may be superfluous from the standpoint of protecting children's interests if there are also compulsory school attendance laws. On the conflict of interest between parents and children that may justify child protection laws, see *supra* §3.12.

8. On the subject of "human capital" see, e.g., Gary S. Becker, Human Capital (1964).

§8.2. 1. Cf. §16.4 *infra.*

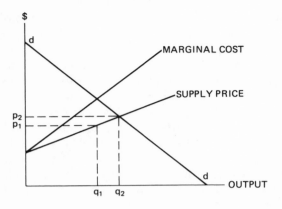

Figure 5

ginal cost and demand) where the marginal man-hour costs him exactly what it is worth to him. His preferred quantity is therefore q_1, which he can obtain at a price of p_1. If the workers had good substitute employment (that is, if the employer were not a monopsonist), they would hold out for price p_2 and the employer would purchase the corresponding quantity of labor, q_2.

When a monopolistic supplier of labor confronts a monopsonistic buyer of labor, the exact price and quantity that will be set depend upon the parties' relative skills at bargaining, ability to use intimidation or bring political pressures to bear, and perhaps other factors. In the end, the quantity of labor supplied may be no greater than it would be if the workers had no monopoly power, since the union wants to limit supply too.

How common is, or was, labor monopsony? Adam Smith thought conspiracies of employers to reduce wages common.[2] And during the Pullman strike the government invoked the Sherman Act against the organizers of the strike but not against the conspiracy of the employers to refuse to grant wage increases.[3] Labor monopsonies might appear to be common today in the form of multi-employer bargaining but since the union must consent to such bargaining, this is a poor example.

§8.3. *The economic effects of labor law.*   The relationship between the provisions of federal labor law, on the one hand, and

2. Adam Smith, An Inquiry into the Nature and Causes of the Wealth of Nations 66–67 (Edwin Cannan ed., Modern Library, 1937).
3. See Almont Lindsey, §8.1 *supra,* note 3, at chs. 6–7, 14.

the monopoly power of unions and monopsony power of employers, on the other, is various. The prohibition against employers' circulating blacklists of union activists is apparently directed against monopsony: blacklists are a traditional method of enforcing a cartel, here directed against workers. Provisions forbidding employers to discriminate against or otherwise punish employees for engaging in union-organizing activities also limit the monopsony power of employers. The employer who had no such power would find it difficult to threaten workers credibly with reprisals for such activities, for by hypothesis the worker could at any time obtain an equally good job with another employer at no significant relocation cost.

Provisions outlawing secondary boycotts — strikes against a supplier or customer of a firm with which the union has a dispute — limit a union's monopoly power by preventing it from using a threat to withhold supplies other than labor to induce higher wages. Provisions enabling union-shop agreements, whereby new employees are required to join the union representing the plant's workers, strengthen the union's hand by reducing the danger of defections from the cartel. The situation is symmetrical to that of seller cartels. The seller who remains outside the cartel obtains higher profits, at least in the short run, than the members, for he sells at (or just below) the cartel price a larger quantity than if he abided by the quotas established by the cartel. The worker who continues to work while his fellows are striking will, if the strike succeeds, have the benefit both of the new wage scale and of the interim wages that he received while the others were striking.

The economic effect of some other provisions of labor law is obscure. An example is the duty of the employer to bargain in good faith with the union representing his employees. The law does not prescribe the terms of a collective bargaining contract, so an employer who does not feel compelled to yield to the union's demands can evade an order to bargain in good faith by holding out for terms unacceptable to the union.

SUGGESTED READINGS

1. Albert Rees, The Effects of Unions on Resource Allocation, 6 J. Law & Econ. 69 (1963).

2. George J. Stigler, The Economics of Minimum Wage Legislation, 36 Am. Econ. Rev. 358 (1946).

PROBLEMS

1. What, precisely, does the leadership of a union try to maximize? The average hourly wage of its members? The average yearly wage? The total wages of workers employed in the unionized activity? What different effects might these various maximands have on the size of the union? Why might the union's leadership be concerned with the size of the union as well as with the incomes of its members?

2. Wages have risen faster in nonunionized occupations, notably domestic service, than in unionized occupations. Does this indicate that unionization is ineffective in raising wages above competitive levels?

Chapter 9

PUBLIC UTILITY AND
COMMON CARRIER REGULATION

§9.1. *Natural monopoly.* Let us take a closer look at the situation where monopoly is inevitable because it is the cheapest way of organizing an industry. This situation is depicted in Figure 6. Observe that average costs are declining at the point where

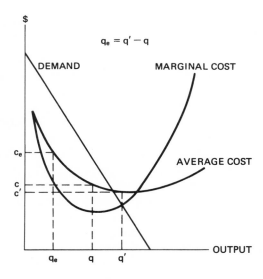

Figure 6

demand intersects marginal cost. Suppose that there is one firm in the market, producing q units at an average cost of c. Efficiency would be increased by carrying production to q'. There are two ways to reach the larger output. One is for the existing firm to produce $q' - q$ more units. Another is for a new firm to enter the market and produce q_e units $(= q' - q)$. At q', the existing firm's average cost is c'. The new entrant would have to incur an average cost of c_e to produce q_e units, and c_e is higher than c'. It is cheaper for the existing firm to supply the additional units, not because the firm is more efficient in the sense that its cost curve lies below those of other firms (indeed, the cost schedules for the existing firm and the new entrant are identical in Figure 6), but because one firm can supply the entire output demanded at a lower cost than could more than one firm. This is the condition known as "natural monopoly."

The condition arises when fixed costs — those that do not vary with output — are very large in relation to demand. If the fixed costs can be spread over the entire output of the market, a firm supplying that output may have a lower average cost of production than, say, two firms, each of which incurs the same fixed costs but spreads them over only one half the output. A plausible example of natural monopoly is local electrical service, where the market is limited in extent due to the cost of transporting electricity over long distances, while fixed costs (generating equipment, a city-wide grid of wires, etc.) are high.

Natural monopoly presents three problems that have been thought to warrant regulation of one kind or another. One is monopoly pricing. The firm that supplies a natural monopoly market has the same incentive as any other firm to maximize profit by limiting supply and a much better opportunity to achieve this goal since it need not incur the legal and administrative costs of collusion or corporate acquisition to do so. The antitrust laws, as we have seen, are ineffectual in this situation.[1]

The second problem — encouragement of inefficient entry — is depicted in Figure 7. The monopolist sells quantity q at price p, as determined by the intersection of marginal cost and marginal revenue. A new entrant, seeing that he can supply a portion of the market, q_e, at an average cost (c_e) lower than the market price set by the existing firm, has an inducement to enter. When he does so, the existing firm must either reduce its price or curtail its output, and if it follows the latter route the average cost of production will be higher than necessary. (What will happen if it reduces price instead?)

The third problem is the difficulty of devising an efficient price structure. At the point in Figure 7 where marginal cost intersects demand, the firm's average cost is greater than its marginal cost. In other words, the last unit of output costs less to produce than

§9.1. 1. See §7.10 *supra*.

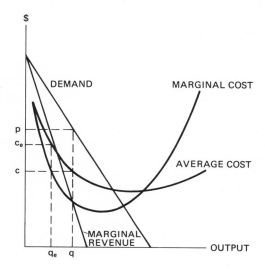

Figure 7

the average cost of all of the units produced. If the firm were to
sell its entire output at the cost of the last unit (marginal cost),
its total revenue would be less than its total cost.[2] But if it sells
at a price equal to average cost, it will induce the marginal purchaser[3] to switch to substitute products, even though they cost
more than it would cost to carry production of the first product
to the point at which price just equals marginal cost; thus, the
marginal purchaser is confronted with a false alternative.

The law's answer to the problem of natural monopoly is public utility and common carrier regulation, which has three primary elements: profit control (the regulated firm's rates may not
exceed the level necessary to enable the firm to cover its cost of
service, including a reasonable return on invested capital); entry
control (a firm may not provide a regulated service without first
obtaining a certificate of public convenience and necessity from
the regulatory agency); and control over price structure (the
firm may not discriminate in its rates). The three controls

2. Total cost is equal to average cost times quantity sold. If marginal cost is
lower than average cost, then the product of marginal cost times quantity sold
will be less than total cost.
3. That is, the purchaser who is willing to pay the marginal cost of the
product, but no more.

(which are discussed in the following sections) relate to the three problems of natural monopoly sketched above; a major question is whether they solve them.

§9.2. *Control of profits and the problem of reasonable return.* There is a standard method by which public utility agencies attempt to limit the profits of regulated firms. The agency first selects a recent and presumably representative year of the company's operations and computes the total costs incurred by the firm that year in rendering the regulated service, less all capital costs, including interest on long-term debt. The included costs are the company's "test-year cost of service." To the cost of service the agency then adds a "reasonable return" on invested capital (long-term debt plus equity). The return component is determined by multiplying the company's "rate base," which is the value of the capital assets used by it in rendering the regulated service, by the firm's "reasonable rate of return," a weighted average of the long-term interest rate plus some rate of return to the equity shareholders that the agency considers appropriate in light of the risk of the investment, the rate of return enjoyed by shareholders in comparable firms, and perhaps other factors. The return component is added to the cost of service to form the company's "revenue requirements." The company submits to the agency a schedule of rates designed to generate just this amount of revenue, on the assumption that the quantity demanded of the firm's service will be the same as in the test year. When approved, these rates are the maximum that the firm may charge.[1]

Determination of the test-year cost of service is relatively straightforward, although some monopoly profits may get concealed in expense items such as managerial salaries and perquisites.[2] Determination of the return component presents significant difficulties. The issue that has preoccupied courts and legal scholars is whether the rate base should be measured by the depreciated original cost of the firm's capital assets or by their replacement cost. The issue is most important in periods of inflation (or deflation, but that is not a current concern), when the

§9.2. 1. There are two different procedures by which rates may be changed. First, the agency may initiate a proceeding, such as that described in the text, to review the firm's rates. Second, and more commonly, the firm may initiate a proceeding for permission to make a rate increase. This is ordinarily a more abbreviated proceeding than the one described in the text. The burden of justifying an increase is on the firm.

2. Cf. §12.4 *infra.*

cost of replacing a long-lived capital asset may greatly exceed the asset's original cost.

An example will illustrate the nature of the problem and point us toward the economically correct solution. Suppose that in year one a firm buys a machine with a capacity to produce 1000 units per year. The machine costs $10,000 and has a useful life of 20 years. Operating costs are $1 per unit and the annual cost of the capital used to purchase the machine is five percent. Average cost is therefore $2.[3] Demand for the firm's product increases and midway through the useful life of its machine the firm decides to buy a second machine. But prices have risen. The identical machine now costs $15,000, and while operating costs are unchanged the cost of capital has increased to six percent. The average cost of production on the second machine is therefore $2.65. What should the firm's *price* be: $2.00, $2.65, or the average of the two costs? The answer given by economic analysis is $2.65. At any lower price, the firm will be induced to make incorrect investment decisions. Suppose the price is set at $2.325. People who value the product at more than $2.325 but less than $2.65 will try to buy it. Faced with excess demand the firm will buy another machine. When it then raises its price to cover the cost of production on the machine (which is $2.65), it will lose most of its new customers; it will have overexpanded.

If replacement (i.e., current) cost is the correct economic standard, why has the issue of original vs. replacement cost been so controversial? There are three reasons, besides confusion and the greater ease of determining original costs. First, replacement cost is not always the correct economic standard. If it is plain that an industry's major capital assets (e.g., railroad tracks, locomotives, and terminals) are not going to be replaced, due to declining demand for the industry's product, a price based on replacement costs, far from preventing the creation of unnecessary new capacity, will simply discourage the utilization of the existing capacity. The proper standard in such a case is the opportunity costs of the industry's assets; if, as in the railroad case, the assets are highly specialized (cannot readily be shifted to an alternative use), those costs may be much lower than the costs of replacing them.[4]

Second, where original cost is lower than replacement cost, the

---

3. Depreciation is $10,000 ÷ 20, or $500 a year, which is equal to $.50 a unit. The annual cost of capital, five percent of $10,000, is another $.50 per unit, and operating costs are $1 per unit, making the total cost $2 per unit.

4. Cf. §9.4 *infra*.

use of replacement costs to determine the firm's revenue require-ments results in an excess of the firm's revenues over the costs carried on the firm's books (i.e., depreciated original costs), which looks like a windfall for the firm's shareholders. The wind-fall may be an illusion created by inflation[5] and is in any event balanced by the losses to the shareholders and creditors of firms in other industries, such as railroads, where the value of special-ized resources has plummeted because demand for the industry's output has declined.

Third, the legal issue of current vs. replacement costs arises in a form that obscures the economic questions. The constitutional guarantee of just compensation for governmental takings has been held to entitle the shareholders of a public utility to a "fair" return on their investment. Two questions are relevant to a de-cision whether the use of original cost in determining a public utility's rate ceiling prevents the shareholders from earning a fair return. The first is, did the shareholders have notice of the standard to be applied when they invested? If they knew the regulatory agency applied an original-cost standard, they can hardly charge confiscation. Presumably, even with this feature, their investment in the regulated firm was more attractive than their alternative investment opportunities, or they would not have made the investment.[6] If they invested on the reasonable assumption that the agency would apply a replacement-cost standard, the argument of confiscation is more compelling. The second question is whether the additional returns to the share-holders resulting from the application of a replacement-cost standard are within the scope of the just-compensation guaran-tee. This may depend on whether or not they are characterized as windfalls.[7] Either inquiry deflects attention from the question of the economic soundness of the original-cost standard.

Another major difficulty in determining the return component in the regulated firm's revenue requirements involves ascertain-

5. Or it may result from a change in underlying supply or demand conditions, unrelated to inflation, that has caused the real price of the good to increase. In the latter case, the "windfall" represents a form of "economic rent," a concept explained in §16.3 *infra*.

6. If the investors are bondholders, the regulated firm is presumably paying them a rate of interest sufficiently high to compensate them for the disadvantages that the original-cost standard may impose upon them. If they are stockholders, the rate of return on equity capital expected to be allowed by the agency pre-sumably was, when they invested, sufficiently high to make the investment re-munerative in spite of the agency's use of the original cost standard.

7. On which see note 5 *supra* and the accompanying text.

ment of the cost of equity capital. But we postpone our discussion of this problem to a subsequent chapter in which we discuss capital market theory.[8]

§9.3. *Other problems in the control of the regulated firm's profits.*   The use of past rather than current costs means that the rates approved by an agency may be inappropriate in current conditions. If costs have risen since the test year, the rates will be too low to cover the firm's current costs; if costs have declined, the rates will be too high. If demand has increased, the rates may again be too high, since they are calculated by dividing the revenue requirements by the test-year output and the average cost of a higher output may be lower if the firm is operating in a region of declining average costs. (What if costs have declined? What if demand has declined?) Observe also that the lag introduced by the use of a test year creates opportunities for a regulated firm to cheat: by reducing the quality of its output, it can reduce its current costs below its test-year costs and thereby increase its profits.

The popularity of the original-cost standard and of the test-year-of-service concept is evidence of the constant struggle between economic theory and feasibility in rate regulation. Both methods facilitate use of the company's own books of account as the basic source of information for the rate-making process. Both lead to serious departures from efficient pricing.

It does not follow that the regulatory process has no effect on monopoly pricing. The evidence that regulation is ineffectual [1] is better explained by reference to the incentives of regulators.[2] The process itself seems as likely to depress the rates of the regulated firm below the firm's costs — especially during inflation when regulatory lag works against the firm — as to permit them to rise to the level at which profits are maximized. It is important to note that mistakes involved in regulatory attempts to limit profits do not cancel out. An agency may err either by setting rates too high in relation to costs or too low, and from an economic standpoint either error is equally serious. If rates are too high, consumers will be induced to purchase substitute products that in fact cost society more to produce. If rates are too low, consumers will be deflected from substitute products that cost society less to produce; again resources will be wasted.

8. See §13.2 *infra.*

§9.3. 1. See, e.g., George J. Stigler & Claire Friedland, What Can Regulators Regulate? The Case of Electricity, 5 J. Law & Econ. 1 (1962).

2. See Chapter 23.

The attempt to control profits has some interesting side effects. First, to the extent that public utility regulation succeeds in its formal aim of placing public utility pricing on a cost-plus basis, it threatens to impose costs greater than the benefits by reducing the regulated firm's incentive to minimize costs. The penalty to the monopolist who fails to minimize costs is that his profits are lower than otherwise. The tendency of public utility regulation is to reduce that penalty. (Regulatory lag may hold this tendency in check, however.)

Second, the regulatory agency's success in monitoring the regulated firm's costs will inevitably be uneven. Since it is easier for the agency to police salaries than perquisites, the management of a regulated firm may substitute the latter for the former. The substitution reduces value if a dollar spent on perquisites is worth less to the recipients than the same dollar given them in cash. Similarly, it is doubtful that the cost of equity capital is constrained as effectively as labor costs; this gives the regulated firm an incentive to substitute capital for labor in production even if inefficient to do so.[3]

Finally, the ability of the regulatory agency to control a firm's pricing is less if the firm has unregulated affiliates, for it may be able to allocate to them some of the profits of its regulated service; so we would expect regulation to create incentives to diversify even when diversification is inefficient. This could be prevented by forbidding a regulated firm to operate in unregulated markets; but such a prohibition might prevent efficient diversification.

§9.4. *Regulation of entry and of the structure of rates.*   The conjunction of profit control and entry regulation seems at first glance odd. The danger of inefficient entry is created by monopoly pricing. If monopoly pricing is eliminated, the danger disappears — the new entrant can gain a foothold in the monopolist's market only if his costs are lower than the monopolist's costs. Either the regulation of entry rests on a sophisticated awareness that control of the overall price level of regulated monopolists is often ineffectual or perverse, or, more plausibly, it has different purposes altogether. One purpose may be to support the third major element of public utility and common carrier regulation, which is control over price structure — how the firm's revenue needs are translated into specific prices.

---

3. See Harvey A. Averch & Leland L. Johnson, Behavior of the Firm Under Regulatory Constraint, 52 Am. Econ. Rev. 1052 (1962).

There is no entirely satisfactory answer to the question, raised earlier, of the optimal pricing of services when marginal cost is below average cost.[1] It used to be thought that the optimum solution was to sell the service at marginal cost, with the government making up the deficit resulting from the firm's inability to recover its total cost out of general tax revenues; in some versions, the government was to provide the service directly at a price equal to marginal cost, again making up the deficit out of general tax revenues. But this solution has a serious drawback. It encourages consumers to substitute services produced under conditions of declining average cost for services produced under conditions of increasing average cost, even when the former services are more costly to provide. To illustrate, suppose that the total cost of providing transportation across a river by means of a bridge is $1 million and the marginal cost $.02 per passenger mile, and the total cost of providing an equivalent substitute service by ferry is $500,000 and the marginal cost $1 per passenger mile. If both services are sold at marginal cost, consumers will choose the bridge even though the same service could be provided by ferry at lower cost.

An alternative possibility is multipart pricing. A user of the bridge in our example would be required to pay (1) an initial one-time fee so calculated that the sum of such fees defrayed the fixed costs of the bridge, and (2) a toll, equal to marginal cost, payable every time he crossed the bridge. This method of pricing enables both the fixed costs of the bridge to be covered and the marginal purchase to be made, but unfortunately it does not enable the marginal purchaser to obtain service. He might be willing to pay the marginal cost of his use of the bridge but not to contribute the standard share of fixed costs. Suppose the one-time charge is $10 and the toll (equal to marginal cost) as before is $.02. Our marginal purchaser is willing, let us say, to pay a $1 one-time charge but no more, because he does not expect to use the bridge often. If he is denied service, the bridge company is worse off since he would have made *some* contribution to its fixed costs, albeit less than the usual, and he of course is worse off, too. The maximization of value in this situation requires that the contribution to fixed costs be allowed to vary among potential customers, or, more realistically, among classes of potential customers, in accordance with willingness to pay.

§9.4. 1. An illuminating discussion of the problem is Ronald H. Coase, The Marginal Cost Controversy, 13 Economica (n.s.) 169 (1946).

Multipart pricing should be distinguished from price discrimination, at least in the sense in which we have used the term.[2] Under price discrimination, too,. price varies with willingness to pay. But the purpose of price discrimination is not to enable fixed costs to be recouped in a manner that permits marginal purchasers to be served; it is to maximize the excess of revenues over costs. Multipart pricing is designed to maximize output consistently with avoiding a deficit; price discrimination is designed to maximize profits regardless of output consequences. Observe, however, that multipart pricing can, like discrimination, create competitive distortions in the purchasers' markets. Even when each purchaser is assessed the same share of the fixed costs, the average price will vary between purchasers depending on the quantity purchased (the greater the quantity, the lower the average price). But there is no actual difference in the unit production cost of serving the two customers. If they are in competition, one will have a competitive advantage unrelated to superior efficiency.

Multipart pricing is fairly common in the regulated industries, but this is so despite rather than because of regulation. Regulatory statutes forbid discrimination in rates and the tendency in the interpretation of these statutes — as in the interpretation of the Robinson-Patman Act, a general antidiscrimination statute — is to equate discrimination with difference in rates and nondiscrimination with rate uniformity.[3] Under this, a noneconomic view of discrimination, multipart pricing has been suspect and average-cost pricing, although less efficient, encouraged. An example is provided by the Supreme Court's "ingot molds" decision,[4] in which the Court upheld the Interstate Commerce Commission's position that railroads may not use prices lower than average cost to attract business away from barge lines. At first glance rail-barge competition seems just like our bridge-ferry example. Railroads, like bridges, have heavy fixed costs (the rights of way, the track, rolling stock, etc.) and low marginal costs; barges, like ferries, have low fixed costs and high marginal costs. But this is not an argument for requiring the railroads to use average-cost pricing (unless the concern with competitive distortion in the purchasers' markets is considered overriding); it is rather an argument for requiring railroads to use multipart

2. See §§6.3, 7.8 *supra*.
3. See Kenneth W. Dam, The Economics and Law of Price Discrimination: Herein of Three Regulatory Schemes, 31 U. Chi. L. Rev. 1 (1963).
4. American Commercial Lines v. Louisville & N.R.R., 392 U.S. 571 (1968).

rather than marginal-cost pricing. But in fact the analogy is deceptive and railroads, unlike the bridge in our example, should be permitted to charge prices equal to marginal cost.

The concern about a pricing system under which the users fail to pay the fixed costs of the bridge is that it creates false signals with respect to the efficient allocation of resources. Travelers use the bridge rather than the ferry so it is assumed that resources should be shifted from ferry building to bridge building. But they prefer the bridge not because it is really cheaper but because they do not pay its full costs. The problem of false signals is unimportant in the case of railroads. It is unlikely that any new railroad lines will be built, or rolling stock replaced as it is used up. Railroads are a declining industry and a shift of some business from barge lines to railroads is not going to induce economically unjustified railroad expansion.

Suppose the bridge company in our example, after experimenting with various forms of multipart pricing, found that it could not cover its fixed costs. Then it should abandon multipart pricing and reduce all prices to, although not below, marginal cost, if that is necessary to attract business. If the bridge is unused, resources will be diverted to the provision of unnecessary ferry service. No false-signal problem is presented, for it is plain that the bridge will not be replaced. This is the situation of the railroads in their competition with the barge lines.[5]

§9.5. *Digression on pay television.*   An interesting variant of the bridge-ferry problem is presented by the controversy over whether pay television should be permitted.[1] The Federal Communications Commission has now taken the first steps toward permitting the development of this service, but it continues to hedge it about with many limitations. The argument against pay television — at least, the argument from efficiency — is that since the marginal cost of broadcasting to another viewer is zero once the transmitter is in operation, viewers should be able to purchase television programs at a zero price, as under the present system of free (to the viewer) television. However, when

---

5. Compare the discussion of original vs. replacement cost as a rate-making standard in a declining industry *supra* §9.2.

§9.5. 1. For a lively debate between economists on the issue see Jora R. Minasian, Television Pricing and the Theory of Public Goods, 7 J. Law & Econ. 71 (1964); Paul A. Samuelson, Public Goods and Subscription TV: Correction of the Record, *id.* at 81; James B. Buchanan, Public Goods in Theory and Practice: A Note on the Minasian-Samuelson Debate, 10 J. Law & Econ. 191 (1967); Paul A. Samuelson, Pitfalls in the Analysis of Public Goods, *id.* at 199; Jora R. Minasian, Public Goods in Theory and Practice Revisited, *id.* at 205.

marginal cost is zero, the problem of financing undertakings priced at marginal cost is acute. The solution of the television industry has been to sell television time to advertisers rather than to viewers. At first glance this seems an ideal solution, for it enables the costs of broadcasting to be defrayed without either a government subsidy or a departure from marginal cost pricing. But it is not clear that advertisers are an adequate proxy for viewers. Since television as an advertising and sales promotion medium has fairly good substitutes, advertisers will not pay more than a few cents per viewer for television time and it is consequently impossible to defray the costs of expensive programming unless an audience of tens of millions of people can be assembled. Advertisers will not support an opera broadcast that costs $400,000 to produce if it will draw a nationwide audience of only one million, for then it is paying $.40 per viewer and it could reach consumers at lower cost through other means. Yet it is possible that a million viewers would be willing to pay the $.40 apiece necessary to defray the cost of the program. The unavailability of pay television compels them to substitute a less desired or more costly entertainment. The vociferous opposition of the movie houses to pay television is not surprising. They fear that under a system of pay television the networks would bid the distribution rights to new movies away from them.

§9.6. *Taxation by regulation.*[1]   In the "ingot molds" case the inefficient rate structure subsidized a group of competitors. In other cases such rate structures subsidize particular classes of customers. Sometimes regulated firms actually provide service below marginal cost: this was apparently true of intercity railroad passenger service prior to Amtrak. But rates above marginal cost may still be inefficiently low. Suppose a firm has fixed costs of $500 and marginal costs of $1 per unit. And suppose that if it uses an average-cost system, it can sell 1000 units at $1.50 per unit, while if it uses a multipart system, under which each customer contributes $10 to fixed costs but may then buy as many units as he wants for $1 per unit, it can sell 2000. The multipart system favors the large purchaser. The average price to a purchaser of 100 units, for example, is $1.10, whereas with average-cost pricing he would pay $1.50. But the purchaser who buys only one unit is worse off. He pays $11 instead of $1.50. He would be better off under the average-cost system, even though

§9.6. 1. See Richard A. Posner, Taxation by Regulation, 2 Bell J. Econ. & Management Sci. 22 (1971).

that system is inefficient since it induces consumers willing to pay between $1 and $1.49 to substitute other products that cost society more than $1. The system in effect subsidizes those users who would contribute more heavily to the fixed costs of the enterprise under a multipart pricing system. The railroad industry again contains examples of this form of inefficient pricing. Traditionally, agricultural commodities have paid less than the share of fixed costs properly (that is, according to the intensity of their demand) allocable to them. The result has been to increase the fixed-cost assessment against commodities, such as manufactured goods, for which there are good substitute modes of transportation, with the result that shippers of such goods have largely abandoned rail transportation.

In both examples — pricing below marginal cost and failing to concentrate fixed costs on the customers willing to pay them — one group of customers is in effect taxed to defray a subsidy for the benefit of another. The taxation analogy brings out the essentially public nature of the income transfer worked by the pricing scheme. An unregulated firm would not sell below marginal cost (except in the rare case of predatory price cutting). The railroads would have abandoned passenger service long before Amtrak were it not for the fact that they could not abandon service without the Interstate Commerce Commission's permission. Nor would an unregulated firm use average-cost pricing when it could increase its profits with multipart pricing.

Internal subsidization is easy to condemn as inefficient, because it results in just the kind of inefficient substitutions that we identified in discussing the consequences of inaccurate profit controls. But if we assume for the moment that the object of the internal subsidy is a laudable one and then ask what alternative methods for providing the subsidy are available, we shall see that the condemnation is superficial. Suppose the money for the subsidy were to be obtained by increasing the federal income tax rate. This would be inefficient in the same sense that internal subsidization is inefficient, for just as internal subsidization makes the value of a product seem higher than it is, so income taxation makes leisure, and nonpecuniary income such as a housewife's imputed earnings, seem more valuable than they are.[2]

Internal subsidization can be criticized as an unnecessarily costly method of taxation. By requiring regulated firms to maintain high price-cost spreads in some markets in order to defray

2. See §§16.7, 16.8 *infra*.

the cost of subsidizing service in other markets, it encourages inefficient entry. Suppose the regulated firm's costs in the high-price market are $2 but its price $3 — not because its profits are not effectively controlled by the regulatory agency but because in another market it is selling the same $2 service at a price of only $1. A firm that could serve the high-price market at a cost of $2.50 would have an incentive to enter that market. To prevent the waste of resources that such entry would involve, as well as the collapse of the subsidy program, the regulatory agency must establish entry controls. These would be unnecessary were it not for internal subsidization, but could be eliminated, without doing away with internal subsidization, by substituting an explicit excise tax on the high-price service, with the proceeds earmarked for the support of the low-price service. Entry would no longer have to be regulated except that every firm entering the high-price market would be subject to the excise tax. This would eliminate the inefficient advantage of the new entrant in our last example.

Internal subsidization can also be criticized on the grounds that the recipients of such subsidies are often unworthy and that the wealth effects are often regressive. For example, the rate structure of the airline industry subsidizes passengers on short-haul routes at the expense of those on long-haul routes; it is difficult to see what social policy such subsidization promotes. Internal subsidization of intercity railroad passenger service transferred wealth from shippers — and hence mainly from consumers — of agricultural products, mineral fuels, and other products shipped heavily on railroads to railroad passengers, many of them well-to-do exurbanites. But the same criticisms to which internal subsidies are vulnerable can also be leveled against many, perhaps most, direct subsidies.

§9.7. *Excessive competition.*   The traditional rationale of public utility and common carrier regulation is the existence of natural monopoly. Yet we frequently find such regulation in markets that are not naturally monopolistic, markets such as long-distance telecommunications service, motor trucking, air transportation, and natural gas production, which can and do efficiently support more, and often many more, than one seller. The imposition of the same regulatory controls in competitive as in monopolistic markets is defended on the ground that, in the absence of regulation designed to limit price cutting and new entry, there would be excessive competition, resulting in bankruptcy and deterioration of service. But there is neither theoretical nor empirical basis for the view that competition in these industries, if unregulated, would produce inefficiency. Competition does not have a tendency to bankrupt an industry, for no firm (except the very occasional predator) will knowingly sell below its marginal cost. To be sure, those firms with high marginal costs relative to their competitors may, and under a criterion of efficiency should, go under, but the efficient producers will not. When businessmen complain about excessive competition, what they usually mean is that they would be happier if their prices were higher than their marginal costs.

§9.8.   *The demand for regulation.*   The deficiencies of public utility regulation viewed as a method of regulating profits, the degree to which it seems deliberately aimed at bringing about inefficient rate structures, and the frequency with which it has been imposed in naturally competitive industries, may lead one to wonder whether its actual purpose is to respond to the economist's concern about the inefficient consequences of unregulated natural monopolies. Another and perhaps more realistic hypothesis is that regulation is a product, much like other products except supplied by the government, that is demanded by and supplied to effective political groups.[1] Under this view, there is no presumption that regulation is always or even often designed to protect the broad consumer interest in the efficient supply of the regulated services. The generalized consumer interest that would be promoted by such a policy is only one of many competing interests that regulation might serve. Particular consumers may demand a rate structure that, while inefficient overall, gives them benefits greater than the costs that it imposes on them in common with other consumers. Members of a competitive industry can benefit from the imposition of public utility controls since minimum rate regulation provides greater assurrance of effective cartel pricing than private agreement — while placing the cartel beyond the reach of the antitrust laws — and regulatory control of entry can remove one of the principal threats to the success of a cartel — the entry of new sellers attracted by the hope of monopoly profits. Coalitions between special-interest consumer groups and members of an industry may be especially effective in manipulating the regulatory process.

But there is a latent paradox here. In Part I we explained the main common law doctrines as a system designed (in the main)

_____

§9.8. 1. See George J. Stigler, The Theory of Economic Regulation, 2 Bell J. Econ. & Management Sci. 3 (1971).

to promote efficiency. Here we use economic analysis to refute the view that another branch of law, public utility regulation, has the same objective, and to propose, indeed, that it pursues a conflicting objective. There is no necessary inconsistency; but there is a challenge to discover why the legal system is guided by such contrary objectives in different areas.[2]

SUGGESTED READINGS

1. Utility Regulation: New Directions in Theory and Practice (William G. Shepherd & Thomas Gies eds. 1966).
2. The Crisis of the Regulatory Commissions, An Introduction to a Current Issue of Public Policy (Paul W. MacAvoy ed. 1970).
3. David Boies, Jr., Experiment in Mercantilism: Minimum Rate Regulation by the Interstate Commerce Commission, 68 Colum. L. Rev. 599 (1968).
4. A. Henderson, The Pricing of Public Utility Undertakings, 15 Manchester School Econ. & Soc. Studies 223 (1947).
5. Richard A. Posner, Taxation by Regulation, 2 Bell J. Econ. & Management Sci. 22 (1971).
6. George J. Stigler, The Theory of Economic Regulation, 2 Bell J. Econ. & Management Sci. 3 (1971).

PROBLEMS

1. Among other rules governing public utilities that have not been discussed in this chapter, there is the rule that a public utility may not arbitrarily refuse to serve a customer, the rule that a public utility may not charge a price other than one contained in a published price list (tariff), and the rule that a public utility may not undertake the construction of additional plant without the permission of the regulatory agency. Can you explain the function of these rules? On the theory that the purpose of public utility regulation is to promote economic efficiency? On the theory that its real purpose is to subsidize particular groups of customers? On the theory that its real purpose is to facilitate monopoly pricing by regulated firms?

2. Most hospitals in the United States today are "voluntary" (nonprofit) hospitals. These hospitals are widely believed to be mismanaged. They run huge deficits and, it is argued, are plagued by chronic excess capacity. In an effort to solve these problems, it has been proposed that hospitals be made public utilities subject to the usual public utility controls, in particular control over new construction (see problem 1 supra). What do you think of this proposal? Would you consider na-

2. See Chapter 23.

tionalization of the hospital industry a better or a worse proposal from an economic standpoint?

3. *Analyze the following proposition: internal subsidization in the railroad industry in the nineteenth century made good economic sense because it promoted more rapid development of the railroad system and thereby increased the rate of the country's economic growth.*

4. *Is the problem of encouraging inefficient entry into a natural monopoly market likely to be serious when the monopolist employs multipart pricing?*

5. *The airline industry has been complaining recently that it has a great deal of excess capacity, as measured by seat occupancy rates (which on many routes are less than 50 percent). The Civil Aeronautics Board, which regulates the industry, establishes minimum as well as maximum fares, and has traditionally been hostile to price competition; it also limits entry into the industry. How might the industry's excess capacity problem be related to the board's regulatory activities?*

CHAPTER 10

THE CHOICE BETWEEN
REGULATION AND COMMON LAW

§*10.1.* *The concept of market failure revised.*   Monopoly, pollution, fraud, mistake, mismanagement, and other such by-products of the market process are conventionally viewed as failures of the self-regulatory mechanisms of the market and, therefore, as appropriate occasions for public regulation. This way of looking at the matter is misleading. The failure is ordinarily a failure of the market *and* of the rules of the market prescribed by the common law. Pollution, for example, would not be considered a serious problem if the common law remedies, such as nuisance and trespass, were efficient methods of minimizing the costs of pollution. The choice is rarely between the market and public regulation. Ordinarily the choice is between two methods of public control, the common law system of privately enforced rights and the administrative system of direct public control. The choice between them should depend upon a weighing of their strengths and weaknesses in particular contexts. We illustrate this point with examples involving consumer fraud, pollution, and the regulation of cable television.

§*10.2.* *Consumer fraud revisited.*   We noted in the chapter on contracts that there are market forces working to give the consumer information about the products that he buys but that these forces may not always work well. Clearly, in the absence of any legal protection, fraud would sometimes be attempted and succeed. Among the predisposing characteristics for successful consumer fraud are a product that is either complex or purchased infrequently (so that the consumer has little opportunity to become acquainted with its characteristics); an inexpensive product (so that it does not pay the consumer to invest substantial time in investigating its qualities); an ignorant consumer; a seller who does not depend on repeat business (so that he is less concerned about developing a reputation for dishonesty).

The defrauded consumer, in principle, has a perfectly adequate common law remedy: he can sue the seller for breach of contract. However, since litigation is costly and the costs are not an allowable item of damages, it is not a realistic remedy in most consumer fraud cases. Also, many defrauding sellers are fly-by-night operators, difficult to catch up with and often judgment-proof. And the defrauded consumer may never discover that he has been had.[1]

The inadequacy of the common law remedy is the usual justification offered for the Federal Trade Commission's (FTC) program of policing the accuracy of representations made in advertising, labeling, and other sales materials.[2] But before the justification is accepted, the possibilities for improving the common law remedy should be explored. The possibilities are many. Defrauded consumers could be permitted to obtain their legal fees, plus a penalty as an additional incentive to sue, in any successful action against the seller. Consumer class actions, which permit a number of insignificant individual claims to be aggregated into a single large claim, could be encouraged.[3] The right of firms that suffer sales losses as a result of misrepresentations in the sales materials of their competitors could be clarified.[4]

These possibilities seem attractive in part because the commission's record of performance has not been impressive. We shall not elaborate this well-documented conclusion[5] here, but we shall suggest some economic reasons for the commission's problems. One is that consumers have little incentive to invoke the commission's enforcement machinery. The commission cannot award any damages or penalty to a defrauded consumer. The threat of a complaint to the commission may sometimes induce a seller to buy off an angry consumer but once the commission begins proceedings the seller will have no further incentive to come to

§10.2. 1. If he never discovers the fraud, can it still be argued that the fraudulent transaction reduced value?

2. Yet, curiously, the converse of this proposition — that common law remedies are adequate where the injury is substantial enough to warrant the expenses of litigation — is rejected. Were it accepted, there would presumably be no Food and Drug Administration.

3. See §24.5 *infra*.

4. As urged in Richard A. Posner, The Federal Trade Commission, 37 U. Chi. L. Rev. 47, 66 (1969).

5. See *ibid.* and sources there cited at 47 n.1.

terms with the consumer; this must limit consumers' interest in filing complaints with the FTC. Competitors of the seller do have an incentive to complain to the commission, since the commission can, by issuance of a cease and desist order, bring to an end a practice that is diverting business from them. But since the commission bears the entire expense of prosecution, the complaining seller has no incentive to avoid lodging with the commission essentially frivolous complaints designed to harass a competitor rather than to dispel consumer misinformation.

The combination of the consumer's lack of incentive to complain with the competitor's incentive creates a serious imbalance in the nature of the pressures that are brought to bear on the commission. It hears less from defrauded consumers than from labor unions concerned about the effect of cheap Japanese imports on the sales of their employers, from furriers concerned about the competition of cheap synthetic furs, from diamond merchants concerned about the competition of synthetic diamonds; given the nature of these inputs it is not surprising that so much of the commission's output of rules and decisions seems so tenuously, if at all, related to actual problems of consumer deception.

In addition, the commission lacks the weapons necessary to be effective against the fly-by-night operator, who is probably the major defrauder of consumers. He preys on people who are the least likely to complain to the commission and the commission lacks sanctions appropriate to deal with firms that lack continuity of operation, that conceal their activities, or that are financially irresponsible.[6]

The distinctive characteristics of the commission as an agency — its lack of a damage remedy or criminal sanctions and the fact that it shoulders the responsibility and expense of prosecution — are sources of weakness in combating consumer fraud, as is the fact that it is a federal agency with its operations highly centralized in Washington (most fraudulent selling is done by local sellers). The commission could be made a more effective agency for fighting consumer fraud. It could be given the power to award reparations to defrauded consumers, to mete out penal sanctions, to assess the costs of prosecution against competitor complainants, and to grant autonomy to its local field offices. But observe

6. On the nature of the requisite sanctions to deal with such cases, see §§25.2, 25.4 *infra*.

that the effect of such changes would be to bring the administrative model closer to the common law model!

§10.3.   *Pollution revisited.*   The common law enforcement problem with respect to pollution is, in part anyway, the same as with respect to consumer fraud: the individual injury may be too slight to justify the expense of litigation to the victim. Again, improvements in the common law machinery are possible, but again, the emphasis has been placed on public regulation instead.

There are three approaches in the public regulation of pollution. The first is for the legislature or an administrative agency to prescribe the specific measures that the polluter must take to avoid the sanctions of the law (or, what is the same thing, to entitle him to a subsidy). For example, a municipality might be required to install a certain kind of sewage treatment plant, a steel mill to build its smokestacks four feet higher, automobile manufacturers to install a particular type of emission control device. Specification of the particular method of pollution control discourages the search for the most efficient method. In the deliberations before the legislature or agency leading to the formulation of the standard, the affected industry has an incentive to propose the cheapest pollution-control method, regardless of its efficacy, and to deny the existence of any more costly devices (even if they are more efficient because of the amount of pollution eliminated). Once the specified measure is adopted, the industry has no incentive to develop better devices unless they also happen to be cheaper. Worse, the members of the industry have an incentive to collude to withhold from the legislature or agency information concerning the technical and economic feasibility of pollution control and even, as alleged in recent antitrust actions against the automobile manufacturers, to conspire to delay the development of pollution control technology.

A second approach is to establish the level of pollution emissions deemed tolerable, to compel the polluters, under penalty of injunction or fine, not to exceed that level, but to leave the choice of method to the industry. This is a better approach than the first but it is not so simple or efficient as it seems. When enforcement is attempted, the industry will argue that the cost of compliance is prohibitive — meaning disproportionate to the benefits from reduced pollution. Such an argument cannot be ignored unless society wants to reduce pollution below efficient levels. It then becomes necessary to weigh the benefits of reduced pollution against the cost of reduction — an analysis similar to that in a common law nuisance case. And the dangers of collusion mentioned above remain under this approach.

The third approach, not yet employed in this country but a great favorite of economists, is to tax pollution. The tax rate for each pollutant would be set equal to the estimated costs imposed by the pollutant. A firm subject to a pollution tax would compare its tax costs with the costs of reducing the tax by installing pollution control equipment, reducing its output, or otherwise changing its operations to reduce pollution. If a net tax saving would be possible through one of these measures, it would adopt it; otherwise it would pay the tax and continue to pollute.

This approach is actually quite similar to the imposition of strict liability in tort.[1] The tax corresponds to the damages (costs) of the victims of pollution. The polluters are required to pay those costs (though, under the tax approach, not to the victims) whether or not there are methods of pollution control that would avert them at lesser cost. This gives polluters an incentive to search for and to adopt cost-justified pollution preventives, but not to adopt any methods of pollution control that cost more than the value they create by reducing pollution.

One problem with this approach is the difficulty of quantifying the costs of pollution — a necessary step in fixing the tax rate. But this is a problem common to all methods of pollution control, so it is not an objection to the tax approach as compared with others. A second problem is that the approach makes no provision for those situations, which may be quite common, where the cheapest pollution avoider is the victim (by installing air conditioning, living farther from the factory, etc.). The polluter will spend on pollution control an amount equal to the estimated tax saving even though victims could have reduced pollution costs by the same amount at lower cost.[2] Third, if we assume that much, if not most, pollution is and will remain cost justified — that it would be prohibitively costly to have absolutely clear air and clean water — then the major effect of the tax will not be to reduce pollution, but to increase the tax bills of polluting enterprises. The tax is in the nature of an excise tax

§10.3. 1. See §4.15 *supra*.

2. In principle, the pollutee could — and should — be taxed also; the analogy is to contributory negligence in a strict liability case. And it is not necessary actually to collect the tax on the pollutee; to complete the analogy to strict liability, the pollutee's tax liability need only be deducted from the polluter's to produce the economically correct amount of pollution control. See William J. Baumol, On Taxation and the Control of Externalities, 62 Am. Econ. Rev. 307 (1972). The problem is measurement.

since it is roughly proportional to output. Excise taxes are regressive. To assure the overall proportionality or progressivity of the tax system, the imposition of comprehensive pollution taxes would require compensating changes elsewhere in the tax system. These changes might not be made; or might be made at great cost. Fourth, the tax approach eliminates private enforcement of pollution standards. (Why? Why might this be a bad thing?)

§10.4. *Copyright and cable television.*[1]   Cable television is a method of delivering television signals to the home by wire rather than by broadcasting them over the air from a transmitter. The cable system may obtain its signals either from a master antenna that picks them up from nearby broadcast stations or from a microwave relay system that brings them in from a distant antenna that receives the signals of broadcast stations proximate to it. When it brings in a distant signal the cable system increases the number of different signals available in the local market in which it operates. The local broadcast stations do not like this because they lose viewers to the new signal and with them advertising revenues. The people who own the copyrights on the programs carried on the distant signal do not like (free) importation either, even though it enlarges the audience for the programs and hence the royalties they can charge the originating station, because it undermines their ability to sell exclusive program rights. A station will not pay more for an exclusive right if the cable system in its market can show the same program brought in from a distant station.

There are two methods of regulating the importation of distant signals: private law property rights (copyright), and federal regulation of cable television operations (by the Federal Communications Commission). The FCC adopted limitations on importation pending the decision by the courts of the copyright question. When the Supreme Court held that importation was not a copyright infringement,[2] the commission continued its limitations.

The question of the appropriate scope of copyright (as of patent) protection is like the bridge-ferry problem in the last chapter. Once a book has been written, the marginal cost of each reader's obtaining a copy is its manufacturing and distribution

§10.4. 1. This section and the next draw on Richard A. Posner, The Appropriate Scope of Regulation in the Cable Television Industry, 3 Bell J. Econ. & Management Sci. 22 (1972).
2. Fortnightly Corp. v. United Artists Television, Inc., 392 U.S. 390 (1968).

cost. If a royalty to the author is included in the price of every book, then some people to whom the value of the book was greater than the cost of getting it into their hands will be deflected to less efficient expenditures. If, however, authors received no royalties, their incentive to produce books would be reduced, just as, if the bridge company received no contribution from its users toward its fixed costs, it would not be able to replace the bridge when it wore out.

The difference is that since the bridge can be duplicated the bridge company is (or at least may be) prevented by competition from charging a price that not only returns its fixed costs but also generates monopoly profits.[3] The effect of copyright is to forbid duplication, so the copyright holder may obtain a return that is in excess of opportunity costs. The question whether to recognize copyright in distant signals thus depends on one's view of the balance struck by the copyright laws between the value of enabling authors to recover their opportunity costs and the costs of enabling them to charge monopoly prices. If one thinks copyright protection is already too generous, one will have little sympathy with the effort to extend it to distant signals. Unfortunately, no one knows whether it is too great or too small. (The high incomes of successful authors are no evidence that it is too great. Although the returns to the successful author are large, most authors fail, so the *expected* return to authors is probably no higher than in other occupations.)

The Court, in rejecting copyright in distant signals, did not discuss these issues. It "reasoned" that the construction of a cable television system is like the erection of a very tall antenna by the individual viewer.

The commission's consideration of the distant-signal issue was biased by the fact that the parties before it included the local television stations as well as the copyright owners. Competition as such is not a common law tort; but a regulatory agency may and often does consider the interest of a firm in being free from competition as one entitled to sympathetic consideration. The major brunt of cable competition, it was believed, would be borne by independent stations, mostly those utilizing the Ultra High Frequency bands of the radio spectrum. Since the commission in its allocation and licensing policies had for many years assiduously nurtured the growth of UHF television, it was natu-

---

3. Whether duplication is economically feasible depends, however, on the size of the market in relation to the cost of duplication.

rally inclined to view sympathetically the complaints of the UHF independents against the competition of cable television.

In sum, the distant-signal question involves a genuine controversy over the assignment of property rights. But transferred from the courts to the regulatory agency, the controversy becomes complicated by the interjection of another argument for limitation based on the interest of one group of firms in freedom from the competition of a new service.

§10.5. *The problem of local monopoly in cable television.* A company desiring to provide cable television service must obtain a franchise from the municipal authorities. Its rates to subscribers may also be subject to regulation by the state public utility commission. Because the distribution of television signals by wire into the home has at least a superficial resemblance to local gas, water, and electric service — the standard examples of natural monopoly — it is not surprising to find wide support for regulation of subscriber rates. But there is an alternative approach, based on contract law. Any number of companies can build and operate a cable television system anywhere in the country. Were there no entry limitations, we would expect several companies to vie for the privilege of serving each community where a substantial demand for cable television service existed. The company that offered the best package of price and service would sign up the most customers. If in fact local cable television service is a natural monopoly, that company would have lower average costs than its competitors and would eventually drive them from the market.

At this point the successful firm would have a monopoly. Would the subscribers therefore be at its mercy? Not if the promised level of price and service had been specified in a contract with each potential subscriber. Competition among rival aspirants to the local market should assure, moreover, that potential subscribers do receive a contract — rather than a promise that the prevailing firm can repudiate as soon as it has obtained the monopoly. Nor is there reason to expect that the process of determining which firm would prevail would impose substantial costs in the form of duplicate facilities that turned out to be redundant. It is unlikely that any firm would commence construction of its cable grid until the completion of an initial period of solicitation. If in that period a strong consumer preference for one firm was indicated, the other firms would probably sell their subscriber contracts to it. If the period of solicitation revealed no strong preference for one firm, and each had subscribers scattered throughout the market, the firms presumably would exchange subscribers until each had a compact market area to serve.

Since contracting costs would not be negligible and might be quite high, it is possible that a pure contract approach would be unsatisfactory. But it may be possible to structure a regulatory approach that preserves the essential elements of the contractual approach. The municipality, acting as the contracting agent of its residents, could solicit bids from competing applicants for the cable television franchise (or franchises). It would compare these bids and enter into a firm contract with the applicant that promised the best combination of low price and generous service. If it had difficulty choosing between different price-service packages, it might conduct a preference poll among the residents following a campaign by the applicants.

The modified contractual approach may seem quite like the existing system of franchising, for the franchisee is usually chosen from among several applicants. The difference is that the municipality under the present system ordinarily does not set as its goal the obtaining of the best possible contract for the subscribers. The approach, rather, is to extract concessions from the franchisee as the price of permitting him to charge a monopoly price. A typical cable franchise will provide that the franchisee must remit a percentage of his gross revenues to the municipality and also dedicate a certain number of channels, free of charge, for municipal services such as education. The residents gain something as taxpayers from the franchise, but they lose as consumers. They pay a monopoly subscription rate that is higher, due to the concessions, than it would be if the cable television company were an unfettered monopolist, let alone a company contractually obligated to provide service at a price equal to cost. This is illustrated in Figure 8, which compares the monopoly price with and without a gross receipts tax.[1] The example points

---

§10.5. 1. To understand the effect of the tax, we must bear in mind that, from the seller's standpoint, the demand schedule is a schedule of average revenue, of price received rather than price charged, at various levels of output. The effect of the tax is to alter the firm's demand (average revenue) schedule, reducing it by a uniform percentage at every level of output as shown in Figure 8. Its marginal revenue schedule is also altered, as shown in the diagram, and the resulting profit-maximizing output is lower and price (including tax) higher than before the tax was imposed.

Suppose the municipality in our example, instead of imposing a gross receipts tax, charges a flat tax per unit of output. What would be the effect on the price and output of a profit-maximizing monopolist? (See §16.4 *infra*.) Now suppose

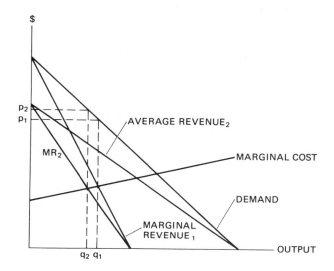

Figure 8

out the difference between taxation by regulation and consumer welfare maximization by contract. It also reminds us of the important question that we have postponed to a later chapter:[2] the comparative political characteristics of common law versus direct public regulation. Possibly the specific techniques of the two institutions are similar or even, in many cases, interchangeable. The difference may be the likelihood that these techniques will be used to promote efficiency rather than some other purpose.

PROBLEMS

1. The federal truth-in-lending statute requires lenders to disclose their interest charges as annual percentage rates. There is evidence that a similar statute enacted in Massachusetts sometime earlier had little effect on consumers' borrowing behavior. (See Note, 9 B.C. Ind. & Com. L. Rev. 1020 (1968).) Can you think of a reason why the annual percentage rate might not be the most meaningful form of stat-

the municipality simply auctions off the cable franchise to the highest lump-sum bidder. What would be the price and output effects? Would it make a difference whether the franchise was exclusive or nonexclusive?
    2. Chapter 23.

ing the interest charge for many consumers, especially poorer ones?

2. If transaction costs between copyright holders and cable television companies were low, would the FCC's distant-signal rules have any significance for the output of copyrighted material? Would it make a difference if many of the copyrights were owned by television networks, which own television stations?

CHAPTER 11

PRICE CONTROLS

At this writing, the economy is subject to comprehensive wage and price controls. They have recently been relaxed and may eventually be removed altogether, but the issue of controls is likely to remain in the forefront of public policy debate for some time.[1]

Controls superficially resemble public utility maximum rate setting but are primarily designed to deal with inflation rather than with monopoly. The current controls, however, are frequently defended by reference to monopolistic conditions in labor and product markets. Let us begin by examining the nature and cause of inflation.[2]

If the number of dollars in the economy and the amount of production remain in constant proportion to each other (as would be true if the supply of money expanded at the same rate as output), a rise in the price of one product would have to be offset by a fall in the price of another product and the overall price level would remain unchanged. Suppose there were 100 dollars in the economy and 100 units of output, each priced at $1. If the price of one of the units increases to $2, the money supply and output remaining unchanged, the price of the other units must fall by a total of $1, for consumers cannot be induced to pay $101 when they have only $100. If the overall price level does

1. In any event, repeal of the Economic Stabilization Act would leave intact New York City's rent control program, state usury laws, and other pockets of price control.

2. The discussion of the economics of inflation that follows is extremely superficial, but the complexity of monetary theory is disproportionate to its importance to an understanding of the characteristic institutions and concerns of the legal system. For contrasting views on monetary theory see, e.g., Milton Friedman, The Optimum Quantity of Money, in The Optimum Quantity of Money and Other Essays 1 (1969), and Fischer Black, Active and Passive Monetary Policy in a Neoclassical Model, 27 J. Fin. 801 (1972).

rise, it means that the ratio of dollars to goods is increasing. A common situation where this occurs, and the occasion for previous imposition of controls in the United States, is during wartime, when production is diverted from civilian to military goods, reducing the amount of goods available for purchase by the private sector. No inflation would result if the government paid for all of its purchases out of higher taxes: the number of dollars in the hands of private consumers would be reduced proportionately to the reduction in the goods they could buy. But governments are reluctant in wartime to impose taxes sufficient to pay for the entire costs of the war, and so inflation results. Inflation could be permitted to take its course: prices would be bid up and the limited supply allocated in accordance with willingness to pay. But this too is politically inexpedient, so prices are frozen. In the resulting scramble for goods, some people who have money are nonetheless unable to obtain goods. Queuing — waiting in line — takes the place of money as the basis for allocating goods among consumers. Queuing is an inefficient method of economic exchange compared to money, because it involves costs in time that are likely to be much greater than the printing and paper costs involved in the use of money. An alternative to queuing is rationing. The government issues scrip that entitles the holder to purchase a specified quantity of a given good. The effect is much like taxation: the scrip buys less than the dollars it replaces, thus eliminating excess demand by reducing the effective money supply. If the scrip is salable, we are back to the price system as the method of allocation, with the difference that the scrip increases the real wealth of the poorer consumers. If the scrip is not salable, the only method by which goods can be shifted from lower valued to higher valued uses is by governmental decision to issue additional scrip to those who convince the government that a particular good would be more valuable in their hands. Economic allocation is replaced by legal allocation, an inefficient substitution.[3]

The current wage-price controls were not imposed because of excessive demand. Indeed, when they were imposed American industry was operating substantially below its full capacity and unemployment was relatively high. Yet inflation seemed to be persisting. Two reasons were offered to explain this; the second was apparently the rationale accepted by the administration. The first was monopoly. Under very special conditions, monopoly might have inflationary effects. If we assume a constant money

3. Cf. §§2.5 *supra* and 23.1 *infra*.

supply, the price rise that would follow the creation of a monopoly would have to be offset by a fall in the prices of other products. However, the creation of a monopoly results not only in a price increase but also in a contraction of the output of the monopolized product, and while the contraction would eventually be offset by increased production of substitute (albeit less valuable) products, there would be an interval during which total output was smaller than before the monopoly. With the supply of money unchanged, this would result in an increase in the general price level.

For monopoly to create inflation requires the simultaneous creation of enough monopolies to have a noticeable effect on the economy as a whole. After the formation of the monopoly and the resulting price increase and output contraction the monopoly has no further effect on inflation. The monopolist will, to be sure, increase prices from time to time in order to offset the effects of inflation, but so would a competitive firm. Recent inflation is difficult to explain in terms of the simultaneous creation of many new monopolies, whether in labor or in product markets.

The second explanation is that the inflation persisted because workers' representatives and sellers believed that the monetary authorities would continue to inflate the money supply in order to increase consumer demand and, derivatively, output and employment. Governments frequently do use inflation as a deliberate device for increasing economic activity, although the long-term effectiveness of such a policy seems doubtful. To be sure, if the consumer is given more dollars he will try to buy more goods and his increased demand will evoke a corresponding increase in supply — but only if prices do not increase as fast as consumer income. Sellers, if rational, will respond to inflation by increasing their (nominal) prices in order to prevent a reduction in their real income. The increase in the consumer's income will thus be offset by an increase in the price of goods; his purchasing power will be no greater than before; therefore he will not demand a greater number of goods. The theory that inflation stimulates economic activity depends crucially on sellers' being shortsighted, which is inconsistent with the usual assumption of economic analysis.

Be that as it may, the theory of the latest wage-price controls was that business and labor needed a demonstration of the administration's determination not to use monetary policy to stimulate the economy and that imposition of controls would make the point in the most dramatic way. An alternative policy would have been to limit the growth of the money supply so tightly that any increase in wages or prices in anticipation of further inflation would be promptly offset by a reduction in wages and prices elsewhere in the economy. But this policy might have created painful short-term dislocations in the economy.

The objective of the controls, at least in "Phase II" (now Phase III) which followed a three-month freeze, was not to supplant the price system as a method of allocating resources, as in wartime programs, but to prevent wage and price increases motivated solely by an anticipation of continued inflation. On the wage side, this was to be done by limiting wage increases to roughly the rate at which productivity was rising. Productivity is the ratio of output to hours worked. The higher a worker's productivity, the more valuable his labor is to his employer. A wage increase strictly limited to the increase in the worker's productivity would not increase the employer's average labor cost at all (and so would in no sense be inflationary) since it would be completely offset by his higher output. On the price side, price increases were to be permitted in proportion to any increase in the firm's average costs.[4] This was intended to prevent a firm from increasing its price not on the basis of higher costs but because it anticipated a reduction in the value of the dollars that it was receiving for its product.

The principal danger that such a program poses to the efficient operation of the economy arises from the tacit assumption, basic to the program, that all firms and markets were in competitive equilibrium, with price equal to opportunity costs, on January 1, 1971. A price increase, to be lawful under the program, must be based on a cost increase incurred after that date. If a firm sustained cost increases before that date, which for one reason or another it had failed to offset by a higher price, the effect of the price control program might be to prevent it from establishing a price high enough to cover its full costs. "Might," not "would," because the firm despite the unrecovered cost increase might be selling above cost and because price increases are not the only

---

4. Why proportionate? Why were not firms allowed only to pass on cost increases dollar for dollar to the consumer? (Hint: the difficulty of measuring the cost of equity capital is relevant here.) In addition, firms were forbidden to increase their profit margin, measured as a percentage of sales revenues, above the level prevailing in any two out of three of the firm's fiscal years prior to August 1971. What is the purpose of this constraint? Could a firm that complied with the rule stated in the text violate this additional constraint?

method by which a firm can increase its revenues in relation to its costs. But some firms, and some entire industries, might find themselves in a position where a higher price was necessary to cover full costs but be unable to charge that price because it could be justified only by reference to higher costs incurred before January 1, 1971. In such industries, price control would impose a ceiling price that, while moving, would still be too low to induce expansion of capacity to meet growing demand.

The more traditional type of price control program, which establishes specific price limits below market-clearing levels, creates additional inefficiencies.[5] First, a large multiproduct firm is in a better position than a small single-product firm to practice various methods of evading price controls. Two examples are the tie-in sale, whereby a firm that sells two products, one controlled and one uncontrolled, can evade the price ceiling on the controlled product by charging a premium for the uncontrolled; and reciprocal buying, whereby a firm can extract an above-ceiling price for its product by purchasing a product from its buyer at a discount.[6] In addition, the existence of a ceiling price induces a firm to reduce the amount of service it renders as a way of increasing its profit. An attractive way to do this under conditions of excess demand is to turn away new customers, since they usually require more service (credit checking, etc.) than old; and this is feasible since the existence of excess demand implies that there are plenty of old customers. The new customers will include a disproportionate number of small firms.

Second, new customers include a disproportionate number of new entrants. So the effect just described reduces the effectiveness of competition. Third, price controls facilitate cartel pricing. The existence of excess demand creates a need for allocative machinery that usually involves cooperation among the sellers of the product affected. The pattern of cooperation may persist after controls are lifted.

It remains to note one curious and, it would seem, self-defeating feature of the Phase II controls — the repeated threats by the price controllers to tighten the controls. The effect of such a threat on a rational self-interested businessman is to induce him to seek price increases even if he does not think that a price in-

5. As explained in Harold Demsetz & George J. Stigler, The Theory of Public Price Control (U. Chi., Grad. Sch. Bus., mimeo., Nov. 25, 1968).
6. Cf. §7.6 *supra.*

crease is appropriate under current market conditions, for he can expect that if controls are tightened it will be for the future and that any price increase already in effect will be permitted to stand.

PROBLEMS

1. *To what extent, if any, does the Phase II method of price control create the three dangers that we have said the traditional method of price control creates?*

2. *The price of retail goods normally has two components: cost of goods sold (i.e., the wholesale price paid by the retailer to his supplier); and the retailer's markup, computed as a percentage of the retail price. In Phase II, retailers' markups were frozen. Since the freeze was of a percentage figure, the retailer remained free to raise prices in proportion to any increase in his cost of goods sold. Does this method of control protect the retailer against the effects of inflation in his input costs?*

PART III

THE REGULATION OF BUSINESS ORGANIZATIONS AND FINANCIAL MARKETS

CHAPTER 12

CORPORATIONS

§12.1.   The nature of the firm.   Transaction costs — the costs involved in ordering economic activity through voluntary exchange — are a recurrent concept in this book. Here we use it to explain why so much economic activity is carried on by firms rather than by individuals.[1]

Contrast two methods of organizing the production of (say) mobile homes. In one, the entrepreneur contracts with one person to supply the component parts, with another to assemble them, and with a third to sell the finished product. In the second method, he hires them to perform these tasks as his employees under his direction. The first method of organizing production is the traditional domain of contract law, the second of master-servant law. The essence of the first method is that the entrepreneur negotiates with each of the three contractors an agreement specifying the price, quantity, quality, due date, credit terms, etc., of the contractor's performance. The essence of the second method is that the entrepreneur pays them wages, not for a specific performance, but for the right to direct their performance.

Neither method of organizing economic activity is costless. The first method, contract, usually requires that the details of the supplier's performance be spelled out at the time of the signing of the contract, which may require protracted and costly negotiations, elaborate bidding procedures, etc. And should changed circumstances require modification of any term of the agreed-upon performance, the agreement must be renegotiated. The

§12.1. 1. The discussion in this section is based primarily on Ronald H. Coase, The Nature of the Firm, 4 Economica (n.s.) 386 (1937). See also Armen A. Alchian & Harold Demsetz, Production, Information Costs, and Economic Organization, 62 Am. Econ. Rev. 777 (1972); George J. Stigler, The Division of Labor Is Limited by the Extent of the Market, in The Organization of Industry 129 (1968).

second method, the firm, involves incentive, information, and communication costs. Since the supplier is now no longer paid directly for his output, he has less incentive than before to minimize his costs: for the contractor a dollar saved in costs is a dollar gained in profit; for the employee the dollar saved may simply increase the employer's profit by a dollar. Information about costs and value is obscured in the firm since the employees do not bid for the various resources that they use in production, a process that would indicate where those resources could be employed most valuably. And since performance in the firm is directed by the employer's orders, machinery for minimizing failures of communication up and down the chain of command is necessary[2] — machinery that may be both costly and imperfect. In sum, the contract method of organizing economic activity encounters the problem of high transaction costs, the method of organizing economic activity through the firm the problem of loss of control. It is the control problem rather than the law of diminishing returns that places an upper limit on the efficient size of firms. Diminishing returns limit the amount of any single product that a firm can efficiently produce. The limit on the number of products is a function of the costs of directing performance in very large organizations.[3]

The point about contract and firm as alternative methods of organizing production is frequently overlooked in discussions of the antitrust legality of vertical integration — the common ownership of successive stages of the production-distribution process. Even if vertical integration led to efficiency costs by increasing the probability of monopoly pricing,[4] these costs might be offset by the efficiency gains from using the firm rather than contract to coordinate successive stages of production. All firms are vertically integrated, in the sense that their operations could be decomposed into successive stages coordinated by contract. A firm that does not contract out its typing is vertically integrated.

§12.2.   *The financing of large undertakings.*   The theory of the firm tells us why so much economic activity is organized in firms but not why most of those firms are corporations. There is

---

2. Is the communication point an amalgam of the incentive and information points just mentioned? Why?

3. In speaking of a limit on the size of firm, we have in mind the firm as an economic, not as a legal, entity. It is unclear what, if any, limitation there is to the size of the firm as a legal entity, since management is free to direct the operations of any part of the firm through contract rather than command.

4. But see §7.6 *supra.*

a clue in the fact that firms in which the inputs are primarily labor rather than capital are frequently organized as partnerships or individual proprietorships. The corporation is primarily a method of solving problems encountered in raising substantial amounts of capital for a venture.[1]

Consider the dilemma of the impecunious entrepreneur who has a promising idea for a new venture. How is he to raise the capital necessary to launch the venture? Borrowing the money is probably out of the question. If the normal interest rate is 6 percent but the venture has a 50 percent chance of failing, the lender, if risk neutral, will charge an interest rate of 56 percent. High interest, plus amortization, will impose heavy fixed costs on the venture from the outset and this will increase the danger of failure, and in turn the interest rate. Moreover, if the venture's prospects cannot be predicted with reasonable confidence, it will be very difficult even to calculate an appropriate interest rate.

These difficulties could perhaps be overcome by careful and imaginative drafting of the loan agreement, but the transaction costs might be very high. An alternative procedure is for the entrepreneur to admit a partner to the business who is entitled to receive a portion of the profits of the venture, if any, in exchange for contributing the necessary capital to it. The partner's compensation is determined automatically by the fortunes of the business. There is no need to compute an interest rate although this is implicit in the determination of the fraction of any future profits that he is to receive in exchange for his contribution. And there are no fixed costs of debt. The partner receives his profits only if and as earned.

But there are still problems. A partnership can be dissolved by, and is automatically dissolved on the death of, any partner. The impermanence of the arrangements may deter the commitment of large amounts of money to an enterprise in which it may be frozen for many years. Again, the partners may be able to negotiate around this hurdle but not without incurring transaction costs that may be high. Moreover, to the extent that they agree to limit the investing partner's right to dissolve the partnership and withdraw his money, the liquidity of his investment is reduced and he may be placed at the mercy of the entrepreneur.

Further, each partner is personally liable for the debts of the partnership. In deciding whether to invest money, therefore, a

§12.2. 1. Today there are also tax reasons for adopting the corporate form, but we will not discuss those reasons here.

prospective partner, if prudent, will need to ascertain the likely extent of the enterprise's potential liability. He may want to go further and participate in the actual management of the firm in order to assure that it does not run up huge debts. This pretty much limits investment to people willing to devote considerable time to active participation in the running of the enterprise. In principle the problem of unlimited liability could be solved by appropriate transactions. The enterprise could include in all of its contracts with customers and suppliers a clause limiting its liability to the assets of the enterprise (some business trusts do this). But the negotiation of such waivers would be costly. And it would be utterly impracticable to limit most tort liability in this way.

The corporate form is the normal solution that the law and business practice have evolved to meet these problems.[2] The corporation can be given perpetual existence so as to obviate the need for a special agreement limiting withdrawal or dissolution. The shareholder (as the investor in a corporation is known) is protected against being exploited by the entrepreneur or promoter by two methods. The first consists of a complex of legal rights vis-à-vis management and any controlling group of shareholders, such as the right to cast votes for candidates to the board of directors (which oversees management) in proportion to the number of shares owned by the shareholder.[3] The second protection lies in the fact that equity interests in a corporation are broken up into shares of relatively small value which can be, and in the case of most of the larger corporations are, traded in organized markets. The shareholder need not make a large investment and if he wants to liquidate his investment by selling his shares he can do so quickly and cheaply. Finally, the corporate form encourages passive investment. The shareholder's liability is limited to the value of his shares. The owner of a share of stock knows that whatever debts the corporation may incur, he can at worst lose what he paid for his shares. In sum, the corporate form greatly broadens the market for investment capital.

2. But not the inevitable solution. An alternative that would be quite similar to the corporation would be a partnership with nonredeemable and freely transferable partnership shares, plus comprehensive insurance against tort and other business liability of the partnership.

3. These rights can be modified by the corporate charter: a corporation can for instance have nonvoting shareholders. The purpose of corporation law is not to force business enterprises into a straitjacket but to minimize transaction costs by establishing a framework suitable to most enterprises in which substantial capital must be raised.

§12.3.   Abuse of limited liability.   Limited liability may be an essential element in the financing of large undertakings but it creates an economic problem illustrated by a series of accident cases involving taxicabs in New York State. The owners of large fleets of cabs, in order to minimize accident liability, formed separate corporations for each cab. The only asset of each corporation was the cab it owned and the value of the cab was often less than the cost of the accident. The scheme largely eliminated the incentive to take cost-justified precautions and so fostered inefficiency.

Solution of the problem does not require the elimination of limited liability. Other, less costly situations are possible. In several cases courts "pierced the corporate veil" and deemed the series of taxi corporations rather than the individual corporations the relevant entity for applying limited liability.[1] Alternatively, corporations could be required to file bonds guaranteeing their ability to answer in damages for any legal wrong they commit. But no method is foolproof: the corporation that filed a bond and later became insolvent would have no financial incentive to avoid dangerous or otherwise costly conduct.[2]

§12.4.   The separation of ownership and control in the modern corporation.   We have laid the groundwork for an economic analysis of the major controversy that has shaped contemporary corporation law — the controversy over the alleged separation between ownership (the shareholders) and control (the management) in the publicly held corporation. The preceding discussion should have illuminated the difference between *firm* and *corporation*. The firm is a method, alternative to contracting, of organizing production; the corporation is a method, like a bond indenture, for attracting capital into the firm. It is because the typical business is both firm and corporation that a confusion over ownership and control has arisen. The control of the firm resides in a management group which gives orders to those who

§12.3. 1. The cases are summarized in Harry G. Henn, Handbook of the Law of Corporations and Other Business Enterprises 254 n.25 (2d ed. 1970). In practice, piercing the corporate veil is an infrequent — perhaps too infrequent — remedy.

2. A solution that might seem quite similar would be to eliminate limited liability for torts. The taxi company would buy liability insurance to protect the shareholders. This would appear to give the shareholder the essential benefits of limited liability, but the appearance is somewhat deceptive. The shareholder would have to worry that if the insurance company for any reason refused to honor the insurance contract, he might have to pay part or all of a tort judgment against the corporation.

buy the firm's inputs and produce and market its output. The group consists of people who are experienced in the business and involved in it on a full-time, day-to-day basis. In contrast, the typical shareholder (except in the closely held corporation or where one shareholder owns a very large percentage of the shares of the corporation) is not knowledgeable about the business of the firm, does not derive an important part of his livelihood from it, and neither expects nor has an incentive to participate in the management of the firm. He is a passive investor and, because of the liquidity of his interest, has only a casual, and frequently quite brief, relationship with the firm. His interest, like that of a creditor, is a financial rather than managerial interest. In a technical sense the shareholders "own" the corporation, but they do not own it in the same sense in which they own their own automobiles; it would be better to speak of their owning the common stock of the corporation.

It is no more anomalous that shareholders do not manage or control "their" corporation than that bondholders do not manage or control the corporations whose bonds they hold, or trust beneficiaries the trustee. All three groups have an investment interest. The difference lies in the greater vulnerability of the shareholder (as of the trust beneficiary) compared to the bondholder.[1] Since the bondholder has a fixed interest rate (and, for what it is worth, the cushion of the equity investment), his concern is not that the firm be well managed but that it not be so mismanaged that it defaults on its interest payments or is unable to repay the principal when the bond matures. In contrast, the shareholder's return is directly related both to how well the firm is managed and to how scrupulously the managers allot to the shareholders an appropriate portion of the firm's income, which is to say everything above the competitive return to the managers for performance of the managerial function.

The danger of mismanagement is less serious than the danger that the managers will not deal fairly with the shareholders. Mismanagement will lead eventually to the bankruptcy of the firm (and of the managers' future employment prospects), as a result

§12.4. 1. The essential continuity between shareholder and bondholder is underscored by the hybrid character of the preferred shareholder's interest. Also, while the position of a shareholder is always more vulnerable than that of a bondholder of the same corporation, the position of a shareholder in a large and prosperous firm is often more secure, in fact, than that of a bondholder in a weaker firm.

of the competition of better managed rivals. The managers thus have a strong incentive to manage the firm well or, if they are unable to manage it well themselves, to sell their offices[2] to those who can. The incentive to deal fairly with shareholders is weaker. To be sure, managers who do not deal fairly with the shareholder will have to pay a premium should they ever want to raise additional capital by a new issue of common stock. But the cost of the premium will not be borne by the managers; it will be borne by the original shareholders in the form of a dilution of their interest.[3] There is thus sufficient conflict of interest between management and shareholders to lead us to predict that shareholders would normally insist upon the inclusion of protective features in the corporate charter.[4] Corporation law has the purpose, by now familiar to the reader, of reducing transaction costs by enacting the framework of rights and duties that the parties could be expected to negotiate anyway.

The most important shareholder right is the right to cast votes, equal to the number of shares he holds, for membership in the corporation's board of directors. The board does not manage the firm. Composed usually of representatives of management plus outsiders who, having full-time employment elsewhere, devote only sporadic attention to the affairs of the corporation, normally the board ratifies — often in a quite perfunctory way — the actions of the management. The importance of the board lies in the fact that it, and through it the shareholders, can fire the existing managers and hire new ones. The essential power of the shareholders is the power to vote out the existing board and vote in a new one that will replace the incumbent management with one more attentive to the shareholders' interests.

The separation of ownership and control is thus a false issue. Separation is efficient, and indeed inescapable, given that for most shareholders the opportunity costs of active participation in the management of the firm would be prohibitively high. What

2. They are not permitted to do this directly; but there are indirect methods of sale, especially as part of a corporate acquisition. See next section.

3. Does the question whether any part of the cost will be borne by the managers depend on how the managers are compensated? On anything else?

4. There is a similar conflict of interest between the beneficiaries of a trust and the trustee, and not surprisingly we find a similar set of protective features (fiduciary duties) in both contexts. There is an important difference, however. The trustee is responsible for diversifying the investments of the beneficiary. The corporation is ordinarily a nondiversified enterprise; it is left to the shareholder, by buying shares in a number of corporations, to achieve the amount of diversification that he desires. But this gets us ahead of our story. See §§13.1, 13.3 *infra*.

is necessary in the interests of the shareholders is not participatory shareholder democracy but machinery for discouraging management from deflecting an inappropriate proportion of the firm's net income from the shareholders to itself. Whether such machinery is effective depends on the actual mechanics by which the control of the firm is transferred through the votes of the shareholders — a question to which we now turn.

§12.5. *The transfer of corporate control.*   If management is disregarding the interests of the shareholders, the market price of the firm's common stock will fall. When this happens alert investors will realize that the stock is underpriced — i.e., its price would be higher if the firm were being managed with the object of maximizing the shareholder's return. They can exploit this knowledge in several ways.

(1) A single investor (normally a large corporation) or a syndicate of smaller investors can offer to purchase a majority of the outstanding shares in the corporation from the existing shareholders at a price somewhere in between the current market price and the price to which the stock would rise under proper management and control. If the offer succeeds, the investor will have enough votes to elect his own board of directors, which will then replace the present management.

(2) The investor can buy enough shares (a) to form a base from which to wage a campaign for the voting proxies of the other shareholders and (b) to enable him to profit handsomely from the increase in the market price of the firm's common stock when the old board and management are overthrown.

(3) The investor (if a corporation) can try to persuade the current board of directors to cooperate in effecting a merger of the two corporations that will give control to the acquiring firm. The acquiescence of the incumbent directors and managers of the acquired firm can be secured by promises of generous compensation in the form of lucrative consulting contracts, etc.

To the economist, to repeat, the coalescence of ownership and control is not a necessary condition of efficient performance. What is necessary (and largely sufficient) is that there be methods — the tender offer, the proxy fight, voluntary acquisition — by which investors (usually, in this context, other large corporations) can obtain control of the board of directors and oust the present management.[1] It is unimportant whether these

§12.5. 1. See Henry G. Manne, The Market for Corporate Control, 73 J. Pol. Econ. 110 (1965).

mechanisms are employed often; indeed, the more effective as a deterrent a threat is the less often it has to be carried out.

The law, however, places several obstacles in the way of effective use of the mechanisms of corporate takeover. The Securities and Exchange Commission forbids an investor bent on takeover to buy up a substantial portion of the target firm's shares without disclosing his purpose. Such disclosure tends to increase the price of the stock and thus to reduce the gain from takeover and therefore the incentive to attempt it.[2] The antitrust laws, as currently interpreted, are a significant obstacle to takeovers. Ordinarily a large corporation can be taken over only by another large corporation, but large corporate acquisitions are highly vulnerable to antitrust challenge. Today one often finds corporate management resisting a takeover on the ground that the resulting acquisition would violate the antitrust laws. There would be another obstacle if proposals were adopted which forbid a controlling shareholder, in selling his shares, to charge a premium for the control of the corporation that the sale bestows on the purchaser. The underlying theory is that the controlling shareholder has fiduciary obligations to the minority shareholders. The theory has merit in cases where there is a conflict of interest between majority and minority shareholders, but in the usual takeover situation the latter will be more injured than benefited by a rule that, by reducing the controlling shareholder's incentive to sell his control, retards the reallocation of the assets of the corporation to people who can use them more productively, to the benefit of all of the shareholders.

The procedures for effecting a takeover are unduly cumbersome. Ordinarily, before an acquisition can be made the shareholders of the firm to be acquired must approve by a two-thirds vote. The firm's board of directors must also approve. Why is not a simple majority of the shareholders (weighted, of course, by number of shares owned by each) sufficient? Conflicting interests of minority shareholders can probably be protected by remedies that do not impede the transfer of corporate assets. The rule requiring the directors of the acquired firm to consent to the acquisition seems particularly anomalous. Probably its main effect is to increase the price that an acquiring firm must pay for the acquiescence of the acquired firm's management (which will generally be in control of the board) in the takeover. That price,

2. Cf. the discussion of a somewhat similar point in the context of eminent domain, *supra* §2.5.

paid ultimately by the shareholders of both firms, increases take-over costs.

The law may thus be faulted for paying insufficient attention to the role of transactions and the market in assuring that corporations are controlled by those who can use that control most productively. Too much emphasis has been placed on creating "corporate democracy" and not enough on creating an efficient market in corporate control. Actually, the political metaphor that underlies the phrase "corporate democracy" reinforces this point. Voters do not manage the government, but political entrepreneurs can use the electoral process to wrest control from the incumbents and this possibility helps keep the incumbents on their toes.[3] The corporate context differs from the political in that the methods of acquiring control are more various, a point obscured by the political metaphor. The pure proxy fight, waged by an individual who has not acquired a substantial ownership position, most closely resembles the electoral process but is the least feasible method of effecting a takeover, in part because it is difficult for such an individual, not owning shares, to recoup the costs of the campaign with a profit commensurate with the risk of failure. Yet facilitating the use of the proxy machinery has been at the forefront of regulatory concern.

§12.6. *Insider trading and the problem of entrepreneurial reward.*   We have identified two forces that operate to keep managers in line. One is competition in the market for the firm's product, which penalizes mismanagement. The other is competition in the market for corporate control. There have also been efforts to forbid managerial practices thought inimical to dealing fairly with the shareholders. An example is the rule that forbids "insider trading" (the practice by which a manager or other insider uses information not yet disclosed to other shareholders or the outside world to make profits by trading in the firm's stock). This rule has been attacked on the ground that such trading, while in a sense a fraud on the other shareholders (who sell to the insider at a low price, or buy from him at a high price, only because he has failed to tell them what he knows), is an important incentive device.[1] This argument would be more forceful as

---

3. See Gary S. Becker, Competition and Democracy, 1 J. Law & Econ. 105 (1958).

§12.6. 1. See Henry G. Manne, Insider Trading and the Stock Market (1966). The leading case applying the doctrine, Securities and Exchange Commission v. Texas Gulf Sulphur Co., 401 F.2d 833 (2d Cir. 1968), illustrates the practical difficulties of its application.

applied to stock options, which create a genuine community of interest between management and the shareholders and make managerial compensation to a significant degree a function of the corporation's profitability. Insider trading does not reward efficient management as such. It rewards the possession of confidential information, whether it is information favorable or unfavorable to the corporation's prospects. One can thus imagine cases where managers would have an incentive to take steps to *accelerate* the demise of their firm, possibly at significant social cost. Nor is the objection to insider trading met by forbidding only short selling on the basis of inside information. Managers would have an incentive to manipulate the disclosure of information about the firm in a manner calculated to produce sharp, if temporary, spurts in the price of the firm's stock. Their energies would be deflected from managing the firm so as to maximize its present worth to managing publicity about the firm so as to maximize the volatility of its stock.

A more forceful objection to insider trading is that it reduces the efficiency of the stock market since the insider's decision to buy or sell provides information about the firm's prospects that permits the stock to be revalued accurately. But this advantage must be balanced against the loss of efficiency that is created when managers conceal information or disseminate misinformation, as they would have greater incentive to do were insider trading permitted.

The costs of enforcing the rule against insider trading are probably high. Not only are concepts like "insider" and "inside information" slippery, but devices for evasion of the rule abound. For example, it is said that insiders in different companies simply trade inside information about each other's companies. This loophole would be difficult to close — except by forbidding insiders and their families to trade in any corporate stock!

The question of managerial incentives that underlies the debate over the propriety of insider trading is of course an important one. It can be argued that the manager is the modern counterpart of the classical entrepreneur of economic theory and should have an opportunity to receive entrepreneurial gains over and above a mere salary. But it is important to distinguish two types of corporate leader. The first is the founder or promoter, who corresponds most closely to the classical entrepreneur. He always receives a large bloc of shares and thereby participates substantially in any increase in the value of the corporation. The second is the exceptionally successful manager of the established concern. His risks are lower than those of the founder or promoter, and so his appropriate reward less; but if he has unusual skills — more precisely, if the corporation cannot find an equally good substitute at a moderate salary — then he will command a very high return, whether in the form of salary, bonus tied to corporate profits, stock options, or other compensation. There is no presumption that extraordinary productivity, whether a business manager's or an opera singer's, will not be fully compensated.

§12.7. *What do corporations maximize?*   In classical economic analysis, the firm is considered an indivisible unit and the question that introduces this section does not arise. The firm maximizes utility and the utility of a firm is the present value of its assets; the firm maximizes profits. Once it is recognized that a firm is actually a collection of individuals, each with his own utility function, the question of what the firm maximizes becomes more problematic. The main concern of this chapter has been to explore ways in which the individuals who manage corporations are prevented from substituting personal goals for that of maximizing corporate profits.

The conflict of interest between management and shareholders involves both an efficiency and a distributive question, and they must be kept separate. The efficiency question is whether the managers have adequate incentives to maximize the present value of the corporation. The distributive question is whether they have adequate incentives to allocate all income in excess of expenses (including their own opportunity costs) to the shareholders, although as with many distributive questions, this one has an efficiency dimension: if managers systematically receive more than a competitive return for their services, excessive resources will be attracted into business management.

Economists have speculated that managers, rather than attempting to maximize the present worth of the corporation, often attempt to maximize sales, growth, staff, perquisites, prestige, leisure, power, etc.[1] There has been no empirical verification of these hypotheses and the previous sections in this chapter present some theoretical reasons for believing that the market and the law do impose penalties on managers who substitute personal goals for the shareholder's interest in profit maximization. Fur-

§12.7. 1. See, e.g., William G. Baumol, Business Behavior, Value and Growth (rev. ed. 1967); Oliver E. Williamson, The Economics of Discretionary Behavior: Managerial Objectives in a Theory of the Firm (1964). A good critique of the literature is Armen A. Alchian, The Basis of Some Recent Advances in the Theory of Management of the Firm, 14 J. Ind. Econ. 30 (1965).

thermore, managerial utility maximization may actually depend upon corporate profit maximization. Consider, first, growth of corporate sales as a maximand. To grow rapidly a firm must either generate large amounts of cash from current operations or obtain money from the capital markets. For either purpose it needs large profits (current or expected). Growth maximization thus blends insensibly into profit maximization. Consider now personal power as a maximand. The most powerful corporate executive is generally the one who controls a highly profitable enterprise. He is least likely to encounter criticism from shareholders, let alone a threat of a takeover.[2] In addition, large profits generate capital (and enable additional capital to be obtained on favorable terms) that he can use for additional ventures. The reader is invited, as an exercise, to consider the compatibility of other personal goals with profit maximization. The debate over whether modern corporations are really profit maximizers may not have much operational significance.

Do we *want* managers to maximize corporate profits? From an economic standpoint, the answer is yes. Assuming adequate social controls to prevent abuses of the competitive process, such as monopolization, profit maximization leads to the maximization of efficiency. Firms are induced to produce those goods that consumers value the most (and hence are willing to pay most for) and to minimize the costs of producing them. Resources are thereby freed, to the maximum extent compatible with efficiency, for use in the production of other goods.

§12.8.   *The question of the corporation's social responsibility.* There are those who believe that profit maximization should not be the only goal of corporate managers. Corporations have long made charitable donations. Why, then, should they not devote a portion of their revenues to other social needs, such as pollution control, the training of members of disadvantaged minorities, and even the regulation of United States military activity?

Charitable donations are not a strong precedent. Especially when made in the localities where the corporation's plants or headquarters are located, they can usually be justified to shareholders as efficient public relations or advertising expenses. Precedent aside, there are economic reasons for questioning both the feasibility and appropriateness of major corporate commitments to social goals other than profit maximization. First, in competi-

---

2. Question: why is a highly profitable company unlikely to be an attractive target for a takeover bid?

tive markets, a sustained commitment to any goal other than profitability will lead to bankruptcy unless collusion is permitted. The firm that channels profits into (say) pollution control will not be able to recoup its losses by charging higher prices to its customers. The customers do not benefit as customers from such expenditures; more precisely, they benefit just as much from those expenditures if they purchase the lower priced product of a competing firm that does not incur them. The firm will therefore have to defray the expenses of pollution control entirely out of its profits. But in a competitive market there are no "profits" in an economic sense. There are accounting profits but they are just equal to the cost of attracting and retaining capital in the business. If these "profits" decline, the firm will eventually be forced out of business. (Under what conditions might a firm be able to survive a cost increase not borne by competitors, and by what change in its behavior?)

The prospects for social responsibility are only slightly brighter in monopolistic markets. If the firm has no rivals, it will be able to shift a part of the cost of pollution control equipment to its customers, but only a part: as shown in Figure 9, its profits will decline. To the outsider, the result is a reduction in monopoly profits (from ABCD to EFGH). To the shareholder, however, it is a loss. The price of a share of stock is equal to the present

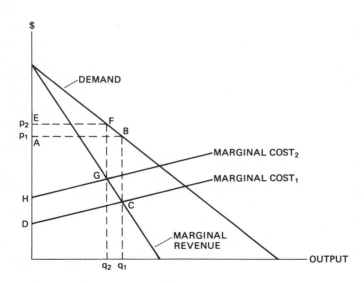

Figure 9

value of the anticipated future earnings of that share.[1] If the firm has a monopoly with a prospect of continued monopoly profits of a certain level, the share price will be higher than if a lower level of profits were expected. Suppose the firm decides to incur pollution control costs that had not been expected. Its anticipated future earnings are now lower, so the price of its shares will fall. This will be felt as a loss to the shareholder. In the usual case he will neither know nor care whether the corporation has monopoly profits. All he knows or cares about is that the value of his holdings has declined. Managers will be reluctant to visit such consequences upon their shareholders.[2]

Observe the tension between different social goals, here pollution abatement and competition. The more competitive a market is, the more difficult it will be to induce any of the sellers to adopt costly pollution control equipment, for unless his rivals follow suit — and their incentive will be to hang back — he will be unable to recoup the costs of the equipment.[3]

The essential point is that neither in a competitive nor a monopolistic market is it realistic to expect much voluntary effort to subordinate profit maximization to social responsibility. Nor is this necessarily to be regretted. An economist would point to the costs of underspecialization that would be incurred in combining economic and social responsibilities in business management. The manager who tries both to produce for the market at lowest cost and to improve society is likely to do neither very well.[4] There are three other problems: (1) a problem of standards: how are managers to decide what is a politically or ethically correct stance? (2) a problem of delegation: is it appropriate for political authority to be exercised by people outside of the political system? and (3) a problem of distributive justice: is it proper that the costs of social responsibility be borne (mainly) by consumers in the form of higher product prices, a

§12.8. 1. We exclude cases where liquidation value is important. Another qualification that we need not worry about here is discussed *infra* §13.1.

2. See also §13.2 *infra*.

3. Parenthetically, observe that not only is a monopoly market more tractable in terms of enforcing antipollution policy but the output of pollutants in such a market will normally be less. When a market is monopolized production is reduced and with it the by-products of production such as pollution. However, production of substitute products will increase and may involve as much or more pollution.

4. The firm could, to be sure, have different divisions for profit-maximizing activities and social improvement activities, but at some level the activities of the two divisions would have to be coordinated.

form of taxation that is usually regressive? [5] Finally, the exercise of social responsibility by the corporation reduces the ability of the shareholders to exercise social responsibility themselves. Profit maximization increases the wealth of the shareholders and so the resources they can devote to political contributions, charitable gifts, and the like. Has the manager any comparative advantage in making such allocations? Arguably, individual choice and decentralization of power are maximized when social responsibility is vested in the shareholders rather than in management.

SUGGESTED READINGS

1. Armen A. Alchian, The Basis of Some Recent Advances in the Theory of Management of the Firm, 14 J. Ind. Econ. 30 (1965).
2. Ronald H. Coase, The Nature of the Firm, 4 Economica (n.s.) 386 (1937).
3. Henry G. Manne, Mergers and the Market for Corporate Control, 73 J. Pol. Econ. 110 (1965).
4. ———, Our Two Corporation Systems: Law and Economics, 53 Va. L. Rev. 259 (1967).

PROBLEMS

1. Suppose that, before the recent reorganization of the postal service, when the post office was still an executive department, you had been asked to design an appropriate organizational form for the postal service. Would you propose a private corporation? A public corporation? Would either form be an advance over the executive department?

2. The Communications Satellite Corporation (Comsat) is a private corporation, but the President of the United States appoints several of the directors (a minority). Do you expect the firm to behave differently from other private corporations by virtue of these "public" directors?

3. Under German law, workers are entitled to elect some of the members of the counterpart (roughly speaking) to our board of directors. Would you consider this a worthwhile innovation in our corporate form? (Cf. Detlev F. Vagts, Reforming the "Modern" Corporation: Perspectives from the German, 80 Harv. L. Rev. 23 (1966).) Does your answer depend on what union leaders maximize (see problem 6)? Suppose workers were given shares of corporate stock: would it make a difference whether it was stock of the company for which they worked or stock of some other company?

5. Because the poor spend a larger fraction of their income than the rich. See §16.2 *infra.*

4. Discuss this proposition: corporation law should be wholly permissive with respect to the allocation of power in the corporate charter between shareholders and directors.

5. It is sometimes argued that managers are more likely to want to maximize corporate sales than corporate profits. How could a manager benefit from adopting a goal of sales maximization? Does your answer depend on whether the market for managers is competitive? Whether buyers in that market are well informed?

6. Would you expect the problem of managers' substituting their personal goals for organizational goals to be more acute in a university, labor union, or government regulatory agency than in a business firm? Can it be argued that the personal goals of the management of any type of organization generally coincide with the goal of maximizing the present worth of the organization?

7. Should "insider," for purposes of applying the rule against insider trading, include only corporate officers, their families, and people to whom they sell inside information, or should it include anyone who in fact possesses inside information? Why might the expanded definition be extremely costly, quite apart from administrative and enforcement costs?

CHAPTER 13

CAPITAL MARKETS

§*13.1.* *Capital market theory.* A share of common stock is
a right to a future stream of income. This suggests that the price
of the share is equal simply to the share's expected earnings discounted to present value. It is true, and for some purposes sufficient, that the price of a share will rise if expected earnings rise
and fall if they fall but it is incorrect that stock prices are a function solely of expected return. Most investors have an aversion
to risk. Between two stocks having identical expected earnings,
they will pay a higher price for the stock that is less risky. Stated
differently, risky stocks have a higher expected return than less
risky stocks.

Another word for risk in this context is *volatility* and a popular
measure of the risk of a stock is to compare its volatility with
that of the market as a whole. A stock whose price on average
rises one percent when the market rises one percent is no riskier
than the market average and has a risk of one. If it rose one-half
percent when the market rose one percent it would be less risky
than the market average, and if it rose ten percent when the
market rose one percent it would be a much greater risk and
would be priced below the safer stock even if both stocks had the
identical expected earnings.[1]

Risk has another important dimension in the securities market.
Compare two investors, one of whom has purchased shares of a
stock the volatility of which is equal to the average of the market
and the other shares of all of the stocks in the market (appropriately weighted). The portfolios comprise shares of the same
average risk; but the first portfolio is a greater risk than the
second portfolio. The first investor has no protection against the

§13.1. 1. A stock that moves *against* the market has a low risk and commands
a high price, because it can be paired by a purchaser with a high risk stock to
produce an investment of very low volatility.

vicissitudes of the particular firm whose shares he owns and of the particular markets in which that firm operates. A labor strike, a sudden shift in demand, the appearance of new competitors, a change in tariff levels or tax laws could greatly affect the expected earnings and hence price of his shares. The owner of a diversified portfolio is shielded against factors operating to depress earnings of one firm or in one market because such factors usually improve earnings of some other firm or in some other markets. Since a strike that reduces the production of one firm may increase the production and profits of a competing firm, the investor who holds shares of both firms in his portfolio is largely insulated against the effect of the strike.

Although the nondiversified portfolio is thus riskier than the diversified portfolio, it will not yield a higher return than the diversified portfolio (unless, contrary to our assumption, the average stock in the nondiversified portfolio is more volatile than the average stock in the diversified portfolio). The prices of volatile stocks are bid down because otherwise they could not be sold, given the prevalent risk aversion of investors. The seller must compensate the buyer for the risk that the buyer assumes. The return to the holder of a portfolio of stocks, however, is simply the sum of the returns of the individual stocks. No one compensates the holder of a nondiversified portfolio. Not only is diversifiable risk uncompensated, but it can ordinarily be eliminated readily. The holder is free to diversify and can do so at moderate transaction cost; the small investor can diversify by purchasing shares in common trust or mutual funds that hold diversified portfolios.

The investor who desires an expected return higher than the market average can obtain it by concentrating on stocks of above-average risk. The price he pays for the higher expected return is a level of risk higher than the market average. The investor who desires a lower level of risk than the market average can obtain it by concentrating on stocks of below-average risk; the price he pays for a lower level of risk is a reduction in his expected return.

The investor can achieve the same objectives by combining the purchase of stocks of average risk with borrowing or lending, instead of purchasing stocks that are above or below the average in risk. Suppose the investor has $100,000 of his own money to invest and a target rate of return of 12 percent. He can select stocks whose average expected rate of return is 12 percent; these stocks would have a greater risk than average. Or, assuming the average expected return for the market as a whole is 10 percent and the applicable interest rate 6 percent, he can borrow $50,000 and invest his total capital, now $150,000, in a portfolio having an average risk equal to that of the market as a whole. His expected return, 10 percent of $150,000 ($15,000), minus his interest cost (6 percent of $50,000, or $3000), will be $12,000, which represents a 12 percent return on his investment. This "levered" portfolio, however, will be riskier than an unlevered market portfolio. If the market falls by 5 percent, the value of his portfolio will decline by 7.5 percent; if it rises by 5 percent, the value of his portfolio will increase by 7.5 percent.[2]

Many investors attempt to increase their expected return not by the manipulation of risk but by trying to outguess the market. They may try to anticipate general market movements, or pick stocks that they think the market has valued incorrectly (undervalued stocks to buy, overvalued stocks to sell). A number of economists now believe that the costs of search and execution and the almost inevitable underdiversification entailed by efforts to beat the market generally exceed the returns.[3] Some evidence for this position is provided by the performance of the mutual funds, which employ highly skilled, or at least well-remunerated, financial analysts in an effort to outperform the market. Not only have the mutual funds as a whole been outperformed by the market in many years, but a mutual fund that ranks first in its risk class one year is as likely to rank last next year as it is to place near the top again.

This suggests that the stock market is an *efficient* market, in which new information about a stock is disseminated so rapidly that possession of such information in advance does not enable an investor to clean up. (Another problem is knowing whether the advance information is really true.) The implication is not that every stock is correctly valued at every moment in time but that the cost of finding out whether or not it is correctly valued will usually exceed the profit to be made from knowing its true value.

§*13.2. Monopoly again.*   Let us proceed now to some legal applications of capital market theory. In the chapter on monop-

2. What should the investor do if he wants to reduce the risk of his portfolio below the market risk?

3. For a lucid exposition of this view see Fischer Black, Implications of the Random Walk Hypothesis for Portfolio Management, Financial Analysts J. 1 (Mar.-Apr. 1970). Stock picking leads to underdiversification because the investor cannot follow closely many stocks at once.

oly, we noted the argument of some economists that monopoly impairs the incentive to reduce input costs and to innovate; or, as a distinguished English economist once put it, that "the best of all monopoly profits is a quiet life." [1] Neither he nor later economists suggested a theoretical or empirical basis for the proposition and there is a theoretical reason against it. As soon as a monopoly is anticipated, the price of the firm's common stock will increase as a method of discounting the expected monopoly profits until the ratio of expected earnings to market price is just equal to the normal rate of return of stocks in the firm's risk class. Thereafter, none of the shareholders will be conscious of receiving monopoly profits. Shareholders who purchased after the formation of the monopoly will clearly not receive such a return. If the managers of the firm are indolent, the price of the stock will rise more slowly than other stocks (it may, of course, not rise at all, or it may fall). The fact that the firm is still earning some monopoly profits will be of small comfort to the shareholders, who will consider themselves losers, or the managers, who will be thought to be slipping (or just plain bad, if they are merely the successors to the management that obtained the monopoly). The firm will be an attractive target for a takeover bid by someone who thinks he can increase its monopoly profits by reducing costs.

Capital market theory may also have a contribution to make to the control of regulated monopolists' profits. The elimination of monopoly profits by regulation is complicated by the difficulty of ascertaining the true cost of equity capital, due to the absence of a directly observable price. The present approach of regulators is a largely circular process of basing the permitted rate of return on the rates of return of other regulated companies. If the regulators were instead to begin by measuring the volatility of the regulated firm's stock, they could fix a level of permitted earnings such that the expected return to the firm's investors was equal to that of investors in nonregulated firms of the same risk (volatility) level. This would be the true cost to the regulated firm of attracting equity capital without diluting the value of the shares held by existing shareholders. The problem, however, is that regulation itself may have reduced the stock's volatility, so there is still circularity.

At the least, capital market theory might be useful in deflect-

§13.2. 1. J. R. Hicks, Annual Survey in Economic Theory: The Theory of Monopoly, 3 Econometrica 1, 8 (1935).

ing regulatory agencies (and their critics) from what are largely spurious issues, such as the optimum debt-equity ratio. It is tempting to argue, in the case of a regulated firm with a very low debt-equity ratio (such as AT & T until recently), that if only the firm would increase its debt-equity ratio its cost of capital would decline — since the interest rate is lower than the return on common stock — and its prices could be reduced. This reasoning is fallacious. It is equivalent to arguing that regulated firms should be more highly levered. But we saw in the first section of this chapter that the use of debt increases the volatility of the equity. A firm that increased the proportion of debt in its capital structure would experience an increase in the cost of its equity capital. The interest rate on its debt would also rise, since a reduction in the proportion of equity increases the risk to the holders of the debt. Not only is there no reason to think that the overall cost of capital would be lower with a higher debt-equity ratio, but, as we shall see, there is reason to believe that were it not for certain tax advantages associated with debt financing the cost of capital to the firm would be identical for any debt-equity ratio.[2]

§*13.3.   The prudent man rule of trust law.*   There is an extensive body of law governing the trustee's duties in managing trust funds. Our interest here is in the principle that in managing such funds the trustee must act prudently and cautiously with the primary purpose of preserving the principal of the trust. The assumption is that the beneficiaries of trusts are, in general, risk averse and therefore prefer to receive a lower expected return in exchange for taking fewer risks. The assumption is reasonable, at least in many trusts. The usual beneficiaries are widows and minor children, whose alternative income opportunities may be highly limited. If as a result of risky investments of the principal the trust income declines steeply, their position may become extremely awkward. Risky investments are more attractive to people who have regular salaries or other stable sources of basic income that protect their standard of living if the investments go sour.[1]

The creator of a trust who desires the trustee to make risky investments can so provide by appropriate language in the trust instrument. The prudent man rule serves the now familiar function of reducing transaction costs by implying a provision in

2. Or at least for most debt-equity ratios. See §14.2 *infra.*
§13.3. 1. Cf. §15.2 *infra.*

every instrument (unless there is language to the contrary) that the parties otherwise would incorporate by express language.

While the general principle underlying the prudent man standard makes economic sense, the way in which the standard is applied frequently does not. In particular, the standard is erroneously applied to individual investments rather than to portfolios. However well the portfolio performs, the trustee may be held accountable for the poor showing of one of the investments in the portfolio if he failed to verify the soundness of that investment before making it. This approach has three bad consequences. First, trustees are induced to spend time and money in investigating the prospects of individual securities even though, if the securities markets are efficient markets, the costs of search and execution involved in identifying and acquiring undervalued securities and in continuously reviewing one's portfolio for overvalued securities to sell will usually exceed the benefits. Second, trustees are deterred from investing in perfectly good securities merely because the company that has issued the securities has poor earnings prospects. There is no presumption in economic theory that the stock prices of bankrupt or declining firms are typically overvalued. Rather, one expects those prices to be bid down to the point where the company's expected earnings (whatever they may be) will yield the investor a normal return on his investment for securities with the stock's volatility, which may be low.[2] Yet a trustee who knowingly bought the shares of a bankrupt firm would probably be considered to have acted imprudently. Third, and probably most serious, the investment-by-investment application of the prudent man rule induce trustees to hold underdiversified portfolios. If the trustee is to investigate every stock that he purchases and monitor it continuously after purchase, the number of different stocks that he can hold in the portfolio may be quite limited. The portfolio will not be well diversified and as a result the beneficiary of the trust will be exposed to a high level of uncompensated risk that could have been diversified away at low cost. There is some recognition in the cases of the benefits of diversification, but it is generally held that an underdiversified portfolio is proper if the trustee has "carefully" selected the securities in it, whereas a broadly diver-

2. The firm may have a positive value even if its present earnings are zero or negative: its assets may have salvage value, or it may have the prospect of earnings in the future.

sified portfolio would still expose the trustee to legal risk if he has not (as, for the reasons just stated, he could not have) investigated each stock in the portfolio.

One manifestation of the law's misconceived preoccupation with care in the selection of individual investments is the concept, embodied in many state statutes and judicial decisions, that whole categories of investments are unlawful for a trustee unless expressly permitted to him in the trust instrument. For a long time trustees were not permitted to invest in common stocks. This naturally led them to invest heavily in bonds. What was overlooked was that a long-term bond exposes the owner to a risk that he would avoid if he invested in stock (or a short-term debt instrument): the risk that the rate of inflation will increase. A bond is perfectly good protection against the existing and expected rate of inflation, for the interest rate fixed in the bond will include an offset for that rate. But should the inflation rate unexpectedly increase during the term of the bond, the resulting reduction in the real (net of inflation) value of the bond will be borne entirely by the bondholder.[3] A risk-averse investor would not want to, and does not have to, bear that risk.

Even today, the law in many states limits the authority of trustees to purchase shares in mutual funds. Yet where the assets of a trust are small it may be impossible to achieve reasonable diversification other than by purchasing shares in a mutual fund. The basis of the rule limiting the trustee's authority in this respect is the notion that by purchasing mutual fund shares the trustee abdicates to the mutual fund's managers his key responsibility of selecting the investments for the trust. This notion rests on the false premise that a trustee by careful selection can outperform the market by a margin greater than the expenses he incurs in the exercise.

With the law so out of phase with economic reality, we would predict that the draftsmen of trust instruments would commonly include language waiving the limitations that are imposed by trust law in the absence of appropriate language. While there is no systematic evidence that this has happened, the impression is that it has. Most current trust instruments waive the detailed

---

3. The inflation will lead to an increase in the market rate of interest. See §4.10 *supra*. The price of the bond will be bid down until the interest it pays yields the market rate of interest on the price of the bond. Those who bought the bond when the market rate of interest was lower will therefore suffer a loss.

limitations of trust law and vest broad discretion in the trustee: thus the remarkable paucity in recent years of reported litigation involving alleged breaches by trustees of their investment duties under trust law. The major significance of this body of law today may lie in increasing the legal costs incidental to the creation of trusts.

§13.4.   *The regulation of the securities markets.*   We have thus far treated the efficiency of the securities markets as a given. But in fact there is an extensive body of regulations administered by the stock exchanges and the Securities and Exchange Commission that is founded on the premise that, without such regulation, the securities markets would not function satisfactorily.

Why have securities markets been singled out for unusually extensive regulation? The reason is not that securities markets are naturally less efficient than most other markets, but is perhaps that they are associated with a misconception about the Depression. It was natural to think that the 1929 stock market crash must have been a cause of the Depression: *post hoc ergo propter hoc.* The theoretical basis for such an inference is unclear. A precipitous decline in stock prices is much more likely to result from the expectation of a decline in economic activity than to cause the decline.

The regulation of the securities markets has two principal aspects, both intended to reduce the likelihood of a recurrence of a 1929-type crash. First, new issues of stock may be sold only by means of a prospectus, approved by the SEC in advance, that contains certain required information (including adverse information) deemed material to a purchaser. Second, trading in securities is subject to a variety of restrictions designed to dampen "speculative fever" and increase public confidence in the securities markets.

There is serious question whether either branch of regulation is effective in achieving its formal objectives. Capital markets are competitive and competitive markets generate, without government prodding, information concerning the products sold. It is especially plausible to expect the capital markets to generate abundant and, on the whole, accurate information about new issues in view of the presence of (1) sophisticated middlemen — the underwriters who market new issues — between issuer and purchaser, (2) sophisticated purchasers such as trust companies, mutual funds, and pension funds, and (3) the many financial analysts employed by brokerage firms and by independent investment advisory services.[1] Indeed, since prospectuses are written in a forbidding legal and accounting jargon, they are of no direct value to the unsophisticated stock purchaser. Nor is it obvious that the disclosure requirements imposed by the SEC in fact increase the flow of information. By limiting selling efforts to the prospectus, and by taking a restrictive view of what may be properly included in a prospectus (for example, the SEC is hostile to earnings projections), the SEC limits the amount of information communicated by the issuer.

In a famous study George J. Stigler showed that purchasers of new issues before the registration system was initiated in 1933 fared, on average, no worse than purchasers of new issues today.[2] Although the details of the study are controversial, the general conclusion — that the effect of regulation on the market in new issues is negligible — is widely accepted by economists.

Much securities law is intended to reduce speculation in stock. We have already remarked the deep-rooted although economically irrational hostility to speculation.[3] In stock trading as elsewhere, speculation serves the salutary purpose of enabling rapid adjustments of prices to current values. The speculator is the eager searcher for undervalued and overvalued securities. The information that he uncovers diffuses rapidly throughout the market (the rapidity with which information spreads in the stock market is the principal reason why it is so hard to outperform the market consistently), enabling other traders to adjust as rapidly as possible to the changed conditions discovered by the speculator. (Oddly, the expected returns of speculators are relatively low compared to the risks involved, suggesting that they are recruited from among the ranks of the risk preferring: society thus buys the important social function of speculation at a low price.)

The law discriminates against people who speculate on a downturn in the market, for example, by forbidding shares to be sold short at a price lower than the most recent price at which the share has traded. The legal attitude resembles the ancient practice of punishing a bearer of bad tidings, since that is who the successful speculator on a market downturn is. One who sells

§13.4. 1. Too many, perhaps? As mentioned later in this section, stock brokerage is a cartelized activity. What relevance? Cf. problem 5 at the end of Chapter 9.

2. George J. Stigler, Public Regulation of the Securities Market, 37 J. Bus. U. Chi. 117 (1964).

3. See §2.3 *supra*.

a stock short (i.e., agrees to deliver at the current market price, hoping that the price of the stock will fall so that he can buy it when delivery is due at less than he has sold it) will lose money unless he has correctly predicted a decline in the price of the stock. He cannot bring about that decline. The short sale signals to other traders the short seller's forecast; but he has no power to coerce their agreement. The legal attitude toward short selling is especially odd in view of the concern with avoiding panics. To the extent that short selling is discouraged, market declines are likely to be more rather than less precipitous. The making of short sales is a signal that some traders believe the stock or stocks being sold short are overvalued. The signal facilitates prompt, continuous adjustment to the changed conditions underlying the decline in the stock's price.

A major endeavor to contain speculative fever is the limitation on the purchase of stock on margin. In our vocabulary, it is a limitation on the amount of leverage that may be employed in the purchase of stocks. On the basis of our earlier discussion of leverage, we would predict that margin limitations would have little or no effect on risky or speculative behavior. Leverage is one way of increasing the risk and expected return of a purchase but an alternative that the margin limitation does not reach is to hold a portfolio of high-risk securities. Indeed, if there is sufficient taste for risk, we would expect to find publicly traded companies increasing their debt-equity ratios in order to create more risky, and hence to some investors more attractive, securities. (As we discuss in the next chapter, this may indeed have happened.)

Like many partial controls, the margin limitation may be worse than ineffectual. Some economists believe that it has created an artificial demand for the more volatile stocks listed on the exchanges, resulting in the bidding up of the prices of those stocks to the point where the expected return is below that of less volatile stocks, after correction for the difference in volatility.[4] It may seem contradictory to posit a class of highly risk-preferring investors in view of our earlier statement, offered as a basic premise of capital market theory, that most investors are risk averse. The statements are consistent. While most investors are risk averse, the stock market also attracts a certain number of risk preferrers, including a number of outright gamblers. The

4. See Fischer Black, Michael C. Jensen, & Myron Scholes, The Capital Asset Pricing Model: Some Empirical Tests (U. Rochester, Coll. Bus. Adm., Systems Analysis Program, Wkg. Paper Ser., No. F7030, Nov. 1970).

stock market is an attractive gambling medium, in part because the overhead — the "house take" (consisting primarily of brokerage commissions) — is very low compared to a Las Vegas gambling casino, for example. The SEC's efforts to limit gambling on the stock market are probably unsuccessful, and distort the relative values of different risk classes of stock.

One of the most questionable features of the SEC's regulation of the capital markets is its condonation of the long-existing cartel of stock brokers.[5] The price of a seat on the New York Stock Exchange is simply the capitalized value of the monopoly profits received by a member of the cartel. The asserted justification for the cartel is safety. Yet public confidence in the securities markets has survived the recent and well-publicized bankruptcies of several large brokerage firms. Further, there is now a federally supported program of insurance for investors against losses due to brokerage firm failures.

SUGGESTED READINGS

1. Richard A. Brealey, An Introduction to Risk and Return from Common Stocks (1969).
2. Fischer Black, Implications of the Random Walk Hypothesis for Portfolio Management, Financial Analysts J. 1 (Mar.-Apr. 1971).
3. John W. O'Brien, How Market Theory Can Help Investors, Financial Analysts J. 91 (July-Aug. 1970).
4. Economic Policy and the Regulation of Corporate Securities (Henry G. Manne ed. 1969) (relevant to Chapter 14 also).

PROBLEMS

1. You want to set up a mutual fund that will be based on the teachings of modern capital market theory. What will be the investment policy of the fund? Sketch the main provisions of the fund's corporate charter. A, a wealthy individual, is interested in investing money in the fund. What doubts is he likely to express? What arguments might you use to allay those doubts? B, a trustee, is interested in the possibility of investing trust funds in your fund. What doubts is he likely to raise? What arguments might you use to allay his doubts? Does it make a difference who the beneficiaries of the trust administered by B are — whether widows and minor children, a hospital, members of an employees' pension plan? How would your answers to any of these questions be different if the fund proposed to employ leverage?

5. For an excellent discussion see William F. Baxter, NYSE Fixed Commission Rates: A Private Cartel Goes Public, 22 Stan. L. Rev. 675 (1970).

2. *Should a trustee be permitted (in the absence of explicit language in the trust instrument) to invest in real estate equities? In real estate mortgages? Should he be permitted to operate a business with the trust funds, as opposed to mere passive investing?*

3.[1] *The absolute priority rule of federal bankruptcy law is designed to assure that the claims of bondholders are fully satisfied before shareholders are permitted to receive any money from the corporation. Suppose Z Corp. is undergoing reorganization under Chapter X of the bankruptcy act, having defaulted on its bonds, which are now owed $100 in principal plus accrued interest. If Z Corp. is liquidated immediately, it will realize only $50 from the sale of its assets. However, if Z Corp. continues as a going concern, it can operate for one more year, at the end of which time its assets will have been all used up, with the following table of possible earnings from one year's operations:*

EARNINGS ($)	PROBABILITY
0	*1/3*
110	*1/3*
220	*1/3*

The expected earnings figure — the weighted average of all possible earnings outcomes — is $110. Assuming that a discount rate of 10 percent is appropriate for the level of risk associated with Z Corp.'s possible outcomes, its present going concern value is obtained by discounting the expected outcome of $110 at the end of one year by 10 percent. Thus its going-concern value equals 110/1.10, which is $100.

On the basis of this estimate of Z Corp.'s future earning capacity, two alternative plans for reorganization are proposed.

(1) PLAN A, proposed by Z Corp.'s old bondholders. The present going concern value exactly equals what the bondholders are owed. Therefore, they propose a plan under which all the ownership interests in the new corporation go to them. Under PLAN A, of course, the old common stockholders are wiped out completely. If PLAN A is adopted the securities received by the old bondholders will have a table of possible outcomes identical with that for the company as a whole.

(2) PLAN B, proposed by Z Corp.'s common stockholders, who make the following argument: "Since the appropriate rate of return for Z Corp.'s risk is 10 percent, the bondholders who are owed $100 should not be allowed to receive any more than $110, in one year. Therefore, PLAN A overcompensates the bondholders in the event the company succeeds beyond expectations and earns $220. The absolute priority rule simply requires that the bondholders receive the first $110 which Z Corp. earns at the end of one year. Any residue over that amount rightfully belongs to the old common stockholders." Under PLAN B, the old bondholders are to receive new bonds, entitled to a maximum of $110 out of the earnings available at the end of the year's operations,

Problems. 1. This problem is borrowed from Stephen B. Cohen.

while the old common stockholders are to receive new common stock which entitles them to any residue once the new bonds have been paid off.

Which plan is closer to the spirit of the absolute priority rule?

CHAPTER 14

THE PUZZLE OF THE CONGLOMERATE CORPORATION

The rise, and abrupt decline, of the conglomerate corporation is a fascinating episode in the financial history of the 1960s. An analysis of the conglomerate phenomenon will serve to bring together a number of the themes in this part of the book.

A conglomerate corporation is one that sells in many seemingly unrelated product lines. Such corporations were formed and grew, mostly through merger, at a smart pace during the 1960s. Many explanations have been offered for the success of the conglomerate, and they have different implications for appropriate legal policy toward this type of firm.

§14.1. Managerial aspects of the conglomerate form. It has been suggested that improvements in managerial techniques have increased the span of control that can be efficiently exercised by an individual or small group. This could be expected to result in a growing concentration of corporate assets in the hands of those possessing presumably scarce managerial skills, since they can now exercise these skills over a broader range without loss of control — the factor that limits the size of firms. A variant of this suggestion is the idea that a large conglomerate corporation can adopt a decentralized, in place of the normal hierarchical, form of organization more easily than a single-product firm.[1] The suggestion reverses the common sense expectation that decentralized forms of organization are adopted to cope with the control problems created by large and diversified organizations. Decentralization is a response to unwieldiness and should be unnecessary in a compact organization.

§14.2. Diversification and leverage. A second efficiency

§14.1. 1. See Oliver E. Williamson, Corporate Control and Business Behavior 141–145 (1970).

argument is that the conglomerate corporation overcame certain inefficiencies in the financial structures of many firms. This argument has two points. The first is that a highly diversified firm, by reducing the risk to the investors, enables capital to be acquired at lower cost than if the firm were not diversified. This seems doubtful. A shareholder whose portfolio consists of shares in single-product firms active in different markets enjoys the same benefits of diversification that he would enjoy if those firms were consolidated into a single conglomerate corporation and he exchanged his shares for the equivalent amount of stock in the new firm. As emphasized in the previous chapter, what is important to an investor is the diversification of his portfolio, not whether individual stocks are diversified.

The second point under financial structure is that many firms purchased by conglomerate corporations had low debt-equity ratios and that the conglomerate, by increasing that ratio, increased the return to the shareholders. This point is often coupled with the first in the argument that the conglomerate's diversification enables it to minimize the risks associated with high debt-equity ratios.

It is doubtful, however, that the value of the shareholders' equity can be increased by tinkering with the debt-equity ratio.[1] Consider a hypothetical firm that has one million shares of common stock outstanding, no debt, and an annual net operating income of $3 million that is expected to continue at that level. Since the value of a firm is the present discounted value of its expected income, the value of our hypothetical firm will be some multiple of $3 million. Suppose it is ten times $3 million or $30 million. (What determines the multiple?) The price of a share of stock in the firm is then $30, the earnings per share $3, and the price-earnings ratio ten to one. Now suppose the firm borrows $15 million, at six percent interest, and uses it to buy back one half of the outstanding shares of common stock, which it then retires. The operating net income is unchanged but there is now an interest expense of $900,000, which reduces the shareholders' earnings to $2.1 million. This is $4.20 per share (since the number of shares has been reduced from 1 million to 500,000). If the price-earnings ratio is unchanged at ten to one, each share of stock will be worth $42 and the aggregate shareholders' equity

---

§14.2. 1. But cf. discussion *supra* §13.4 of the effect of the SEC's margin limitations on investor interest in risky securities, and discussion *infra* this section of tax advantages of debt financing.

will be $21 million. The value of the firm will therefore be $36 million ($21 million equity plus $15 million debt). It seems that the change in the debt-equity ratio has created a new value of $6 million.

But something must be wrong. The net assets of the firm were worth $30 million originally because they generated net operating income of $3 million a year. Nothing has happened to make those assets more productive; they still generate $3 million in annual income. Why would a purchaser now pay $36 million for the assets? The answer is that he would not.

The fallacy in the hypothetical is the assumption that the price-earnings ratio is unaffected by the amount of debt in the firm's capital structure. But we know that the addition of leverage increases the risk to the shareholder. Formerly, if one year the firm's net operating income declined by one half, the shareholder's return also declined by one half. Now, should the firm's net operating income decline from $3 million to $1.5 million, the earnings of the shareholder will decline from $4.20 per share to $1.20 per share (a fall of more than 70 percent), due to the fact that the firm's interest expense is fixed. Therefore we can expect the price-earnings ratio of the stock to be lower than before the addition of leverage. Indeed, since the value of the firm's assets is unaffected by how the firm chooses to arrange its capital structure, we would expect the firm's price-earning ratio to fall to 7.14 to 1, for this is the ratio at which the value of the firm is unchanged from before.[2]

There is no reason to expect the purchaser of a firm to pay a premium because its capital structure contains leverage, even if he prefers a high risk investment with a high expected return. The purchaser of a firm that has zero leverage can create his preferred debt-equity ratio by purchasing some of the stock with borrowed money. Or he can pair his purchase with investments in highly levered or otherwise highly risky firms. Why, in our example, should he pay $6 million more for a firm (or some fraction for shares of its stock) in order to obtain a level of risk and expected return that he can create for himself, at relatively small cost, in a variety of ways?

The purity of the analysis is impaired by the differential tax treatment accorded interest and earnings. The government subsidizes the raising of capital through borrowing rather than the

---

2. It may, however, remain somewhat higher if the suggestion, made *supra* §13.4, that risky stocks are often overpriced is correct.

issuance of stock by permitting corporations to deduct the cost of borrowed, but not of equity, capital from their taxable income. In addition, when a firm's debt-equity ratio is very high, the risks both to the holders of debt and to the shareholders may become so great that the firm will be unable to attract either sort of investor. The amount of leverage in its capital structure is therefore not a matter of complete indifference to the shareholder. Some firms may not have enough debt in their capital structure to maximize their after-tax earnings, adjusted for risk. These firms might be attractive candidates for takeover by a sophisticated conglomerate. It seems unlikely, however, that this factor provides an adequate explanation of the conglomerate movement.

§14.3.   *The conglomerate as a device for facilitating takeover.* As discussed earlier,[1] a takeover of a large firm by individuals is very difficult to accomplish. They must either wage a costly proxy campaign or obtain enough cash to purchase a controlling interest in the firm. A corporation is in a much better position to take over the firm at reasonable cost since it can offer its own stock instead of cash and since, should cash be necessary, it can raise the required amount more easily than an individual or group of individuals.

One might expect takeovers to be attempted normally by firms in the same product field, for they are more likely to know when a firm in that field is undervalued than outsiders. But the takeover of a firm in the same field as the acquiring firm is frequently prohibited by the antitrust laws. We would therefore expect takeovers very commonly to take the form of conglomerate acquisitions.

§14.4.   *Monopoly arguments.*   The explanations thus far examined assume that the conglomerate firm promotes efficiency in the use of resources. It has also been claimed that the growth of the conglomerate is a subtle form of monopolization. Three arguments are made. The first is that a conglomerate acquisition eliminates the acquiring firm as a potential competitor in the market of the acquired firm. But a reduction by one in the number of potential competitors in a market is unlikely to make a difference in the pricing behavior of the firms in the market. The significance of potential competition is that should the firms in the market form a cartel, the resulting high rate of return would induce one or more of the potential competitors to enter the mar-

§14.3. 1. See §12.5 *supra*.

ket, and their sales, by increasing the output of the market above the amount established by the cartel, would force the market price back down. A potential competitor is thus any firm that will be induced to enter the market by a significant increase in price above cost. So defined, most markets must have a large number of potential competitors, given the tendency of resources to gravitate toward more profitable employments. The elimination of one firm should make little difference either to the returns to cartelization or to the rate at which a cartel will be eroded by new entry.

The second argument is that the formation or expansion of a conglomerate firm increases the opportunities to practice reciprocal buying. This is true (why?) but we saw in the chapter on antitrust law that reciprocal buying is generally a harmless (and sometimes a beneficent) practice.[1]

The third argument is that a conglomerate firm, by virtue of the variety of markets in which it operates, is in a stronger position than a single-product firm to exercise political influence. Although there is some spicy anecdotal support for this view, it is not especially persuasive. The diversity of the conglomerate firm's interests is a source of weakness as well as strength, since with respect to many governmental policies a conglomerate will find that some of its divisions are hurt and others benefited. The precipitous decline in conglomerate stock prices in the late 1960s, coupled with the inability of the conglomerates to ward off either antitrust prosecution or disadvantageous changes in accounting conventions, casts doubt on the idea that they possess significant political influence.

If the foregoing analysis is correct, the vigorous prosecution of conglomerate mergers by the Department of Justice represents a misallocation of law enforcement resources. But more than waste is involved. The crackdown has made it more difficult to take over firms — and has been applauded on this very ground by many businessmen.

§14.5. *Fraud.*   It is widely believed that the conglomerate "bubble" was the result of a fraud on the investing public. The precipitous decline in conglomerate stock prices, the near collapse of some conglomerates, and the voluntary spin-off of many conglomerate divisions lend at least superficial credibility to the charge.

According to the fraud theory, the conglomerate firms were

§14.4. 1. See §7.6 *supra.*

able to pull the wool over the investing public's eyes in at least three respects. First, they convinced the public, contrary to our earlier discussion, that they could increase the value of acquired assets by adding or increasing leverage. Second, they persuaded the public not to reduce the price-earnings ratio of their stock when they acquired firms with low price-earnings multiples. Suppose before its acquisition of firm B conglomerate firm A's stock was selling at a price 20 times earnings (which, let us say, were $3 per share). As a result of acquiring B, A's earnings per share increase by $1. Before the acquisition B had a price-earnings ratio of only 10 to 1. A gullible public, it is argued, would bid up the price of the conglomerate's stock to $80 (20 times $4) thereby in effect revaluing the assets of the acquired firm at twice their value before the acquisition. Third, it is alleged that the conglomerate firms, in effecting acquisitions, used complex types of security the implications of which eluded the investor. An example is the convertible debenture, a bond that can be converted at the holder's option to a share (or shares) of common stock. The firm's earnings per share will vary depending on whether or not the convertible debentures are counted as shares of stock. It is alleged that the public failed to take the conversion possibility into account in appraising the earnings statements of the conglomerate firms, which reported per-share earnings on an unconverted basis.

The fraud theory is difficult to reconcile with the view, developed earlier, of the stock market as an efficient market in which information is rapidly diffused and acted upon. Investors would have to be awfully gullible to fail to readjust price-earnings ratios when a firm having a low ratio was acquired, or to ignore the dilution possibilities inherent in the issuance of convertible debentures. A more convincing explanation for the collapse of conglomerate share values in the 1969 bear market may be that it was the natural consequence of the fact that the conglomerates were highly levered. In a period of general stock market decline, the prices of conglomerate stocks could be expected to fall more rapidly than the average share in the market. Another possibility is that the fall in share values represented a correction of unrealistic expectations of corporate performance generated by misconceptions concerning the managerial skills of the conglomerates' leaders.

PART IV

LAW AND THE DISTRIBUTION OF INCOME AND WEALTH

CHAPTER 15

INCOME INEQUALITIES AND DISTRIBUTIVE JUSTICE

The first chapter of this book distinguished between the income and the resource effects of a transaction, and in subsequent chapters we have from time to time touched on the effect of legal policies on the distribution of income and wealth. The emphasis in this part will be upon legal policies that reflect an explicit concern with a just distribution.

What has the economist to tell us about the distribution of income? He can tell us something about the existing distribution, how it has changed over time, its determinants, and the effects of legal policies designed to change it. Whether he can supply criteria, comparable to value or efficiency, for preferring one distribution over another is quite another question, but one that in many practical contexts does not have to be answered.

§15.1. *The measurement of inequality.* Money income is distributed unevenly among the people of this country (as in all countries). Economists have various ways of measuring this inequality. In Figure 10, percentage of income received, cumulated from lowest to highest, is expressed as a function of percentage of household units, cumulated from lowest to highest. Were income distributed evenly among all the household units in the country, the function would be the straight line labeled "line of equality." At every point on that line, the fraction of income enjoyed by a given percentage of the household units in the country is exactly equal to that percentage: 20 percent of the units have 20 percent of the income, 55 percent of the units have 55 percent of the income, etc. The more bowed the actual distribution the less equal it is. In 1929 the poorest 40 percent of the household units had, in the aggregate, less than 13 percent of the nation's family personal income. Today, the poorest 20 percent of the nation's families have less than 6 percent of the nation's family

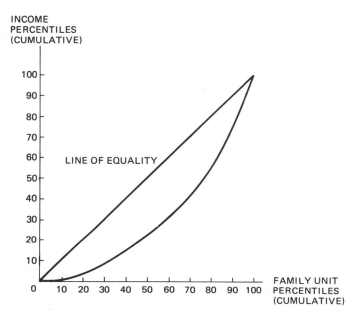

Figure 10

Source: U.S. Dept. of Commerce, Bur. of the Census, Statistical Abstract of the United States 1971, at 317 (1969 data).

personal income, while the richest 5 percent have almost 15 percent.[1] The distribution of income changes slowly and appears to be quite similar for different countries in the same stage of economic development, such as Sweden and the United States, even though the former is usually thought to be a more socialistic society.[2]

Statistics on income inequality do not provide clear-cut guidance for the formulation of social policy. To begin with, being limited to pecuniary income, such statistics ignore many factors that are highly important to welfare but difficult to quantify. For example, compare the following households. In the first both husband and wife work and each earns $10,000 per year. In the second only the husband works; he earns $20,000. The pecuniary

§15.1. 1. See U.S. Dept. of Commerce, Bureau of the Census, Statistical Abstract of the United States 1971, at 317; id., Historical Statistics of the United States 166 (1960). Current figures are for 1969.
2. See Robert M. Solow, Income Inequality Since the War, in Inequality and Poverty 50, 60 (Edward C. Budd ed. 1967).

income of the households is the same, but the real income of the second household is greater. The wife stays home because her services in the home are worth more to the household than the income she would obtain from an outside job. If she is intelligent, energetic, and well educated, her alternative income may be quite high — as high as, or higher than, her husband's. It is because the same qualities may make her an especially competent housewife and mother that her value at home may exceed the pecuniary income she might obtain outside. The real income of the second household may be $40,000 or more.

Even in paying jobs, an important part of the remuneration is often nonpecuniary. Teachers, for example, have traditionally received a part of their income in the form of vacations; pecuniary income figures understate their real income. Conversely, people who set little value on leisure and work very hard may have high pecuniary wages but their real income may be no greater than people with lower money wages and greater income from leisure. Similarly, people in dangerous or unpleasant jobs will, other things being equal, receive higher wages than people whose jobs lack these undesirable characteristics. But the real income of the two groups is the same. Risk (in the sense of economic uncertainty rather than danger) is also important. Suppose that the income of a successful inventor is $100,000 a year and of an unsuccessful inventor zero, and that the likelihood of an inventor's succeeding is one in ten (we ignore intermediate possibilities). The expected income of inventors is then $10,000 and is equal to that of civil servants certain to earn $10,000 every year. If we placed a $10,000 ceiling on the earnings of successful inventors, very few people would choose a career in inventing, for their expected income would be only $1000; they could better that in almost any other occupation.

Taste for risk is an important (and distinct) factor. People who are risk averse will pay (in the form of a lower-than-average expected income) to have less than average volatility in their earnings. Consequently, in a given year their income may be much less than that of the risk preferrer who is having one of his boom years and yet they might be unwilling to change places with the "higher income" risk preferrer.

Another important factor is the temporal distribution of income. A carpenter and a baseball player may have the same lifetime incomes but there will be some years in which the baseball player has a higher income than the carpenter. Lifetime comparisons are complicated by the fact that people have different discount rates.[3] Suppose a young person is choosing between an occupation that requires a long period of educational preparation, during which his income will be zero, and an occupation that he can enter immediately. His lifetime income in the first occupation may be larger than in the second even though the receipt of any income from the first is deferred for a period of years. But if he has a very high discount rate — meaning that future dollars are worth relatively little to him compared to dollars now — the present value of the expected lifetime earnings in the second occupation may be higher than the value of the expected lifetime earnings in the first. He would be worse off if he chose the higher-paying occupation. Another point applicable to the professions is that the high incomes of professionals represent in part repayment of their (or their parents') investment in education, and is thus a return of capital rather than income.[4]

Still another important factor in gauging real equality is the distribution of economic benefits, pecuniary and nonpecuniary, that are not included in most measurements of income. Federal and state government, and to a lesser extent other institutions (hospitals, foundations, etc.), provide a variety of benefits, such as education, police protection, health care, pensions, poor relief, and recreational facilities, without any direct charge. These benefits may have a differential impact on the welfare of different income groups. Not only is it important to measure this impact but it is equally important to determine how the costs (primarily taxes) are distributed among income classes. If, for example, the burden of public education of poor children is borne primarily by poor families, no net transfer of wealth from wealthier classes in society may be accomplished by public education.

For these reasons the proper interpretation of the inequality in money incomes revealed by Figure 10 is unclear. Inequality of real incomes may be greater than Figure 10 reveals, or smaller. Certainly the equalization of pure money incomes would create a great many new income inequalities.

§15.2. Is inequality inefficient?   Let us suppose that real incomes are highly unequal. Can we, as economists, prove that instituting policies designed to move the society closer to equality would increase welfare? In general, the answer is no, and it holds even if the costs of income redistribution are assumed to

---

3. The concept of discounting is explained *supra* §4.10.

4. Of course, if the education was paid for by the state rather than the family, the "repayment" of capital is actually a contribution of capital and is better regarded as a gift than as a form of amortization.

be zero. Income equality is not a criterion, like efficiency, that is linked logically to the economic concept of value. Monopoly is inefficient in the sense that were transactions between monopolists and consumers costless, the consumers would pay the monopolists to increase output and this payment would make both groups better off. Such a payment is possible because the loss to the consumers exceeds the gain to the monopolists.[1] But if two families have different incomes, it cannot be said that a transfer that equalized their incomes would make them better off than before the transfer. The gain to one would be equal to the loss to the other.

Yet many economists used to think that equal incomes would maximize welfare (ignoring incentive effects and other possible costs). Their argument was based on the idea of diminishing marginal utility. Suppose I have one easy chair and then receive a second as a gift. My total utility, the sum of my satisfactions, will be increased, but the second easy chair may well be worth less to me than the first. If I receive a third, and then a fourth, and then a fifth easy chair, the marginal utility to me of easy chairs will probably diminish sharply. Money is a more versatile possession than easy chairs. But the principle of diminishing marginal utility should still hold. I am likely to be more willing to work hard to increase my income from $5000 to $6000 than from $50,000 to $51,000, even if there were no progressive income tax. I am likelier to stake $1000 on a bet if I have $100,000 than if I have $1000.

Given the diminishing marginal utility of money, it is tempting to conclude that a transfer of money from a wealthy man to a poor one is likely to increase the sum of the two men's total utilities: a loss of a dollar hurts the millionaire less than the gain of a dollar helps the pauper. But there is no theoretical basis for this conclusion. In Figure 11, utility is plotted on the vertical axis, money income on the horizontal. The curve on the left shows Mr. A's utility as a function of his money income. His present income is $7000. The area under the curve to the left of $7000 is his total utility. The curve is negatively sloped in accordance with the principle of diminishing marginal utility. Thus, if A's income increased from $7000 to $8000 the increase in his utility (the area under the curve between these two figures) would be smaller than would be the increase in utility if his in-

§15.2. 1. See §6.1 *supra*.

come had been $6000 and rose to $7000. Mr. B's income is $3000. His total utility is the area under the curve on the right-hand side of the diagram to the right of $3000 on his scale.

If $1000 of income is transferred from A to B, A's utility will decrease by the area under his marginal utility curve between $7000 and $6000 on his scale, while B's utility will increase by the area under his marginal utility curve between the same two

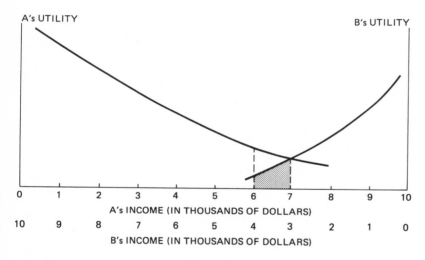

A's UTILITY

B's UTILITY

A's INCOME (IN THOUSANDS OF DOLLARS)

B's INCOME (IN THOUSANDS OF DOLLARS)

Figure 11

points ($3000 and $4000 on his scale). This area (hatched in the diagram) is smaller than the area that measures the diminution in A's utility as a result of the transfer. The transfer has resulted in a diminution in total utility. The reason is that while both A and B have a diminishing marginal utility function, A's is higher than B's in the relevant region (A gets more utility from a dollar than B in that region).

Since the shape and height of people's marginal utility curves are unknown, and probably unknowable, the possibility that wealthier people's marginal utility curves are often higher than poorer people's cannot be negated. Unless we assume that the marginal utility of income is the same regardless of income class, we cannot prove that attaining the line of equality would increase economic welfare. Conversely, unless we assume that marginal utility of income is positively correlated with total income (i.e., that rich people's marginal utility curves are generally higher than poor people's), we cannot conclude that equalizing incomes would reduce total utility.

The entire discussion has ignored the crucial fact that redistributing income is not a costless process, as we shall soon see. Even if it could be shown that redistribution would increase total utility if the costs involved in effecting it were zero, it would be necessary somehow to weigh those costs, which are positive, against the gain.

§15.3. *The contract theory of distributive justice.*   A philosopher, John Rawls, has proposed a theory of justice that, while generally regarded as antithetical to economic theory, may in fact be compatible with it.[1] His view is that the distribution of income and wealth is just if there is no alternative distribution that would make the worst off people in society better off. The optimum distribution may thus be highly unequal, if, for example, the negative impact of a more equal distribution on the incentive to work would be so substantial that the larger slice received by the worst off was smaller in absolute value than the relatively smaller slice that they received under the less equal distribution.

To make the interests of the worst off paramount may appear to violate the principle, developed in the preceding section, that "interpersonal comparisons of utility" are arbitrary. Rawls' justification is that it is plausible to suppose that, if one could somehow poll all of the people who have ever composed or will ever compose the society, in their "original positions" (that is, before they knew what their place in society would be), it would turn out that they preferred a set of arrangements that maximized the position of the worst off. This assumes, of course, that most people are risk averse. Risk preferrers would prefer a set of arrangements that made the payoff from holding a winning ticket in life's lottery higher. The assumption may be plausible,[2] but there are degrees of risk aversion and the degree assumed by Rawls in deriving his principle of justice seems too high. Compare two sets of social arrangements, A and B. A leads to a distribution of income in which the average income of the poorest ten percent of the people in the society is $1000 a year and the

§15.3. 1. John Rawls, A Theory of Justice (1971), especially pt. 1. In view of the remarks about the nature of economic inquiry made in Chapter 1 of this book, his remark that "on the contract view the theory of justice is part of the theory of rational choice" is significant. Id. at 47.

2. See id. ch. 3, especially §29.

average income of all of the people in the society is also $1000. B leads to a distribution of income in which the average income of the poorest ten percent is $900 but the average income of all of the people in society is $3000. These distributions are compared in Figure 12. Is it obvious that people in the original position, although risk averse, would choose A? Surely not.[3] But all

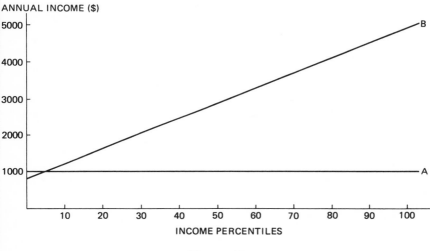

Figure 12

this shows is that the specific form of Rawls' principle of justice is not established. His basic point, that justice requires that society take some measure to improve the lot of the worst off in society, is not affected.

Rawls' approach ingeniously breaks the impasse that arose in

3. Especially since Rawls assumes that no one in the original position is afflicted by envy. If envy were assumed to be an important part of people's psychological makeup, the utility of a larger income in a society in which incomes were highly unequal might be less than that of a smaller income in a society in which incomes were equal (why?). Incidentally, Rawls is aware of the problem discussed in the text, but dismisses it, primarily on the ground that large increases in the welfare of the better off would almost certainly also increase the welfare of the worst off, at least when other safeguards incorporated into his principle of justice (such as open competition for positions) are taken into account. See id. at 157–158. This seems to leave out of consideration, however, the possibility that substantial reductions in the welfare of the better off might lead to a trivial improvement in the welfare of the worst off, in which event a set of institutional arrangements that bore very heavily on the well-to-do might be required by his principle of justice.

the previous section when we tried to compare the utilities of people *after* the lottery tickets had been drawn. An individual's utility may be diminished when his winning ticket is taken away from him and given to someone else even though the lottery was not conducted fairly. If A slices a cake and gives B the largest piece, B may be reluctant to give a portion of it to C, who received the smallest piece, but his reluctance is irrelevant to whether the method of slicing the cake was fair. Rawls' approach embodies the intuitively appealing principle of fairness that if one person slices the cake and the other gets first pick the division of the cake will be fair even if it is unequal.

Rawls asks us to do what we have done many times in this book: imagine the content of a contract that cannot be made in the market because of high transaction costs. People in the "original position" know that the wealth of the society may be divided up in many ways. They presumably want some protection against getting a very small slice (unless the pie is very large), or no slice at all. Rawls' principle, like the rule for dividing cakes (which it resembles), provides them with such protection.

Unfortunately, Rawls' theory of distributive justice has little operational content.[4] There is the problem, mentioned earlier, of determining what degree of risk aversion to assume. There is also the problem of deciding who shall be counted as worst off, which Rawls recognizes but does not attempt to resolve.[5] If the worst off is a single person, some measures will be deemed unjust that would be just if the worst off were, for example, the poorest income decile. Whether the relevant universe is a single society or the entire world is also critical (why?), as is whether "worst off" is to be understood strictly in money income terms, with all the problems that measure involves,[6] or more broadly. Moreover, as we shall see, it is extremely difficult to determine in advance the effect of a change in policy on the worst off, except in the case of policies (such as farm price supports) that almost every observer agrees *both* harm the worst off *and* are inefficient — and so are outside the area of debate.

§*15.4. The practical issue.*   Our inability to come up with an operational concept of optimum distribution is a less serious problem than one might at first suppose. A great many policy matters can in practice be disposed of quite easily once the distributive effects are identified, which the economist can often do.

4. But cf. §19.2 *infra.*
5. See John Rawls, *supra* note 1, at 98.
6. See §15.1 *supra.*

A policy is not likely to be supported today, at least explicitly, if it increases the inequality of income. And while the economist cannot offer reasons for seeking to attain more equal distribution of income, he can sometimes offer efficiency reasons for various redistributive policies. For example, there is some reason to believe that severe inequality of income within an area may increase the crime rate; redistribution of wealth may therefore be a cost-justifiable measure for reducing the inefficiency caused by a high crime rate.[1] In practice, then, the economist's inability to establish a normative criterion of income distribution may not prevent him from contributing to the solution of social problems related to income inequality.

SUGGESTED READINGS

1. Inequality and Poverty (Edward C. Budd ed. 1967).
2. Milton Friedman, Price Theory, ch. 12 (1962).
3. Amartya K. Sen, Collective Choice and Social Welfare, ch. 9 (1970).
4. Henry C. Simons, Personal Income Taxation, ch. 1 (1938).

PROBLEMS

1. Suppose that society desires to bring about a greater equality of incomes. Suppose further that there is a measure that can be expected to reduce the average income of the wealthiest decile in society by one percent and increase the average income of the poorest decile by ten percent. However, the policy is costly: it will reduce the total income of the society by one percent. How does one trade off benefits in greater income equality against costs in reduced efficiency?

2. If the principle of the diminishing marginal utility of money is accepted, does it follow that a corporation that obtains a monopoly and thereby increases its profits will become less concerned with minimizing its costs? Is the principle applicable to organizations at all?

3. Can the principle of compensating victims of accidents for the injuries that they have sustained be derived from principles of distributive justice? Do those principles help one to decide how common law rights and liabilities should be assigned? Is your answer to this question dependent upon a solution to problem 1?

5. You are legislative assistant to a U.S. Senator. He asks you to advise him whether to vote for certain pending bills. He wants your views on the merits, not the politics, of the bills. Advise him. The bills are as follows:

§15.4. 1. We return to this point later. See §25.5 *infra*.

(a) A bill to improve coal-mine safety by requiring the installation of early-warning devices against mine explosions and more frequent safety inspections of mines. The annual cost of these measures is estimated to be $500,000 and is to be defrayed by a special tax on the mining companies.

(b) A bill to provide an annual subsidy out of general tax revenues for railroad passenger service on routes of less than 80 miles, in the amount of $10 million per year.

6. Appraise the following passage, which was written by John Stuart Mill: "[T]he Distribution of wealth . . . is a matter of human institutions only. . . . The rules by which it is determined are what the opinions and feelings of the ruling portion of the community make them, and are very different in different ages and countries; and might be still more different, if mankind so chose." Principles of Political Economy, bk. II, ch. I, §1, at 200 (W. J. Ashley ed. 1926).

CHAPTER 16

TAXATION

§*16.1. Taxation and efficiency.* Taxation is sometimes used as a device for changing resource use (recall our discussion of pollution taxes) or the distribution of wealth, but mainly it is used to pay for public services. An efficient revenue tax would be one that required the user of a public service to pay the opportunity costs of his use, but this would be treating public services just like private goods, whereas they are public services precisely because it is judged infeasible or inexpedient to sell them. In the case of some public services, such as national defense, free-rider problems prevent the use of the market to provide the service: the individual who refused to buy his share of the cost of our nuclear deterrent would receive the same protection from it as those who paid for it. In the case of other public services, such as education, the provision of the service by the government rests on a judgment that unwillingness to pay the cost of the service should not disentitle the individual to use it.[1]

The heavy emphasis placed on distributive considerations in discussions of tax policy explains why the chapter on taxation appears in this part of the book. But efficiency considerations also weigh — or should weigh — heavily. The imposition of a tax on an activity creates an incentive for people engaged in the activity to substitute another activity that is taxed less heavily. But presumably they were more productively employed in the first activity; otherwise the imposition of a tax would not have been necessary to induce them to switch to the second. This implies that the tax has caused a reduction in the efficiency with

§16.1. 1. Recall our discussion (§3.12) of the conflict of interest between parents and children. Observe, however, that the government could require children to attend school, defray part or all of the costs of education for children whose parents lacked monetary means, and establish minimum educational standards — all without actually operating the schools.

which resources are employed. The inefficiency might have been avoided, without revenue loss, had the tax been designed to minimize substitution effects. Unfortunately, attempts to minimize such effects may clash with the distributive goals of tax policy. A flat head tax, for example, has minimum efficiency effects (minimum, but not zero, because it will induce some people to leave the taxing jurisdiction to avoid the tax even though the value of their economic activity may have been greater had they stayed; depending on how it is measured, it may also induce people to reduce family size, again regardless of efficiency). But a flat head tax would be highly oppressive to poor people unless it were very low, in which event it would generate little revenue.

We will discuss the distributive and efficiency consequences of several different forms of taxation in this chapter. Death taxes are touched on in the next chapter, and some special problems of tax policy resulting from the federal structure of our governmental system are discussed in Chapter 20.

§16.2. *Excise taxes.*   We begin with a retail sales tax: for every widget sold the producer[1] must remit 30 percent of the price to the government. If the widget industry is competitive, meaning that before the imposition of the tax the price of a widget was equal to its marginal cost, the price must now rise if the industry is not to sell at a loss. The effect of the tax is to shift the industry's demand schedule (viewed here as the schedule of average revenue to the industry rather than of average cost to the consumer) as shown in Figure 13. The industry's price will be determined by the intersection of the marginal cost schedule with the new average revenue schedule. That price is p_2 and is higher than p_1, the price before the tax was imposed. At the higher price the amount demanded by consumers, q_2, is less than the amount demanded before the tax was imposed. The higher price induces some consumers to shift to other products that now seem cheaper, although in fact they are either more costly to produce than or inferior to widgets (otherwise the substitution would have occurred before the tax led to an increase in the price of widgets). The tax has the same kind of substitution effects as would monopoly pricing of widgets.

The magnitude of the effect depends on the responsiveness of output to changes in price — the elasticity of demand.[2] If de-

§16.2. 1. For simplicity, we assume that the producer sells directly to the consumer. What modifications in the analysis might be necessary if the tax were imposed on a retailer who purchased from the producer?

2. Defined *supra* §7.1.

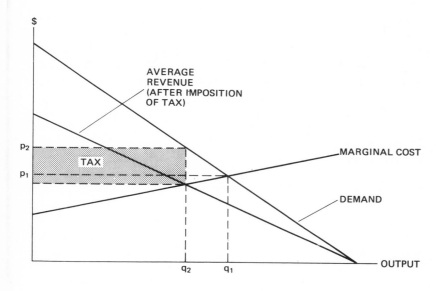

Figure 13

mand is highly elastic, a relatively small increase in price induced by the tax will lead to a relatively large reduction in output. The revenue generated by the tax, being a function of sales, will also be smaller than if the tax had been levied on a product for which the demand was less elastic. Thus, the goals of minimizing the substitution effects of taxation and of maximizing the government's tax revenues both argue for taxing price-inelastic industries or activities.

But what of the distributive effects of the tax? The government revenue generated by the tax is represented in Figure 13 by the hatched area. Notice that most of the tax, $q_2 \times (p_2 - p_1)$, is borne by the consumers of widgets.[3] Taxes on consumption tend to be regressive, that is, to take a larger fraction of the income of the nonwealthy than of the wealthy, because the nonwealthy consume a larger fraction of their income. To be sure, the nature of the product — whether it is more likely to be bought by a wealthy than by a nonwealthy person — is important: a tax on yachts would presumably be progressive. Products in heavy de-

3. How else are consumers hurt by the tax?

mand by the wealthy, however, are not necessarily those for which demand is inelastic, so an efficient excise tax will often be regressive and a progressive excise tax often inefficient.

We said that most of the widget tax was shifted to consumers. The remainder comes out of rents received by the owner of certain factors of production used in making widgets. The concept of "rent" is explained next.

§16.3. Economic rent. Economic rent (not to be confused with rental) is a return, over and above opportunity costs, that the owner of a resource obtains due to its scarcity. The traditional example is the rent of land. Suppose that the price of a bushel of corn is $1 and is equal to the marginal cost of producing corn. The marginal cost includes (1) the opportunity costs of the farm labor, fertilizer, and other labor and capital inputs into corn production and (2) the opportunity cost, equal to the net benefit forgone of its next best alternative use, of the land on which the corn is grown. Suppose I own an acre of especially good cornland. At an annual cost of $50, composed of (1) $30 in various direct costs and (2) $20, the net income I would obtain from devoting the land to its next best use (pasture), my acre yields a corn crop with a market value of $120. The difference ($70) between the price of the crop and its cost is the rent of the land. Marginal cornland, where, let us suppose, a crop worth $80 can be grown at a direct cost of just $80, would yield no rent. Observe that the amount of rent is a function of the price of the crop and that a change in the amount of rent does not affect the use to which the land is put, so long as the rent is nonnegative. If the price of corn rises, the rent of my land will increase and I will keep it in corn. But even if the price of corn plummets, so that my crop is worth only $50.01, I will keep the land in corn since I could not obtain a higher return from an alternative use of the land.

Economic rents are not limited to land. A monopolist obtains rents by creating an artificial scarcity of his product. The difference between him and the landowner is that the scarcity of good cornland is a natural condition that cannot readily be overcome. If the supply of good cornland were unlimited, competition between owners of such land would drive down the price of corn until rents were zero. Star entertainers receive economic rents because their services are in short supply and the supply cannot be expanded readily.

In our widget example, there are economic rents because the industry's costs (in Figure 13, the area under the marginal cost schedule to the left of q_1, before the tax is imposed, and to the left of q_2, after the tax is imposed) is less than the industry's revenue (p_1q_1 or p_2q_2). The divergence results from the fact that marginal cost increases with output in this industry. Evidently, some units of output can be produced at lower cost than others, just as good cornland yields corn at a lower unit cost than marginal cornland. A resource — well-located land, a patented process, skilled management, machinery constructed when costs were low[1] — that enables these units to be produced cheaply must be in short supply, or else it would have been duplicated and used in all of the industry's production, causing the marginal cost curve to flatten out. The owners of these resources (who may be the stockholders of the widget producers or outsiders from whom the producers lease the resource) will obtain economic rents. Just as rents of the owner of cornland will decline if revenue from the sale of corn declines, so in our widget example a reduction in the revenues of the widget industry results in a reduction of rents. The rentiers bear some of the burden of the tax on the sale of widgets.

A tax that fell entirely on rents would have attractive features. There would be no substitution effects. Rents are a return over and above opportunity costs, that is, alternative returns, so a reduction in rents will not induce a shift of the resource to an alternative use. And a tax on rents would be progressive since the recipients of rent are usually, although not invariably, well-to-do.

§16.4.   *Excise taxation of monopoly.*   The taxation of goods produced by monopolists might appear to be a method of applying the preceding observations. A practical problem is to detect monopoly prices and profits. Observe that if monopoly profits could be detected and measured, they could be taxed directly, and since they are rents the tax would have no substitution effects. An *excise* tax on monopolies, however, has essentially the same substitution and distributive effects as excise taxes on the goods of competitive sellers. As shown in Figure 14, the excise tax confronts the monopolist with a new demand (average revenue) schedule, which causes him to recompute his marginal revenue schedule. His new price, at the intersection of his marginal cost and new marginal revenue curves, is higher than the old price and his profit-maximizing output is smaller. The tax (the hatched area in the diagram) is borne by consumers, by the monopolist

§16.3. 1. See §9.2 *supra.*

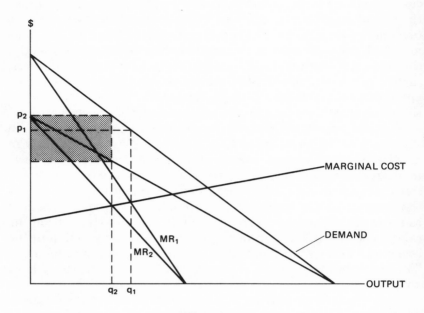

Figure 14

in the form of reduced monopoly profits, and by owners of resources, the supply of which is inelastic, used in the production
of the product.[1]

§16.5. Real estate taxes.   Henry George's famous proposal
to replace all taxes with a single tax on land was an attempt to
limit taxation to pure rents. It is doubtful whether today the
rent of land is sufficiently great to meet all government revenue
demands. There is also a problem of measurement, arising from
the fact that land is more likely to be used by the owner than to
be rented. If I own a piece of land, build an apartment house on
it, and rent the apartments, part of the rental I receive will consist of the rent of the land, but part will consist of revenue from
the improvements on the property and this revenue may not include any rent at all. Or suppose I own and occupy a house on my
land: I receive an imputed rent equal to the rent that I could
have obtained by leasing the land. Still another problem is that
many rentiers are not wealthy people. A heavy tax on the rent

§16.4. 1. Figure 14 depicts an excise tax computed as a percentage of the firm's
gross receipts. What if the excise tax were computed as a flat tax (e.g., two cents
per widget)? Cf. §10.5 *supra*, note 1.

of land would impoverish many farmers, workmen, and retirees who had purchased land at a price that capitalized the expected rents. Suppose a farmer, using borrowed money, buys good farmland for $1000 that yields an annual rent of $100, net of property taxes. A tax of $90 a year is later imposed on the property. His return will fall to $10. If he sells the land, he will recover only a small fraction of the money that he paid for it.

Real estate taxes tax the rent of land but much else besides. Indeed, the improvements to land are usually taxed much more heavily than the land itself. One result is to give landowners an artificial incentive to avoid (or postpone) improving their land. More important, a tax on land improvements has much the same effect as our widget excise tax. Consider apartment house developments. If the real estate tax is proportioned to the rent rolls, the owners of developments will treat it in the same way that our widget manufacturers treated the sales tax: as reducing average revenue by a uniform percentage at all levels of output. To maximize return in these circumstances, they will raise price and reduce output. The burden of the tax will be shared between consumers — the people to whom apartments are rented — and rentiers — the owners of the land. Such a tax may be quite inefficient and regressive.[1]

The real estate tax subtly undermines the property rights system. Suppose I am a farmer in an area where more and more land is being developed for residential purposes. My land is worth only $100 as farmland but a developer offers me $200. I refuse because the land is worth more to me than to him — I am sentimentally attached to the land and do not want to move. At what value should the real estate tax assessor appraise the land? If he assesses it at the higher value he may force me to sell to the developer, since my farm income may be insufficient to pay a tax assessed on the basis of a use of the land that yields a larger pecuniary income. From the assessor's standpoint this forced exchange is a good thing because it increases the tax base. But the land is more valuable to me than to the developer. The real estate tax has the same effect here as eminent domain, which also systematically extinguishes land values in excess of market price.[2]

§16.6.   *Corporate income taxation.*   The corporate income tax is in one aspect a crude device for taxing rents, here the rent

§16.5. 1. Cf. §18.6 *infra.*
2. See §2.5 *supra.*

that consists of the difference between a firm's total revenues and its total costs.[1] The trouble is that the tax does not permit a deduction for the cost of equity capital and so falls not only on profits, in the economic sense, or other rents but on the cost of equity capital as well. The result is an incentive to substitute exempt forms of capital such as debt and human capital, to substitute labor for capital inputs, and to substitute other forms of business organization for the corporate form. Moreover, to the extent that the cost of equity capital is a marginal cost, part of the corporate income tax is passed along to consumers in the form of higher product prices, much like an excise tax. Figure 15 illustrates this effect.[2]

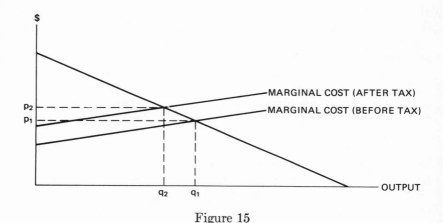

Figure 15

§16.7. The quest for an optimum tax.   We may define an optimum system of taxation as one that (1) has a large tax base, which facilitates the raising of the large amounts of revenues that modern governments demand; (2) taxes an activity the demand for which is highly inelastic, so that the substitution effects of the tax are minimal; (3) does not increase inequality[1] or offend equity;[2] and (4) is inexpensive to administer. The tax-

§16.6. 1. The corporate income tax also serves to limit exploitation by taxpayers of the favorable treatment accorded capital gains. See §16.10 *infra*.

2. There is a large and inconclusive literature on the incidence of the corporate income tax. An important study is Marian Krzyzaniak & Richard A. Musgrave, The Shifting of the Corporation Income Tax (1963).

§16.7. 1. We postpone to §16.11 the question to what extent a tax should attempt to reduce inequality. No one thinks it should increase it.

2. A tax on red-haired people would offend equity; it probably would not increase inequality.

ation of personal income has seemed to many the system that most closely approximates this optimum. The tax base is large, the demand for income is presumably inelastic, income is a broad measure of welfare, and collection is facilitated by the fact that most people are the salaried employees of large organizations. However, the second and third desiderata cannot be attained in fact because they depend on a definition of income so broad as to involve prohibitive administrative costs. Moreover, even if it were feasible to tax all real income (including leisure), income taxation might deviate from our ideal tax. Income includes money that the recipient saves rather than spends. If such income is not taxed, the tax is not an income but a spendings tax. The exclusion of saved income from taxation would violate the third criteria of optimal taxation by favoring wealthy people, who save a larger fraction of their income than the poor; income saved is part of a person's real wealth. However, the taxation of savings creates an economic problem. As we have remarked in another context,[3] there is a conflict of interest among generations. Money saved is used to invest in activity that frequently does not yield its full benefits until after the death of the investor, who has thus sacrificed his own consumption to increase that of future generations. An obligation to save may be derived from the contract theory of distributive justice discussed earlier in this part: people in the original position, not knowing to what generation they belong, would presumably make some provision to assure that all of the resources of society were not consumed by the first generation. However, part of the larger problem of the lack of operational content in the contract theory is that we do not know what the bargained-for rate of savings is, and so we cannot say that a tax on savings violates the contract.[4]

§16.8. *Personal income taxation: The problem of definition of income.* The degree to which the income tax approaches the optimum tax defined in the previous section depends on the feasibility of including, at reasonable administrative cost, the various forms of real income. The exclusion of income reduces the tax base, creates incentives to substitute activities that yield the excluded form of income, and may, depending on the wealth of those who receive the excluded form of income, increase inequality. The broadest definition of income would be all pecuni-

3. See §3.12 *supra*.
4. Are there any market arrangements by which unborn generations can in effect buy from the present generation resources for their use?

ary and nonpecuniary receipts, including leisure and gifts, but if our principal concern is with the avoidance of substitution effects a slightly narrower definition will suffice and gifts, especially within the family, can be excluded. Since they are not a reward for a particular activity, their exclusion from taxable income will not create an incentive to substitute less productive activity.[1]

Administrative costs preclude a comprehensive definition of income for tax purposes, and some of the necessary exclusions, notably that of leisure, may have significant substitution effects. It biases the choice of activities in favor of those that yield leisure instead of pecuniary income. These activities include jobs such as teaching in which long, paid vacations[2] are an important part of the compensation for the job. A similar bias is introduced by the necessary exclusion of fame, prestige, comfort, excitement, and other intangible yields of activity. But many of the exclusions cannot be justified in terms of overwhelming measurement costs. We shall discuss three examples: services that are not sold in a market; the imputed rental of owner-occupied premises; and perquisites.

(1) Often there is a choice between contracting for a service in the market and providing it within the household. An income tax law that counts only pecuniary receipts as income biases the choice in favor of household provision. Probably the most important such bias created by the present income tax law arises from the failure to include the considerable real (but not pecuniary) income generated by housewives' services within the home. Suppose a woman could earn $10,000 outside the home, on which she would pay an income tax of $2000, while if she stayed home her services would be worth only $9000. The value of her work would be increased if she worked outside, but the effect of the incomplete definition of income in the tax law is to induce her to stay home. There are of course serious difficulties in valuing nonmarket services; we pointed out earlier the error of equating the value of a housewife's services to the wages of a domestic ser-

§16.8. 1. Moreover, the exclusion of gifts from the income tax need not reduce the tax base, since gifts can be (and are) taxed to the donor. See §17.1 *infra*. It is sometimes argued that gifts should be excluded because they are not a part of the national income (why not?). Why is this irrelevant? Another question: does the reason for not taxing gifts to the recipient as income suggested in the text help to decide when a "gift" to someone in a commercial relationship to the donor should be taxed as income? Cf. Commissioner v. Duberstein, 363 U.S. 278 (1960). Finally: is the problem discussed in this section similar to the measurement problem discussed *supra* §15.1?

2. What does "paid vacation" mean to an economist?

vant.[3] But since those wages represent a minimum estimate of the value of (most) housewives' services, the inclusion of that amount as income imputed to every household in which the wife did not work would reduce the incentive to remain at home that the present law creates for women who would be more productive in jobs outside of the home.

(2) A man gives his two sons, A and B, $10,000 each. A puts his $10,000 in a savings bank that pays 5 percent annual interest, which he uses to pay the rent on the apartment that he leases. Because he is in the 20 percent federal income tax bracket, he pay $100 of the interest he receives each year to the government. B, who is in the same tax bracket as A, uses his $10,000 to purchase an apartment that has the same rental value as the apartment rented by A. B pays no income tax although he has put the same amount of money to the identical use as A. He is simply better off than A to the extent of $100 a year. This arbitrary difference in treatment creates an incentive (increased by the interest deduction) for people to own rather than rent their homes and for lawyers to create complex legal forms, such as the condominium, designed to enable rental properties to be recast as fee simple properties.

There would of course be administrative difficulties in estimating the real but nonpecuniary rental income that people derive from owning their homes rather than renting them from other people, but even a crude estimate, biased downward, would reduce the incentive to substitute home ownership for rental. Observe that once this step were taken, the deductibility of home mortgage interest payments would cease to be objectionable, for the payments would then be an expense for the production of taxable income.[4] The most serious objection to the inclusion of imputed rental income is distributive: it would bring about a sudden and substantial transfer of wealth from owners of homes to owners of rental property. (Is this an economic objection?)

(3) The exclusion of perquisites and fringe benefits from taxable income gives executives an incentive to take part of their compensation in the form of perquisites — a fancy office, a company car, etc. — even if they are worth less to them (excluding tax considerations) than their cash equivalent; the difference is pure waste. It gives all employees an incentive to take part of

3. See §4.10 *supra*.
4. The deduction of expenses incurred in the production of income is discussed in the next section.

their compensation in the form of fringe benefits such as life and health insurance, vacations, and pension benefits,[5] even if they would prefer, tax considerations aside, the cash equivalent. In many cases, the inclusion of the cash value of the benefits in taxable income would not impose substantial administrative expenses.

§16.9. *Income tax deductions.*   We defined income as ideally including all pecuniary and nonpecuniary receipts. The presumption should be against permitting the taxpayer to deduct expenses in figuring his taxable income, for in general an expenditure is not a reduction in welfare but the necessary step by which people transform money into an increase in welfare: a man is richer, not poorer, after he has exchanged cash for a new television set. Expenditures designed solely to produce income, however, are not of this character. They increase welfare only insofar as they generate income, so if the income is fully taxable the deduction of business expenses is necessary to avoid double taxation (why?). The principal problem with this deduction is that some business expenses simultaneously involve a consumption expenditure. The restaurant meals and hotel lodging that I purchase on a business trip represent expenses that are normally indispensable to the production of the income that I obtain from the trip. At the same time, they represent consumption activities that I would have engaged in in some form had I not gone on the trip. The law has dealt with the problem in an arbitrary manner by permitting the complete deduction of expenses (unless "lavish") incurred in overnight business trips while forbidding as "personal" any deduction for commuting and certain other expenses incurred in business activity not involving an overnight stay away from one's usual place of business (restaurant expense is deductible in either case). A better approach, at least in principle, would be to permit all business-related expenses to be deducted, but to include in taxable income any savings in personal consumption expenditures enabled by the business expense. Suppose that I take a three-day business trip to San Francisco, stay in a hotel that charges $30 a night, and eat meals costing me a total of $50. Under the suggested approach, $80 would be deductible, but only after subtracting the saving in personal consumption expenditures made possible by the trip. The lodging component of the offset will usually be small, and for administra-

---

5. Pensions are taxable. In what sense therefore is there a tax incentive to take income in the form of pension benefits rather than current salary?

tive convenience should probably be set at zero, since the marginal cost (cleaning, wear and tear, electricity, etc.) of spending one more night at home is usually trivial. The meal offset will be larger, but it will be less than $50 in my example because the cost of meals prepared at home is generally much less than the cost of restaurant meals. To be sure, the choice of the cost of the home meal and lodging as the appropriate measure of the amount to be offset is somewhat arbitrary since it ignores quality differences. A $20 meal at a restaurant would presumably be worth more to the diners than the $3 meal that they would have eaten at home; otherwise they would have stayed home. But since very few people eat frequently at expensive restaurants, the $50 that I spent on meals away from home in my hypothetical example probably yielded me a good deal less than $50 in value as measured by willingness to pay. Thus, while the cost of the meals I would have had at home is probably less than the personal consumption value of the restaurant meals I had on the trip, the price of those meals is undoubtedly greater than that value. Perhaps use of a compromise figure, such as 50 percent of the price of business meals, would be an appropriate way of implementing the suggested reform.[1]

Some of the other familiar deductions from federal income tax may be justifiable on various grounds. The deduction for state taxes is a form of federal revenue sharing with the states that may be appropriate in view of certain incentive problems, discussed in a subsequent chapter, created by the federal structure of our governmental system.[2] An interesting case is the deduction for children. If children are considered a form of pet, the deduction is unjustifiable; on this view people are presumed to spend money taking care of children because they derive greater pleasure from this than from any alternative use of the money expended. But this would seem to involve the fallacy pointed out earlier[3] of regarding children as the property of their parents. The parents should rather be considered trustees of not yet responsible human beings.

The charitable deduction presents a difficult case. A gift to charity contributes to the satisfactions of the donor, and in that sense is indistinguishable from an expenditure on himself. As mentioned in Chapter 1, the economic assumptions regarding

§16.9. 1. How should commuting expenses be treated under this approach?
2. See §20.6 *infra.*
3. See §3.12 *supra.*

human behavior do not distinguish between selfish and altruistic behavior. As a practical matter, however, the charitable deduction may be defended as a method of reducing the role of government in important activities such as poor relief and education in which private markets may not work satisfactorily, a matter to which we return in a later chapter.[4]

A number of deductions — the medical-expense and casualty-loss deductions are perhaps the best examples — appear to be motivated by an effort to distinguish between expenditures that increase personal well-being and expenditures (for medical care, or for replacement of an uninsured item of personal property destroyed by fire) designed merely to restore the taxpayer to a former state of well-being.[5] The goal is presumably to equalize tax burdens among individuals who may have identical pecuniary incomes but different real incomes. One can sympathize with the goal but question both its feasibility and the specific means adopted to attain it. Consider the wage premium paid to people who have dangerous jobs. The premium does not increase their well-being compared to people who have safe jobs; it merely compensates them for the danger. But clearly it would be infeasible to permit deduction of such wage premiums. Or consider two families of equal income, one more efficient at consumption than the other and so obtaining a higher well-being from the same amount of money; again a deduction to equalize the after-tax well-being of the two families would be infeasible. In these and many other ways relative pecuniary income distorts relative well-being,[6] and since most of these distortions cannot be corrected, it is doubtful whether an attempt to correct one or two contributes measurably to the goal of "horizontal equity." The specific deductions, moreover, are badly designed in terms of the goal. The measure of the medical deduction should be the cost of illness to the taxpayer rather than the cost of medical treatment. Some illnesses may be very costly but, either because of the state of the medical art or the taxpayer's financial situation, may not evoke substantial expenditures on treatment. And medical expenditures are sometimes incurred to increase well-being (e.g., a

4. See §18.2 *infra*.
5. The effort is defended in two interesting recent articles: William D. Andrews, Personal Deductions in an Ideal Income Tax, 86 Harv. L. Rev. 309 (1972); Richard A. Epstein, The Consumption and Loss of Personal Property Under the Internal Revenue Code, 23 Stan. L. Rev. 454 (1971).
6. On the inadequacy of pecuniary income as a measure of real income see *supra* §15.1.

face-lifting operation) rather than to treat an illness or other deprivation of well-being; the example suggests, moreover, how frequently tenuous is the distinction between increasing and restoring well-being. As for the casualty-loss deduction, its effect is not so much to compensate people whose well-being has been impaired as to compensate people who have lacked the foresight to insure. The deduction also reduces the cost of self-insurance (why?), primarily to the benefit of wealthy taxpayers.

§16.10.   *The special treatment of capital gains.*   The federal income tax taxes earnings only when they are realized. Thus, if a corporation does not distribute all of its earnings to the shareholders in the form of dividends, the undistributed earnings are not taxed as personal income. This is proper: retained earnings are not the property of the shareholder. Except in liquidation they enrich him only insofar as they increase the value of his shares. It is the increment in that value that is income to him. When the stockholder sells his shares he must pay tax on the appreciation including that part of the appreciation attributable to the retention of earnings. But this is not an adequate substitute for taxation of the appreciation as it occurs since the postponement of tax in effect gives the taxpayer the interest on the tax he would have paid had the appreciation been taxed when it occurred. Moreover, the taxation of capital gains, as realized appreciation is known, is at a lower rate than ordinary income; and if the taxpayer owns the shares at death the appreciation escapes the income tax altogether.

These factors have a number of inefficient consequences. In part in order to reduce shareholder windfalls Congress has imposed the corporate income tax which, as mentioned in a previous section, is an inefficient tax. The special treatment of capital gains gives corporations an incentive to retain rather than distribute earnings; by making corporations less dependent on new stock issues to finance expansion this reduces the discipline of the capital market. People are induced to cling to property until death, even if it would be more valuable in other hands, by the desire to avoid tax that grows larger every year as the property appreciates. And they are led to substitute activities that yield capital gains for more productive activities that yield ordinary income, which has resulted in overinvestment in activities such as real estate speculation and cattle raising.

The special treatment of capital gains is sometimes defended on the ground that it promotes risk taking. But it is unclear whether the amount of risk taking without such encouragement would be less than the efficient amount, or whether the argument is not really one in favor of reducing the marginal tax rates of people with large incomes, a question we touch upon in the next section. The taxation of retained earnings would present formidable practical difficulties, especially in the case of corporate earnings that had to be allocated among different classes of securities;[1] but taxation of unrealized appreciation would not present these problems (why not?). It would present other problems, however. Taxpayers would find it difficult to predict their tax liability. Liquidity problems would frequently force taxpayers to sell securities or other property in order to pay taxes on unrealized appreciation. And provisions for averaging income from year to year would have to be expanded greatly (why?).

The differential treatment of capital gains could be reduced significantly, and at little administrative cost, by two reforms: taxing capital gains at the same rates as ordinary income; and treating death as a realization of all of the taxpayer's capital gains. The latter proposal has been criticized on the ground that the value of a long-held asset will often include a large proportion of phantom appreciation due to inflation; but this argument is oversimplified, as an example will illustrate. Suppose the real interest rate is 5 percent, the rate of inflation 3 percent, and the market rate of interest therefore 8 percent.[2] At the end of ten years a bond that cost $10,000 and that accumulates interest (compounded annually) will be worth $21,589. Suppose the tax rate is 25 percent and the tax therefore $2897. Net of inflation, the appreciation is only $6289, and after tax only $3392. Had there been no inflation, the market interest rate would have been 5 percent and the value of the bond would have been $16,289 at the end of the period, the tax $1572, and the bondholder's net appreciation after tax $4717 — more than in the case of inflation, which shows that some of the appreciation taxed in that case was indeed phantom appreciation due to inflation. But there is an offsetting factor. By being able to postpone the tax, the bondholder was able to earn interest on income that he would otherwise have had to pay out in taxes. Thus, compare the position of a bondholder who receives annual payments of interest of $800 (8 percent of $10,000) on which he pays a tax of 25 percent with that of a bondholder who pays the same tax on such payments but only at the end of the ten-year period. The first bondholder

§16.10. 1. E.g., between holders of convertible debentures and of common stock. (Why is there a problem?)
2. See §4.10 *supra*.

in effect receives a 6 percent return which, compounded at the same rate, amounts to $7908 by the end of the period. The second bondholder has an 8 percent compounded return, which, as we know from the previous example, yields a total of $11,589 in interest during the period. After tax, his return is $8692, which is larger than the return of $7908 obtained by the bondholder who was not able to defer the tax. The longer the tax is deferred, the larger will be the amount of taxation of phantom appreciation but, at the same time, the larger will be the amount of interest earned by the taxpayer as a result of being able to defer the payment of tax.

§*16.11. The question of progressive taxation.* We have thus far implicitly assumed that the income tax is proportional: everyone pays the same percentage of his income. Once the tax rate is made to increase with the taxpayer's income, a number of serious problems arise. One is a timing problem. Under a proportional tax, the man who earns $10,000 one year and $100,000 the next pays the same total tax as the man who earns $55,000 both years. Under a progressive income tax system, the first man is likely to pay much more than the second. Hence, a provision for tax averaging of incomes between years becomes necessary. Also, the disincentive effects of excluding leisure from taxable income are magnified. Suppose a person who earns $50,000 a year pays $15,000 in taxes but income above $50,000 is taxed at a rate of 75 percent. If he earns $55,000, his income after tax will increase from $35,000 to $36,250, an increase of about 3 percent. The effort involved in raising his before-tax income by 10 percent, which was presumably substantial, is poorly recompensed under the assumed tax rates. But the effects of progressive income taxation on work incentives are more complex than this example suggests.[1] The taxpayer with little taste for leisure may be induced by a high marginal tax rate to work all the harder so that his money income does not fall. And since the substitution of a progressive for a proportional tax (holding tax revenues constant) will reduce some taxpayers' marginal rates, it may increase their work incentives by more than it reduces those of the taxpayers whose marginal rates are increased.

The progressive tax will sometimes increase rather than reduce wealth inequalities. The charitable deduction exemplifies this effect. If a taxpayer in the 20 percent marginal tax bracket con-

---

§16.11. 1. See Richard A. Musgrave, The Theory of Public Finance 232–246 (1959).

tributes $1000 to charity, the cost to him is $800, so in effect an expenditure of $800 controls resources worth $1000. If a taxpayer in the 50 percent marginal tax bracket donates $1000 to charity, his donation controls the same amount of resources as the poorer taxpayer's but at a cost of only $500. For the same price that the poorer taxpayer must pay to control $1000 in charitable resources — $800 — the richer taxpayer can "buy" control of the use of $1600 in resources.

Finally, it is arguable that a highly progressive income tax generates substantial waste in the form of legal and accounting expenditures designed to avoid or evade taxation. If the marginal tax rate were 90 percent for income in excess of $50,000, someone with an income of $200,000 would be willing to spend just short of $135,000 on measures to avoid having to pay any tax on his last $150,000 of income, and the resources consumed as a result of this expenditure, like the costs incurred by the thief in carrying on a career of stealing, would be unproductive. The analysis is somewhat complicated, however, by the fact that a very high marginal tax rate has an income as well as an incentive effect. The high earner will have less money to spend on avoiding taxes if the taxation system is at least partially effective.[2] But this effect is offset to some extent by the fact that tax-avoidance expenses are tax deductible.[3]

Observe that an increase in the marginal rates of high income taxpayers will result in a decrease in the marginal rates of low income taxpayers and hence in a reduction in the incentives of the members of the latter group to avoid taxation; but they may have fewer opportunities for successful avoidance.

Even if it were clear that a progressive tax suffered from serious drawbacks in comparison to a proportional tax, at least one contrary consideration might be decisive. Most taxes other than income taxes are regressive, that is, proportionately they tax the poor more heavily than the rich. If the tax system is to be proportional overall, income taxes should be progressive — although an even better solution might be to replace all taxes with a proportional federal income tax.[4]

Let us now consider the question whether the overall incidence of the tax system should be progressive or proportional. It has

2. Is this conclusion invalidated by the fact that lawyers can frequently be hired on a contingent-fee basis to obtain a reduction in the taxpayer's liability?
3. Should they be?
4. But cf. §20.6 *infra*.

been argued that progressive taxation is peculiarly subject to abuse because it permits the electorate to shift the burden of taxation to a numerical minority, composed of people with high incomes.[5] However, the practical ability of the poorer half to shift the burden of taxation to the wealthier half is limited by three factors. First, those in the poorer half who expect to be in the wealthier half some day will be reluctant to support a steeply progressive income tax, especially since income taxation discriminates against the new rich. Second, the poorer half may be reluctant to adopt a method of taxation that (at least at some level of progressivity) must impair incentives to work, since they benefit from the productivity of hard-working wealthy (or aspiring-to-be-wealthy) people. Third, simple voter majorities frequently do not decide public policy.[6] It is not surprising that our income tax system is only moderately progressive, and the overall tax system at best proportional.

A traditional justification for progressive taxation is the greater benefit that the wealthy are presumed to derive from government. Governmental protective services such as national defense and police and fire departments are arguably more valuable to the wealthy than to the nonwealthy: the wealthy man disabled by a criminal suffers a larger earnings loss than a poor man. But an increasing part of the federal, and also of state and local, budgets is devoted to services that benefit the poor and here the benefits-received rationale breaks down. A more basic criticism is that a proportional income tax would adequately serve the purpose of tailoring the burdens of taxation to the benefits, since the absolute tax liability of a wealthy person would be much higher than that of a poor person.

It should be clear from the last chapter that progressive taxation cannot be justified by reference to the principle of diminishing marginal utility of income. It is an open question whether it can be justified on the contract theory, as a measure designed to maximize the welfare of the worst off. They might conceivably be better off under a combination of proportional taxation (which might encourage greater productive activity than progressive taxation and would be cheaper to administer) and special transfer payments to low income groups.

5. Milton Friedman, Capitalism and Freedom 174–175 (1962).
6. See §23.5 *infra*.

SUGGESTED READINGS

1. Boris I. Bittker, et al., A Comprehensive Tax Base? A Debate (1968).
2. Walter J. Blum & Harry Kalven, Jr., The Uneasy Case for Progressive Taxation (1953).
3. Henry C. Simons, Personal Income Taxation (1938).
4. William Vickrey, Agenda for Progressive Taxation (1947).

PROBLEMS

1. Can you think of any economic reasons for or against the following tax rules:

  a. Income splitting by husband and wife.

  b. The treatment of a trust as a taxpaying unit.

  c. The nontaxability of compensatory damages in tort cases.

  d. The taxation of a woman's income at the husband's marginal rate.

2. A company, we saw, may be able to shift an excise tax forward to consumers, backward to suppliers. Can a personal income tax ever be shifted? Suppose that a special surtax were levied on the income of accountants. Would accounting fees increase? Would it make a difference if accountants' incomes included some monopoly profits?

3. Can you see a relationship between the discussion of taxation in this chapter and the discussion of the problem of second best in Chapter 6 (§6.6)?

4. Suppose housewives' imputed income were taxed. Would it be appropriate on economic grounds to permit them to deduct the wages of any maids or nurses whom they hired? The costs of detergents and other household supplies? If the wife works outside the home, should she be permitted to deduct the cost of a child-care center where she leaves her child?

5. Discuss the following proposition: if death were treated as the realization of the decedent's capital gains, an important force for the stability of the stock market would be removed.

6. In Sanitary Farms Dairy, Inc., *25 T.C. 463 (1955), the Tax Court held that the owner of a dairy company could deduct from his income tax more than $15,000 that he had expended on an African safari that he had taken with his wife. He had made movies during the safari which he later used extensively in advertising his dairy business. The court found that "the evidence shows that advertising of equal value to that here involved could not have been obtained for the same amount of money in any more normal way," and concluded: "No part of that cost is taxable . . . as personal travel and pleasure expense. . . . They admittedly enjoyed hunting, but enjoyment of one's work does* *not make that work a mere personal hobby or the cost of a hunting trip income to the hunter." Is this result economically sound? Should the court have allowed no deduction? A partial deduction?*

7. In what circumstances, if any, should a taxpayer be permitted to deduct the cost of legal service incidental to litigation?

CHAPTER 17

THE TRANSMISSION OF
WEALTH AT DEATH

§*17.1. Death (and gift) taxes.* To many students of taxation the taxation of wealth at death seems substantially free from the substitution effects and regressiveness of so many other taxes. Since the distribution of wealth among the population is far more uneven than that of income,[1] death taxes are likely to be highly progressive; and the disincentive to work created by a heavy death tax would seem to be much less than that created by heavy income taxes.

But closer analysis suggests that substitution effects may be serious. Since the accumulation of a substantial estate is one of the motivations that drive people to work hard, a death tax is indirectly a tax on work. There may, however, be an offsetting tendency for the inheritors of substantial wealth to work less hard than they would if they had inherited less. If we assume decreasing marginal utility of money, a person who possesses substantial wealth as a result of inheritance may consider working to increase his income less worthwhile than he would if he lacked a cushion of inherited wealth. Which effect dominates is uncertain. However, other substitution effects can be predicted, at least if death tax rates are very high, with greater confidence.

The simplest method of avoiding a death tax is to give money away during one's lifetime. Gift taxes and special rules for the taxation of gifts in contemplation of death can close this escape hatch to some extent but not completely. A gift tax may prevent father from giving junior a million dollars but will not prevent father from installing junior as executive vice-president of his company. This form of the gift, unlike a simple cash transfer, is

§17.1. 1. See Robert J. Lampman, Changes in the Concentration of Wealth, in Inequality and Poverty 80 (Edward C. Budd ed. 1967).

not costless: nepotism may reduce the company's productivity. Even if all forms of gifts were effectively subject to à heavy gift tax, heavy death taxes would create a substitution effect besides leisure for work (or vice versa): consumption for saving. Since saving would be penalized by the heavy and inescapable tax on accumulated wealth at death, wealthy people would have an incentive to consume a very large fraction of their income and wealth. Frugal living and investment would be discouraged; extravagant consumption would be encouraged. Might not the resulting modification in the style of life of the rich actually exacerbate the social tensions that give rise to proposals for confiscatory taxation of large estates?

Observe that the lighter taxation of gifts than of bequests at death is not necessarily a loophole. An *inter vivos* gift is more costly to the donor than a bequest at death, because the donor loses the interest on the principal of the gift during his lifetime. And should the donee predecease the donor, the result is double taxation. The problems of meshing gift and estate taxes could be avoided, and the objective of promoting a more equal distribution of wealth more effectively attained, if the present gift-estate tax system were replaced by a cumulative gift-inheritance tax designed to limit the total amount of money that any individual could receive through gifts or bequests during his lifetime.

§*17.2.   The problem of the "dead hand."*   An apparent dilemma is presented by the frequent efforts of testators to limit the uses to which the assets of the estate will be put. Some power to limit use is inherent in the right (not wholly unqualified either, but of that more later) to designate the beneficiaries. But if the bequest is otherwise unrestricted, the beneficiaries can apply the funds as they see fit. The problem of a "dead hand" controlling resource use by the living is presented when death does not result in a clean transfer to living persons permitting them to do with the money as they please. The motivation for accumulating a substantial estate may frequently include a desire on the part of the accumulator to project his influence after death by establishing conditions (perhaps perpetual) on the use of the funds in the estate. Consequently, a policy of disregarding a testator's conditions would in some instances have much the same effect on the incentive to accumulate as a heavy estate tax.[1] Yet if conditions, especially perpetual conditions, in

§17.2. 1. And in the case of charitable gifts, where the problem mainly arises, there would be no offset, of the kind mentioned in the last section, from preventing an individual's acquiring great wealth that might reduce his incentive to work.

a will are always obeyed, the frequent result will be that resources controlled by such conditions will be employed inefficiently. Unforeseen contingencies that materialized after the testator's death may require that the resources be redeployed in order to maximize efficiency. If the conditions in the will cannot be altered, there is no way to bring about the reallocation.

The character of the problem is illustrated by a controversy over a park donated to the city of Macon, Georgia, by Augustus Bacon, a United States Senator from Georgia who died in the early years of this century. Senator Bacon's will, drawn during the era of segregationist legislation that followed the end of Reconstruction, stipulated that the park was to be used by white women and children only. In the 1960s a suit was brought against the city charging that the enforcement of the racial condition violated the equal protection clause of the Fourteenth Amendment. The Supreme Court of the United States held the condition void,[2] whereupon heirs of Senator Bacon, the residuary legatees under the will, brought suit to declare (a) the gift of the park void since the city could no longer comply with the racial condition of the gift and (b) the property theirs under the residuary clause of the will. They won.[3]

At first glance, the result may appear to vindicate the policy of enforcing testators' intentions as disclosed by the conditions in bequests. But on closer examination this becomes doubtful. It appears that Senator Bacon may have inserted the racial condition primarily to assure that the city would agree to administer the park. There was no indication that the dominant purpose of the gift was to foster racial segregation rather than to provide a recreational facility for the people of Macon. It seems likely that, if Senator Bacon could be consulted on the matter, he would prefer that the park remain a park, albeit open to nonwhites, rather than that his distant heirs subdivide the property for residential or commercial use. This is especially plausible since the city could always repurchase the land from the heirs and continue to use it for a park — a park that would have to be open to nonwhites. In that event Senator Bacon's discriminatory intentions would not be respected and the only effect of the voiding of the charitable gift would be to confer windfall gains on the heirs, a result Bacon presumably did *not* want since he did not bequeath the property to them.

2. Evans v. Newton, 382 U.S. 296 (1966).
3. Evans v. Abney, 396 U.S. 435 (1970).

As the case suggests, the dilemma whether to enforce the testator's intent or to modify the terms of the will in accordance with changed conditions since his death is often a false one. A policy of rigid adherence to the letter of the donative instrument is likely to frustrate both the donor's purposes and the efficient use of resources. To be sure, in the Macon case itself no significant efficiency issue was involved: if the land was more valuable as a park than in an alternative use the city could always purchase it back from the heirs.[4] But suppose that Senator Bacon had given the city a tuberculosis sanatorium rather than a park. As the incidence of tuberculosis declined and advances in medical science rendered the sanatorium method of treating tuberculosis obsolete, the value of the donated facilities in their intended use would have diminished. Eventually it would have become clear that the facilities would be more valuable in another use. Unlike the park case, there would be no legal obstacle to continuing to enforce all of the conditions of the gift. Yet not only would enforcement be inefficient, but in all likelihood it would be contrary to the purposes of the donor, who intended by his gift to contribute to the cure of disease, not to perpetuate useless facilities.

The foregoing discussion may seem tantamount to denying the competence of a donor to balance the value of a perpetual gift against the cost in efficiency that such gifts frequently impose. However, since no one can foresee the future, a rational donor knows that he will eventually be thwarted by unpredictable circumstances and may therefore be presumed to accept implicitly a rule permitting modification of the terms of the bequest in the event that an unforeseen change frustrates his original intention.[5]

§17.3. *The cy pres doctrine.* The law's solution to the problem in the case of charitable gifts is the "cy pres" doctrine. Where the continued enforcement of conditions in a charitable gift is no longer justifiable, because of illegality (in the park example) or opportunity costs (in the sanatorium example), the court, rather than declaring the gift void and transferring the property to the residuary legatees (if any can be identified), will authorize the administrators of the charitable trust to apply the assets of the trust to a related purpose within the general scope of the donor's intent.

4. By condemnation if they were unwilling to sell at the market price.
5. If a particular donor explicitly rejects such a rule of interpretation, should his wishes be enforced — as a matter of economic theory?

The cy pres doctrine is reasonably well designed to avoid frustration of the donor's intentions and could have been used in the park case as justification for disregarding the racial condition but permitting the gift to stand. To be sure, the interest in efficiency, narrowly conceived, would be as well or better served by a rule providing that when enforcement of the conditions of a gift becomes either unlawful or uneconomical, the gift lapses and the property is transferred to the residuary legatees or (if they cannot be identified) the state. As in the park case the result would be the immediate vesting of the property in a living owner free to apply it to its highest valued use. The court might of course be mistaken in judging the charitable donation to be no longer economical but the only significant consequence of its mistake would be distributive: the charitable institution could purchase the property from the new owner and continue to use it as before. However, we are using "efficiency" here in too limited a sense. The approach just suggested may be inefficient if it reduces the incentive to accumulate wealth by making it virtually impossible to create a perpetual charity with reasonably well-defined purposes.

§17.4. *The problem of incentives of charitable foundations.* Even where there are no unforeseen contingencies, perpetual charitable gifts raise an economic issue that echoes the concern with the separation of ownership and control in the modern business corporation. The concern in its original context may be largely misplaced,[1] but it has considerable force when transposed to the context of a charitable foundation that enjoys a substantial income, in perpetuity, from its original endowment. Such a foundation does not compete in any product market or in the capital markets and it has no stockholders. Its board of trustees is self-perpetuating and is accountable to no one (except itself) for the performance of the enterprise. Although state attorneys general enjoy a nominal authority over the administration of charitable trusts, it is largely formal. There are thus neither sanctions for trustees or managers who are inefficient in investing the principal of the trust or spending the income nor mechanisms for displacing them.

The incentives to efficient management of foundation assets[2] could be strengthened by a rule requiring charitable foundations to distribute every gift received, principal and interest, including

§17.4. 1. See §12.4 *supra.*
2. Are such incentives nonexistent? Why not?

the original endowment, within a specified period of years. The foundation would not be required to wind up its operations within the period; it could continue indefinitely. But it would have to receive new gifts from time to time in order to avoid exhausting all of its funds. Since donors are unlikely to give money to an enterprise known to be slack, the necessity of returning periodically to the market for charitable donations would increase the incentive of the trustees and managers of charitable foundations to conduct a tight operation. Foundations, mostly religious and educational, that market their services or depend on continuing charitable support, and are therefore already subject to some competitive constraints, could be exempted from the exhaustion rule.[3]

§17.5. *Noncharitable perpetuities.*   We have thus far considered the problem of perpetual gifts in the context of charitable donations. But it arises in connection with noncharitable donations as well. Landowners in England once went to great lengths to assure that their holdings would never be divided; and many people, if permitted, would attach conditions to the use of bequeathed property of the form: "I give my daughter my diamond wedding ring on condition that she never sell it."

The power to perpetuate control over assets bequeathed other than for charitable purposes is limited by two doctrines: the rule forbidding restraints on alienation and the Rule Against Perpetuities. The former rule provides that the owner of a fee simple interest may not be prevented by his grantor from transferring the property. If I sell you my automobile I cannot extract from you an enforceable promise that you will not resell it, unless such a condition is necessary to protect a security interest I retain in the property (you may not yet have paid me in full). The rule against restraints on alienation is applicable to bequests. The merit of the rule, at least as applied to bequests at death, is that it prevents the inefficient use of resources that would frequently result from unforeseen contingencies; its now-familiar drawback is that it weakens the incentive to work hard in order to accumulate wealth.

Is the rule against restraints on alienation consistent with the rule permitting perpetual restrictive covenants? The cy pres doctrine (which is applied only to charitable bequests) represents a

---

3. Can the rule proposed in this section be criticized on the ground that donors are free under existing law to insert such a condition in their charitable bequests? On the ground that the efficiency gains of the rule might be offset by an adverse effect on donors' incentives?

middle position between the policies exemplified by the rule against restraints on alienation and by the rule permitting perpetual restrictive covenants.

The common law Rule Against Perpetuities (modified by statute in some states) provides that no interest is valid unless it must vest within 21 years after lives in being when the interest was created. The rule is something of a misnomer. It does not limit the duration of a condition in a bequest, but rather limits the testator's power to earmark gifts for remote descendants.[1] The rule is, however, related to the other limitations on the "dead hand" that we have surveyed, since arrangements for the distant future are most likely to result in an inefficient use of resources due to unforeseen contingencies. The rule has proved impossibly complex in practice, so that its net benefits are quite probably negative.

§17.6.   The widow's share.   Another limitation on the power of a testator is the provision, found in the inheritance laws of all states, forbidding him to disinherit his widow completely. The limitation has an economic justification. The husband's wealth at death is likely to be a product, in part, of the wife's work even if she never had any pecuniary income. As we have pointed out several times now, a wife's work in the home is a source of real, although not pecuniary, family income, and so of the family's net worth. By staying home, she enables money that would otherwise have gone to hire maids and nurses to be saved (or used to defray other expenses, thereby increasing the amount of money from the husband's income that can be saved) — and the husband's estate is simply the amount of savings in his name at his death. Without statutory protection against disinheritance, women could negotiate with their husbands for contractual protection. The statutory provision minimizes transaction costs.

The preceding analysis also demonstrates the economic basis for exempting from the estate tax on the husband's estate a part of the wife's share of the estate. Some of the money she inherits from her husband represents an accumulation of her (usually imputed rather than pecuniary) earnings, not his. Also, she is likely to be an older person, and should she die soon after her husband his estate would be subjected to estate taxation twice in a short period (so what?).

---

§17.5. 1. Today, tax avoidance is the usual motive for attempting such earmarking.

SUGGESTED READING

Carl S. Shoup, Federal Estate and Gift Taxes (1966).

PROBLEMS

1. To what extent would the difficulties discussed in this chapter be reduced or eliminated if the present system of death and gift taxes were replaced by a cumulative gift-inheritance tax on recipients of gifts and bequests?

2. A man dies and in his will leaves one million dollars in trust for his pet cat, with instructions that the income from the trust be used to enhance the cat's comfort and pleasure. From an economic standpoint, should the bequest be upheld?

3. Testator owns a valuable art collection. In his will he orders that the collection be burned. Should his direction be upheld if challenged by the residuary legatee? (See, e.g., Board of County Commissioners v. Scott, *88 Minn. 386, 93 N.W. 109 (1903).) Suppose he had ordered it destroyed while he was living. Should the law restrain the execution of such an order? Would the case be different if he had bought the art collection from a museum and at the time of purchase had disclosed to the museum his intention to destroy the collection? If the property ordered to be destroyed was a manuscript that the testator, a successful novelist, had written?*

CHAPTER 18

LAW AND POVERTY

§*18.1.* *The costs of poverty.* If the goal of equalizing income and wealth has little support in economic theory, and if the methods for achieving the goal, such as confiscatory taxation of incomes and of decedents' estates, seem dubious from an economic perspective, still, there is an economic argument for measures to reduce the gross inequality that creates "poverty."

The definition of poverty is elusive, its identification simpler. It is a relative concept: poverty in India means something different from poverty in the United States. And within the same culture the concept changes over time. If one compares estimates from various periods in our history of the minimum income necessary to place a family of given size above the poverty level, one finds that the level has risen steadily, even after correction for the decline in the value of the dollar due to inflation.[1] Even with a rising floor under what is considered a tolerable income, the incidence of poverty in the United States has apparently declined markedly over the years.[2]

Poverty imposes costs on the nonpoor that warrant, on strictly economic grounds and without regard to ethical or political considerations, incurring some costs to reduce it. For example, poverty in the midst of a generally wealthy society is likely to increase the incidence of crime. One important cost of a criminal career, the forgone income of a legitimate alternative occupation, will be low for someone who has little earning capacity in legitimate occupations, while the proximity of wealth increases

§18.1. 1. See Oscar Ornati, The Poverty Band and the Count of the Poor, in Inequality and Poverty 167 (Edward C. Budd ed. 1967).
2. See ibid.; U.S. Dept. of Commerce, Bureau of the Census, Statistical Abstract of the United States 1971, at 322.

the expected return from crime, or, stated another way, the cost of honesty.[3]

Another cost of poverty is the distress that many people feel either at the visible signs of poverty, such as slum housing, or at the thought that people in the society are living below minimally decent levels. Whether sympathy, condescension, revulsion, or guilt is the predominant emotion is not important. If poverty reduces the satisfactions of many nonpoor, it imposes an economic cost just like damage from pollution, bad weather, or managerial incompetence. There is also the argument that the well-off are "contractually" obligated to help the poor.[4]

§18.2.   *The limitations of charity.*   Although poverty imposes costs, it is not self-evident why efforts to reduce these costs have been preempted by government rather than left to the market. An individual who feels endangered or appalled at the poverty around him can contribute to an organization designed to alleviate that poverty an amount equal to the benefit that he would derive from the reduction of poverty enabled by his contribution (net of administrative costs). If Americans in the aggregate felt that poverty was costing them $10 billion a year, they would contribute up to $10 billion to eliminate it; the poverty not eliminated by the contribution would be the economically optimum amount of poverty. But there are two reasons against relying entirely on voluntary contributions. The first, which is the traditional economic argument, is that due to a free-rider problem the amount contributed to charity will be smaller than the members of society would be willing to contribute were there no free riders. I may want to see poverty reduced yet hang back from contributing in the hope that others will. Unlike an ordinary good, which cannot be consumed unless the consumer purchases it, a reduction in poverty can be enjoyed fully by one who refuses to purchase it, counting on others to do so.

The weakness in this argument is the assumption that the free rider receives exactly the same good as if he contributes, so long as others contribute. This is false. If others contribute $100 in the aggregate and I contribute nothing, poverty is reduced by

3. This analysis is not inconsistent with the observation that crime rates are frequently low in poor countries, even though inequality of wealth is often much greater in those countries than in more advanced ones. If wealth is highly concentrated, the costs of protecting it from criminals may be quite low. It is where wealth is more widely distributed that criminals are presented with an abundance of attractive targets.

4. See §15.3 *supra.*

$100. If others contribute $100 and I contribute $1, poverty is reduced by $101. The reduction in poverty brought about by my contribution is thus unaffected by the amount contributed by others. To be sure, if my desire is only to reduce poverty by $100, if the benefit to me of a greater reduction would be zero, then I may hold back from contributing anything. And that may of course be true in many cases. But if a further reduction in poverty of one dollar is worth a dollar to me, I will contribute that dollar.

The second reason against relying entirely on voluntary contributions to reduce poverty — and it is a "reason" only in the realpolitik sense — is that it places the burden of expense primarily upon the wealthy; it is they to whom the poor naturally look for assistance. It would not be surprising if the wealthy attempted to shift the burden to other members of the society, thereby freeing their resources for other uses (including other charitable uses). A program of poor relief paid out of state and local taxes, which are primarily regressive, and even one paid out of federal income tax, which is only moderately progressive, might accomplish such a shift.

§18.3. *Unrestricted cash transfers vs. benefits in kind.*   For better or worse the government has assumed the principal burden of dealing with poverty.[1] But the proper governmental strategy is debatable. The causes and hence cures of poverty are not well understood. The simplest view is that poverty results from a lack of income and is most effectively treated by unrestricted cash payments to poor people. This approach has growing support, but there are three economic points against it which may explain, in part anyway, why it has not yet been adopted. First, what people are distressed by and want to alleviate may not be poverty itself but certain manifestations of poverty, such as substandard housing, hunger, a high rate of infant mortality, lack of legal representation, or poor education. If so, it would be rational for them to wish to channel governmental efforts toward reducing these manifestations rather than the underlying poverty. If substandard housing is what people especially dislike about poverty, a program directed against such housing may yield a larger margin of benefits over costs than one designed to increase the incomes of the poor generally, since only a portion of their higher incomes would be devoted to purchasing better housing.

---

§18.3. 1. At least if the children of nonpoor parents are not considered among the poor.

Second, perhaps many people are poor because they are incompetent at managing money; if so, unrestricted cash grants may be squandered, without reducing poverty.

Third, the unrestricted cash transfer involves a potentially serious incentive problem. If, for example, every family of four were guaranteed a minimum income of $3500, the head of such a family would have no incentive to take a job paying less than $70 a week. Indeed, he would have no incentive to take a job that paid a good deal higher than that. An $80 job would increase his gross income by only about $10 a week. His net income would probably decline since working is not costless (he would have to pay for transportation, for work clothes, federal and state income tax, etc.). Productive people would be given a strong economic incentive to withdraw permanently from the labor force.

There are two ways around this objection. The first is to point out that the usual methods employed in poor relief for preserving work incentives have their own incentive problems. If, for example, assistance is denied to a family that includes an able-bodied male, an incentive is created for the man to leave his family, since by doing so he maximizes the joint income of himself and his family. The second is to adopt a graduated scale of cash transfers designed to preserve at least some incentive to work. Let the guaranteed minimum income for a family of four be $3500 and let it further be provided that for every dollar earned the government's contribution to the family's income is reduced by only $.50, even if the result is that the family's total income, earned as well as subsidized, exceeds the minimum. The difficulty with this solution is that a 50 percent marginal income tax rate, while better than 100 percent, is still very stiff and can be expected to have disincentive effects. A man with a yearly income of $3500 would retain only $1750, and after deducting the costs of work, including the opportunity cost of forgone leisure, the value of the job to him might be negative. The disincentive to work, moreover, would operate not only on people now on welfare and not working but also on people not on welfare who are working for low wages. They would be attracted to leaving the work force, which would both increase the cost of the program and reduce the supply of labor in low-paying jobs. The reduction in demand for such jobs would lead to an increase in the wages offered, but while this would partly offset the disincentive effect by making work more remunerative, it would also increase the cost and hence price of the goods and services dependent on such labor, much like an excise tax; and excise taxes are generally regressive.[2]

The marginal income tax rate can be varied at will in order to mitigate the disincentive effects just discussed, but a substantial reduction in the rate would greatly increase the cost of the program to the taxpayer. If the marginal tax rate were 25 percent, a family of four in which the head of the household earned $5000 per year would receive an annual income supplement from the government of $2250; if he earned $10,000 he would still receive $1000.[3] Even at a 50 percent marginal tax rate every family of four with an income below $7000 a year would receive some income supplement. A program of such dimensions could be financed only by a substantial increase in federal income tax rates — a step that would create additional disincentives to work and that in any event would exceed the willingness of the taxpaying public to contribute to the reduction of poverty.

The disincentive effects (and other problems) inherent in an unrestricted cash transfer plan with a high marginal tax rate — the "negative income tax" approach outlined above — are not decisive against adoption of the approach. The traditional method of preserving work incentives under poor relief is to confine assistance to those unable to work. This method is crude and costly to administer, ignores the plight of those who are able to work but only for inadequate wages, and creates an incentive for husbands to live apart from their families so that the family will be entitled to public assistance.

Another alternative to the unrestricted cash transfer is the benefit in kind — public housing or rent supplements, food stamps, free legal services or medical care, job training, etc. The question of work incentives is rarely raised in connection with such programs, perhaps because no one has proposed a system of benefits in kind so extensive that the recipients would have no urgent need for cash income. The root problem with benefits in kind is an informational one.[4] The willingness of a consumer, including a poor consumer, to pay the market price for one good over another is evidence of the relative value of the goods to him — it does not matter how he came by the dollars he is using to express his preference. When the price of a good is made zero, it

2. See §16.2 *supra*.
3. $3500 — .25 × $5000 = $2250; $3500 — .25 × $10,000 = $1000.
4. A good recent discussion of benefits in kind is Ralph K. Winter, Jr., Poverty, Economic Inequality, and the Equal Protection Clause, 1972 Sup. Ct. Rev. 41 (Philip B. Kurland ed.).

becomes very difficult to evaluate the worth of the good to him.[5] Government officials who dispense benefits in kind have no direct information on the priority needs of the poor — on whether they need more food or more housing, more medical care or more legal aid, more safety or more education. In a sense, the poor "need" more of everything, but since society is not prepared to devote many resources to poor relief, the need for hard choices is inescapable. When services are dispensed without charge, the officials lack information on which to base such choices. Moreover, even if they had an idea of how in general the poor ranked the various kinds of goods and services, this would enable only an average judgment, which, given the widely varying needs of particular poor families, would lead to superfluity in many individual cases and insufficiency in many others. The resources that are wasted because of lack of information are unavailable for other uses and reduce the total amount of assistance to the poor.

Some examples drawn from specifically legal contexts may help to elucidate the problems that are involved in channeling government assistance to the poor through benefits in kind.

§18.4. *Pay television revisited.*   One of the arguments used to justify the severe restrictions that the Federal Communications Commission has placed on the development of pay television is that if pay television siphoned off the most popular programs from the free service, the poor would be forced to pay for a good deal of costly and popular entertainment on television that they now watch without charge. It is no answer that "free" television is not really free since most of the cost of programming and transmission is borne ultimately by the consumers of the goods and services advertised on television, for poor people pay a disproportionately small share of this indirect cost.[1] However, not only are the restrictions on pay television inefficient because they prevent people from buying a service that is worth more to them than the price, but they probably hurt the poor more than they help them. To be poor in this country is not to be utterly destitute. Poor people in the aggregate constitute a substantial market that television broadcasters have little incentive to serve under current arrangements since they cannot extract payment from it. Under a system of pay television, they would have an in-

5. Cf. our discussion of marginal cost pricing of bridge transportation when marginal cost equals zero, *supra* §9.4.

§18.4. 1. See F. A. Lees & C. Y. Yang, The Redistributional Effect of Television Advertising, 76 Econ. J. 328 (1966). Moreover, is it clear that the cost of goods would be lower without advertising? Why might they actually be higher?

centive to design and market programs of special appeal to the poor. Pay television might also enable poor people to substitute a cheaper, albeit not costless, television service for services that cost them more. If, for example, unrestricted pay television resulted in the replacement of the movie theater as the primary channel for the distribution of first-run motion pictures by pay television, a poor person might be able to see a first-run motion picture at a price that, while greater than zero, was lower than the price of a movie theater ticket plus the cost in time, travel, and baby sitter of going to the theater.

§*18.5. Legal services.* Another example of a service provided to the poor at zero price is the government program of free legal services. As with benefits in kind generally, this method of assistance to the poor actually prevents many poor people from achieving their most efficient pattern of consumption. Since governmental funds allocated to legal services for the poor are unavailable for other programs of assistance to the poor, the cost to the poor person of being entitled to receive $100 in legal services is the benefit that he would have derived from receiving $100 of some other good or service, or in cash. In many cases that cost will exceed the value of the $100 in legal services. Many poor people may get along quite nicely without a lawyer, either because they are fortunate enough not to encounter legal problems or because they are clever enough to cope with them unaided by a lawyer. But since the lawyer is free,[1] they will use him unless the value of his services is zero or very slight. Faced with an excess demand for his time, the lawyer will try to limit his services to those whose needs for legal service seem most acute. Since this requires a difficult judgment, there are bound to be many cases where a poor person receives legal services that cost $100 but are worth only $50 to him. The waste involved in the use of the lawyer in these circumstances would be avoided if poor people were given $100 instead of free lawyers. They would use the $100 to hire a lawyer rather than to buy food, medicine, education, or housing only when the value of legal services to them was at least $100.[2]

There is an additional cost, to society and especially to the poor, involved in a program of subsidized legal services for the poor. Legal services are typically although not invariably utilized

§18.5. 1. Are his services entirely "free" to the client? Why not?
2. Legal assistance to a poor person charged with crime may present a special question. See §19.2 *infra*.

in a dispute — in the case of a poor person, with a landlord, spouse, merchant, welfare agency, finance company, etc. The legal efforts made on behalf of one of the parties to the dispute will increase the costs to the other, who must either increase *his* legal efforts or abandon the stakes in the dispute to the other party.[3] These costs are typically marginal costs — they are a function of output — so that, by a now-familiar analysis, they will be passed on in part to the customers of the enterprise if, like a finance company, merchant, or landlord, it sells its services in the market. If its customers are primarily other poor people, then the costs generated by one poor tenant or customer or debtor's employment of a lawyer will be borne in large part by other poor people. In the case of a lawyer hired to prosecute a divorce, this effect may be offset by the fact that the spouse is also entitled to free legal service. If the dispute is with a government agency, the additional legal expense (or higher grant level) of the agency will not be borne primarily by the poor unless the agency is funded by means of a highly regressive tax. But they may bear it indirectly. The increased cost of the program may result in a reduction in the scale or coverage of the benefits provided by it. The costs thereby imposed on a large number of poor may exceed the benefits to those who employed lawyers in their dispute with the agency.

§*18.6. Wealth redistribution by liability rules: The case of housing-code enforcement.*   Housing codes specify minimum standards of housing. Whether the standards are prescribed in order to ensure a decent minimum level of safety and sanitation or in order to subsidize the building trades is a matter of debate, but certainly the codes, if enforced, would eliminate conditions that most people consider indecent, such as inadequate plumbing and heating. Legal scholarship has been imaginative in suggesting devices by which the violators of housing codes could be subjected to sanctions that would greatly reduce the incidence of violation. To deal with the problem of substandard housing by legal sanction has the additional attraction of enabling, or seeming to enable, a principal manifestation of poverty to be eliminated without any expenditure by the government.

However, if we compare housing-code enforcement with an alternative method of improving the stock of housing available to the poor, such as rent supplements, we find that the former method has serious shortcomings. Compliance with the require-

3. See §§24.4, 26.2, *infra*.

ments of housing codes costs money and there are only two sources, in the absence of government funds, from which the necessary money can be obtained: the rentals paid by tenants or the rent of land obtained by the landlord. Rentals are an unappealing source. If his tenants were willing to pay the cost of higher quality housing, the landlord would presumably have improved the building voluntarily, in much the same way that the food industry will produce scallions, without having to be prodded by the law, if consumers are willing to pay the cost of producing and selling them. Thus, tenants forced to pay higher rentals to cover the cost of compliance with the building code will be made worse off. Economic rent is an especially unpromising source of the funds necessary to comply with the housing code, because the use of land for slum housing generally does not generate substantial rent.[1] In New York and Chicago, where the abandonment of slum buildings by their owners has become a common phenomenon, the value of much land in slum areas, and hence its rent, must be at or near zero. Even if the land itself has some value, the rent from using it for slum housing may be zero, depending on the other uses to which the land might be put. Suppose the revenue from a property used as slum housing is $25,000 per year and the maintenance, depreciation, tax, interest, and other costs incurred to produce that revenue are $20,000. It does not follow that the property produces a rent of $5000 (in which event, even if the landlord were subjected to an annual cost of housing code compliance of $4,999.99 and could recoup no part of it by raising rents, he would not abandon the property or shift it to another use). Perhaps if he upgraded the property to middle income housing it would yield a revenue of $30,000 per year at a cost of $29,000; if so, he would make this shift if the cost of compliance with the housing code exceeded $4000. Or perhaps if used for some commercial purpose instead of housing, the property would yield a revenue of $10,000 at a cost of $9500; then if the cost of compliance with the housing code exceeded $4500 he would shift to this alternative use. In any case, the result of housing code enforcement is quite likely to be a reduction in the stock of housing available to the poor, albeit the housing that is available will be of higher quality than before. There is no assurance that the poor will be on balance better off. Furthermore, the rentiers in this case who bear a part of the cost of compliance are likely to include a number of almost-poor people for

§18.6. 1. See George Sternlieb, The Tenement Landlord (1966).

whom ownership of slum property represents a first step in the escape from poverty.

A recent article suggests that a program of vigorous code enforcement in slum areas would have only one adverse effect on the poor: it would cause some buildings to be abandoned.[2] This is a highly optimistic view. As shown in Figure 16, firms in a market will increase price if their marginal costs increase. The costs of maintenance and repair involved in compliance with housing codes are marginal costs; they vary with the landlord's output (the number of units rented). The demand schedule facing the firms as a group is negatively sloped rather than horizontal (perfectly elastic) since not all the residents of the slum would move out if a somewhat higher rental were charged rather than pay the additional rental, although some would. Figure 16 demonstrates that one effect of stricter housing code enforcement would be higher rentals; and a correlative effect would be a reduction in the number of housing units supplied.

It is not a persuasive answer that the landlord cannot increase

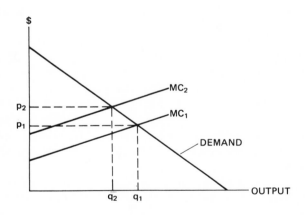

Figure 16

2. Bruce Ackerman, Regulating Slum Housing Markets on Behalf of the Poor: Of Housing Codes, Housing Subsidies and Income Redistribution Policy, 80 Yale L.J. 1093 (1971), criticized in Neil K. Komesar, Return to Slumville: A Critique of the Ackerman Analysis of Housing Code Enforcement and the Poor, forthcoming in Yale L.J. (1973). A recent case suggests that landlords might be forbidden to abandon buildings as an alternative to code compliance if they were "able" to comply. Robinson v. Diamond Housing Corp., 463 F.2d 853, 869 (D.C. Cir. 1972). Would such a prohibition be likely to increase or to decrease the long-run supply of housing to the poor?

rentals (i.e., demand really is perfectly elastic) because the slightest increase would induce many tenants to double up.[3] Since doubling up is costly (it involves forgoing the value of the greater space and privacy of single-family occupancy), tenants would be willing to pay something to avoid being forced to double up — i.e., a somewhat higher rental.

We can predict another effect of housing code enforcement. The higher quality housing resulting from compliance with the housing code can be expected to attract people from other slum areas, especially if rentals do not rise appreciably, and even people who live in middle class areas.[4] The influx of newcomers will operate to bid up rentals, including the rentals paid by the original tenants. In addition, housing code enforcement can be expected to retard the conversion of middle income into low income housing. In sum, it is likely that strict enforcement of housing codes would have an adverse impact on the amount of housing available to the poor. Perhaps the construction industry would be the major beneficiary of such enforcement.[5]

Strict enforcement, public or private, of housing codes is only one of several methods proposed or adopted for increasing the welfare of slum tenants by imposing liabilities of various sorts on landlords. Other methods include the implied warranty of habitability[6] and the right to a hearing before eviction or rental increase. The analysis is the same as in the case of code enforcement. The measures increase the landlord's costs, resulting in higher rentals and a curtailment of the housing supply to the low income tenant. The right to a hearing before eviction is an especially good example of a provision that makes it cheaper for the landlord to deal with a more responsible (normally higher income) tenant against whom a cheap and speedy remedy of eviction is less likely to be needed.

The reader may recall a somewhat similar analysis of efforts to use legal sanctions to redistribute income to poor people. The earlier example was the outlawing of efficient but sometimes (or

3. Bruce Ackerman, note 2 *supra,* at 1105. And doubling up would probably violate the housing code!

4. Might a covert purpose of housing codes be to increase the supply of middle income housing at the expense of people of low income? Cf. George J. Stigler, Director's Law of Public Income Redistribution, 13 J. Law & Econ. 1 (1970).

5. Does this suggest a general explanation of the prevalence of benefit-in-kind assistance to the poor, rather than outright cash transfers? What group benefits from the welfare system besides the welfare recipients?

6. See problem 5 at the end of this chapter.

often) oppressive methods of enforcing debts.[7] Both examples support a general point that should be in the forefront of concern to a generation of socially conscious law students: the use of liability rules or other legal sanctions to redistribute income from wealthy to poor is likely to miscarry. A rule of liability is like an excise tax: it induces a contraction in output and increase in price. The party made liable, even if not poor himself (but that, as we have seen, is possible, too), may be able to shift much of the cost of the liability to the poor in the form of higher prices or reduced opportunities (the housing example). The result may be a capricious redistribution of income and wealth within the class of poor people themselves and an overall reduction in their welfare.[8]

SUGGESTED READING

George J. Stigler, Director's Law of Public Income Redistribution, 13 J. Law & Econ. 1 (1970).

PROBLEMS

1. Is a food stamp program likely to increase the nourishment of poor people? Consider the following hypothetical example: a poor family, before the food stamp program, spent $700 a year on food. The family receives food stamps with a retail value of $500. Would you expect this to affect the family's eating habits more than a cash transfer of $500 would affect them? Might your answer be affected by what restrictions were placed on the use of the stamps (i.e., what specific foods could not be purchased with them)?

2. Contrast from an economic standpoint the following methods of increasing the employment of poor people: a government-subsidized job-training program; a subsidy to employers of poor people; a negative income tax with a low marginal tax rate.

3. Is rent control, as in New York City, likely to help or hurt the poor as a whole? What would be the effect on the supply of housing if rent control were combined with strict enforcement of housing code provisions? (Cf. Edgar O. Olsen, An Economist's Analysis of Rent Control, 80 J. Pol. Econ. 1081 (1972).)

4. Professor Ackerman (see §18.6 supra, note 2) asserts that it is uneconomical to build low income housing today without a govern-

7. See §3.7 *supra.*
8. The problems raised by attempts to use legal rules to reduce poverty are discussed further *infra* §19.2.

ment subsidy. If so, does this support his conclusion that strict en-forcement of housing codes is unlikely to affect the supply of slum housing, except to cause abandonment of some marginal properties?

5. *In* Javins v. First National Realty Corp., *428 F.2d 1071 (D.C. Cir. 1970), the United States Court of Appeals for the District of Columbia Circuit, in an opinion by Judge J. Skelly Wright, held that there is a warranty of habitability, measured by the standards set forth in the housing code of the District of Columbia, that is implied by operation of law in all leases. The suit was a landlord's suit for possession on the ground of nonpayment of rent. The court held that it was for the jury to determine what portion if any of the tenant's obligation to pay rent was suspended by the landlord's breach. In the course of its opinion the court stated:*

> *The inequality of bargaining power between landlord and tenants has been well documented. Tenants have very little leverage to enforce demands for better housing. Various impediments to com-petition in the rental housing market, such as racial and class discrimination and standardized form leases, mean that landlords place tenants in a take it or leave it situation. The increasingly severe shortage of adequate housing further increases the land-lord's bargaining power and escalates the need for maintaining and improving the existing stock. [Id. at 1079 (footnotes omitted).]*

What does Judge Wright mean by "shortage"? By "bargaining power"? Assuming that the quoted statement is accurate and coherent, would you expect the court's decision to make tenants in general better off, or worse off, than if no implied warranty of habitability were recog-nized? How about the particular tenants who brought the suit?

6. *Does a rule forbidding the garnishment of welfare checks increase or decrease the real income of welfare recipients?*

PART V

THE CONSTITUTION AND THE FEDERAL SYSTEM

CHAPTER 19

ECONOMIC DUE PROCESS

§*19.1.* *Liberty of contract as a constitutional principle.* For more than 50 years, until the late 1930s, "liberty of contract" was a key element of the concept of due process under the Fifth and Fourteenth Amendments to the Constitution as interpreted by the Supreme Court, and was the ground upon which the Court invalidated a variety of state and federal statutes regulating economic activity.[1] Classical economic theory was thereby elevated to the status of constitutional principle, for the idea that voluntary transactions almost always promote welfare and regulations that inhibit such transactions almost always reduce it is an implication of classical economic analysis. To be sure, the Court upheld the antitrust laws and laws subjecting monopolists to maximum rate controls, but these laws are commonly thought to be necessary to preserve or simulate the results of free markets.

Today the liberty of contract decisions are commonly viewed as grotesque distortions of constitutional principle; but it is possible to argue that they are not, or at least no more so than contemporary constitutional decisions. Thus, while it is said that there was no source for a doctrine of liberty of contract in the text or history of the relevant constitutional provisions, the same criticism can be (and has been) made of the Court's decisions in a wide variety of other constitutional areas, such as reapportionment. It is also said that economic questions are more difficult for courts to decide sensibly than questions involving the rights of criminal defendants, political dissidents or members of racial minorities; yet in fact less is known about those questions than about the analysis of conventional economic problems. It is said that economic rights are less important than other rights; even if

§19.1. 1. The era is analyzed in Robert G. McCloskey, Economic Due Process and the Supreme Court: An Exhumation and Reburial, 1962 Sup. Ct. Rev. 34 (Philip B. Kurland ed.).

so (a question to which we return later),[2] it does not follow that the Court should give them no protection. It is said that the Court's mistake in the liberty of contract cases was to be out of step with dominant public opinion. But this was true only toward the end of the era (and is the reason why the era ended when it did). Moreover, the criticism can easily be turned into a compliment to the Court for its steadfastness in the face of contrary popular opinion. It is said that the victims of economic controls are businessmen well able to protect themselves without the Court's help, unlike the powerless minorities typically involved in a noneconomic constitutional case. Yet, as we are about to see, the burden of the economic legislation challenged during the liberty of contract era was often borne by politically unorganized groups such as consumers. And it is not correct to say that racial and religious minorities are unable to compete effectively in the political arena.

Finally, and most pertinent to an economic analysis of law, it is commonly believed that the Court's liberty of contract decisions were economically unsound. An early criticism based on this view is found in Justice Brandeis' dissenting opinion in *New State Ice Co. v. Liebmann.*[3]

The case involved the constitutionality of a state statute that required anyone who wanted to manufacture and sell ice to obtain a certificate of public convenience and necessity, and provided that a certificate would be denied if existing service was adequate. New State, which had such a certificate, sought to enjoin Liebmann, who did not, from entering the ice business in New State's territory. Liebmann's defense was that the statute was unconstitutional. The Court invalidated the statute, on the basis of an analysis in which most economists today would concur:

Stated succinctly, a private corporation here seeks to prevent a competitor from entering the business of making and selling ice. . . . There is no question now before us of any regulation by the state to protect the consuming public either with respect to conditions of manufacture and distribution or to insure purity of products or to prevent extortion. The control here asserted does not protect against monopoly, but tends to foster it. The aim is not to encourage competition, but to prevent it; not to regulate the business, but to preclude persons from engaging in it. . . . It is not the case of a natural monopoly, or of an enterprise

2. See §22.4 *infra.*
3. 285 U.S. 262 (1932).

in its nature dependent upon the grant of public privileges. The particular requirement before us was evidently not imposed to prevent a practical monopoly of the business, since its tendency is quite to the contrary.[4]

The Court likened the certification provision to an attempt of one shoemaker, under state authority, "to prevent another shoemaker from making or selling shoes because shoemakers already in that occupation can make and sell all the shoes that are needed." [5]

Brandeis' economic argument begins with the proposition that the ice business may be "one which lends itself peculiarly to monopoly" since "the business is conducted in local plants with a market narrowly limited in area" due to the weight and perishability of the product.[6] This is error: the fact that a firm has only a local market area does not preclude competition (witness grocery stores). Brandeis' opinion reveals, moreover, that prior to the passage of the challenged statute there was competition in the ice business in many localities in the state. To be sure, he argues that "even in those localities the prices of ice were ordinarily uniform," [7] but since, as he stresses elsewhere in his opinion, the product is uniform one is not surprised to find competitive sellers charging the same or nearly the same price.

The test of natural monopoly is the size of the market in relation to the conditions of supply: if one firm can supply the whole demand of the market at lower cost than more than one firm, it is a natural monopoly.[8] On the critical issue of the supply conditions in the ice business, however, the opinion is obscure and contradictory. Brandeis remarks on "the relative ease and cheapness with which an ice plant may be constructed" and on the fact that increased production of ice has not "had the effect of greatly increasing the size of plants in the ice business." [9] These remarks suggest that competitive provision of ice is no more costly than monopolistic. But he also states that "ice plants have a determinate capacity, and inflexible fixed charges and operating costs," [10] which seems to imply production under conditions of declining average cost.

4. Id. at 278–279.
5. Id. at 279.
6. Id. at 291–292.
7. Id. at 293.
8. See §9.1 *supra*.
9. 285 U.S. at 292.
10. Ibid.

A more likely explanation for the statute (than that it was aimed at preventing wasteful duplication under conditions of natural monopoly) is that it was designed to foster cartelization of the Oklahoma ice industry. As Brandeis himself curiously emphasizes,

Trade journals and reports of association meetings of ice manufacturers bear ample witness to the hostility of the industry to such competition, and to its unremitting efforts, through trade associations, informal agreements, combination of delivery systems, and in particular through the consolidation of plants, to protect markets and prices against competition of any character.[11]

He also notes: "the ice industry as a whole in Oklahoma has acquiesced in and accepted the Act and the status which it creates." [12]

If, as seems quite likely, the true purpose and effect of the Oklahoma statute was to facilitate monopoly pricing of ice, then Brandeis, in viewing the case as one in which Liebmann's economic rights were pitted against the interests of the poor people of Oklahoma who cannot afford refrigerators, got it backward. The "right" that he would have vindicated was the interest of New State Ice and other established ice companies in being free from competition, to the enrichment of their shareholders. The people actually wronged by the statute were the poor, who were compelled to pay higher prices for ice than if free entry had been permitted; the well-to-do, as Brandeis pointed out, were more likely to have refrigerators.

If the ice business were a natural monopoly, the Brandeis position just might be economically defensible, since (as we saw in an earlier chapter) the effort of a natural monopolist to maximize his profits by establishing a monopoly price might lead to a wasteful duplication of facilities. However, not only is the premise (that the ice business is a natural monopoly) false, but it appears from the latter part of Brandeis' opinion that the natural monopoly language of the earlier part is a makeweight and that he was prepared to embrace the sweeping proposition that ruinous competition is a common phenomenon of economic markets and was a major factor behind the Depression. The case was decided in 1931, and, although the Oklahoma statute predated the Depression, Brandeis discusses extensively, and with at least tentative approval, the proposition that the philosophy embodied in

11. Id. at 292–293.
12. Id. at 294.

the Oklahoma limitation on entry into the ice business might be a remedy of general application to the economic dislocation created by the Depression.[13]

The view of the Depression as rooted in the excesses of competition and curable by reducing competition is discredited.[14] Of course, when demand declined during the Depression much of the existing industrial capacity, geared as it was to supplying a larger demand, seemed excess. But limiting competition would not have increased purchasing power and therefore demand; its principal effect would have been to reduce the efficiency of economic activity at its reduced level. Nonetheless the cartel remedy for depressions, as we may call it, was tried in the early New Deal statutes, such as the National Industrial Recovery Act which authorized industries to fix minimum prices. The notion was that higher prices would encourage economic activity to pick up; the notion is unsound. Higher prices might increase the wealth of shareholders but would not encourage them to invest that wealth in additional production. The act was invalidated in the *Schechter* decision,[15] albeit on grounds of excessive delegation of legislative authority rather than interference with liberty of contract. The decision was widely condemned as a further example of the Court's backward thinking about matters of economic policy. As in the ice case, however, the Court had the better of the economic argument than its critics.

It is an interesting footnote to the *Schechter* decision that afterward the pendulum of opinion swung to the opposite extreme and it was argued that monopoly rather then competition had been responsible for the Depression, or at least for its severity. The argument is no more convincing than its predecessor. It is true that a monopolist may reduce his price more slowly than a competitive firm when the volume of demand declines.[16] But then prices must fall faster in other markets, for the relatively high price that the consumer continues to pay for the monopolized

13. In fairness to Brandeis, it should be noted that under his view of the proper scope of constitutional adjudication, a justice's responsibility was to decide whether there was a rational basis for challenged legislation rather than to decide whether he himself agreed that the legislation was sound. There is accordingly a problem of distinguishing between his own views in the opinion and views he rejected personally but considered respectable.

14. Cf. §9.7 *supra*.

15. Schechter Poultry Corp. v. United States, 295 U.S. 495 (1935).

16. See Richard D. Reimer, A Comment on Oligopoly Pricing Practices and Economic Theory, 38 J. Bus. U. Chi. 210 (1965); cf §7.1 *supra* (discussion of *American Tobacco* case).

product reduces the amount of money that he can spend on competitively produced products, thereby accelerating the decline in the demand for and (assuming a rising marginal cost schedule) [17] price of such products. The aggregate effect of monopoly on the reduction in consumer purchasing power during a depression is likely to be zero.

The *New State Ice* and *Schechter* decisions are not isolated examples: many of the statutes struck down by the Court in the period when it was guided by liberty of contract notions were attempts to suppress competition under the guise of promoting the general welfare. Indeed, as we shall see in Chapter 23, economic theory teaches that the promotion of special interests at the expense of the larger public interest is a normal rather than aberrational feature of economic regulation. Since the Court's repudiation of the liberty of contract touchstone, it has frequently upheld statutes designed to facilitate monopolization. A state statute that, on grounds of public health, forbids opticians to replace eyeglass *frames* without a prescription signed by an optometrist or ophthalmologist can have no real purpose other than to increase the incomes of optometrists and ophthalmologists at the expense of opticians — and consumers.[18]

Not all statutes challenged on liberty of contract grounds, however, were quite of this type. *Muller v. Oregon*[19] involved a state statute fixing a maximum work day of ten hours for women employed in laundries. This statute — which the Court upheld — was more plausibly related than our previous examples to a genuine purpose of preventing the exploitation of a vulnerable group. Even here, economic analysis induces skepticism. Unless the state enacting such a statute also had a minimum wage law and the wages of women employed in laundries were not significantly higher than the minimum, the statute would have little effect: if forced to reduce the work day, the employer would compensate by reducing the daily wage. If the employer is prevented from reducing the daily wage, he will treat the statute as having increased the cost of his labor (he gets less output for the same wage), and, under a now familiar analysis, will adapt by purchasing a smaller quantity of labor, by raising prices, or by taking both steps. The reduction in employment will harm

17. Why is this assumption necessary?
18. See Williamson v. Lee Optical Co., 348 U.S. 483 (1955). For an extreme example of the Court's tolerance see Kotch v. Board of River Port Pilot Commrs., 330 U.S. 552 (1947).
19. 208 U.S. 412 (1908).

any workers he lays off who do not have equally good alternative employment opportunities and the increase in prices will harm consumers — and usually poor consumers more than rich. The welfare effects of the statute are thus ambiguous.

The irony of *Muller* is that statutes that purport to grant special protection in employment to women are now being challenged as discriminatory. Students of economic regulation will not be surprised if it turns out that frequently the real purpose of a statute purportedly concerned with protecting the safety or health of women is to limit their opportunities in the job market.

§*19.2.   Economic due process revived: The poor as a constitutionally protected class.*   In *Griffin v. Illinois,*[1] the Supreme Court held that the requirement that a criminal defendant buy a transcript of the record at trial as a precondition to appellate review of the record discriminated against those who could not afford the payment. The Court could have reached the same result — the provision of transcripts without charge to indigents — by holding that due process in criminal proceedings requires that the defendant have an opportunity, if necessary at the expense of the state, for a meaningful appellate review of the conduct of the trial.[2] But if, as the *Griffin* opinion seems to hold, a poor defendant is entitled to a free transcript simply in order to neutralize an advantage that the affluent defendant would otherwise enjoy over him, new vistas of constitutional obligation are opened up. If the state must neutralize the advantages conferred by the possession of money in this area, why not in others? It has in fact been argued that *Griffin* was the first in a series of cases that can best be explained on the theory that government is required, as a matter of constitutional principle, to satisfy the "minimum just wants" of people regardless of their ability to pay.[3] Another in the series is said to be the *Harper* decision, which invalidated the poll tax.[4]

The argument amounts to saying that government is required to provide certain benefits in kind, and is based on John Rawls'

§19.2. 1. 351 U.S. 12 (1956).

2. Or, even more narrowly, that in a system where appeal is important, opportunity for a meaningful appeal must be afforded all defendants. This would leave states free to adopt criminal procedure systems like the English, where appeals are relatively unusual.

3. Frank I. Michelman, On Protecting the Poor Through the Fourteenth Amendment, 83 Harv. L. Rev. 7 (1969), criticized in Ralph K. Winter, Jr., Poverty, Economic Equality, and the Equal Protection Clause, 1972 Sup. Ct. Rev. 41 (Philip B. Kurland ed.).

4. Harper v. Virginia Bd. of Elections, 383 U.S. 663 (1966).

theory of justice, discussed in an earlier chapter.[5] Rawls' theory implies that society should establish a floor beneath the worst off, but it does not specify the particular form that the floor should take — whether unrestricted cash transfers or specific benefits in kind [6] — and the latter is in general a wasteful method of providing assistance to poor people.[7] Possibly, however, the provision of certain minimum procedural privileges to the indigent criminal defendant is an appropriate in-kind method of poor relief. This conclusion, which implies a narrow interpretation of *Griffin* that assimilates it to the cases guaranteeing counsel for indigent criminal defendants, is based on a recognition that the individual who (suppose, through no fault of his own) is destitute still has a valuable property right: his freedom of action. If the government can take it away arbitrarily, which is one way of characterizing a criminal proceeding in which only the government has counsel or in which the defendant realistically cannot appeal an adverse judgment at trial, the value of that property right is diminished. To be sure, poor people might be even better off if, rather than having a specific right to counsel in a criminal proceeding, they had a right to a minimum cash income at a level that permitted them to purchase legal insurance. The proponents of legal benefits in kind do not consider this alternative. However, since the proposal of a guaranteed income is recent, and legal insurance still generally unavailable,[8] the right to counsel may represent the second-best solution (likewise with certain other benefits in kind that the Court has recognized).[9]

The *Harper* decision, however, seems unrelated. Voting, like prayer, can be viewed either as an act of production or as an act of consumption (one prays either for results, or because of religious feeling or duty). Viewed as an act of production, voting is rarely cost justified. Although the costs (mostly the opportunity costs of the time spent in registering to vote and in voting) are not large, the benefits, in all but the smallest elections, are negligible. Rarely will a single vote noticeably affect even the size of the winner's plurality: it requires about 700,000 votes to make up one percent of the presidential vote. It is not surprising that a substantial fraction of the electorate does not bother to vote.

---

5. See §15.3 *supra*.

6. See John Rawls, A Theory of Justice 275 (1971).

7. See §18.3 *supra*. For an alternative economic rationale of the right to counsel to that suggested in the text below see §26.3 *infra*.

8. Can you think of a reason why?

9. See, e.g., Boddie v. Connecticut, 401 U.S. 371 (1971).

Since voting is already so costly an undertaking (at least when viewed as an instrumental rather than final act), a moderate poll tax might substantially deter poor people from voting — even if they were interested rather than apathetic with regard to the issues or candidates. But our political system presupposes the desirability of broad participation in the electoral process. This is a ground for the poll tax decision that is unrelated to a concern with distributive justice.

The furthest development to date of the implications of the *Griffin* decision is the invalidation of the financing of public education by local property taxes by the Supreme Court of California, in *Serrano v. Priest*.[10] Under such a system of financing, the amount of money per pupil spent for public education in each school district is a function in part of the value of property in the district. It is contended that since wealthier districts as a rule contain more valuable properties, the children of wealthier parents receive a more expensive education than the children of poorer parents. There are two practical objections to this reasoning. The first is that the correlation between the real estate tax base and the income of the families who patronize the public schools may often be negative. In New York City, for example, there are many wealthy people and enormously valuable real estate. But since the wealthy people do not send their children to public schools and much of the property tax is levied on commercial rather than residential property, the effect of this method of school financing is to redistribute income to the poor. If expenditures per pupil were equalized on a state-wide basis, New York City would be classified as a wealthy district and its expenditures per pupil reduced, although many of these pupils are poor. The primary beneficiaries of equalization would be rural inhabitants.

Second, equalization would weaken the public school system by reducing the incentive of wealthy communities to tax themselves heavily to pay for high quality public education. No community is entirely homogeneous. Invariably some of its residents will be drawn from lower income strata, and they will enjoy a high quality education subsidized by their wealthy neighbors. This effect will become especially pronounced if current govern-

10. 5 Cal. 3d 584, 487 P.2d 1241 (1972). For a critical examination of this case and of cases following it, see Note, A Statistical Analysis of the School Finance Decisions: On Winning Battles and Losing Wars, 81 Yale L.J. 1303 (1972). The United States Supreme Court has recently declined to follow *Serrano*. See San Antonio Independent School Dist. v. Rodriguez, 93 S. Ct. 1278 (1973).

ment policies of dispersing public housing into suburban areas make any headway. Indeed, one reason why suburbs resist such dispersion may be that it would require them to bestow the costly public education that their residents demand for their own children on children whose parents are not able to defray the costs.

§19.3. *The constitutional rights of consumers.* The judicial reawakening of interest in economic rights is further illustrated by a line of cases that at first glance seem conventional in their insistence on purely procedural safeguards. The recent *Fuentes* decision[1] will illustrate. There the Supreme Court invalidated state statutes authorizing, upon the posting of a security bond, the replevy (repossession), without prior notice or hearing, of property that the plaintiff in the replevin suit claims is rightfully his. The plaintiffs in the case were sellers under installment sales contracts; the defendants were buyers who allegedly had defaulted. The Court reasoned that since the buyers had a right to the possession of the goods sold under the contract, the goods were their "property" within the meaning of the due process clause of the Fourteenth Amendment and they could not be deprived of them by state action without notice and an opportunity for a hearing in advance.

The basic premise of the Court's decision — that a person's "right to enjoy what is his, free of governmental interference," is a right worthy of judicial solicitude[2] — is congenial to economic analysis; the conclusion the Court drew is not. The Court did not question that repossession is an appropriate remedy for defaulting on an installment sales contract. The issue was how best to prevent the remedy from being invoked as a method of harassment when there is no default in fact. The best method is to create an economic disincentive to replevy groundlessly. The statutes in issue did this. They required the sellers to post bonds. Although the replevin procedure, like the procedure for obtaining a preliminary restraining order, is summary initially, a final decision cannot be rendered without a hearing. If, at the hearing, it appears that the property was wrongfully replevied, the seller must return the property and make good the damages, if any,

---

§19.3. 1. Fuentes v. Shevin, 407 U.S. 67 (1972).

2. Id. at 81. An even more extravagant paean to property rights may be found in Mr. Justice Stewart's opinion for the Court in Lynch v. Household Finance Corp., 405 U.S. 538, 552 (1972). The Court's reawakened interest in economic rights is discussed in Gerald Gunther, The Supreme Court 1971 Term — Forward: In Search of Evolving Doctrine in a Changing Court: A Model for a Newer Equal Protection, 86 Harv. L. Rev. 1, 23–46 (1972).

suffered by the buyer; the seller is also out of pocket the cost of the bond. Thus he has nothing to gain and money to lose from invoking the remedy groundlessly. Nor have many buyers anything to gain from having a right to a prior hearing. The requirement that the seller post a bond should both discourage frivolous invocations of the remedy and protect the buyer when mistakes are made.

The Court noted the economic incentive of the seller to avoid invoking the remedy groundlessly but held that such an incentive is no substitute for the judgment of a neutral official. The preference for authority over self-interest as a regulator of human conduct is curious, at least to an economist. He would also think it odd that the Court should draw so sharp a distinction between the particular thing replevied and its economic equivalent. By their requirement that the seller post a bond and justify the replevin at a subsequent hearing, the statutes protected the value of the buyers' interests if not the continuous possession of the specific good. In the case of the common consumer products involved in these cases, the good and its monetary value are interchangeable.

The *Fuentes* decision protects economic rights of a sort but it does not vindicate economic freedom, as is further shown by the Court's refusal to give effect to the express provisions of the sales contracts authorizing repossession in the event of default, among other reasons because they were "adhesion contracts." [3] The effect of the *Fuentes* decision is to increase the cost of the installment sales contract: a dubious blessing to consumers, especially those who have no alternative to such contracts if they wish to purchase consumer durables.

This does not conclude our consideration of the constitutional protection of economic rights. The Supreme Court's recent decision invalidating state welfare residency requirements is examined in the next chapter, and later we return to the fundamental question whether liberty of contract is in fact distinguishable from other forms of personal liberty. [4]

SUGGESTED READING

Ralph K. Winter, Jr., Poverty, Economic Equality, and the Equal Protection Clause, 1972 Sup. Ct. Rev. 41 (Philip B. Kurland ed.).

3. That is, standard or form contracts. See §3.7 *supra*.
4. See §22.4 *infra*.

PROBLEMS

1. Do the Supreme Court cases discussed in this chapter suggest to you that the Court simply mirrors the prevailing economic ideology, whatever it may be?

2. Does the Court use the same economic premises in the decision of antitrust cases as in the decision of the recent economic rights cases, such as Fuentes v. Shevin?

3. Suppose that it was convincingly demonstrated that the federal minimum wage law, at present levels, significantly impairs the employment opportunities of poor people. (See, e.g., Yale Brozen, The Effect of Statutory Minimum Wage Increases on Teen-age Employment, 13 J. Law & Econ. 109 (1970).) (Why, incidentally, might this be so?) Could the minimum wage law be successfully challenged as a violation of the equal protection clause?

4. Were a negative income tax to be adopted, would — or should — the Court reexamine the question of the constitutional right to a transcript in a criminal case? Other questions involving the rights of the poor?

CHAPTER 20

THE ECONOMICS OF FEDERALISM

The division of the United States into quasi-sovereign states, each with its own regulatory and taxing authority and revenue needs and each governed by officials who are not accountable to inhabitants of other states, is a source of fascinating and important economic problems. We discuss four examples that look more disparate than they are: the regulation of state taxation under the commerce clause, conflicts among state pollution-control schemes, interbasin transfers of water resources, and the challenge to residency requirements in state welfare laws. We conclude with a discussion of the significance of competition among the states.

§20.1. State taxation: Excise taxes. Each state has an incentive to impose taxes the burden of which will fall, so far as possible, on residents of other states. Such an incentive is undesirable because it deflects the state from the search for taxing methods that maximize efficiency and distributive criteria for the nation as a whole. States may also use taxation not to raise revenue but to protect producers or sellers from nonresident competitors. Such a tax will harm the resident consumers as well as nonresident sellers of the out-of-state goods that are taxed. Indeed, the loss to the resident consumers will usually exceed the gain to the resident sellers.[1] But since special interests frequently obtain legislation that reduces efficiency we should not be surprised to find that, with states as with nations, taxes that discriminate against importers are sometimes imposed.

The Supreme Court has adequate formal authority under the

---

§20.1. 1. The tax raises the price of the imported good relative to that of the local good, and so induces consumers to substitute the latter. The substitution benefits the local seller while harming the consumer. But not all consumers make the substitution. Some continue to buy the imported good at the higher price, and their loss is not captured by the resident seller.

commerce clause, and the due process and equal protection clauses of the Fourteenth Amendment, to prevent states from imposing taxes that have the uneconomical features just identified. It has exercised this authority to forbid clearly extraterritorial taxes and tariffs on goods imported from other states. But it has failed to prevent the states from reimposing such taxes and tariffs under names that conceal the true economic effect.

If Texas imposed a tax on the sale of gasoline in Illinois, the invalidity of the tax would be clear; yet a tax on the extraction of petroleum from the ground in Texas (a severance tax) is clearly valid. The dichotomous treatment does not make good economic sense. If the demand for Texas petroleum is relatively inelastic — a plausible assumption in view of the restrictions on the importation of petroleum imposed under the oil import quota program — and if the ultimate consumers of Texas petroleum are mainly nonresidents of Texas, then the Texas tax on production, assuming it is proportional to the output produced, will in fact be paid mostly by nonresidents of Texas in the form of higher prices for petroleum products (Figure 17).[2]

One could argue that the severance tax is in fact a royalty, to which the state, as the original owner of the natural resources found within its boundaries, should be entitled. And it is true (as we shall see when we discuss the problem of interbasin water transfers) that efficiency is promoted by vesting the state with ownership of natural resources in which private individuals or firms have not yet obtained property rights: that initial vesting is the first step to creating markets in the resources. But suppose the state either retains ownership of all of the rights to a resource or sells them all to a single purchaser: the result — if there are no good substitutes elsewhere for the resource, as in our Texas oil example — will be monopoly. Monopolization is not inherent in state ownership of its natural resources, because the state can disperse the rights sufficiently broadly to assure competition.[3] But a severance tax, imposed on a resource that lacks good substitutes produced in other states, is monopolistic. The tax leads to an increase in price above the competitive level and

2. We ignore in the example the fact that there are intermediate sellers between the producer and the consumer. Does this make a difference? Observe also that the example assumes a flat tax (e.g., two cents a barrel). Would it make a difference if the tax were in the form of a percentage of the producers' revenues from the sale of oil? Cf. §16.2 *supra*.

3. Is this a possible reason why actual diversion is required to establish a property right in water? See §2.11 *supra*.

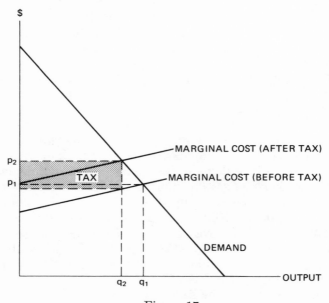

Figure 17

a reduction in output below it, and generates large, supracompetitive revenues (received, however, by the state rather than by the rights holders).

Not every excise tax monopolizes. Were there good substitutes for Texas oil, so that the demand schedule in Figure 17 were horizontal, the excise tax would merely reduce the output of Texas oil and the value of Texas oil land, leading to a compensating increase in output and land values elsewhere.[4] It would be a tax on economic rent.[5] It would be a responsible form of taxation (as well as an efficient one) because the residents of the state imposing the tax would be the taxpayers.[6]

An intermediate case is one where, although demand for the resource taxed is inelastic due to lack of good substitutes elsewhere, there is a substantial market within the state so that the major burden of the tax falls on the residents of the taxing state. One could still object that the tax was monopolistic in its effects,

4. Figure 18 illustrates this effect.
5. See §16.3 *supra*, for a discussion of this term.
6. This assumes, however, that the oil-producing land is owned by residents of Texas.

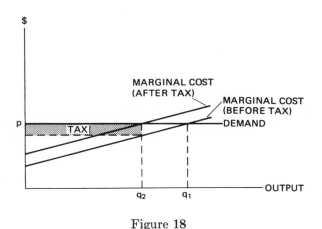

Figure 18

How would you draw the diagram if the tax were a percentage of gross receipts?

but the objection would not be very forceful. Most taxes have some substitution effects. The revenues of government cannot be raised by taxes on economic rent alone, which do not have such effects.

If a state imposed a tax designed to exploit a locational monopoly — say, Louisiana levied a heavy toll on all ships using the part of the Mississippi River that is wholly within the state — the element of extraterritoriality would be unmistakable. The natural resource tax, in cases such as our Texas oil example, is identical in its economic character, the only difference being that the state's monopoly is founded on possession of scarce natural resources rather than on strategic location. The vice of the tax in both cases is to shift the burden of taxation to people who have no control over the level of the tax, which weakens the incentives to economize on government spending.

The Supreme Court has been more critical of state import taxes. Early decisions held that a state could not levy its general sales tax on sales made by out-of-state sellers to its residents. The reader may wonder how the uniform levy of a sales tax could discriminate against out-of-state sellers. But consider two states, one that raises revenue primarily by a sales tax (state A), the other primarily by a property tax (B). Since the value of property is normally based on its capitalized earnings, the net income from sales to residents of state A by a firm located in B will probably be capitalized in the property tax paid by the firm to state B. The firm thus pays to B a tax on its sales in A. Its competitors in state A do not pay a similar exaction but simply a straight sales tax. If the firm in B is also subject to state A's sales tax it will pay more tax than its competitors in A although presumably it receives no greater governmental services. The tax differential, which is unrelated to any difference in costs, discriminates against the out-of-state seller, although the effect may be offset to some extent by the fact that state A's sales tax reduces the value of the firm's property and hence the amount of tax it pays to B.[7]

To perceive the element of discrimination in general sales taxes required some subtlety on the part of the Court. But confusion returned and the Court upheld a clearly evasive device known as a compensating use tax. This is a tax, equal to sales tax, on goods that residents of the taxing state purchase but on which they do not pay sales tax. In our example, the residents of state A who purchased from the firm in B would have to pay A a tax equal to the sales tax they would have paid if they had bought the same goods from a seller located in A. The Court has also permitted states to compel the out-of-state seller to collect the compensating use tax, which completes the functional identity of the two taxes.

Perhaps the reason why the Court has failed to "see through" severance and compensating use taxes is that it phrases the question as whether the state has placed a tax "on" interstate commerce. The petroleum as it comes out of the ground and the good after it has been received by the resident purchaser are reassuringly present, in a physical sense, within the boundaries of the state. But from an economic standpoint the issue is not whether a tax is "on" interstate commerce or where the nominal subject of the tax is physically located. The economic issues are whether

7. But not completely offset. Suppose that the sales tax in state A is 3¢ on the dollar, the out-of-state seller's normal profit is 10¢ on the dollar, and state B's property tax is equivalent to 30 percent of the seller's normal profit, and hence also 3¢. If state A's sales tax is not imposed, the out-of-state seller obtains net profits of 7¢ on the dollar. If the sales tax is imposed, the seller's profit before imposition of the property tax is only 7¢. The property tax is 30 percent of this amount, or 2.1¢, and so the seller's total tax burden is 5.1¢, leaving a profit of only 4.9¢. It is plain that if sellers in state A are subject only to sales tax, the imposition of that tax on the out-of-state seller gives them a competitive advantage unrelated to efficiency, for we are assuming that the out-of-state seller receives no greater governmental services, although his taxes are more than 40 percent greater than the local sellers. It is also plain that the out-of-state seller's additional tax burden (2.1¢) is less than the sum of the two taxes to which it is subject.

the tax is in fact paid by nonresidents and whether the effect of the tax is to increase, without justification based on higher costs of governmental services, the prices of imported compared to domestic goods.

In some instances the Court's emphasis on whether a tax is "on" interstate commerce may give unjustified tax breaks to out-of-state sellers, thereby creating an opposite but equally inappropriate incentive to substitute interstate for intrastate goods and services. Suppose a firm located in a state that relies primarily on a sales tax to raise revenues makes most of its sales in other states that rely primarily on property taxes to raise revenues. The domiciliary state may not be permitted to apply its sales tax to the firm's interstate sales because those sales are made in interstate commerce. As a result the firm will pay lower taxes than competitors who make mostly intrastate sales, although it receives no fewer governmental services than they.

The essential point here — that the consumption of governmental services is not necessarily related to the destination of a firm's goods — implies that our criteria of suspect state taxes may conflict in particular cases. The criteria are whether the tax falls primarily on nonresidents and whether it creates arbitrary differences in the prices charged by competing firms depending on their location. In the last example the first criterion would imply a policy of prohibiting taxation of the firm's interstate sales by the domiciliary state, since the burden of the tax would fall primarily on nonresidents. But the second criterion would lead us to *approve* such a tax so that the taxes paid by an interstate firm will not be lower than those paid by a local firm due to the difference in their status rather than any difference in the amount of governmental services that they receive.

Can the criteria be reconciled? One approach might be (1) to permit all states to impose a general sales tax applied indiscriminately to interstate and intrastate sales by sellers in the state but (2) to forbid taxes on particular products that are primarily export goods when products of equivalent importance sold primarily in the local market are not taxed as heavily. Under this approach severance taxes would be dubious[8] and the last vestige of justification for compensating use taxes would be removed since the out-of-state seller would be subject to sales tax in his state of residence even with respect to his out-of-state sales.

§20.2.   *State taxation: Real estate and corporate income taxes.*

8. If it is true that these are mostly export taxes.

The Supreme Court has tended to treat real estate taxes as inherently local. They would be if (1) they were taxes solely on the rent of land and (2) all land were locally owned. But when a state taxes a railroad's real estate, for example, it is more likely to proportion its tax to the railroad's revenues than to the rent of land. The railroad will treat such a tax as an excise tax and shift a large part of it to the railroad's customers, most of whom will be nonresidents. And to the extent that the tax is on rents, the burden will again be borne primarily by nonresidents — the railroad's shareholders.[1] Thus, real estate taxes on the property of firms that are owned by and do business mainly with nonresidents should be subject to careful scrutiny like severance taxes. Yet, perhaps because the physical characteristics of land place it so firmly within state boundaries, the Court has not critically scrutinized real estate taxes on railroads and similar commercial properties.

Similar dangers inhere in state corporate income taxes. The burden of such a tax is normally shared between consumers and shareholders.[2] In the case of a corporation doing business in several states, the consumers and shareholders will usually be composed primarily of nonresidents. The temptation to impose a heavy corporate income tax on the multistate corporation is therefore great. It might appear that so long as each state has a uniform tax rate for all the corporations that do business in the state, local as well as multistate, there is no danger of discrimination. However, the Supreme Court has allowed states, within the broadest limits, to choose the formula for the apportionment of a multistate corporation's income that attributes the largest possible share to the taxing state. If a state in which a railroad has a lot of track but runs relatively few cars apportions the railroad's income by track mileage, while a state in which the railroad has relatively little track but runs a great many cars apportions the railroad's income according to cars, the railroad's combined income tax bill will be larger than that of any pair of similar but local firms one of which is located in the first state and the other in the second. The effort of both states to export their tax burdens results in the multistate firm's being compelled to pay a higher tax than if it operated only in one state, although it does not require relatively greater governmental services. The

§20.2. 1. This assumes that the land was owned by the railroad before the tax was anticipated. What difference does this make?
2. See §16.6 supra.

result is an arbitrary disincentive to do business in more than one state.[3]

§20.3. *State regulation of pollution.*   Taxation is not the only method by which a state can shift costs to residents of other states and secure local sellers against competition in the local market from nonresident sellers. The Court long ago held that a state could not impose minimum price regulations on out-of-state sellers; as we have seen, however, a similar result is permitted when brought about by a compensating use tax. The Court in several notable cases has looked through regulations ostensibly concerned with protecting health to the exclusionary purpose animating them. For example, it has forbidden a city to require that all milk sold there be pasteurized within a five-mile radius of the city's center.[1] The public health rationale of the law was tenuous; the purpose of preventing competition by nonresidents with local milk producers, inescapable.

Possible examples of cost-shifting regulation are provided by the recent burst of regulatory activity in the states relating to the control of pollution. The production of a good, such as paper and electricity, and of its pollution by-products will often take place in a different state from the principal markets for the good. Where this is so, the state of production — which will also be the state most affected by the pollution generated by the production process — may have an incentive to impose stringent pollution control requirements on the producers. The benefits of reduced pollution will be enjoyed primarily by the residents of the state. The costs of compliance with the pollution requirements will be borne in major part by the nonresident consumers of the product — although workers and taxpayers in the regulating state will also suffer to some extent. If Maine can prevent an electric utility from building a generating plant in the state to serve Boston residents, the effect is much like a severance tax. Benefits (reduced pollution, in the one case, and tax revenues in the other) are conferred on the residents of the regulating (or taxing) state at the expense of residents of other states.

The pollution case is more difficult than the milk case. The concern with public health in the milk case was a fairly transparent sham; the concern with pollution by the residents of Maine, like the desire for tax revenues of the residents of Texas,

3. Recent proposals for reform in the control of state taxation are discussed in Gerald Gunther & Noel T. Dowling, Cases and Materials on Constitutional Law 747–751 (8th ed. 1970).
§20.3. 1. Dean Milk Co. v. City of Madison, 340 U.S. 349 (1951).

is not fraudulent. But the measures animated by that concern may be excessive, if the residents of Maine can escape most of the costs, in reduced output of electricity, that result from not building the generating plant.[2]

State pollution control provides interesting examples of a distinct problem inherent in a federal system: the problem of effecting major interregional redeployments of resources. Suppose two states lie along the same river. In one state the river is primarily used by municipalities to dump sewage; in the other it is used primarily for swimming. Suppose that the added value to swimmers in the second state if the river were clean would exceed the added cost to the municipalities in the first state of disposing of sewage in some other manner. Then efficiency would be increased by inducing the first state to adopt alternative sewage-disposal methods. Suppose further that the costs of transactions preclude the swimmers in the second state from negotiating with the municipalities in the first. If there were no states, and the municipal sewage systems were owned either privately or by the federal government, there would be some hope for a political solution that improved efficiency. The swimmers would bring pressure to bear on the government to adopt alternative sewage-disposal methods if it owned the systems itself, or to require the private owners to shift to the alternative methods.

The existence of the federal system reduces the likelihood of an efficient solution. The swimmers have no political influence in the polluting state. The second state, acting on behalf of the swimmer, might attempt to sue the first on a nuisance theory. The Supreme Court has rendered judgments in a few such cases but has generally been unable to enforce its decrees against the losing state. Another possibility is for the second state to pay the first state to abate the pollution; by hypothesis, the first state could be induced to do this for a price lower than the cost to the swimmers of the dirty river. Such transactions, however, are extraordinarily rare. Perhaps the allocation of the proceeds among the affected municipalities would be very difficult. Perhaps the paying state would be unable to extract an enforceable commitment from the polluting state to cease polluting. At all events, while in principle it would seem that the federal system might actually facilitate transactions by creating large institutional representatives (i.e., the states) of benefited or harmed individuals

2. Does the existence of such costs presuppose that it is cheaper to produce electricity in Maine than elsewhere?

and individual firms, in practice it appears that efficient solutions are unlikely in cases such as we have described unless imposed by the federal government.[3]

§20.4. *Interbasin water transfers.*   Let us take a closer look at the problem of large interregional transfers under the federal system, using as our example water resources.[1] Since water is a surplus commodity in many states and a deficit commodity in others, there would appear to be promising opportunities for increasing the overall value of the resource by transferring some water from the surplus to the deficit regions. The cost of transporting water over large distances is substantial; however, the major obstacle to interregional transfers may be legal and institutional factors deriving from the structure of the federal system.

Were it feasible for the out-of-state purchaser to obtain the quantity of water he needed by purchasing individual appropriative rights owned by residents of the state or states having a water surplus, no special problem would be presented, since a state may not forbid the sale of an appropriative right to an out-of-state purchaser. But in view of the heavy transaction costs involved in the purchase of even a single appropriative right,[2] the costs of attempting to aggregate a large number of such rights by individual purchase would probably be prohibitive.

An alternative that gets around the cost of having to deal with a multitude of small rights holders is the purchase of unappropriated waters, which are found in large quantities in some states, especially in the Pacific Northwest. But there is a major problem. No one can convey a clear title to such waters, because it is only by the act of appropriation that a property right is created. A nonresident could attempt an appropriation but he would be met by the argument that the rents of unappropriated waters belong to the residents of the state within which they are located. And more than rents are involved. Unappropriated waters are not necessarily unused waters. There are many economically valuable but nonappropriative uses of water, such as recreation and the dilution of pollutants, that a major transfer to another water basin might impair.

The problem could be overcome by the payment of appropriate compensation by the out-of-state user to the state of origin.

3. The representative role of the state is discussed further *infra* §24.5.

§20.4. 1. The discussion in this section draws on Charles J. Meyers & Richard A. Posner, Market Transfers of Water Rights, pt. 4 (Natl. Tech. & Info Serv. 1971).

2. See §2.11 *supra*.

But the allocation of the compensation among affected residents would pose substantial administrative difficulties. There is also the conceptual problem that there is no recognized owner prior to appropriation. Most important, any title conveyed by the state would be clouded by the extensive but unquantified interests of the federal government and of other states. The United States has rights — the extent of which has never been determined — to use the waters of the rivers on the extensive federal public domain in the western states (Indian reservations, national parks and forests, military bases, etc.). The United States also has ill-defined but extensive interests in the waters of all navigable rivers by virtue of its "navigational servitude." A substantial interbasin diversion would therefore require the approval of the federal government, and probably only Congress itself could give this approval. It would also require the approval of the other states in the river basin, since the diversion of a substantial quantity of water from one point in a river system can affect recreational, environmental, and other valuable economic interests up and down the river system. A definition of each state's interests would require an apportionment by the Supreme Court, by interstate compact, or by Congress.

Clearly, a major problem with interbasin water transfers is the absence of clear-cut property rights in the waters that would be suitable for such transfers. The difficulty derives in part from the nature of a federal system, but it would be a mistake to put too much weight on this factor. A single owner of all of the property in the United States would still find it difficult to measure in advance the opportunity costs of a substantial interbasin water transfer and, if he found those costs to be smaller than the value of the water after transfer, to allocate appropriate compensation among those of his "tenants" who were adversely affected by the transfer and distribute it to them. The existence of dual and overlapping sovereignties and the resulting absence of clearly defined property rights are merely aggravating factors.

§20.5. *The exportation of poverty.*   One cost that states have found occasionally feasible to shift to other states is that of supporting the nonworking poor. The cost of the governmental services that the nonworking poor consume is higher than the tax revenues that they contribute to the support of those services: they are a deficit item in the public finance of the state. If in addition they have little political power, there will be strong support for attempting to export them. A cheap and easy method of doing this is to establish a level of welfare benefits so low that the beneficiaries are induced to migrate to states that grant higher benefits.

This is a very old problem. It plagued the English administration of poor relief and led to prohibitions against paupers' leaving their original parish. The solution of our states, a milder version of the English practice, was to require that an individual reside in the state for a period of time, usually one year, before he could receive welfare benefits. Notwithstanding this rule, many indigents from extremely low welfare benefit states such as Mississippi migrated to high welfare benefit states such as New York, scraping by with the help of relatives or friends during the one-year waiting period. But others doubtless were discouraged. To survive for a year in New York without any public assistance is a difficult challenge for an indigent family.

In *Shapiro v. Thompson*,[1] the Court invalidated the residency requirement on the ground that it inhibited interstate travel. However, some of the travel inhibited was induced by the prospect of receiving larger welfare payments than available in the migrant's state of origin. Migration for such an object would appear to distort rather than to promote the efficient geographical distribution of population. Society is no better off if indigents move from Mississippi to New York merely because New York has more generous poor relief. In fact, it is probably worse off economically because indigents can be supported decently at lower cost in Mississippi than in New York; the cost of living is lower in Mississippi. It is not even clear that indigents as a group are made better off by such migration, although individual indigents are. Free migration encourages the low welfare benefit states in their policy of inducing emigration by inadequate public assistance. Its effect in the high welfare benefit states is more complex. On the one hand, the increase in the number of its indigent residents may augment the political influence of the poor of the state, resulting in still higher levels of support. On the other hand, each increase attracts new welfare recipients from other states and eventually the state must realize that it is allowing itself to be used by the low welfare benefit states to relieve them of the burden of supporting the poor of those states. Once the high welfare benefit state stops increasing its welfare budget, the average welfare benefits of its residents will decrease, for indigents will continue to arrive, drawn by a level of support that, while static, and in average terms declining (the pie is not

§20.5. 1. 394 U.S. 618 (1969).

growing but it is being divided into more pieces), is still higher than in their own states.

The basic problem, both in English poor relief and in ours, is regional organization, which creates socially unproductive incentives: the incentive of states to shift the cost of welfare to other states, the incentive of the poor to migrate to areas where welfare benefits are more generous. A residency requirement is a crude and only partially effective method of dealing with this problem: crude, because it may often discourage the migration of a poor family that is motivated by superior employment opportunities in the high welfare benefit state but requires modest public assistance during the first few weeks or months of residence in a new state;[2] only partially effective, because the requirement invites fraud and because, as noted earlier, an indigent family may be able to scrape by for a year without public assistance. By undermining the regional approach to welfare administration, the *Shapiro* decision may hasten the national solution[3] that seems essential to overcome the locational inefficiencies that traditional decentralized welfare schemes create.

§20.6. *Competition among state governments.* As we have just seen, interstate mobility of people and resources limits the ability of a state to effectuate its policies. If indigents are highly mobile, a state cannot maintain a generous level of welfare benefits without attracting indigents from other states and, eventually, perhaps bankrupting the program. Mobility works the other way too. It limits the ability of a state to impose taxes that are disproportionate to the value of the public services financed by the taxes and is thus a powerful force for economy in state and local government. With complete mobility, import taxes would not be feasible. As mentioned earlier, the residents of the state imposing such a tax usually lose more than the producers in the state gain; therefore the residents would migrate to states that did not impose such taxes. Were nonhuman resources also completely mobile, states would be unable to impose monopolistic severance taxes: the oil producer would move his well to a state that did not impose such a tax.

People and resources do not enjoy complete interstate mobility — relocation to another state is not generally costless — and

2. Could such a poor person borrow the necessary assistance? Observe also that the residency requirement discourages indigents in high welfare benefit states from seeking employment in other areas (why?).

3. Is an appropriate national solution a uniform level of benefits regardless of location? Why should a cost of living differential *not* be included?

therefore competition among the states is not a complete answer to the problems of extraterritorial and protectionist taxes and regulations. But the consumers of state services have enough mobility to impede, at least, the efforts of the states to implement their policies. Welfare is one example. Another is taxation. A tax on railroad boxcars found in the state, assessed on one day of the year, is unlikely to be an effective revenue measure: the railroad can move most of the cars out of the state on tax day. This is an extreme example because the railroad continues to enjoy the benefit of whatever governmental services the state provides it out of the tax revenues; it simply escapes their costs. But even where the taxpayer cannot escape the tax without forfeiting the public services of the state (for example, he would have to move to a different school district to escape a heavy school tax) he will have an incentive to relocate whenever the additional taxes he pays are excessive in relation to the services that the taxing district confers on him. This may lead to inefficient relocations, just as in the welfare case: the taxpayer may have received a higher wage (net of taxes) in the state that taxed him more heavily, because his services were more valuable there.

There would be little cause for concern were it accepted that taxes should always be proportional to benefits received; the mobility of taxpayers exerts pressure in this direction. But that cannot be the operative principle of taxation, if only because it would not permit the use of public revenues to support the poor. It is thus inevitable that some taxpayers will derive no greater benefits in governmental services received in a state where the tax rate is high than in one where it is low. The incentive of such taxpayers to migrate to states where tax rates are low undermines the efforts of states, say, with a large number of poor people, to provide adequate levels of poor relief.

The economic case for the sharing of federal tax revenues with the states, either directly or by permitting state taxes to be deducted from federal income tax, is thus simply that international mobility is much less than interstate.[1] The optimum form of federal revenue sharing might appear to be a system in which the *only* taxes were federal taxes. This would eliminate the incentive to change residence solely in order to take advantage of lower tax rates. But there is a serious drawback to such a plan. Since the expenses of state government would no longer be defrayed by the

---

§20.6. 1. By the same token, interstate mobility is less than local. What implications does this have for the tenable scope of local taxation?

state's taxpayers, an important incentive for economizing on government expenses would be impaired. Although the extravagance of one state would increase the overall federal tax burden, the extra cost would be spread among all federal taxpayers. The residents of the state in question would pay only a small share of the costs of their improvidence, and would have correspondingly little incentive to take corrective steps through the political process.

SUGGESTED READINGS

1. Developments in the Law — Federal Limitations on State Taxation of Interstate Business, 75 Harv. L. Rev. 953 (1963).
2. Charles J. Meyers & Richard A. Posner, Market Transfers of Water Rights, pt. 4 (Natl. Tech. & Info. Serv. 1971).
3. George J. Stigler, The Tenable Range of Functions of Local Government, in Staff of Joint Econ. Comm., Federal Expenditure Policy for Economic Growth 213 (Jt. Comm. Print 1967).

PROBLEMS

1. *Why should Texas, in our severance tax example, be restrained from taxing nonresidents? Do not nonresident consumers of oil products benefit from the services that the State of Texas renders to the oil producers located in the state?*

2. *Can economic theory help you to devise a formula for apportioning a firm's movable property (e.g., an airline's aircraft) among the states for state tax purposes?*

3. *Should states be permitted to impose corporate income taxes? Suppose states that impose such taxes were required to adopt a uniform formula for apportioning corporate income among the states. What would be a better formula: percentage of corporate revenues derived from sales to residents of the taxing state or percentage of employees within the taxing state? To what extent is apportionment of corporate income among states arbitrary from an economic standpoint?*

4. *In Baldwin v. G.A.F. Seelig, Inc., 294 U.S. 511 (1935), the Supreme Court held that a New York State law fixing a minimum price for milk sold in the state could not constitutionally be applied to milk produced in Vermont and imported into New York. The Court's strong condemnation of New York's attempt to subject such milk to its minimum-price law has been criticized as follows: "New York's interest was not simple economic bias against out-of-state competitors; it dealt primarily with local economic well-being and health." Gerald Gunther & Noel T. Dowling, Cases and Materials on Constitutional*

Law 651 (8th ed. 1970). Can "economic bias against out-of-state competitors" be differentiated from "local economic well-being"? Is the criticism tantamount to asserting that states should be permitted to create some tariffs?

5. Why do some states have higher welfare allowances than others? Is it because the taxpayers in those states attach a greater value to reducing poverty? If so, can it still be argued that efficiency is reduced rather than increased if the poor gravitate to these states?

6. A railroad brakeman, a resident of state A, is injured in an accident in state B. He sues the railroad in state A. The railroad sets up the defense that the brakeman was injured by the negligence of a fellow worker. This is a good defense under the law of B but not under the law of A. Which rule should govern? (See Alabama Great So. R.R. v. Carroll, *97 Ala. 126, 11 So. 803 (1892).) Does the analysis in this chapter help you to answer conflict-of-law questions such as these?*

CHAPTER 21

RACIAL DISCRIMINATION

§21.1. The economics of discrimination.[1]   Many people
would prefer not to associate with the members of particular
racial, religious, or ethnic groups different from their own and
would pay a price to indulge their taste. Thus, although there are
pecuniary gains to trade between blacks and whites — to blacks
working for whites (or vice versa), whites selling houses to blacks,
and so forth — much as there are pecuniary gains to trade among
nations, by increasing the contact between members of the two
races such trade imposes nonpecuniary, but real, costs on those
members of either race who dislike association with members
of the other race. These costs are analogous to transportation
costs in international trade, and like transportation costs, they
reduce the amount of trading (and of the association incidental
to it).

What is the impact of reduced exchange on the wealth of the
groups involved? Assume that whites do not like to associate with
blacks but that blacks are indifferent to the racial identity of
those with whom they associate. The incomes of many whites
will be lower than they would be if they did not have such a
taste.[2] They forgo advantageous exchanges: for example, they
may refuse to sell their houses to blacks who are willing to pay
higher prices than white purchasers. The racial preference of the
whites will also reduce the incomes of the blacks, by preventing
them from making advantageous exchanges with whites. The reduction in the blacks' incomes, however, will be proportionately
greater than the reduction in the whites' incomes, given that, independent of bigotry or discrimination, the economy of the

§21.1. 1. This section draws very heavily on Gary S. Becker, The Economics of
Discrimination (2d ed. 1971).
2. Some whites — those who are not prejudiced — will have higher incomes
than they would if other whites were not prejudiced (why?).

United States is dominated by white people. Because blacks are only a small part of the economy, the number of advantageous exchanges that blacks can make with whites is greater than the number of advantageous transactions that whites can make with blacks. The white sector is so large as to be virtually self-sufficient; the black sector is much smaller and more dependent on trade with the white.

The international trade analogy can help clarify the point. The United States constitutes so large an aggregation of skills, resources, and population that it could survive a substantial reduction of its foreign trade in relative comfort. Switzerland could not. Its markets are too small and its resources too limited to permit it to achieve economies of scale and of specialization without trading with other countries. The position of the black minority in the United States is similar to that of Switzerland in the world economy. The reduction of commercial intercourse between blacks and whites brought about by discrimination reduces the money income of whites some, but the incomes of blacks greatly.

The effect on blacks' money incomes would be the same if the reduction in trading between blacks and whites were brought about not by whites' distaste for association with blacks but by blacks' distaste for association with whites.[3] But the reduction in the blacks' money incomes would be in a sense self-imposed (would their economic welfare be any higher?).

Discrimination is consistent with competition, just as a reduction in international trade due to higher costs of transportation would be no evidence that international markets were not competitive. In a competitive market, however, there are economic forces working to minimize discrimination that are blunted in a market either monopolized or controlled by government. In a market of many sellers one can expect the intensity of the prejudice against blacks to vary considerably. Some sellers will have only a mild prejudice against them. These sellers will not forgo as many advantageous transactions with blacks as their more prejudiced competitors. Their costs will therefore be lower and this will enable them to increase their share of the market. The least prejudiced sellers will come to dominate the market in much the same way as people who are least afraid of heights come to dominate occupations that require working at heights: they demand a smaller premium for working at such a job.

3. To some extent this is true today, due to the rise of black nationalism.

Under monopoly, the tendency for the market to be dominated by firms with the least prejudice against blacks is not so strong. The single seller in the market will be, on average, as prejudiced as the average, not as the least prejudiced, member of the community. To be sure, there will be a tendency for monopolies that are freely transferable (such as patents) to come into the hands of the least prejudiced. The efficient exploitation of a monopoly which requires association with blacks is less valuable to a highly prejudiced owner, who suffers either a reduction in his pecuniary income by forgoing advantageous transactions with blacks or a nonpecuniary cost by making such transactions, than it would be to a less prejudiced owner. Therefore the less prejudiced will tend to purchase monopolies from the more prejudiced. But not all monopolies are freely transferable.

If the monopoly is regulated, the market forces working against discrimination are apt to be weakened still further. One way to evade a profit ceiling is by substituting nonpecuniary for pecuniary income, since the former is very difficult for a regulatory agency to control. One form of nonpecuniary income is that which people receive from not associating with the minorities against which they are prejudiced. Stated otherwise, the cost of discrimination is less where, due to regulation, the pecuniary income forgone as a result of discrimination is smaller than it would be without regulation.[4]

Labor unions that have monopoly power seriously impair the effectiveness of competition in minimizing discrimination. A monopolistic union will increase the incomes of its members above their alternative incomes in other occupations. This disparity in turn will induce workers in other occupations to seek entry into the union. The union cannot take all comers since if it increases the supply of labor it will be unable to maintain the monopoly price that it is charging employers. Thus the need arises to ration membership in the union. The union could auction off vacancies as they occur or permit members to sell their membership (this is the method used to fill vacancies on the New York Stock Exchange, a cartel of stockbrokers). Or it could adopt various nonprice criteria, such as nepotism or race. The usual practice has been to use nonprice criteria, including membership in the white race. In effect, the members of the union take a part of their monopoly

---

4. For some evidence on this point see Armen A. Alchian & Reuben Kessel, Competition, Monopoly, and the Pursuit of Money, in Aspects of Labor Economics 157 (Natl. Bur. Econ. Research 1962). But cf. §21.3 *infra*, note 2, and accompanying text.

profits in the form of freedom from a type of association distasteful to them. In the absence of monopolistic unions, the least prejudiced workers would have an advantage in the job market comparable to that enjoyed by the least prejudiced sellers in product markets. Employers would not have to pay them so high a premium to work with black employees whom the employers might for reasons of efficiency want to hire.

Thus governmental policy, which is responsible for profit controls on monopolists and in part for strong labor unions, may increase discrimination above the level that would exist in an unregulated market. The effect is even greater when the government enacts and enforces laws that require discrimination, as was long the practice in the southern states. To be sure, such laws will not be enacted unless there is a strong preference in the community for not associating with blacks. But it does not follow that the law adds nothing to private feeling. There may be a minority of whites who have relatively little taste for discrimination and might be unwilling to bear the expense involved in maintaining separate public rest rooms, schools, and other facilities in their community. In a southern state that had no law against integrated public schools, we might still expect most school districts to maintain segregated schools if permitted by federal law; but some — those in which the white residents were not prepared to pay a significant price to avoid association with blacks — would not. The total amount of discrimination in the state would be less.

All this is not to say that the effect of government is invariably to increase the amount of discrimination. Government regulations that reduce competition or reduce the cost of forgoing pecuniary income have this effect as do laws enacting discriminatory policies. But if the opponents of discrimination control the governmental machinery, they can use the powers of government to reduce discrimination.[5]

§21.2. *School segregation.* In *Brown v. Board of Education*,[1] the Supreme Court declared unconstitutional state laws either requiring or permitting racial segregation of public schools. The Court held that segregated education was inherently unequal because it instilled a sense of inferiority in black children. The analysis in the preceding section suggests an economic as distinct from a psychological basis for rejecting the notion of

5. See §21.4 *infra*.
§21.2. 1. 347 U.S. 483 (1954).

"separate but equal." Segregation reduces the opportunities for valuable associations between races and these associations would be especially valuable to the blacks because of the dominant position of the whites in the society. The Court had explicitly recognized this point in an earlier case, *Sweatt v. Painter*,[2] which held that blacks must be admitted to state law schools. The Court observed that black students in a segregated law school would have no opportunity to develop valuable professional contacts with the students most likely to occupy important positions in the bench and bar after graduation. It rejected the argument that this disadvantage was offset by the disadvantage to white students of being barred from association with black law students, noting that the weak position of the blacks in the profession made such associations less valuable to white students.

If our earlier analysis is correct, the laws invalidated in *Brown* that forbade local school districts to integrate the schools made discrimination greater than it would have been in the absence of such laws — but perhaps not much greater. While the federal courts, the United States Department of Justice, and other agencies were eventually able to compel the southern states to desist from enforcing their segregation laws, many whites were willing to pay the additional costs necessary to perpetuate school segregation. They sent their children to segregated private schools or moved to school districts containing few black residents. The Supreme Court had made discrimination more costly but since the white population valued school discrimination very highly, the effect of the Court's action on the amount of school discrimination was (until recently) small. Further, since the white population controlled the public finance of the states it could deflect the force of the Court's action, in part at least, by reducing appropriations for public education and by directly subsidizing private education through tuition grants and tax credits. These measures made the shift of white children to segregated private schools less costly to parents.

The Court could have exploited the value that the whites attached to school segregation by requiring, as a condition of maintaining segregated schools, that the southern states devote much larger sums to the education of blacks than was their practice. As it did in invalidating public school segregation, the Court would have been increasing the cost of discrimination to the whites;

2. 339 U.S. 629 (1950).

and it would have been increasing the incomes of the blacks in compensation for continued segregation. It is at least arguable that the blacks might have been better off under such an arrangement, even if the *Brown* decision had received prompt and wholehearted compliance. Suppose a community composed of 200 blacks and 800 whites, where the average income of the blacks is $5000, and of the whites $10,000. The elimination of segregated education would, let us assume, increase the income of the blacks by an average of $2000 (we will not worry about the lag between changed educational conditions and better employment). The black community would therefore gain $400,000 from desegregation. Suppose that the whites in the community would be willing to pay an average of $1000 apiece not to integrate the schools. They would therefore be willing to spend a total of $800,000 on better education for the blacks as the price of continued segregation, an expenditure that might well increase the blacks' incomes by more than $400,000.

The major significance of the *Brown* decision may not have been its impact on the educational system at all. While economists usually treat tastes as givens, external to their analysis, the character of much advertising suggests that the creation of new tastes and the alteration of old may be an important part of economic activity. One purpose of many advertisements appears to be the creation of a pleasant association between the product and the viewer or reader's other tastes (for romance, pleasant countryside, outdoor activity, etc.).[3] The major practical effect of the Court's *Brown* decision may have been to create an association between discrimination and the invasion of highly regarded values enshrined in the Constitution that reduced the taste for discrimination.

Reinforcement or alteration of taste may be an important part of the intended effect of law and hence of legal decisions, especially when the decisions invalidate laws. Many laws — notably present-day laws regulating deviant sexual practices — are not seriously enforced but are nevertheless retained on the books. Such laws have negligible effects on incentives but may have an

---

3. Other purposes are to remind the potential customer of the product's availability and to assure him that the producer is an established and financially responsible concern. (The latter is presumably one reason why people prefer Bayer aspirin although all aspirin have the same chemical composition; better quality control may be another and related reason.)

effect on tastes, just as a celebrity's opinion on the latest fashion in women's dresses may affect taste.[4]

The *Brown* decision has been criticized on the ground that it denied freedom of association to the whites at the same time that it promoted the freedom of association of the blacks and that there is no "neutral principle" by which to choose between the associational preferences of whites and blacks.[5] However, economic analysis suggests an important distinction between the associational preferences of prejudiced whites and nonprejudiced blacks. Because blacks are an economic minority, the pecuniary costs to them of the whites' prejudice are proportionately much greater than the pecuniary costs to the whites. This distinction in the distributive effects of prejudice is perfectly general. It applies to any economic minority — such a minority pays a higher price for being the object of discrimination than the economic majority that discriminates against it.

§21.3. *The requirement of state action.* We have seen that laws requiring discrimination increase its incidence even in communities where the taste for discrimination among the white residents is high. The distinction between state and private action in the Fourteenth Amendment (which provides that no *state* shall deny equal protection of its laws or deprive anyone of life, liberty, or property without due process of law) is thus consistent with the economic analysis of discrimination. That analysis also clarifies the issues involved in defining state action.

Three levels of state involvement in discrimination may be distinguished. The first is a law or other official action that orders discrimination. The second is the practice of discrimination by a public enterprise. The third is state involvement in private enterprises that practice discrimination but not in the decision of the enterprise to discriminate. Both the first and second levels of state involvement were involved in the *Brown* case, but they were not distinguished. One aspect of the Court's decision is the invalidation of laws requiring all public schools in a state to be segregated. Such laws may be presumed to enact the prejudices of the more prejudiced half of the population and thus to produce greater discrimination than if the decision to segregate were left up to each individual public school district. The second aspect of

4. This may explain the Court's decisions attributing to the state private discrimination pursuant to official statement or ordinance, though admittedly void. See, e.g., Peterson v. Greenville, 373 U.S. 244 (1963).

5. Herbert Wechsler, Toward Neutral Principles of Constitutional Law, 73 Harv. L. Rev. 1 (1959).

the decision is the invalidation of state laws permitting local school districts, at their option, to segregate. When the decision whether or not to segregate is left to each local school district it is not so obvious that the result will be a different amount of discrimination from what there would be if all education were private; but probably there will be more discrimination. A public school system is a nontransferable monopoly (private education is a substitute, but it is not so good a substitute as to deprive the school district of all monopoly power), and we saw earlier that nontransferable monopolies may be expected to discriminate more, on average, than competitive firms or freely transferable monopolies. Since most governmental services are in the nature of nontransferable monopolies, this point has general application to state agencies. The reader may object to equating a political body like a public school system with a private monopolist. However, the equation is valid if it can be assumed that the political body is apt to be representative of the average level of discrimination in the community.[1] A further point is that public enterprises may in general be less sensitive to the costs of alternative policies than private firms and hence less sensitive to the pecuniary costs that a policy of discrimination imposes.[2]

The analysis is different where the decision to discriminate is made by a private individual or firm, albeit the state is involved to some extent in the private activity. Here the question should be whether the nature of the state involvement is such as to make a decision to discriminate more likely than if the state had not been involved. Where state involvement takes the form of public utility or common carrier regulation, then, as we saw earlier, the likelihood that the firm will follow discriminatory policies is greater, and so the firm's discrimination could be viewed as action by the state (in the legal sense). However, where the involvement of the state does not increase the likelihood of discrimination, there is no basis in principle for attributing to the state a private decision to discriminate. The state maintains an extensive system of land title recordation and is otherwise deeply involved in the regulation of land use, but the state's involvement in the real estate industry does not make it more likely that

§21.3. 1. This assumes the whites dominate the political process of the community.

2. How does the point about the agency's relative insensitivity to pecuniary cost cut if the agency is controlled by people less prejudiced than the average of the community in which the enterprise is operating? This is quite plausible if the agency is federal rather than local.

a white homeowner will refuse to sell his house to a black buyer because of distaste for association with blacks than if the state did not regulate the industry.

The proposed distinction suggests not a narrower but a different definition of state action from what the courts have employed. It would support a prohibition under the Fourteenth Amendment of racial discrimination by trade unions, for the governmental policies that have fostered the growth of monopolistic unions have thereby increased the likelihood that they would practice racial discrimination. It would not forbid discrimination by the private concessionaire in a public office building[3] unless the public authority had encouraged the concessionaire to discriminate.

An interesting question is presented when the state involvement takes the form of legal enforcement of a private decision to discriminate. May racial covenants be enforced? [4] May the City of Macon as trustee of the park donated by Senator Bacon comply with the racial condition in the gift? [5] Does the equal protection clause forbid civil and criminal remedies for trespass to the shopkeeper who does not want black customers? It can hardly be shown that, in the absence of legal protection of property rights, there would be less discrimination. There might well be more, at least in communities in which the taste for discrimination was widespread, since without a system of legally protected property rights more economic activity would have to be directed by political decision rather than by the market. It is true but trivial that if the state enforced all private decisions except those to discriminate, the cost of discrimination would be higher and the incidence lower. This is equivalent to saying that the state's failure to punish private discrimination is discriminatory state action, a view that would set at naught the constitutional requirement of state action.

To be sure, in the restrictive covenant and charitable gift cases the effect of enforcing a racial condition would be to create more discrimination than the members of society today want, assuming a secular decline in the taste for discrimination. To return to the international trade analogy, it is a little as if nations had agreed in the nineteenth century that they would never permit international trade to be conducted other than in sailing ships. But

---

3. Burton v. Wilmington Parking Authority, 365 U.S. 715 (1951).
4. See Shelley v. Kraemer, 334 U.S. 1 (1948).
5. See Evans v. Newton, 382 U.S. 296 (1966); §17.2 *supra*.

the result is simply a particular application of the broader problem discussed in an earlier chapter: a perpetual condition in a deed or gift may cause resources to be employed inefficiently if an unforeseen contingency, in this case a decline in the taste for discrimination, materializes. It is pure accident whether the result of a perpetual condition is more discrimination than contemporaries want — or less. Were there a secular increase rather than decline in racial discrimination, the result of enforcing racially motivated deed or gift restrictions (such as a provision in a foundation charter declaring the purpose of the foundation to be to promote racial integration) might be less discrimination than contemporaries wanted.

§*21.4. Antidiscrimination laws.* The decisions of the federal courts invalidating the segregation laws of the southern states and compelling the integration of publicly owned facilities did not eliminate discrimination in the South. Where there is a strong taste for discrimination, one expects to find widespread discrimination even if the government is effectively prevented from encouraging it. Further, a strong taste for discrimination — which, stated otherwise, is a willingness to forgo substantial pecuniary gains in order to avoid association with the members of a particular group — makes people willing to pay a price in punishment costs for noncompliance with a federal court order directing integration; this too occurred in the southern states.

Such was the background for the enactment of federal laws forbidding private discrimination, notably in the sale and rental of real estate, in employment, and in restaurants, hotels, and other places of public accommodation. The usual justifications advanced for such laws, at least in legal argument, are first, that they are necessary to eliminate the effects of centuries of discriminatory legislation, and second, that they promote interstate commerce. The second justification strikes many people as rather contrived, yet it makes economic sense. Discrimination reduces transactions between blacks and whites and many of the transactions that are prevented would be in interstate commerce, even narrowly defined. It is the first justification that is dubious, because of its nigh infinite reach. If the comparison of·legislation and advertising as molders of taste is accepted, then there is a realistic sense in which today's private discrimination may be said to be a result in part of discriminatory legislation now invalid. This is the kernel of sense in the Supreme Court's decisions holding that private discrimination may be attributed to the state when it is required by law even though the law has been declared unconstitutional.[1] The trouble is that virtually *any* deprivation from which black people suffer today may be a result in part of past discrimination fostered by discriminatory laws or other governmental policies. If black children on average do not perform well in northern schools, it may be because the returns to education for black people have traditionally been low due to particularly severe discrimination in employment against educated blacks; this in turn may have been influenced by the discriminatory governmental policies of the southern states from which many northern blacks originated.

Economic analysis is helpful in explaining the variance in compliance with antidiscrimination laws. Where the interracial associations brought about by the law are slight or transient, the costs of association even to prejudiced people will be low and they will not be willing to sustain large pecuniary costs, in the form of punishment or legal expenses incurred in resisting compliance, merely to indulge their taste. It is not surprising that there has been general compliance with laws forbidding people to refuse to sell real estate on racial grounds, although few resources have been allocated to enforcing these laws. Unless the seller plans to remain in the neighborhood, his association with a black purchaser is limited to the negotiation of the sale. Similarly, the association between a hotel owner and staff on the one hand and the guests of the hotel on the other are rather impersonal except where the establishment is very small — and for just this reason small establishments were exempted from the public accommodation law — so again it is not surprising that widespread compliance was rapidly and easily achieved. School integration is different. Not only is the association among school children intimate and prolonged but to the extent that black children, for whatever reason, on average perform worse in school than white children, integration may involve costs to whites over and above the nonpecuniary costs imposed by an undesired association.

§21.5. *Job discrimination.*   Laws forbidding discrimination in employment involve interesting problems of proof, statutory purpose, and remedy.[1] A firm may have no black employees, even if

§21.4. 1. See §21.2 *supra*, note 4.

§21.5. 1. There is an excellent literature on employment discrimination laws. See, e.g., William M. Landes, The Economics of Fair Employment Laws, 76 J. Pol. Econ. 507 (1968); Ralph K. Winter, Jr., Improving the Economic Status of Negroes Through Laws Against Discrimination: A Reply to Professor Sovern, 34 U. Chi. L. Rev. 817 (1967); Owen M. Fiss, A Theory of Fair Employment Laws, 38 id. 235 (1971). The Landes article is an empirical study of the effects of state employment discrimination law on black employment and income.

it is located in an area having a large black population, for reasons unrelated to discrimination by either the management of the firm or the white workers. There may be no blacks with the requisite training or aptitude or they may not like the type of work or they may simply be unaware of job openings at the firm. If any of these reasons are operative it becomes necessary to decide whether the purpose of the law is simply to prevent current and future discrimination in employment or whether it is more broadly designed to improve the condition of blacks. There are economic reasons for preferring the narrower reading even if the appropriateness of redistributing wealth in favor of blacks is accepted. If an employer is compelled to hire unqualified blacks, or pay them a premium to induce them to do a type of work that they do not like, or advertise in the black community openings for jobs in which very few blacks are interested, the firm sustains costs in excess of the benefits to the blacks who are hired. The unqualified black employee imposes productivity losses that he does not recoup in higher wages. The premium paid to the black employee who does not like to work in this type of job is a cost to the firm but not a benefit to the black employee: it only offsets the nonpecuniary cost of the job to him. The expense of advertising jobs in the black community may not confer a commensurate benefit on the blacks if the advertising fails to generate a significant flow of qualified applicants. Since the major part of the additional costs will be passed on to the firm's consumers, these methods of improving the welfare of black people tend to be regressive as well as costly.

Even limited to the discriminating employer, antidiscrimination laws impose costs. The employer may have to pay a higher wage to those white workers who have both a taste for discrimination and attractive alternative opportunities for employment in firms that do not have black employees. If they lack such opportunities, the elimination of discrimination may impose no pecuniary costs — by hypothesis the workers have no choice but to accept association with blacks — but it will impose nonpecuniary costs, in the form of an association distasteful to the whites. And the costs are unlikely to be offset by the gains of black workers for whom jobs in the firm are superior to their alternative job opportunities, or by the economic advantages that increased trading with blacks brings to the firm and hence to its customers: were there these offsetting gains, the blacks would have been hired without legal pressure (can you see why?).

Let us consider now the question of the appropriate remedy

in a job discrimination case in which a violation has been adjudged. There is relatively little problem in the case where the employer has discriminated against blacks, either because he has a taste for discrimination or because his white workers do. If he is the guilty party, he should be required to pay the damages of any black person against whom he has discriminated, perhaps doubled or trebled to facilitate enforcement where damages are small.[2] If the employees are the guilty ones (for example, because they have refused to permit blacks to join their union), an appropriate remedy is to order the employer to hire the black workers thus wronged, if necessary laying off some white workers. (Observe, however, that the employer may have to pay higher wages to the remaining white workers; what would be the economic consequences of his doing so?)[3]

The problem of remedy becomes acute if the law is interpreted to require that the employer have some minimum number or percentage of black employees regardless of whether he or his white employees have been guilty of discrimination. To comply, the employer must lay off workers or, what amounts to the same thing, favor black over white job applicants for as long a period of time as is necessary to attain the quota. In either case white employees untainted by discrimination are made to bear a high cost in order to improve the condition of black workers. The result is a capricious and regressive tax on the white working class.

SUGGESTED READING

Gary S. Becker, The Economics of Discrimination (2d ed. 1971).

PROBLEMS

1. In this chapter we suggested a neutral principle for forbidding discrimination. Is it possible to argue that discrimination is inefficient? In economic terms, are the costs of interracial associations, given prejudice, any different from the crop damage caused by the interaction of railroading and farming?

2. There is an interesting litigation in process in the City of Chicago between a number of blacks who bought homes on land contracts and the developers who sold the homes to them. The blacks defaulted on the contracts. They claim, however, that they should not be held liable for the default because the prices charged them for the homes were

2. Cf. §25.2 *infra.*
3. Cf. §2.12 *supra.*

excessive. They contend that they were forced to pay higher prices than white purchasers of similar property, due to discrimination against blacks. The developers contend that the blacks should be grateful that they were willing to sell them such desirable property. What light can economic analysis shed on the issues in the litigation? Would the welfare of blacks as a whole be increased or reduced if the developers lost the lawsuit?

3. Can it be argued that racially restrictive covenants might increase efficiency? If so, would it follow that they should be enforced?

CHAPTER 22

THE MARKETPLACE OF IDEAS, AND
THE PRIMACY OF POLITICAL
OVER ECONOMIC RIGHTS

§22.1. *The economic basis of freedom of speech.* The First Amendment forbids government to prevent or punish the expression of ideas or opinions even if it can make out a good case that they are wrong and pernicious. There are exceptions, which we examine in a moment, but the unquestioned core of the principle is substantial.

The principle may be restated in a form that brings out its economic character: government may not limit competition in ideas. Ideas are a useful good produced in enormous quantity in a highly competitive market; the marketplace of ideas of which Holmes wrote is fact, not merely a figure of speech.[1] This market-place determines the "truth" of ideas (other than purely deductive propositions such as the Pythagorean theorem), for when we say that an idea (the earth revolves around the sun) is correct we mean that all or most of the knowledgeable consumers have accepted ("bought") it. Research in the history of science supports this view of how truth is established. Even in science — the traditional domain of objective validity — ideas are discarded not because they are demonstrated to be false but because competing ideas give better answers to the questions with which the scientists of the day are most concerned.[2] If competition among ideas is the method by which truth is established, the suppression of an idea on the ground that it is false is irrational. An idea is false only if rejected in the marketplace, and if rejected there is no occasion to suppress it. For the government to declare an idea to be "true" when it has suppressed the competing ideas would

§22.1. 1. Abrams v. United States, 250 U.S. 616, 630 (1919) (dissenting opinion).
2. See Thomas Kuhn, The Structure of Scientific Revolutions (1962).

be comparable to its declaring a brand of beer to be the "most popular" brand when it had suppressed the sale of the other brands.

§22.2. *The scope of the protected activity: Incitement, defamation, and obscenity.* Not all statements communicate ideas. If I say "I am going for a walk now" or "I am going to rob a bank" or "I am organizing an armed insurrection," I am not expressing an idea but merely describing my intention. To punish me for such utterances would not be an interference with the marketplace of ideas, although it might be objectionable on other grounds. But the line between inciting on the one hand and marketing ideas on the other is a fine one: to say "armed insurrection tomorrow would be a good thing" is to compete in the marketplace of ideas unless the circumstances are such that the statement is intended as a signal for action, like firing the opening gun at a racetrack.

Defamatory statements constitute a difficult case. Damaging statements about individuals are an important part of the marketplace of ideas and can be validated in the same way as other ideas — by competition. But they are special in that they inflict costs that are both concentrated and at least crudely measurable. On an economic analysis, producers and sellers of ideas, as of other goods, should not escape the costs of their activity. Thus it can be argued that they should be liable for injuries to reputations and other property, although punitive damages should be disallowed since they might induce the suppression of an idea the benefits of which exceeded the costs (the costs being the actual damages, fairly estimated, of the victims of the defamation).

The difficult question is whether truth should be a defense to a defamation charge. One can argue no, because truth is what the market, rather than a court or jury, decides to believe, and because the costs of a defamatory utterance are no less — they will in fact usually be more — when it is true (believed). But there are serious problems with this position. If the market in ideas were just like the markets in other goods, the damages awarded in cases involving true defamatory utterances, although normally larger than in cases of false defamatory utterances, would not result in suppression of the true defamatory utterance more often than the false. The benefits of the true utterance would be greater than the benefits of the false, for by "true" we mean widely believed. The true utterance is like the brand of beer that commands 95 percent of the market, and the false like the brand with only 5 percent. The problem is that the producer of an idea often cannot appropriate its full social benefits. If a reporter gets a scoop, his newspaper will capture in higher sales revenues a part of the value that the public attaches to the news, but only a part, because the item will be carried in all competing papers with only a slight time lag. If the reporter and the newspaper that employs him are faced with the prospect of large damages, they may be reluctant to publish the item even though the total social benefits, as measured by the willingness of all newspaper readers to pay to read the item, may exceed those damages.

There are various ways of coping with this problem. One is to exempt from liability those defamatory utterances that are highly valued because they are likely to be universally accepted. The defense of truth provides a method, crude but as applied to simple questions serviceable, of predicting the degree of acceptance of a particular defamatory idea. An alternative efficient approach would be to recognize more extensive property rights in news. The *Associated Press* decision,[1] which held that a news service could enjoin the unauthorized publication of its dispatches by a rival service, would be a helpful precedent in this regard had it not been eroded by subsequent decisions.[2] However, even if there were more extensive property rights in news, a defense of truth would remain clearly appropriate in at least some cases. The corrupt official, for example, should not be permitted to collect damages for the exposure of his malfeasance, since public humiliation is part of the system of sanctions for official misconduct.[3] Since the consequence of construing the right of privacy as protecting people from disclosure of genuinely discrediting information is to reduce the cost of discreditable conduct, the fundamental question is when impairment of reputation should be utilized as a method of social regulation; in those cases a defense must be recognized.[4]

The question whether to exact a price for ideas that inflict cost is acutely posed by pornography. Even those most hostile to censorship accept the propriety of punishing lewd public displays — an obscene billboard, for example. As a belching factory chimney imposes costs on nonparties to the sale of steel, so an obscene

§22.2. 1. International News Service v. Associated Press, 248 U.S. 215 (1918).

2. See Edmund W. Kitch & Harvey S. Perlman, Legal Regulation of the Competitive Process 25–28 (1972).

3. Cf. §2.10 *supra*. What if the information relates to past crimes for which the official has already been punished?

4. Do you see an analogy here to the question whether contributory negligence should be recognized as a defense to strict liability for accidental harms? Cf. §4.15 *supra*.

billboard imposes costs on nonparties to the sale of pornography. If the costs exceed the advertising benefits, the billboard represents an inefficient use of resources. But pornography may impose costs on consumers even though it is distributed without offensive advertising or promotion. Nonconsumers may be disgusted at the thought that pornography is publicly available or fearful that their children will be corrupted or that the incidence of sex crimes will rise. Such disgust and fear are a cost, but a different kind of cost, one not based primarily on personal injury but rather on concern for community welfare.

The analysis of nuisance in Chapter 2 is relevant in framing the issues here. A rule that permitted pornography to be sold but not publicly displayed would impose some costs on the sellers and consumers of pornography but probably less than the costs of public display to those hostile to pornography. A rule that forbade all distribution of pornography would, if we may judge by the size of the market for pornography and the absence of close substitutes, impose very heavy costs on people who have a taste for pornography. These costs might exceed what knowledge of the availability of pornography would cost those hostile to pornography.

It cannot be assumed that a community's laws relating to pornography express the preferences of the members of the community, aggregated by their willingness to pay, for and against pornography. If 75 percent of the voters are mildly hostile to pornography and 25 percent extremely favorable, the willingness of the minority to pay to have it may exceed the willingness of the majority to pay not to have it. But unless the 25 percent can form a coalition with other voters, whose support for pornography is obtained by a promise to support some position about which these voters feel strongly, the economic preferences of the community will not be reflected in the political process.[5] By the same token the absence of laws forbidding pornography might not reflect the preferences of the population as they would be expressed in a market.

Unfortunately, in the case where pornography is available but not advertised publicly, the nuisance approach tends to break down, for we are in an area where freedom of expression is sought to be restricted less because it imposes costs on specific individuals than because it is thought to be dangerous to the community

5. The expression of preference through the political process is discussed at greater length in the next chapter.

at large. This reason for suppression implies, contrary to the usual assumptions of economic analysis, that the consumer of ideas may not be able to make rational choices among them, for putting aside the special problem of children it would seem that if pornography corrupts the character the way poison corrupts the body (or, in the political arena, if certain ideologies are unwholesome, like tainted meat), the consuming public will refuse to buy them. In fact the government regulates the sale of dangerous products, so perhaps the real basis for the nonregulation of dangerous ideas is not faith in consumer sovereignty in the realm of ideas but the difficulty of agreeing on which ideas are unwholesome.

§22.3.   The regulation of broadcasting.   One of the exceptions to freedom of speech deserves special attention because it is an explicit application of economic theory. This is the principle, reaffirmed by the Supreme Court recently in the *Red Lion* case,[1] that the government may regulate the content of broadcasting because of the physical limitations of the electromagnetic spectrum. The regulation in question was the "fairness doctrine," under which a broadcaster is required to present all sides of a controversial question. The regulation is not so intrusive an interference with the marketplace of ideas as would be one punishing the expression of particular ideas, but it does reduce the freedom of the broadcaster to select the ideas that he will disseminate. It has been assumed that a similar regulation, applied to newspapers, would violate the First Amendment.

The difference, the Court has reasoned, is that broadcasters, unlike newspaper owners, enjoy a monopoly position in the dissemination of ideas due to the limited capacity of the electromagnetic spectrum to support competing broadcasters in the same community. Since two broadcasters could not broadcast on the same frequency in the same area without creating intolerable interference, the award by the Federal Communications Commission of a license to use a particular frequency in a particular area confers a monopoly of that frequency that has no counterpart in other media of expression.

The Court's use of the term "monopoly" in this context is odd, at least from an economic standpoint. While it is true that every frequency is unique and that only one can be used in the same

---

§22.3. 1. Red Lion Broadcasting Co. v. Federal Communications Commission, 395 U.S. 367 (1969). See also National Broadcasting Co. v. United States, 319 U.S. 190, 226 (1943).

area at the same time, the result need not be monopoly, since different frequencies are, within a range, perfect substitutes for one another. The Federal Communications Commission (FCC) generally licenses more than one television station in each market. Most markets have at least three or four stations and a few have nine to eleven. This is invariably more than the number of newspapers in the same market.

Nor does the fact that the electromagnetic spectrum is limited distinguish it from other resources. The inputs into the alternative methods of communicating ideas are also limited. The range of frequencies at which electromagnetic waves can be propagated is vast, its use in broadcasting limited only by opportunity costs and by government policy. If other uses of the spectrum, such as mobile communication, were valued less highly, the number of channels available for television broadcasting could be increased substantially. The viewer would also receive more television signals if the FCC adopted a different policy for the allocation of television frequencies. Instead of seeking to promote local stations, the FCC could license only stations that would broadcast to a large regional market. By careful engineering of a system of regional broadcasting the FCC could eliminate the many dead spaces necessary to prevent interference between stations in adjacent markets that reduce the number of different signals that viewers receive. Thus the scarcity of television channels differs from the scarcity of other natural resources only in the fact that it is to a significant extent the product of deliberate governmental policies. Newspapers suffer from more acute scarcities that, in conjunction with the pressure of substitute competition, have brought about a degree of local monopoly much greater than we find in broadcasting. The Court's attempted distinction is untenable.

Now let us suppose that a broadcaster does have an effective monopoly of the market in which he operates and consider what impact on the dissemination of news and opinion we might expect. He might, in order to maximize his revenues, limit the amount of time he broadcasts. This would reduce the distribution of ideas to the people in the market. But the fairness doctrine is not calculated to increase the broadcaster's output of ideas. On the contrary, it penalizes him for presenting controversial ideas by requiring him to present all sides of a controversy. The element of penalty lies in the fact that the doctrine comes into play only when the broadcaster's welfare would be maximized by his not presenting all sides.

The real concern is that the monopoly broadcaster will distort the news and suppress opinions he disagrees with in an effort to convert people in his market to his own views. Any broadcaster could do this. The significance of monopoly is that the cost to the broadcaster is less than in a competitive market, both because there are no substitutes to which his audience can turn and because his control of information may prevent the audience from realizing that it is being misinformed. And the cost to the audience is greater: with competing broadcasters, the partiality of one would not deprive the audience of access to a broad range of competing ideas. In effect, monopoly here operates to suppress the demand for competing products.[2]

It is important to bear in mind, however, that the broadcaster is a middleman between the producers of ideas and the consumers, so that even the monopolist broadcaster, if he wants to maximize his pecuniary income, will provide the mixture and diversity of ideas deemed optimum by his customers rather than propagate his own ideas. Only if he is willing to sacrifice pecuniary income in order to propagate ideas that his customers do not want to buy will he become a monopolist of ideas.[3] This is most likely to occur in a small or family-owned station. The management of a large publicly held corporation will have difficulty finding issues on which a partisan stand would not alienate large numbers of shareholders.

§22.4.   *False advertising and the relationship between political and economic rights.*   A discussion of one other exception to freedom of speech will help clarify a fundamental perplexity of constitutional law. The First Amendment has been held not to forbid the government to regulate comprehensively the communication of information and ideas in connection with the sale of goods or services. If the seller of a drug advertises that it can cure arthritis, the Federal Trade Commission can enjoin the claim if it is shown to be probably false. If the same claim were made in a book, it would be clear that the First Amendment forbade the Commission to enjoin it, at least if the author were not the seller of the drug.[1] The different treatment of the two cases is curious.

2. See §6.2 *supra.*
3. To be sure, he will be buying time with his own money. The objection, however, is not to his promoting his own ideas in the marketplace but to the lack of competition in his particular geographical area.
§22.4. 1. Cf. Rodale Press, Inc. v. Federal Trade Commission, 407 F.2d 1252 (D.C. Cir. 1968).

Since the claims are identical, the difference cannot be that advertising claims are either obviously true or obviously false; clearly, they often are neither. Nor can the presence of a commercial motive in one case but not in the other be the distinguishing factor. The author of a book on health will have a strong incentive to make false claims if he believes that they will increase his income from the book, unless he thinks exposure would harm him more — but the risk of exposure is the same for the seller of the drug. Political candidates have an incentive to make false claims if they think they will bring them closer to power, and so with professors and academic reputation.

Perhaps the essential point is that commercial advertising is not a vehicle for the presentation of political arguments and that the Supreme Court has seen protection of the political process as the primary function of the free speech clause of the First Amendment. This would also explain why the Court for so long ignored the censorship of obscenity and why its concern with the scope of liability for defamation has been limited largely to defamation of public officials and other political figures.

The dichotomy between political and nonpolitical speech is closely related to a larger dichotomy, between the protection of competition in goods and the protection of competition in ideas, that is characteristic of constitutional law today.[2] The classical liberals believed that both product markets and political debate should be free. The Court's preference for the latter form of freedom cannot easily be justified on principled grounds.[3] It may reflect the special importance that political rights have in the minds of lawyers, judges, and constitutional scholars — people with a strong interest [4] in the public and political arenas of action. But economic rights may be as or more important to a larger if less articulate segment of the population; and economic legislation frequently infringes these rights. Legislation may limit choice of occupation (an example is a city ordinance limiting the number of taxi licenses that may be granted). It may transfer wealth from consumers to shareholders (the enforcement of the airlines' cartel by the Civil Aeronautics Board is a case in point). It may prevent people from obtaining services that they want and for which they are willing to pay (restrictions on pay tele-

2. The discussion that follows is based on Aaron Director, The Parity of the Economic Market Place, 7 J. Law & Econ. 1 (1964).
3. See §19.1 *supra*.
4. In both senses of the word.

vision are an example). The Court's lack of concern with deprivations of this sort may betoken a certain insensitivity to the needs and concerns of most people.

There is also a question whether political and economic rights are as neatly separable as the Court believes. Political dissent requires substantial financial resources. In a society where activity was completely controlled by government — in which paper was rationed, printing was licensed, and the state, directly or indirectly, was the principal employer — it would be extremely difficult to organize and finance political activity in opposition to the. government. In the McCarthy era, people believed to be sympathetic to communism were barred from government employment, even in nonsensitive jobs. These people did not starve. They found jobs in the private sector and today some of them are again active in politics. The costs of dissent would have been greater had the government been the only employer so that the consequence of holding unpopular views might be denial of all opportunity to obtain a livelihood. Although no single economic regulatory measure brings us measurably closer to complete governmental control of economic activity, the Court has been unwilling to tolerate even slight encroachments on First Amendment freedoms.

Political and economic rights converge in another sense. The trend in constitutional adjudication is toward recognition of the special claims to constitutional protection of groups other than the traditional racial, religious, and political minorities, notably poor people and women. Their interests, however, are frequently identical to the broader public interest in economic liberty. The invalidation of restrictions on women's occupational choices would promote efficiency as well as women's rights. The abrogation of laws restricting economic freedom would often benefit the poor more than other groups.

PROBLEMS

1. If the economic analysis of freedom of speech were accepted, would blackmail be a protected activity?

2. "Blockbusting" is the practice by which real estate brokers allegedly attempt to frighten white homeowners into selling their homes at distress prices, by telling them that the neighborhood is becoming black. Should the practice be protected by the First Amendment? Should it make a difference whether the information that the broker tells the homeowner is true?

3. Is political freedom a necessary condition of economic freedom? Is economic freedom a necessary condition of political freedom? A sufficient condition?

4. Many courts have held that a funeral parlor in a residential neighborhood is a nuisance. (See Comment, 20 Syracuse L. Rev. 45 (1968).) Is this an appropriate application (or extension) of the economic theory of nuisance (see §2.6 supra)? Suppose it could be shown that the introduction of a pornographic bookstore in a community reduced property values. Should the bookstore be deemed a nuisance?

PART VI
THE LEGAL PROCESS

CHAPTER 23

ALLOCATION OF RESOURCES BY THE MARKET, THE ADVERSARY SYSTEM, AND THE LEGISLATIVE PROCESS

§23.1.   Law and the market as methods of resource allocation.
If the analysis in Part I of this book is correct, the ultimate question for decision in many lawsuits is, what allocation of resources would maximize efficiency? The market normally decides this question, but it is given to the legal system to decide in situations where the costs of a market determination would exceed those of a legal determination. The criteria of decision are thus the same, but what of the decision-making processes? Here we find some surprising parallels, together with significant differences.

Like the market (although less extensively) the law uses prices equal to opportunity costs to induce people to maximize efficiency. Where compensatory damages are the standard remedy for a breach of legal duty, the effect of liability is not to compel compliance with law but to compel the violator to pay a price equal to the opportunity costs of the violation. If that price is lower than the value he derives from the unlawful act, then efficiency is maximized if he commits it, and the legal system encourages him to do so; if higher, efficiency requires that he not commit the act. Again the damage remedy provides the correct incentive. The legal system, like the market, confronts the individual with the costs of his act but leaves the decision whether to incur those costs to him.

A quite different method of regulation is to command obedience to the legal precept under pain of penalties greater than the actual social costs of disobedience. Penalties of that kind are sometimes prescribed by the legal system but in circumstances, as we shall see,[1] normally consistent with the creation of the correct economic incentives.

Again like the market, the legal process relies for its administration primarily on private individuals motivated by economic self-interest rather than on altruists or officials. Observe that from the standpoint of imparting correct economic incentives to defendants and potential defendants it is immaterial who receives the damages that are assessed; the price of the unlawful conduct is unaffected.[2] Payment of the damages to the person injured by the unlawful act is significant primarily because it gives him an incentive to shoulder the principal burdens involved in the enforcement of law. Through the lawyer that he hires, the victim of conduct that may be unlawful (inefficient) investigates the circumstances surrounding the allegedly unlawful act, organizes the information obtained by the investigation, decides whether to activate the machinery of legal allocation, feeds information in digestible form to that machinery, checks the accuracy of the information supplied by the defendant, presses if necessary for changes in the rules of allocation applied by the courts, and sees to the collection of the judgment. The state is thereby enabled to dispense with a police force to protect people's common law rights, public attorneys to enforce them, and other bureaucratic personnel to operate the system. These functionaries would be less highly motivated than a private plaintiff, since their economic self-interest would be affected only indirectly by the outcomes of particular cases. The number of public employees involved in the protection of private rights of action is remarkably small considering the amount of activity regulated by the laws creating those rights, just as the number of public employees involved in the operation of the market is small relative to the activity organized by the market.

A closely related point is that the legal process, like the market, is competitive. The adversary system, with its rules against ex parte contacts, its elaborate rights of cross-examination, and its rituals of partisanship, places the tribunal in the position of a consumer forced to decide between the similar goods of two fiercely determined salesmen. To be sure, most cases are settled before trial, but those cases do not enter into the process by which legal rules are created and modified. The critical stage

§23.1. 1. See §§25.1, 25.2 *infra.*
2. Subject to the possibly important qualification mentioned *supra* §4.9, note 3.

of the legal allocation process is dominated by the competition between plaintiffs and defendants for the favor of the tribunal.

Finally, law resembles the market in its impersonality, its subordination of distributive considerations. The invisible hand of the market has its counterpart in the aloof disinterest of the judge. The method by which judges are compensated and the rules of judicial ethics are designed to assure that the judge will have no financial or other interest in the outcome of a case before him, no responsibility with respect to the case other than to decide issues tendered by the parties, and no knowledge of the case other than what the competition of the parties conveys to him about it. Jurors are similarly constrained. The disappointed litigant will rarely have grounds for a personal animus against the tribunal, just as the consumer who does not find a product he wants at a price he is willing to pay will rarely have grounds for a personal animus against a seller.

Judicial impersonality is reinforced 'by the rules of evidence, which exclude as irrelevant considerations that go not to the conduct of the parties but to their relative deservedness. The poor man cannot advance poverty as a reason why he should be excused from liability or the wealthy man appeal to the judge's sense of class solidarity. These distributive factors cannot be entirely banished from the courtroom, but perhaps they are sufficiently muted to induce emphasis on allocative considerations. And so it is in the market. Sellers have a strong incentive to ignore distributive considerations and thereby maximize efficiency. The allocation of resources in accordance with the criterion of efficiency, whether done by the law or by the market, affects the distribution of income and wealth. But in both methods of allocation it is primarily the criterion of efficiency rather than of distributive justice that guides decision.

Our emphasis on the allocative function of the legal system suggests a possible economic justification for government's defraying a portion of the costs of the system (judges' salaries, the cost of building and maintaining court houses, etc.). If the function of the legal system were solely to settle disputes, it would be appropriate to impose the entire costs of the system on the disputants. But that is not its only function. It establishes rules of conduct designed to shape future conduct, not only the present disputants' but also other people's. Since the social benefits of a litigation may exceed the private benefits to the litigants, the amount of litigation might be too small if the litigants had to bear the total costs of the suit.[3] The governmental subsidy to litigation is modest. The main expenses — attorneys' fees — are defrayed entirely by the litigants.

There are also important differences between law and the market as methods of allocating resources. The fundamental difference is that the market is a more efficient mechanism of valuing competing uses. In the market people have to back up their value assertions with money (or equivalent sacrifice of alternative opportunities). Willingness to pay imparts greater credibility to a claim of superior value than forensic energy.[4]

The law's frequent inability to identify preferences or relative values has two important consequences. First, it reinforces the tendency of common law courts to avoid major allocative judgments. The treatment of custom as a defense to negligence is a good example. In principle it is not a defense, and this, as we saw in the chapter on torts, is economically correct.[5] But in practice conduct sanctioned by the custom of the defendant's industry is rarely adjudged negligent. The reluctance of courts to condemn customary practices reflects the difficulty of determining value forensically. The plaintiff's lawyer may argue vigorously and persuasively that the gain in accident cost reduction from installation of a 24-inch rubber bumper on every new automobile produced will exceed the cost of the bumper. But since no manufacturer at present produces a car with such a bumper, the estimate of costs will be conjectural and the manufacturers will be able to argue plausibly for a higher estimate. Nor will there be experience with the effects of such bumpers on the severity of accidents, other than experimental evidence that will inevitably be vulnerable to contentions that it does not accurately predict the effects of real-world usage. The vogue of cost-benefit analysis has created inflated notions of the effectiveness of analytical techniques in resolving questions of cost and demand. It is not surprising that judges should view with skepticism arguments so difficult to validate in the absence of willingness to pay for upsetting a customary practice. The cost of overcoming this skepticism is likely to exceed the plaintiff's stake in the outcome of the case.

The second consequence of the law's inability to ascertain pref-

---

3. Cf. discussion of the social benefits of railroading *supra* §5.2.
4. Cf. §2.2 *supra*.
5. See §4.4 *supra*.

erences accurately is a tendency of the legal process to suppress variances in value. Many people place a value on their home that exceeds its market price, but the only convincing evidence of this is a refusal to accept an offer to purchase the house at a higher price. The evidentiary problem is asymmetrical: if the house were worth less to the owner than the market price, he would have sold it. A rule of damages in eminent domain proceedings that entitles the owner to recover no more than the market value of his house is thus biased (as pointed out in the chapter on property rights): it overcompensates very few owners but undercompensates many.[6] Yet a standard of subjective value, while economically correct, would be virtually impossible to administer due to the difficulty of proving — except by evidence of refusal to accept a bona fide offer just below the owner's valuation — that the house was worth more to him than the market price.

The problem of valuation is acute with respect to damages for pain and suffering, which encompass disfigurement and other real, but ordinarily not pecuniary (unless an impairment of earning capacity results), costs of accidents. People's sensitivity to this type of loss must vary widely but proof of above- or below-average sensitivity is virtually impossible, so the tendency is to award a standard or average figure (perhaps the average of the jurors' sensitivities). There is a systematic tendency to inaccurate compensation in the individual case but, unlike the eminent domain example, no tendency to undercompensation or overcompensation across cases: a plaintiff's sensitivities are as likely to be below the average as above.

The deficiencies of legal as compared with market allocation have two implications for policy. The first is that it is desirable, so far as is consistent with achieving efficient use of resources, to minimize the necessity for broad cost-benefit analysis in legal decisions. But it is not always possible. The problem of custom could be attacked by substituting a rule of strict liability for one of negligence liability. The accident costs that could be prevented by a change in customary practices would be made costs to the industry, whose firms would then decide for themselves whether the cost of changing the customary practices would yield a greater accident cost reduction. But such a rule eliminates the incentive of accident victims under a negligence standard to investigate the value in reduced accident costs of changing their cus-

6. See §2.5 *supra*.

tomary modes of behavior.[7] Another step is necessary in order to justify such a rule: the court must decide whether the victims' custom is more likely than the injurers' to be inefficient. But this is the same question that we earlier said was intractable.

The second implication, one by now familiar to the reader,[8] is that people should be prevented from transforming market transactions into legal transactions unless the costs of market transactions are very high. This is the economic justification for punishing theft even where the probability of apprehension is unity — but of this more later.[9]

§23.2.   *The incentives of judges.*   The analysis in the preceding section assumes that judges make their decisions in accordance with the criterion of efficiency. But what is the linkage between the judges' self-interest and the promotion of efficient resource use? This is a difficult question. The economist can predict the reactions of consumers if the price of pork rises relative to that of lamb, because the consumer's choice is presumably motivated by a desire to maximize his satisfactions, a goal affected by relative costs. But the judicial process is carefully designed to insulate the judge from any pecuniary interest in the outcome of the case.

Nonetheless, it may be possible to venture some tentative observations on the incentive structure of the judicial system. Let us begin with systems, common in many of the states, where the judges do not have lifetime tenure and frequently aspire to higher office, judicial or political. It seems appropriate to view these judges as the agents of the executive or legislative organs of the state. In such systems the analysis of judicial behavior becomes a branch of the analysis of political behavior (the subject of the following sections), but a rather special branch, for we would not expect the state to politicize the judicial decision-making process in all, or indeed in many, areas of judicial decision. If we are correct that a property rights system and a law of contracts, torts, and crimes are important to the efficient use of a society's resources, and if we further assume that society cares about efficiency albeit not to the exclusion of other values, then we should not be surprised to find, even in jurisdictions where judges lack independence from the political authorities, that the judicial process is carried on largely free from gross political in-

7. Cf. §4.15 *supra.*
8. See §§2.5, 4.1, *supra.*
9. See §25.1 *infra.*

terference — that rights and liabilities continue to be assigned, in the main, on the basis of a politically neutral comparison of costs. We should expect this especially in those disputes, which are many, where the distributive or political consequences are not clear-cut. Disputes between farmers and railroads are an example. Since farmers (in the days when railroad cases shaped the law in many common law fields) were the principal customers of railroads, disputes between railroads and farmers did not provide an easy opportunity for advancing the interests of one group over another. Competition among states[1] is an additional force acting in the direction of minimizing political interference in the judicial process (why?).

The United States Supreme Court represents an extreme example of the severance of judicial decision making from political control. The justices have life tenure and normally no aspirations to higher office. They operate within economic constraints — Congress could refuse to appropriate money to pay their salaries and expenses, and, more subtly, could refuse to increase their salaries in times of inflation — but the constraints are loose. It is therefore less appropriate to view the justices as agents for carrying out the desires of the dominant political authority. Models of the firm that stress personal utility maximizing by the executives[2] may be relevant here.

We have thus far assumed that the judge is, at the least, effectively insulated from a narrow personal stake in the outcome of the case. The assumption is not uniformly accepted. It has sometimes been argued, for example, that a judge's decisions can be explained in terms of the interests of the group or class in society to which he belongs — that the judge who owns land will decide in favor of landowners, the judge who walks to work in favor of pedestrians, the judge who used to be a corporate lawyer in favor of corporations. There are two points to be made here. First, where a particular outcome would promote the interests of a group to which the judge no longer belongs (our last example), it is difficult to see how the judge's self-interest is advanced by adopting that outcome. The judge's previous experience may, however, lead him to evaluate the merits of the case differently from judges of different backgrounds. Second, the increase in a judge's income from a ruling in favor of a broad group, such as pedes-

§23.2. 1. See §20.6 *supra*.
2. See §12.7 *supra*.

trians or homeowners, to which he belongs will usually be so trivial as to be easily outweighed by the penalties, mild as they often are (professional criticism, reversal by a higher court, etc.), for deciding a case in a way perceived to be unsound or biased. Even at the level of the United States Supreme Court, the number of decisions that change more than incrementally the fortunes of a particular industry or activity is trivial. It is thus arguable that existing conflict of interest laws are much too strict, and it is not surprising that attempts to link judicial policies and outcomes to the personal economic interests of the judges have foundered.[3]

§23.3. *The legislative emphasis on distributive considerations.* If much of the common law seems informed by an implicit economic logic, the same cannot be said for statute law. Unsystematic as our survey of statute law has been in this book, it does suggest that statutes exhibit a less pervasive concern with efficiency and a much greater concern with wealth distribution.

One possible explanation for the difference in the relative emphasis on efficiency and distribution is that the common law rules crystallized in the nineteenth century, while the statutes discussed in this book are for the most part products of this century. The nineteenth century was one of relatively greater scarcity of economic resources than today, and efficiency may be a more highly prized value under conditions of greater scarcity (at least in Western societies). But this is not a very satisfactory explanation. Much of our least efficient statutory regulation emerged during the Depression, a period of great scarcity; some of it, notably railroad regulation, originated in the heyday of the common law. Another possibility is that the economic issues in common law cases are accessible to intuition, whereas many of the subjects dealt with by statutes, such as monopoly and the capital markets, are not. The "leverage" theory of monopoly[1] is intuitively appealing, but analytically unsound. The concept of the stock market as an "efficient market" is deeply counterintuitive, as is the related idea that capital structure does not affect a firm's value (much).[2]

Two other possibilities, the focus of inquiry in the next two sections, are first, differences in the procedures by which rules

3. Roscoe Pound, The Economic Interpretation and the Law of Torts, 53 Harv. L. Rev. 365 (1940).
§23.3. 1. See §7.6 *supra.*
2. See §§13.1, 14.2 *supra.*

are formulated by judges on the one hand and legislatures on the other, and second, the greater importance of political considerations in legislative compared to judicial policy making.

§23.4. *Judicial and legislative procedures compared.*   In Karl Llewellyn's picture of how appellate judges, the makers of common law, decide cases, the judge first decides what outcome is dictated by good common sense and then drafts an opinion rationalizing the result in terms of precedent and settled legal policies.[1] In deciding what outcome is "right," the judge presumably does not decide which of the parties is the "better" person. He does not know the parties; as we have already discussed, considerations pertaining to their relative deservedness (wealth, poverty, good breeding, etc.) are suppressed; and a judgment based on such considerations would be difficult to rationalize in a judicial opinion. Nor is he apt to view the parties as representatives of warring social classes or political groups (although this is less certain): besides the considerations discussed in previous sections, observe that the judge's comparative immunity from political vicissitudes depends upon public acceptance of his role as a technician and is impaired if he is seen to be operating in the political arena. Almost by default, the judge is compelled to view the parties as representatives of activities — owning land, growing tulips, walking on railroad tracks, driving cars. And where a choice must be made between competing activities, it is natural, and comfortably objective and neutral, to ask which is more valuable in the economic sense.

The legislative process presents a marked contrast to the judicial. There is no rule against the admission of considerations relating to the relative deservedness of the people affected by proposed legislation. There is no commitment to accept the guidance of the efficiency criterion. The adversary system, with its comparison of concrete interfering activities that assures that questions of relative costs are always close to the surface of the controversy, is not employed. Furthermore, the legislative tools for redistributing wealth are much more flexible and powerful than the judicial. Ordinarily a court can redistribute wealth only by means of (in effect) an excise tax on the good involved in the suit. A court that desires to redistribute income from landlords to poor tenants can give tenants a legal right to withhold rents pending repairs but it cannot prevent landlords from passing on

§23.4. 1. Karl N. Llewellyn, The Common Law Tradition: Deciding Appeals (1960).

most of the costs of the resulting repairs to their (poor) tenants.[2] Legislatures are not so limited.

§23.5. The allocation of resources by the political process. There is a further and more fundamental reason why legislatures are less constrained than courts in basing policy on distributive rather than efficiency considerations. It lies in the difference between political and market allocation. The market, and the legal process insofar as it attempts to simulate market processes, provides no machinery for direct redistribution of wealth.[1] Redistributions occur, but purely as incidents to voluntary transactions. Changes in tastes, population, technology, natural resources, and the like alter the relative scarcities of resources (including skills) and therefore the incomes of the owners of resources. But efficiency is the product of the market, and the redistribution of income only a by-product. The political process severs the connection between efficiency and redistribution. The taxing power can be used to transfer income from one group to another without a showing that the transfer increases the efficiency of resource use.[2]

We have suggested why legislatures play a more active role than courts in distributive policy, but we have yet to explore the relative emphasis in legislative activity on efficiency and on redistribution. The second question is vital to a comparison between legislation and common law as methods of preventing abuses of the market process.[3]

There is abundant evidence that legislative regulation of the economy frequently, perhaps typically, brings about less efficient results than the market–common law system of resource allocation.[4] The crucial question is whether this failure is accidental and easily remediable, or perhaps inherent in the nature

2. See §18.6 supra. If the landlord is forbidden to raise rents, then as we saw in the section just cited, the costs of the repairs will still be borne ultimately by the tenant class but in the form of reduced availability of housing.

§23.5. 1. This assumes that monopoly, theft, and other abuses of the competitive process are prevented.

2. Can you think of instances where such a transfer might increase efficiency?

3. See Chapter 10.

4. A few examples of the abundant literature on the question are William F. Baxter, NYSE Fixed Commission Rates: A Private Cartel Goes Public, 22 Stan. L. Rev. 675 (1970); Cabinet Task Force on Oil Import Control, The Oil Import Question (Govt. Printing Office 1970); Edmund W. Kitch, Marc Isaacson & Daniel Kasper, The Regulation of Taxicabs in Chicago, 14 J. Law & Econ. 285 (1971); Paul W. MacAvoy, The Regulation-Induced Shortage of Natural Gas, 14 J. Law & Econ. 167 (1971); Sam Peltzman, Entry in Commercial Banking, 8 J. Law & Econ. 11 (1965); Comment, Is Regulation Necessary? California Air Transportation and National Regulatory Policy, 74 Yale L.J. 1416 (1965).

of political decision making. The latter view is gaining support.[5] The essential problem seems to be that the generalized consumer interest in efficient markets is systematically underrepresented in legislative decision making. Money plays an important role in influencing both the choice of legislative representative and his behavior as a legislator. But acute free-rider problems prevent consumers from contributing significantly to the financing of political activity: the individual consumer benefits from legislation favorable to consumers (or from the defeat of legislation hostile to them) whether or not he has contributed money to the representatives of the consumer interest. More compact groups such as trade associations can overcome the free-rider problem; the transaction costs of organizing financial support are much lower for them.

Even if money played no role in legislative activity, the principle of majority rule would frequently enable coalitions of special interest groups to impose costs on consumers in excess of the benefits to the coalition. Almost every voter has some interest, whether as employee, shareholder, producer, black person, etc., that outweighs, in his calculation of satisfactions, his interest as a consumer. The doctor has more to gain from legislation favorable to doctors than he has to lose if his medical bills are higher as a result of the legislation. He may have more to gain from such legislation even if his taxi fares — and children's tuition, and local taxes, and clothing costs — as well as his medical bills will be higher because the medical profession cannot procure the passage of favorable legislation without enlisting the support of the taxi owners, the teachers, the welfare workers, and the textile manufacturers, in exchange for supporting similar legislation favorable to those groups. A politician may win election with the votes of 51 percent of the voting population because those 51 percent stand to gain more in protective legislation that he favors than they stand to lose as consumers. Yet when the costs of the legislation to the majority, as consumers, are combined with the costs to the other 49 percent of the voting population, who are outside of the coalition altogether, it may turn out that the program is highly inefficient.

The reader may question the assumption that there is leakage or waste in the process of redistribution so that the losses generated by the program are often greater than the gain to the win-

5. A recent and rigorous statement is George J. Stigler, The Theory of Economic Regulation, 2 Bell J. Econ. & Management Sci. 3 (1971).

ning coalition. But one observes that the means adopted by legislatures to redistribute wealth are frequently inefficient. Instead of granting the oil industry an annual subsidy out of general revenues, Congress has authorized an oil import quota program under which the importation of foreign oil is limited (thus increasing the value of oil-producing land in the Southwest) and the oil companies are permitted to import limited quantities of foreign oil (since foreign oil is cheaper than domestic, these quotas are the equivalent of a subsidy equal in amount to the difference between the foreign and domestic price times the quantity specified in the quota). The result is that the price of oil to the American consumer is higher than the cost of oil. This induces the substitution of other products that cost more to produce than oil or are otherwise inadequate substitutes. The loss is captured by no one and amounts to several billion dollar a year.[6]

There are several possible reasons, however, why the indirect approach is preferred. One is that cash subsidies would be difficult to administer since they would create an incentive for every company in the United States to create an oil affiliate. But this could be overcome by limiting the subsidy to designated companies. Another possibility is that the form in which the program is cast increases the cost to consumers, and their political representatives (if any), of determining the net social costs of the program. It can be represented as designed not to enrich oil interests but to promote United States foreign policy by minimizing dependence on the oil produced by the Arab nations, which have close relations with the Soviet Union. The claim is dubious, if only because a goal of limiting the importation of oil could be achieved by a tariff, which would yield revenue to the government rather than to the oil companies (the owners of oil land would still benefit). But since the cost of the oil import quota to the average consumer is only a few dollars per year, it is not worth his while to invest much time in investigating even a flimsy justification.

But most important, there may be no efficient methods of redistributing wealth (save as an incident to market processes). Suppose Congress did provide an annual subsidy out of general revenues to the oil companies in lieu of import quotas. Then it would have to increase its tax revenues by the amount of the subsidy. Any method it used to do this would have substitution effects that would distort the efficient use of resources. If it raised

6. Cf. Cabinet Task Force on Oil Import Control, note 4 *supra*, at 124–125.

federal personal income tax rates, it would aggravate the various misallocative effects of that tax, discussed in Chapter 16; for example, it would increase the relative cost of work to the taxpayer, which might induce him to substitute leisure even though, but for the tax, leisure would have been less valuable to him than activity yielding a pecuniary income. The import quota has much the same effect as an excise tax, and there is no general presumption that income taxes are more efficient than excise taxes.[7] Other methods of increasing revenues (greater government borrowing, inflation, increasing other tax rates, spending additional resources on tax collections) would also involve costly substitution effects.

SUGGESTED READINGS

1. James Buchanan & Gordon Tullock, The Calculus of Consent (1962).
2. Anthony Downs, An Economic Theory of Democracy (1957).
3. ———, In Defense of Majority Voting, 69 J. Pol. Econ. 192 (1961).
4. Mancur Olson, Jr., The Logic of Collective Action (1965).
5. Roscoe Pound, The Economic Interpretation and the Law of Torts, 53 Harv. L. Rev. 365 (1940).
6. George J. Stigler, The Theory of Economic Regulation, 2 Bell. J. Econ. & Management Sci. 3 (1971).
7. ———, Economic Competition and Political Competition, 13 Pub. Choice 91 (1972).

PROBLEMS

1. Should a federal judge be forbidden to serve as a director of a diversified mutual fund?

2. In the part of this book that deals with constitutional law (Part V), we never considered the question why there are constitutional rights — i.e., rights that cannot be abrogated simply by majority vote. Does the discussion in this chapter suggest the outline of an economic theory of constitutionalism? On an economic analysis, what rights do you think are most appropriately placed beyond the power of majority rule?

---

7. See Milton Friedman, Price Theory, ch. 3 (1962).

Chapter 24

CIVIL PROCEDURE AND
JUDICIAL ADMINISTRATION

§*24.1.* *The economic goals of a procedural system.* In this chapter we explore some of the implications of applying economic theory to problems of court procedure and administration. The goal of a procedural system, viewed economically, is to minimize the sum of two types of cost. The first is the cost of erroneous judicial decisions. Suppose the expected cost of a particular type of accident is 100, and the cost to the potential injurer of avoiding it is 90 (the cost of avoidance by the victim, we will assume, is greater than 100). If the injurer is subject to either a negligence or a strict liability standard, he will avoid the accident, at least if the standard is administered accurately. But suppose that in 15 percent of the cases in which an accident occurs, the injurer can expect to avoid liability due to erroneous determinations by the procedural system. Then the expected cost of the accident to the injurer will fall to 85, and since this is less than the cost of avoidance, the accident will not be prevented. The result will be a net social loss of 10.

But the analysis is incomplete — which brings us to the second type of cost that we are interested in minimizing, the cost of operating the procedural system. Suppose that to reduce the error rate in our example from 15 percent to anywhere below 10 percent would entail additional expenditures on the procedural system of 20. Then value would be maximized by tolerating the 15 percent probability of error, for the cost of error (10) is less than the cost necessary to eliminate the error cost (20). In general we do not want to spend $1.00 to eliminate an error in the procedural system that imposes a social cost of only $.50 (or

$.99). That is why we are interested in minimizing the *sum* of error and direct costs of the procedural system.[1]

Elementary as this formulation is, it has the great advantage of making discussable issues of procedure characteristically debated in visceral rather than analytical terms. Consider the question whether there is a right to a trial-type hearing in various administrative contexts, such as exclusion of aliens from the United States. The question is viewed by lawyers as one of "fairness"; the economic approach enables the question to be broken down into objectively analyzable, although not simple, inquiries. We begin by asking, what is the cost of withholding a trial-type hearing in a particular type of case? This inquiry has two branches: first, how is the probability of an error likely to be affected by a trial-type hearing? If the legally dispositive issues are the kind of factual issues for which the trial-type hearing is designed, chances are that the probability of error will be high if such a hearing is denied. The second branch of this inquiry is, what is the cost of an error if one occurs? As a crude first approximation, if the stakes in the case are large, the cost of error in an individual case will be large, so if in addition the probability of error is high, total error costs will be great. Having established the costs of error, we then inquire into the costs of measures that would reduce the error costs. If those direct costs are low — more precisely, if the rate of increase in those costs as a result of adopting a measure to reduce error is less than the rate of decrease in the error costs as a result of the measure — then adoption can be expected to reduce the sum of error and direct costs and thus increase efficiency.

§24.2. *The costs of error.*   Figure 19 depicts the effects of erroneous judicial determinations. D represents the value, in avoidance of accident costs, of a unit of safety equipment as a function of the quantity of equipment purchased. Another name for D is the marginal product of safety equipment. C represents the cost of the equipment. Value is maximized by purchasing the amount of safety equipment indicated by the intersection of D and C—that is, q. If the industry is fully liable for the cost of accidents, then D becomes the industry's demand for safety equipment and the optimum quantity is purchased. If, however, due to error in the legal system, the industry can expect to be liable for only P

---

§24.1. 1. What if the purpose of the substantive rule being enforced is not to improve efficiency, but to redistribute wealth (or accomplish some other non-economic end)? In what sense can we still speak of the goal of procedure as being the minimization of the sum of error and direct costs?

percent of the costs of the accidents it inflicts, then its demand for safety equipment falls to D' (equal to $P \times D$), and it purchases only q_1 amount of safety equipment, resulting in a social loss of L. Observe that the effect of error on the industry's behavior is identical to that of a tax on gross receipts.[1]

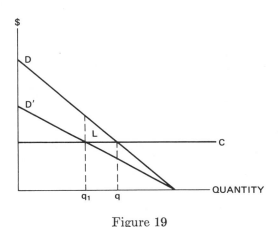

Figure 19

The analysis is incomplete in two important respects. First, whatever causes errors in favor of the industry in some cases (lying witnesses, for example) will probably also cause errors in favor of accident victims in others, and this will tend to shift D' to the right. But it is likely that, on balance, D' will lie below D. All errors in favor of the industry move D' downward, whereas only some errors against the industry move it upward. If the error against the industry takes the form of exaggerating its liability (the accident victim convinces the court that his damages are greater than they really are), it will tend to make safety equipment more valuable to it and thus raise D'. But if the error results in imposition of liability in circumstances where additional safety equipment would not have reduced the industry's liability (the accident may not have occurred at all, or may have been caused by someone other than a member of the industry), the industry will have no incentive to purchase additional safety equipment and D' will not increase.

Second, the social cost of a reduction in the industry's incentive to avoid accidents is likely to be offset partially by the

§24.2. 1. See §§10.5, 16.2, *supra*.

increased incentive of victims to avoid accidents. The effect of a downward shift of D' is to increase the expected uncompensated accident cost to victims and therefore the incentive of victims to prevent accidents. Presumably victim avoidance in these cases will be less efficient than avoidance by the injurers (why?); nonetheless there is some offset.

The analysis of error costs has many interesting applications to problems of civil procedure. Consider the preponderance-of-the-evidence standard which governs civil cases. This standard directs the trier of facts to find in favor of the party who has the burden of proof on an issue if that party's version of the disputed facts is more probably true than the other party's version; thus, to prevail, the party bearing the burden of proof need only establish the validity of his claim by a probability infinitesimally greater than 50 percent. This implies that of cases decided erroneously, about half will be won by undeserving plaintiffs and about half lost by deserving plaintiffs. Whether this result is economically sound depends on whether the costs of each type of error — in favor of undeserving plaintiffs, and against deserving plaintiffs — are about the same; and in general it would seem that they would be the same.[2] To be sure, the principle of diminishing marginal utility of money implies that the benefit to the undeserving plaintiff is smaller than the cost to the deserving plaintiff (can you see why?) — but only if we assume that the marginal utility schedules of deserving plaintiffs are as high as those of undeserving plaintiffs.[3]

In some cases the preponderance standard is not followed literally. Consider the example of the victim of a bus accident whose only evidence linking the accident to the defendant bus company is that the defendant operates 80 percent of the buses on the route where the accident occurred.[4] Most courts would not permit the victim to recover damages without additional evidence of the defendant's liability. There may be a good economic reason for this. If bus accident cases are decided on such a scanty record, the margin of error will be at least 20 percent (why "at least"?). An error of this magnitude is likely to be quite costly, in particular because one consequence will be that defendant's competitors on the route will bear zero liability, resulting in an increase in their market share (why?) and accident rate.

2. But not in a criminal case; see §25.6 *infra*.
3. Cf. §15.2 *supra*.
4. Discussed in Laurence H. Tribe, Trial by Mathematics: Precision and Ritual in the Legal Process, 84 Harv. L. Rev. 1329, 1349–1350 (1971).

The error costs are likely to be large enough to justify the adoption of procedures that create incentives to produce additional evidence. If the plaintiff cannot obtain damages without more evidence, he will tend to introduce more evidence in those cases where defendant is in fact liable (and to abandon the other cases), and the error rate will fall. But observe that since the defendant will have a strong incentive to introduce evidence in cases where it is in fact not liable, a rule that requires the plaintiff to introduce evidence (beyond defendant's market share) is an appropriate economizing measure only if it is cheaper for the plaintiff to introduce evidence than for the defendant to do so.

§24.3. *Settlements.*   Let us turn now to the direct costs of the procedural system. Since settlements are normally cheaper than trials, the settlement rate is an important determinant of the direct costs of resolving legal disputes. That cases are ever litigated rather than settled might appear to violate the principle that when transaction costs are low, parties will voluntarily transact if a mutually beneficial transaction is possible. Since the parties to a legal dispute are ordinarily just two in number, transaction costs should be low; and since, in addition, the costs of litigation are almost always greater than the costs of a settlement out of court,[1] even with the subsidy that the government provides for litigation,[2] it would seem to follow that virtually all cases would be settled out of court. But if *all* cases were settled out of court, the litigation process as a method of generating information and rules concerning the efficient regulation of behavior would have to be superseded; and beyond a certain point, an increase in the settlement rate will result in a sharp rise in the cost of settlements (why?).

In fact the vast majority of legal disputes *are* settled without going to trial; in the automobile accident field, the proportion of disputes settled out of court exceeds 95 percent.[3] This is as economic theory would predict but we have still to explain the small fraction that go to trial.

A settlement negotiation is an example of decision making under conditions of uncertainty. In such a context, successful

§24.3. 1. An exception is that the marginal cost of an appeal, once trial has been completed and a judgment rendered, may not greatly exceed the cost of settlement negotiations that would obviate the need to take an appeal. For some evidence on this point see Richard A. Posner, A Theory of Negligence, 1 J. Leg. Studies 29, 95–96 (1972).

2. See §23.1 *supra.*

3. A recent study found that only two percent of automobile accident claims are actually tried. H. Laurence Ross, Settled Out of Court 179, 216 (1970).

completion of the negotiation is affected not only by the costs of negotiation relative to those of the alternative decision-making procedure (here litigation) but also by the parties' attitude toward risk and by any difference between the parties' judgments on the likely outcomes under the alternative procedure.[4] We begin with an example of a case in which settlement negotiations are successful. Plaintiff claims that defendant owes him $10,000. The cost of litigating the claim would be $1000 for each party; the cost of settling out of court, again for each party, would be $250. Both parties think the plaintiff has a 75 percent chance of recovering $8000 and a 25 percent chance of recovering nothing. If the plaintiff goes to trial, his expected gain is $8000 × .75 — $1000, or $5000, so if he is risk neutral he will settle the case for anything over $5000 plus $250, his settlement costs; his minimum settlement offer is $5250. If defendant goes to trial, his expected loss is $8000 × .75 + $1000, or $7000. If he is risk neutral he will settle for anything less than $7000 minus $250; his maximum settlement offer is therefore $6750. Since any settlement between $5250 and $6750 will make both parties better off than if they litigated, we can expect them to settle.

In the previous example both parties were risk neutral and had identical expectations with regard to the outcome of the case if litigated. Let us now consider what happens if either assumption is altered in certain ways. Suppose the same facts as before except that now the plaintiff has a pronounced taste for risk: a 75 percent chance of recovering $8000 is worth more to him than a certainty of receiving $6000. Say it is worth $7500. Then his minimum settlement offer becomes $7500 — $1000 + $250, or $6750, and there is now no settlement price that makes both parties better off than they expect to be with litigation (assuming the defendant is either risk neutral or risk preferring). If one or both parties are risk averse, the range within which settlement will be preferred to litigation will be greater than if they were risk neutral, as in the first example.[5]

Suppose neither party has a preference for risk but the parties disagree on the likely outcome. Plaintiff thinks that he has a 75

---

4. For the application of this theory to the legal settlement process see William M. Landes, An Economic Analysis of the Courts, 14 J. Law & Econ. 61 (1971); Richard A. Posner, The Behavior of Administrative Agencies, 1 J. Leg. Studies 305, 320–323 (1972), and An Economic Approach to Legal Procedure and Judicial Administration, forthcoming in 2 J. Leg. Studies (1973).

5. Devise a numerical example to demonstrate this. What happens if one party is risk preferring and the other risk neutral or risk averse? Again use a numerical example to explore the effect of this permutation.

percent chance of obtaining a judgment for $8000, as before, but defendant thinks plaintiff's chance of obtaining nothing is 75 percent. Plaintiff's minimum settlement offer is $5250 as in the first example but defendant's maximum settlement offer is now $8000 × .25 + $1000 — $250, or $2750. Again there is no settlement price at which the parties consider themselves better off than they would be litigating the claim.

The three factors thus far identified as affecting the decision to settle rather than litigate — the relative costs of litigation and settlement, the parties' attitudes toward risk, and differences between the parties' judgment of the likely outcome if the case is litigated — are interacting. Thus, the higher the cost of litigation relative to settlement, the larger must be either the risk preference of one or both parties, or the difference between their estimates of the likely outcome of litigation, for settlement negotiations to fail. From this interaction it is clear that, despite the option of settlement, a government subsidy of litigation costs, even if only partial, does increase the amount of litigation.

Up to this point we have assumed that the stakes to the parties in the case are identical. But they need not be. Suppose for example that the parties have different discount rates — different rates at which they translate money to be received in the future into a present value. If the defendant's discount rate is higher than the plaintiff's, the present cost to the defendant of a judgment to be paid sometime in the future may be less than the present value of the same judgment to the plaintiff, and settlement negotiations may fail even though the parties agree on the probability of the plaintiff's prevailing and the cost of settlement is less than the cost of litigation.

In summary, settlement negotiations will fail if the expected utility of litigation to the plaintiff exceeds the expected disutility of litigation to the defendant by more than the difference between the cost of litigating the case and the cost of settling it. We have identified four factors — the relative cost of litigating and settling, the parties' estimates of the likely outcome, the parties' attitudes toward risk, and differences in the size of the stakes to the parties — that affect this inequality.

The economic analysis of the settlement process enables us to predict the effect of particular procedural conditions on the settlement rate. We begin with pretrial discovery. A full exchange of the information in the possession of the parties to a legal dispute is likely to facilitate settlement by enabling each party to form a more accurate, and generally therefore more convergent, estimate of the likely outcome of the case; and pretrial discovery enables each party to compel his opponent to disclose relevant information in his possession. One may wonder why compulsion is necessary, since the exchange of information is a normal incident of bargaining. The reason is that such an exchange is less likely in a settlement negotiation than in an ordinary commercial transaction. If a commercial negotiation fails, the parties go their separate ways, but if a settlement negotiation fails, the parties proceed to trial, at which surprise has strategic value. Each party has an incentive to withhold information at the settlement negotiation knowing that if negotiations fail, the information will be more valuable at trial if the opponent has not had an opportunity to prepare a rebuttal to it.

Although pretrial discovery is likely to increase the settlement rate, the effect of particular discovery provisions is less certain. Consider Rule 35 of the Federal Rules of Civil Procedure, which authorizes a party to compel his opponent to be examined by a physician designated by the party, if the opponent's health or fitness is in issue. (Rule 35 is most often invoked by defendants in personal-injury actions.) Suppose the plaintiff is less seriously injured in fact than defendant would have believed had he not been able to compel an examination by his physician. In such a case the effect of Rule 35 is to reduce the probability of a settlement. The defendant is not willing to make as large a settlement offer as he would if he exaggerated the extent of the plaintiff's injuries; but the plaintiff's minimum settlement offer is not affected since the examination presumably discloses no new information to the plaintiff concerning the extent of his injuries. Suppose before the examination defendant estimated that plaintiff would receive $10,000 damages if he prevailed at trial and that the probability of his prevailing was 75 percent, and on the basis of these computations was willing to pay up to $7500 to settle the case. Plaintiff believed that he would obtain only $5000 in damages if he won at trial and that his probability of winning was 80 percent, and on the basis of these computations was willing to settle for any amount in excess of $4000. There was thus ample room for settlement. But suppose that after the Rule 35 examination defendant reduces his estimate of the plaintiff's damages to $5000, and his maximum settlement offer accordingly to $3750: settlement negotiations will fail. However, in cases where the Rule 35 examination convinces the defendant that plaintiff's injuries were more serious than he (the defendant) had believed, Rule 35 increases the likelihood of settlement (why?).

A well-known study of judicial administration argues that allowing a winning plaintiff interest on the judgment from the date of accident (or other event giving rise to his claim) would not affect the settlement rate, even if the plaintiff had a higher discount rate than the defendant.[6] The argument is erroneous. The addition of prejudgment interest will reduce the likelihood of a settlement, whatever the discount rates. Suppose that, before the addition of interest, and ignoring for a moment litigation and settlement costs, the expected value of a litigated judgment to the plaintiff is 120, and the expected cost to the defendant is 100 (this is the example used in the cited study). If interest is added, say at an annual rate of 6 percent, for one year, the expected value to the plaintiff will increase to 127.2 and the expected cost to the defendant to 106. The difference between expected value and expected cost is larger — 21.2 instead of 20 — and this will increase the likelihood of litigation. (Thus, if the difference between the sum of the parties' litigation costs and the sum of their settlement costs is 21, the case will be settled if prejudgment interest is not awarded and litigated if it is.) Our example assumed zero discount rates. Clearly, if the parties have identical discount rates, our results remain unchanged qualitatively (why?). If the parties have different discount rates — whichever one's is higher — our results still hold: the addition of prejudgment interest increases the likelihood of litigation.[7]

Prejudgment interest increases the likelihood of litigation

6. Hans Zeisel, Harry Kalven, Jr. & Bernard Buchholz, Delay in the Court 133–136 (1959).

7. Assume before interest the judgment is $10,000, plaintiff's subjective probability of prevailing is 80 percent, his discount rate is 15 percent a year, and the expected delay is two years. Defendant's subjective probability of prevailing is 60 percent (i.e., he thinks plaintiff has a 40 percent chance of winning), and his discount rate is 10 percent. Then plaintiff's minimum settlement offer (ignoring litigation and settlement costs) will be $6049 and defendant's maximum offer $3306, a difference of $2743. If we now increase the judgment by 12 percent (two years' interest), the three figures become $6775, $3702, and $3072, respectively. Thus if the excess of the parties' litigation costs over their settlement costs were $3000, the case would be settled if interest were not added, and litigated if it were. If we reverse the parties' discount rates, the plaintiff's minimum offer, the defendant's maximum offer, and the difference, before imposition of interest, are $6611, $3024, and $3586 respectively; after interest, the respective figures are $7405, $3387, and $4017. Discrepancies are due to rounding.

Suppose in our original example the plaintiff's and defendant's best offers were reversed, so that plaintiff's minimum offer was 100 and defendant's maximum 120. Would our conclusions with respect to the effect of adding prejudgment interest hold, or would they be reversed? Why is the altered example not realistic, however?

simply by increasing the stakes. This suggests the important general point that settlement is less likely, the larger the stakes in the case, everything else remaining unchanged. The converse is that settlement is more likely, the smaller the stakes. One thing that reduces the stakes to the parties is delay, assuming that they have positive discount rates (can you see why?). Delay thus has the opposite effect of prejudgment interest. But not quite. If the defendant's discount rate is higher than the plaintiff's, delay may actually reduce the likelihood of a settlement by causing the defendant's maximum settlement offer to shrink faster than the gap between the offers. Moreover, delay increases uncertainty as to outcome, which as we have seen can be expected to reduce the chances of a settlement.

The analysis in this section can cast some light on a question relevant to the chapter on torts — whether the replacement of negligence liability by strict liability would reduce the total costs of tort litigation.[8] Adoption of strict liability can be expected to lead to an increase in the number of claims against injurers, since it increases the scope of liability. Therefore, if the fraction of claims that go to trial remains the same as under a negligence standard, and if each trial is as costly under the new standard, then the aggregate costs of tort litigation would rise. Both "if's," however, are uncertain. Since strict liability eliminates a major issue in tort litigation, the question of negligence, it reduces the amount of uncertainty involved in predicting the outcome of litigation if the claim is not settled; and we have seen that a reduction in the amount of uncertainty about the outcome of litigation should reduce the fraction of claims that go to trial. Simplification of issues might also lead to a reduction in the cost of each trial, and hence in the total costs of accident litigation, although this is uncertain. The elimination of the negligence issue will tend to increase the value of the plaintiff's claim and this may (though it need not) lead him to expend more money on his case rather than less; but the defendant may also spend less.[9] Even if the cost of trial is lower under strict liability, since this will narrow the gap between the cost of litigation and of settlement one result will be to make litigation relatively more attractive than under the negligence standard of liability, so that a larger fraction of claims may be tried. No clear-cut prediction

8. See §4.15 *supra.*
9. The determinants of litigation expenditures are complex. See §§24.4, 26.2 *infra.*

of the impact of a movement to strict liability on the aggregate costs of litigation can be made; empirical study is necessary.

Here we digress momentarily to discuss the criminal counterpart of the civil settlement, the bargained plea. Some people concerned with the rights of criminal defendants argue that plea bargaining is an abuse of the criminal process and that all criminal defendants should have a trial. The abolition of plea bargaining might, however, make criminal defendants as a group — along with the taxpayers who defray the expenses of prosecution and of the judiciary — worse off rather than better off. If a settlement did not make both parties to a criminal case better off than if they went to trial, one or the other would invoke his right to a trial. Thus plea bargaining as such should not result, on average, either in heavier sentences or in lighter sentences than would a system in which everyone had a trial. The bargained plea, like the civil settlement, can be expected to fall somewhere in between the maximum and minimum estimates of the punishment likely to be imposed if the case went to trial. Perhaps most people who profess to object to plea bargaining are really opposed to other features of the criminal system, such as pretrial incarceration, that operate to increase the expected punishment of the defendant and therefore the bargained sentence.

Although a reduction in plea bargaining, with everything else in the criminal justice system unchanged, would not affect the average severity of sentences, the methods suggested for reducing plea bargaining, such as increasing the number of judges, affect the system at other points as well. We discuss these effects later.[10]

Our discussion of settlements is incomplete because we have assumed thus far that the parties' litigation costs are fixed. The significance of this assumption and the consequences of relaxing it are discussed in the next section.

§24.4. *Expenditures on litigation.*   If settlement negotiations fail, there is a trial for which each party purchases legal services and other litigation inputs. The purchase of such inputs increases the expected value of the litigation to the purchaser by increasing the probability that he will prevail, but at the same time increases the cost of the litigation. The party optimizes his litigation expenditures by spending up to the point where a dollar in such expenditures increases the expected value of the litigation to him by just a dollar. The process of arriving at an

10. See §25.6 *infra* for a discussion of this and other questions of criminal procedure.

optimum level of expenditures, however, is complicated by two factors. First, the parties will frequently find it mutually advantageous to agree not to incur a particular expenditure (e.g., by stipulating to a fact so as to obviate the need for testimony on it); since only two parties are involved in the normal lawsuit, we would expect such transactions to be frequent. Second, every expenditure decision by one party affects the expenditure decision of the other by altering the probability and hence expected value of an outcome favorable to the other party, much as every price or output change by an oligopolist alters the optimum price and output of his rivals.[1] If we assume that each party, in deciding how much to spend on the lawsuit, takes account of the effect of his expenditures on the other party's, then (as in the oligopoly case) there is no equilibrium level of expenditures — no level at which neither party has an incentive to alter his expenditures further. If instead we assume that neither party takes account of the effects of his expenditures on the other party in deciding how much to spend, then we must revise the conclusion in the last section that divergent expectations with respect to the outcome of a case are bound to make litigation more likely. Suppose both parties become highly optimistic about the outcome. This leads them to plan to spend more money on the case (why?). The excess of the parties' litigation costs over their settlement costs will grow by the sum of the additional expenditures projected, but the gap between the plaintiff's minimum settlement offer and the defendant's maximum offer may well grow more slowly due to the mutually offsetting character of their additional expenditures; if so, the likelihood of the parties' litigating rather than settling the case will decline (can you see why?).

Many procedural rules are designed to increase the productivity of litigation inputs. A good example is the rule that permits the judge to take judicial notice of obviously true facts so that the party having the burden of proof need not establish the fact by evidence. The rule[2] reduces the cost to the party of establishing his case. Its effect on his litigation expenditures is shown in Figure 20. D is the average value to the party of various quantities of evidence, and S the average (equal to marginal) cost of that evidence. A rule of procedure (such as judicial notice) that reduces the cost of evidence without reducing its value shifts S

§24.4. 1. See §7.3 *supra*.

2. And rules similarly designed to increase productivity of litigation inputs, such as summary judgment, exclusion of merely cumulative evidence, rules governing the burden of production of evidence, and (perhaps) the hearsay rule.

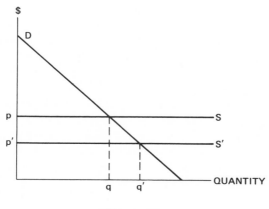

Figure 20

downward, to S'. The party is thereby induced to expand his
purchase of evidence from q to q'. Whether his total expenditures
(price times quantity) will increase, however, depends on the
elasticity of demand with respect to price in the segment of the
demand curve between q and q'. If the elasticity is greater than
one, total expenditures will increase; if it is equal to one, they
will be the same; and if it is greater than one, they will decrease.
Even if total expenditures increase, it does not follow that the
rule is uneconomical, for by increasing the productivity of the
party's litigation expenditures it may reduce the probability and
hence costs of error by more than it increases the resources consumed in the litigation process.

It is often thought that wealthy individuals or large firms
might try to overwhelm their opponents in a litigation by heavy
spending. Our discussion of predatory pricing in an earlier chapter[3] is relevant to an appraisal of this concern. We saw there that
a threat to destroy a rival by below-cost selling would rarely be
credible because it would be so costly to the threatener to carry
out the threat; and the point seems equally applicable in the
present context. We did however identify one case where a credible threat to sell below cost could be made, and it has a parallel
here. If a party anticipates a succession of similar lawsuits, he
may be quite prepared to carry out a threat to overwhelm his
opponent in the first suit by spending heavily on the litigation

3. See §7.5 *supra*.

in order to make a similar threat against succeeding opponents credible.[4]

The discovery process affords opportunities, in principle at least, for a type of predatory conduct. A party could serve demands for discovery on his opponent that were very costly to comply with, as a means of discouraging the opponent from litigating by imposing heavy costs on him at no significant cost to the party demanding discovery. Since, however, the opponent could presumably retaliate, and since the courts are empowered to issue protective orders to prevent such abuses of the discovery process, "predatory discovery" is rare too.

§24.5. *Access to legal remedies.*   The principal litigation input is lawyers' time. The cost of that time is important not only to the direct costs of legal dispute resolution, but also to its error costs. The higher the cost of litigation to the plaintiff the larger must be his stakes in the case for him to be able to obtain legal redress. The point is not that he will be forced to settle if his litigation costs exceed his stakes (discounted by the probability of a successful outcome) but that he will not be able to obtain more than a nominal settlement because he cannot in such a case make a credible threat to litigate in the event that settlement negotiations break down. Hence, where litigation costs are high, the legal system will frequently fail to correct inefficient practices or reduce transaction costs. The resulting inefficiency may be very large even though the individual case is, by hypothesis, one in which the stakes are relatively small; the aggregate stakes involved in many small cases may be substantial.

There is a traditional view that litigation is an evil, a necessary one, but certainly not one to be encouraged. Those who hold this view may be skeptical of any measures that, by reducing the cost of litigation, increase the demand for it. But this view is unsound. If litigation were an inexpensive method of allocating resources, because lawyers were in such plentiful supply that the price of legal service was very low, we might want to *encourage* recourse to litigation as a substitute for costly market processes of allocation.

In fact the practice of law is subject to a web of public regulations that make legal fees higher than they would be in a free market. In order to be permitted to practice law, an individual must have had at least three years of law school and at least two

---

4. How is this point relevant to the question discussed above of the equilibrium level of the parties' expenditures in a lawsuit?

of college. Yet the practice of law encompasses many services that can be performed adequately by people with less extensive schooling and at lower cost since their prices would not include amortization of (and a reasonable return on) a large investment in higher education.[1] The efficient regional allocation of legal resources is impeded by the refusal of many states to recognize qualification in another state as sufficient evidence of fitness to be admitted to the local bar. The prohibition of advertising by lawyers reduces the flow of information to laymen concerning their legal rights, impairs their ability to choose a lawyer intelligently, and reduces competition among lawyers. The prohibition against "lay intermediaries" between lawyer and client reduces the flow of management skills and capital into the legal services industry and impedes experimentation with new forms of delivering legal services. And the rule against lawyers' "fomenting" litigation denies them an important entrepreneurial role in the industry.

Lawyers sometimes attempt to justify these interferences with the free market in legal services on the ground that the practice of law is too arcane and important to be regulated by the self-interest of the consumer of legal services in obtaining the best service at the lowest price. But the premise, even if it were true, would not support the specific regulations that have been imposed. If consumer deception is believed to be a serious problem, close regulation of advertising by lawyers may be warranted; but to forbid all advertising, however informative, can only aggravate the consumer's lack of information. The ban on the involvement of laymen in the management of legal services enterprises is likewise illogical. If the concern is that laymen lack competence to render legal services, it can be allayed by forbidding lay interference in professional decisions, as is the rule in hospital management (many hospitals are owned by nonmedical, profit-making corporations). If the concern is that laymen are not subject to the same sanctions as lawyers, notably exclusion from the profession, it can be allayed by subjecting them to equally harsh albeit different sanctions for misconduct.

The requirements of graduation from an accredited law school and of passing a bar examination are more plausibly related to a genuine concern with protecting the public against incompetent

---

§24.5. 1. Bear in mind that the cost of higher education includes not only the direct costs, although they are considerable, but also the forgone earnings from the job the student would have held had he not been in school.

lawyers. However, the relationship between the completion of these requirements and competence in the practice of law seems tenuous, especially since many dimensions of legal performance, including probity, are not tested in the education and examination process. Less restrictive alternatives would be to require that lawyers disclose their level of educational attainment to prospective clients and to encourage the creation of private certification services. It is consistent with an efficient allocation of resources that some clients would choose the less well-educated, less experienced, or even less intelligent lawyer: his lower quality would presumably be offset by a lower price.

The cost of legal services is occasionally an obstacle to vindication of a claim even when the plaintiff's stakes are very large, but here the legal profession has devised an imaginative solution. Suppose a plaintiff has a claim of $100,000 and a 50 percent probability of vindicating it. The discounted value of the claim is $50,000 and would justify him in expending up to that amount in litigation costs to protect the asset. (He is assumed in this example to be risk neutral.) But suppose the claim is his only asset. Ordinarily this would be no problem: one can borrow a substantial sum against an asset as collateral. But it is not always possible to borrow against a legal claim. Banks and other lending institutions may be risk averse (due to government regulation of financial institutions) or may find it difficult (costly) to estimate the likelihood that the claim can be established in court. These factors may make the interest rate prohibitively high. Most important, many legal claims (for example, a personal injury claim arising from an accident) are by law not assignable — in order to prevent the "fomenting" of litigation — and so are worthless as collateral.

The solution that the legal profession has devised is the contingent fee contract.[2] The lawyer lends his services against a share of the claim. Risk is reduced because the lawyer specializing in contingent fee matters can pool many claims and thereby minimize the variance of the returns. Specialization also enables him to estimate risks more precisely than could a conventional lender.

It has been argued that contingent fees are often exorbitant; but it is easy to be misled here. A contingent fee must be higher than a fee for the same legal services paid as they are performed.

2. See Murray L. Schwartz & Daniel J. B. Mitchell, An Economic Analysis of the Contingent Fee in Personal Injury Litigation, 22 Stan. L. Rev. 1125 (1970).

The contingent fee compensates the lawyer not only for the legal services he renders but for the loan of those services. The interest rate on such a loan is high partly because the interest is accrued during the life of the loan and paid all at once at the end but mostly because the risk of default (the loss of the case, which cancels the debt of the client to the lawyer) is higher than that of conventional loans.

There have always been techniques for aggregating a number of small claims into one large enough to justify the costs of suit — or, stated otherwise, for realizing economies of scale in litigation. A department store performs this function with respect to the claims of its customers against the manufacturers whose products are sold by the store. The customer who purchases defective merchandise may not have enough at stake to sue the manufacturer but he will not hesitate to complain informally to the department store. The store will replace the merchandise or refund the customer's money and, if several customers complain, will pool these complaints and present them to the manufacturer. If the latter is unwilling to reimburse the store for its costs in responding to the customers' complaints, the store will be able to make a credible threat to take legal action against the manufacturer.

The contemporary class action presents an opportunity for generalizing this technique. Suppose the manufacturers of toothbrushes have conspired to charge a monopoly price. Millions of purchasers are harmed; the aggregate cost may be substantial: but the injury to each purchaser may be only a few cents. If all of these claims are aggregated in a class action, the stakes in the action will be large enough to defray the costs of suit and the cartel will be brought to bar.[3]

But the device may have only limited utility in cases where it is most needed — where the individual claim is very small. The defendant can be compelled in such a case to pay a judgment equal to the costs of its violation — but to whom? The costs of identifying the injured purchasers and distributing to them their individual damages may exceed the judgment. To be sure, the most important point, on an economic analysis, is that the vio-

---

3. The federal courts have refused to permit the aggregation of individual claims in a class action for purposes of complying with the minimum jurisdictional amount of $10,000 applicable to some types of federal-court action. If the purpose of the jurisdictional minimum is to keep petty disputes out of the federal courts, the refusal to aggregate individual claims arising from a single, substantial violation seems difficult to justify.

lator be confronted with the costs of his violation — this achieves the allocative purpose of the suit — not that he pay them to his victims. Our earlier emphasis on the importance of receipt of damages by the injured party to motivate him to operate the legal machinery is inapplicable here, since the stakes are too small to induce any victim to bear any of the burden of obtaining legal redress. But there are still problems. First, the costs of actually effecting compensation to the members of a numerous class may be extremely high; in many cases they may exceed the benefits in deterrence yielded by the action. Second, the absence of a real client impairs the incentive of the lawyer for the class to press the suit to a successful conclusion. His profit from the suit is determined by the legal fee he receives rather than by the size of the judgment. No one has an economic stake in the size of the judgment except the defendant and he has an interest in minimizing it. The lawyer for the class will be tempted to offer to settle with the defendant for a small judgment and a large legal fee, and such an offer will be attractive to the defendant.[4]

A class action such as we have described places the lawyer in the position of an entrepreneur rather than an agent, which is good although contrary to tradition, but it also relieves him of accountability, which is bad, because his private incentive diverges from the social goal of obtaining a judgment equal to the social costs of the violation. The problem is not present where the individual members of the class have substantial stakes in the outcome, and this observation provides a strong practical argument for permitting a state to sue as *parens patriae* in cases where a violation of law has inflicted a small harm on each of a great many of its citizens.[5]

The English and Continental practice of requiring the losing party to a lawsuit to reimburse the winning party's attorney's and witness fees might appear to provide an alternative to the class action as a method of vindicating small claims. No matter how small the claim, the claimant should not be deterred from pursuing his legal remedies by the cost of litigation since his litigation expenses will be reimbursed if he wins. There are several disadvantages of the practice, however, in comparison with

4. Of course, the judge must approve the settlement. But the lawyers largely control the judge's access to the information — about the merits of the claim, the amount of work done by the lawyer for the class, the likely damages if pressed to trial, etc. — that is vital to determining the reasonableness of the settlement.

5. We return to the problem discussed in this section in a subsequent chapter. See §26.1 *infra*.

the class action. First, reimbursement is not in fact complete, primarily because the plaintiff's time and bother (which may be considerable in relation to the value of the claim, if it is small) are not compensated. Second, unless the plaintiff is certain to prevail, his expected cost of litigation may easily exceed the expected value of the litigation. Suppose his claim is for one dollar, the probability of his winning is 90 percent, and his litigation expenses are $100. Then the expected gain from litigation is $.90 and the expected cost $20 (assuming his opponent's litigation costs are also $100), so he will not sue. Third, reimbursement of litigation expenses lacks an important economizing feature of the class action and may result in a socially excessive quantity of litigation. The class action permits the amalgamation of a multitude of small claims, enabling economies of scale to be realized. In contrast, reimbursement may create incentives for litigation in circumstances where the total costs of litigation (in the absence of some method of aggregating the separate claims) exceed the benefits. Suppose there are 1000 identical claims for $10 each, the cost of litigating each one is $100, and the probability of prevailing for the plaintiff is 100 percent. If all 1000 claimants sue, as they may since each stands to net $10 from suit, then $100,000 will be spent to vindicate claims worth in the aggregate only $10,000.[6] Had the claims been aggregated in a class action, the expenses of the suit might have been only a small fraction of the expenses of a hundred separate actions.

This is not to deny that reimbursement would be a sensible reform in American civil procedure — although it should not be viewed as a substitute for the class action. Reimbursement has interesting and on the whole desirable properties. By increasing the variance in the expected returns to litigation (why?), the practice encourages settlements, assuming more litigants are risk averse than risk preferring. It should also encourage settlements by giving the parties added incentive to estimate the likely outcome of litigation correctly: the party has more to lose from an incorrect estimate, if one consequence of litigating and losing is that he must reimburse the other party's litigation expenses. The practice also discourages nuisance suits (why?), while encouraging, as we have seen, the bringing of meritorious small claims.

§24.6. *Stare decisis and res judicata.* We are now ready to suggest an economic rationale for the weight that common law courts traditionally attach to conformity with precedent — their

6. Is $10,000 the correct measure of the social benefits of the suits?

reluctance to make new rules except gradually, by small steps — and for their refusal to permit the relitigation of the same claim between the same parties.

If the common law doctrines are intended to promote the efficient use of resources, then we would expect the doctrines to change slowly because the cost and demand conditions that determine which uses of resources are efficient usually change slowly. The pace of economic change has been quickening, however, and perhaps this is one reason why adherence to *stare decisis* appears to be waning even in those common law fields that have been least affected by legislation.

The emphasis on precedent and on small changes makes law more predictable than it would be if every case were decided afresh, on the basis of first principles. Predictability increases the settlement rate and thereby economizes on the costs of the legal system. Without predictability, moreover, property rights would be indefinite, which is the equivalent of saying that there would be few property rights. This too would reduce the efficiency of the economic system. Finally, a system of precedent reduces the costs of litigation by enabling the parties to a case to incorporate the information that has been generated (often at considerable expense) in previous cases. If it has been held in twenty cases that an electric crossing signal is a required (cost-justified) precaution at busy railroad crossings, the marginal gain in knowledge of the relevant costs and values from incurring the expense of a trial in the twenty-first case may be smaller than the cost. A rule of the common law emerges when its factual premises have been so validated by repeated testing in litigation that additional expenditures on proof and argument would exceed the value of the incremental knowledge produced.

The refusal of courts to permit the same claim to be relitigated between the same parties (res judicata) seems at first glance surprising. Having lost once, the party will presumably be reluctant to try again; the loss is evidence of the likely outcome of his second suit. But why should he be forbidden to try, any more than an advertiser should be forbidden to repeat an advertising campaign that failed when first tried a few months previously? The economic theory of legal procedure suggests an answer. The benefit in reducing error costs from relitigation is in general zero; since the costs are positive, relitigation should be forbidden. The reason why the benefit is zero is that we have no way of determining which outcomes in a series of inconsistent outcomes (A sues B and loses; A sues B again and wins; B now sues A to recover A's judgment against B, and wins; etc.) were correct. Wherever we break the chain, we have no reason to think that the last decision is more likely to have been correct than a prior inconsistent decision.

§24.7. *The jury.*   The delegation of a significant part of the judicial function to laymen, each employed very briefly, is consistent with the privatization of legal administration that we mentioned in the last chapter as an example of the affinity between market and legal decision making. It also enhances the impersonality of legal allocation by diffusing the responsibility for the judgment at trial among 13 people, 12 of whom have only a temporary connection with the judicial process.

The analogy to the market breaks down, however, in the method by which a juror's services are obtained. The juror is not hired; he is conscripted.[1] And in contrast to property seizures under the eminent domain power, the state does not pay the market value of the time that it condemns for jury duty. The price paid for a juror's time is low[2] and within each jurisdiction uniform, regardless of the opportunity costs of the individual juror's time. This system is calculated to channel into jury service many people whose time is worth more in alternative employments.

Although the efficiency consequences of jury conscription are presumably most serious with respect to people with high incomes, the distributive consequences may be most serious with respect to poor people. If an individual who earns $100 a day is forced to devote five days to jury duty for which he is paid $6 a day, and if the value to society of his work as a juror is $50, his employment as a juror costs society $250 (what assumptions underlie this cost estimate?). The cost *to him* is different: it is $94 × 5 if his employer does not pay his salary while he is serving as a juror, less if he does.[3] But even a loss of $470 would not be catastrophic to an individual who earned $25,000 a year. Compare the case of a dishwasher who earns $15 a day. His value to society as a juror, let us assume, is $30, so there is no misallocation of manpower resources in conscripting him for jury duty. However, the cost to him is $9 × 5, or $45. The loss of $45 may be more painful to him that the loss of $470 is to the $25,000-a-year

§24.7. 1. See Donald L. Martin, The Economics of Jury Conscription, 80 J. Pol. Econ. 680 (1972).

2. The highest price, $20 a day, is paid in the federal courts. Jury compensation is much lower in the state courts.

3. But as noted below, the ultimate cost may be borne by the employee even if the employer does not interrupt his salary.

man. Also, the dishwasher is less likely to be paid by his employer during jury duty; he may incur unreimbursed transportation costs that substantially increase the cost to him; most seriously of all, he may jeopardize his continued employment in his present job.

Both the efficiency and distributive effects are mitigated, however, by the ease with which a person summoned for jury duty can get excused upon a perfunctory showing of hardship, and by the lack of sanctions for people who simply ignore jury summonses. Perhaps the system is de facto voluntary; yet this conclusion seems difficult to reconcile with statistics on the composition of juries. In a voluntary system, given the low rate of pay for jury service, one would expect juries to be composed disproportionately of retirees, the unemployed, and housewives without young children — people for whom the opportunity costs of jury service would normally be lower than those of people, rich or poor, employed in the regular job market. In fact we find disproportionately few old or unemployed people on juries and disproportionately many professionals and business executives.

A possible explanation is that jury service yields nonpecuniary income, much like voting — an activity that also yields only slight tangible benefits while entailing significant costs for people whose time has any value.[4] Jury duty, like voting, is an obligation of citizenship, and perhaps one felt most strongly by the prosperous employed. They may be willing to accept a lower pecuniary income in exchange for the opportunity to discharge this felt obligation. The pecuniary sacrifice involved in jury duty can be eased by negotiating with one's employer the right to continue employment without interruption of pay during periods of jury duty; but the employee must expect to pay for this concession by the employer since it reduces the value of his work.

§24.8. Delay in court.   The perennial but apparently deepening problem of docket congestion has evoked a spate of suggested reforms and a new discipline — "judicial administration." The most frequent suggestions are for more judges and for greater use of computerized management techniques to smooth the judges' load and permit more cases to be disposed of in a given amount of judge time. As remedies, these suggestions are flawed by the fact that they ignore the role of pricing both in the creation of court delay and in the formulation of effective methods of relieving it.

4. See §19.2 *supra*.

Delay is not due to the fact that the demand for litigation is high and the amount of judge time limited. The demand for potatoes is also high and the capacity to expand production to meet new increments of demand also limited. People queue up to buy litigation but not to buy potatoes because judicial time is not rationed by price and potatoes are. If the demand for potatoes increased faster than the supply, the price of potatoes would rise until demand and supply were equated. An appropriately graduated system of surcharges for people desiring to have their cases heard promptly would have the same effect. If the prices necessary to clear the market (eliminate the queue) were very high, it would be a signal that an investment of resources in hiring more judges would probably be cost justified. The prices might not be high. Perhaps only a small fraction of litigants have sufficient interest in an early trial to pay a surcharge. That would be a signal not to add judges.

To add judges without changing the price of access to judicial time is questionable on two counts. As just mentioned, the additional judges may not in fact be needed. The demand for prompt trials may be weak. But we will never know in the absence of a price mechanism for measuring the intensity of demand. Second, the addition of judges may have little effect on delay other than in the very short run. By increasing the quality of legal redress, at least to those who value speedy trials, the expansion in the number of judges will induce some people to use the courts who previously had been deterred by the delay. The analogy is to the construction of a new freeway to relieve traffic congestion. Significant relief may not be produced. The new freeway may induce people who formerly used other methods of transportation due to dislike for congestion to substitute driving, until the freeway is almost as congested as the roads it replaced had been.

Thus far we have assumed, with the judicial administrators, that court delay is a bad thing and should be the focus of attention by court reformers. In fact delay is an omnipresent feature of social and economic life; in the judicial system as in the restaurant industry, it would be surprising indeed if the optimal amount of delay were zero. Since court delay does not involve the same time costs as waiting in line for a table at a restaurant (why not?), and since some interval is necessary to prepare a case and a defense thereto, some delay must be optimal; on the other hand long delays may be highly inefficient since the decay of evidence would result in an increase in error costs. And of course the costs of delay must be balanced against the costs of shortening the court queue. The advantage of the pricing approach suggested above is that it would obviate the need for attempting to measure directly the costs and benefits of various amounts of court delay.

SUGGESTED READINGS

1. William M. Landes, An Economic Analysis of the Courts, 14 J. Law & Econ. 61 (1971).
2. Donald L. Martin, The Economics of Jury Conscription, 80 J. Pol. Econ. 680 (1972).
3. Richard A. Posner, An Economic Approach to Legal Procedure and Judicial Administration, forthcoming in 2 J. Leg. (1973).

PROBLEMS

1. Can you think of an economic rationale for rules of standing? (See Kenneth C. Scott, Standing in the Supreme Court — A Functional Analysis, 86 Harv. L. Rev. 645, 670–83 (1973).) For the replacement of "notice" pleading by "issue" pleading as in the Federal Rules of Civil Procedure?

2. Should a party to a lawsuit be able to compel the attendance of a witness? Should he be able to compel the production of documents or testimony from the other party to the litigation?

3. In Clauss v. Danker, *264 F. Supp. 246 (S.D.N.Y. 1967), a tort action, the question was whether the plaintiff could seek discovery of the particulars of the defendant's liability insurance policy, albeit those particulars would not be admissible as evidence in the trial of the case. The court said it would be desirable that such discovery be permitted, primarily in order to facilitate settlement, but held that under the existing Federal Rules of Civil Procedure discovery could not be ordered. In 1970 the Rules were amended to permit discovery. The advisory committee noted: "Disclosure of insurance coverage will enable counsel for both sides to make the same realistic appraisal of the case, so that settlement and litigation strategy are based on knowledge and not speculation. It will conduce to settlement and avoid protracted litigation in some cases, though in others it may have an opposite effect." Federal Rules of Civil Procedure for the United States District Courts, as Amended Through July 1, 1971, at 267 (Foundation Press 1971).*

Is the change in the rules likely to increase or reduce the frequency of settlement?

CHAPTER 25

LEGAL SANCTIONS, AND
CRIME CONTROL

§25.1. *Deterrence and the economic theory of remedies.*
The economic content of legal theory is nowhere clearer than in
the rationale of criminal punishment. The usual justification
offered by legal theory for why the state punishes criminal violators is that it is necessary in order to deter people from committing crimes. The justification was proposed by Jeremy Bentham, a lawyer who was also an economist, as an application of
his general theory of human behavior. People, according to
Bentham, are rational maximizers of satisfaction. They will
therefore avoid committing an act that yields them more pain
than pleasure, so crime can be prevented by subjecting the criminal offender to a punishment more painful to him than the
commission of the crime is pleasurable.[1]

Bentham's utilitarianism, in its aspect as a positive theory of
human behavior, is another name for economic theory. Pleasure
is value, and pain cost. People engage in the acts that yield them
the most value net of cost and can be deterred from criminal
activity by a punishment system that makes the cost of criminal
activity greater than the value of that activity to them.

The deterrence theory of criminal punishment is a special case
of a broader economic theory of legal remedies. As emphasized
many times in this book, the function of legal remedies, viewed
in an economic perspective, is to impose costs on people who
violate legal rules. This is as true of simple damages for breach
of contract as it is of imprisonment for rape. The difference is
that the deterrent purpose in the first case is only conditional.
We want to deter only those breaches of contract in which the

§25.1. 1. See Jeremy Bentham, Theory of Legislation 325–326 (R. Hildreth ed.
1864). A recent Benthamite exposition of the theory of criminal punishment is
Herbert L. Packer, The Limits of the Criminal Sanction (1968).

costs to the victim of the breach are greater than the benefits to the breaching party. The correct amount of deterrence is obtained by requiring the breaching party to pay the victim's costs, for then contracts are breached if and only if the benefits to the breaching party exceed the victim's costs. But society does not want to deter only those rapes in which the displeasure of the victim is shown to be greater than the satisfaction derived by the rapist from his act. A simple damages remedy would therefore be inadequate.

The general case in which economic theory suggests that unconditional rather than conditional deterrence is the appropriate goal is where economic allocation is a viable alternative to legal allocation because transaction costs are low.[2] The question whether a particular automobile is more valuable in my hands than in yours can be answered more reliably by negotiations between us than by my taking the automobile subject to an obligation to pay you your damages; and so with the rape victim's body. The question whether my thumb is more valuable to me than as an input into railroading cannot be determined at reasonable cost by negotiation, and therefore subjecting the railroad to severe punishment for inflicting accidental injury would not reserve to the market questions of resource use that the market can most efficiently decide.

A remedy for conversion or rape that prevents people from transforming economic transactions, though feasible, into legal transactions thus increases the efficiency of resource use. A simple damages remedy is not adequate to perform this channeling function. It will not deter the rapist to whom the act has greater value than the cost that he thinks the victim could establish at trial. He can be deterred only by a punishment equal to the value, or profit, of the act to him.

But profit is not quite the correct economic test either; nor is "unconditional" deterrence a precise formulation of the economic punishment goal. The goal of deterring the inefficient substitution of legal for market transactions can be achieved by setting punishment costs equal to the costs to the victim plus the difference between the costs of a market transaction and a legal transaction in the particular activity involved. If the value of the criminal conduct to the criminal exceeds all relevant costs to society, including those of allocation by legal rather than market transactions, the criminal conduct is value maximizing and

2. The discussion in this section reviews and amplifies the analysis *supra* §4.1.

should be tolerated. This is the meaning of Bentham's point that the unnecessary infliction of punishment creates avoidable and therefore wasteful costs. It would be inefficient to punish the thief by cutting off his head: the value of the theft (say, to a starving person) may be greater than the cost of using thievery to allocate resources, and if so, efficiency is promoted by tolerating the conduct.[3] But we shall ignore this important refinement in subsequent discussion.

Although it happens that rape and theft, our examples of the appropriate application of unconditional deterrence, are crimes, the categories of conditional and unconditional deterrence do not completely overlap the categories of civil and criminal remedy. An accounting for profits is an example of a civil remedy designed to deter unconditionally. If the profit of patent infringement to the infringer is greater than the cost to the patentee, a simple damages remedy will not deter infringement. We want deterrence in this case so that people who desire to develop patents owned by others will negotiate with the owners for patent licenses. Deterrence is achieved by requiring that the infringer disgorge his profits if they exceed the patentee's losses (if the losses are greater, simple damages are the appropriate remedy). Injunctions often serve the same purpose: the effect of enjoining me from occupying your land is to compel me to negotiate with you for permission to occupy it.[4]

By now it should be apparent to the reader that the standard example of conditional deterrence, breach of contract, is problematic. An injunction against a breach of contract merely compels the party that wants to be relieved from his obligation under the contract to negotiate mutually satisfactory terms for rescission. It no more prevents dissolution than punishment for rape prevents sexual relations outside of marriage. It compels transacting where, due to fewness of parties, the costs of transacting should not be high. But there are differences between the examples. First, legal allocation is a better substitute for economic allocation in the contract case than in the rape case; the measurement of costs is simpler. Second, parties to a contract have the option of prescribing the conditions under which the contract may be terminated. Their failure to prescribe conditions is some evidence that they considered the cost of negotiating appropriate

3. Also, excessively severe punishment for theft would make the thief indifferent between committing theft and a more serious crime. See §25.5 *infra*.
4. See §2.7 *supra*.

conditions greater than the costs of directing resource use by the law of contract.

§25.2. *The deterrence of concealable acts.* Where the probability that damages will be imposed for a violation is less than unity, a simple damages remedy will fail to deter conditionally (i.e., impose the full cost of violation on the violator). Suppose a group of competing sellers is considering whether to form a cartel. They anticipate that the cost of the cartel to consumers and others adversely affected would be $2 million, and the benefits $800,000. But they also anticipate that the likelihood that the cartel will be discovered is only 25 percent. Under a rule of simple damages, they will (if risk neutral) reckon the cost to them of cartelization as $500,000 and decide to form the cartel. But the costs in fact exceed the benefits. The rule of simple damages provides false signals when the violation is concealable. The proper measure of damages — merely to achieve conditional deterrence — requires that the cost of the violation be divided by the probability of detection and successful prosecution. The proper damage award in the example is $8 million.[1]

Damages so calculated are classified by the law as penal, but this nomenclature is misleading. To be sure, damages awarded in a particular case will, as in our example, exceed the losses to victims in that case; but if the apprehension rate was estimated correctly, the sum of the damages awarded in all such cases will exactly equal the sum of the losses of all of the victims. As in the simple damages case, violators are not deterred from committing violations in cases where the benefits to them from violation exceed the costs to victims. In sum, just as there are civil remedies designed to effect unconditional deterrence, there are "penal" remedies (treble-damage awards in antitrust cases and criminal fines for overweight trucks are examples) designed merely to effect conditional deterrence.

§25.3. *Antitrust remedies.* The foregoing analysis can be used to analyze particular remedial systems, such as that of antitrust law. The violator of a per se antitrust prohibition, such as the prohibition against price fixing, can be imprisoned for a maximum of one year or fined up to $50,000. A variety of injunctive remedies are available to prevent, or undo the effects of, an antitrust violation. And private victims of antitrust violations may

---

§25.2. 1. See Gary S. Becker, Crime and Punishment: An Economic Approach, 76 J. Pol. Econ. 169 (1968); cf. discussion of the appropriate reward for risky undertakings *supra* §§2.2, note 9, and 15.1.

obtain treble their actual damages, plus an allowance for attorney's fees. How adequate is this system?

Conditional rather than unconditional deterrence is the appropriate goal of antitrust enforcement. Conduct forbidden by the antitrust law may, in particular cases, confer benefits greater than the costs, yet the costs of obtaining the victims' consent will ordinarily be prohibitive. But, because many antitrust violations are concealable, a simple damages remedy is not sufficient. Ideally, the damages awarded in an antitrust case should equal the social costs of the violation divided by the probability of apprehension and successful prosecution.

The determinations necessary to translate this ideal into a working rule are difficult to make, perhaps insuperably so. But several things are clear. First, the measure of damages should not be limited to the costs resulting from the substitution of other products for the monopolized product. Since these costs are often smaller than the gains from monopoly pricing, a damage measure limited to these costs would not deter the unproductive activity of monopolizing. What would be missing from such a damage remedy would be the costs to those consumers who continue to buy the product but at a higher price. Those costs are offset by the monopolist's gains but since the latter will enter into his judgment whether to comply, so should the former. We can arrive at the same conclusion by a different route. Since monopolizing as such is an unproductive activity, we want to make it unprofitable. To do this, we must make damages equal to the profits of monopolizing. This is roughly the approach of existing law. To be sure, if the monopolistic conduct yields efficiency gains over and above the profits from monopolizing, damages equal to profits will not deter monopolizing but in this case continued monopolization is the efficient result and we do not want to deter it.

Incarceration (a penalty that, as discussed in the next section, should normally be employed only as a last resort) is an unnecessary penalty in an antitrust case. Antitrust defendants are almost always financially responsible. But the $50,000 maximum fine (although somewhat flexible due to the possibility of multiplying counts) is much too low. And the treble-damage remedy is too rigid. It overdeters in cases where the probability of punishment is higher than 33 percent and underdeters in cases where the probability is lower. The multiple applied to the actual damages should be permitted to vary depending on the particular circumstances of the case.

Structural remedies, such as divestiture and dissolution, are in principle undesirable. A damages judgment against a monopolist that imposed on him costs equal to the social costs of his monopoly would give him a strong incentive to eliminate the adverse consequences of the monopoly and to do so at lowest cost. The lowest cost method might simply be to cease charging monopoly prices. Or, if the monopoly involved diseconomies of scale, tolerable to the firm only so long as they were offset by monopoly profits, the cheapest method might be dismemberment of the firm. To prescribe the method of compliance would appear to be as inefficient as to regulate pollution by prescribing the specific methods of pollution control that are to be used.[1] The appropriate sanction would be to place the cost of illegality on the violator and let him figure out the cheapest way of avoiding that cost. Unfortunately, so little is known about monopolizing that unless a structural remedy is applied there will often be no way of determining compliance. (A rejoinder might be: if we cannot recognize monopoly pricing, on what basis do we prosecute monopolies?)

§25.4.   *Types of criminal sanction.*   A monetary exaction payable out of the violator's current assets is a cheap and effective remedy when those assets are equal to or greater than the costs that society wants to impose as the sanction for the violation. This, rather than discrimination in favor of the wealthy, may be why monetary penalties are relied upon heavily for violations committed by business firms or wealthy individuals. Where the violator has no assets, monetary penalties have no deterrent efficacy and it is necessary to consider alternative forms of remedy. Incarceration is one. It imposes pecuniary costs on the violator by reducing his income during the period of confinement and, in many cases, by reducing his earning capacity after release as well (the "criminal record" effect). It also imposes nonpecuniary costs insofar as people prefer living conditions outside of jail.

Since fines and imprisonment are simply different ways of imposing economic costs on violators, it may seem odd that the Supreme Court should take the view that a sentence which imposes a fine but provides for imprisonment if the defendant cannot or will not pay the fine discriminates against the poor.[1] There

§25.3. 1. See §10.3 *supra.*
§25.4. 1. See Tate v. Short, 401 U.S. 395 (1971); Williams v. Illinois, 399 U.S. 235 (1970).

is no inherent discrimination. A rate of exchange can be found that equates, for any given individual, a number of dollars with a number of days in jail. Perhaps the root of the Court's objection is that most criminal statutes establish a rate of exchange highly favorable to people who have assets. Five hundred dollars is a milder sanction than 100 days in jail,[2] even for people of low income; it is a trivial sanction for people of high income — the people most likely to be able to pay the fine in lieu of serving a jail term.

Had the Court held that the rate of exchange must be realistic, there could be little quarrel with its decisions. By holding that the fine-or-imprisonment form of punishment is inherently discriminatory, however, the Court may have encouraged the penal authorities to place increased reliance on incarceration as a remedy for illegal conduct.[3] This would be unfortunate, since incarceration is a more costly remedy to society than a fine is. The social costs of incarceration include the expense of constructing, maintaining, and operating prisons, the loss of the incarcerated individual's legitimate production (if any) during the period of incarceration, and the likely impairment of his legitimate productivity after release. The last effect in turn increases the likelihood of his resuming criminal activity, an additional source of social cost. Prisons have a tendency to reduce the prisoner's taste, aptitude, and prospects for legitimate employment or, in sum, the income that he can anticipate from "going straight." Since the income from alternative legitimate employment is one of the opportunity costs of crime, a reduction in that income reduces the costs of criminal activity to him and thereby increases the likelihood that he will commit crimes after his release.

Since water cannot be squeezed out of a stone, it may seem that incarceration must continue to be used for indigent offenders, who predominate in theft and in crimes of violence. Yet there are methods, cheaper than incarceration, of imposing costs even on poor offenders. Fines can be made payable in installments (as is now done in many states). They can be proportioned to and payable out of earnings rather than stated as a fixed number of dollars. Exclusion from particular occupations can be used as a sanction, as can compulsory service for an appropriate period of time in a prescribed occupation. Freedom of action can be

2. See Williams v Illinois, note 1 *supra.*
3. As Mr. Justice Blackmun predicted, concurring, in Tate v. Short, 401 U.S. at 401.

restricted in ways that permit productive activity (such as incarceration on weekends only). Some of these methods are not entirely free from the objections advanced earlier to incarceration: a fine payable in installments or proportioned to future earnings would reduce the offender's income from legitimate activity and so also his incentive to choose it in preference to criminal activity.

Incarceration cannot be banished entirely. There must be a method of coercing the payment of required monetary penalties, compliance with occupational conditions, etc. Incarceration has, moreover, a significant advantage in relation to alternative remedies that impose the same cost on the individual. It prevents the offender from committing crimes during the period of his incarceration. It is the indispensable remedy for those who are undeterrable (for example, because insane).

There is one crime for which neither fines nor incarceration may provide an adequate remedy: murder. The cost to the victim is very high, and may indeed approach infinity, since as mentioned in an earlier chapter many people would be unwilling to surrender their lives on the spot for any finite sum of money.[4] Even very heavy fines may not provide the correct amount of deterrence — and of course the problem is aggravated if the murderer has little money or earning capacity. Even prolonged incarceration may not impose on the murderer costs equal to those of the victim. This suggests a possible economic justification for capital punishment, a form of punishment that imposes on the defendant a cost roughly commensurate with the cost of his conduct. But other considerations must be weighed. Because of the severity and irrevocability of the penalty, the cost of mistaken imposition of capital punishment is very high, and so substantially greater resources are invested in the litigation of a capital case. The additional resources may not be justified if the incremental deterrent effect of capital punishment compared, say, to life imprisonment is small. There is recent evidence, however, that it may be substantial.[5]

§25.5. *Additional implications of the economic model of criminal behavior.*   Our discussion of sanctions may have left the

---

4. See §4.11 *supra.*
5. Isaac Ehrlich, The Deterrent Effect of Capital Punishment (unpublished manuscript, U. of Chi., Grad. Sch. of Bus.). Assuming the same burden of proof in capital as in other criminal cases, would you expect the probability of an erroneous judgment (either acquittal of a guilty defendant or conviction of an innocent one) to be greater or smaller in a capital case, or the same?

impression that the control of illegal conduct is a matter simply of choosing the remedy that, at least cost to society, imposes costs of a desired level on the offender. But severity of sanction is only one of the variables determining the incidence of crime. An exposition of the economic model implicit in our discussion of remedies will help make this point clear.

To the economist, a criminal is someone who has chosen to engage in criminal activity because the expected utility of such activity to him, net of expected costs, is greater than that of any legitimate alternative activity.[1] His calculation of advantages can be altered by changing any of a number of factors that affect the expected utilities and costs of alternative occupations. Expected punishment cost is one of these factors and the severity of the punishment, in the event punishment is imposed, in turn affects the expected punishment cost. But there are others. For example, one of the considerations affecting the attractiveness of committing crimes for pecuniary gain (such as robbery, in contrast, say, to rape, which is a consumption activity), relative to other activities, is the wealth of the community. And one of the things that depresses the legitimate earning capacity of an individual, quite plausibly, is a background of poverty. Low earning capacity also reduces the cost of incarceration to the offender. Thus, a highly unequal wealth distribution within a wealthy community[2] (or between communities, if mobility is high) can be expected to produce a higher incidence of pecuniary crimes than if the wealth were more equally distributed, by increasing the expected return to such crimes while decreasing both the opportunity costs of legitimate income forgone and the punishment cost. Income redistribution is thus a possible instrument of crime control.

Another factor that affects the relative utilities of alternative occupations is the risk, or variance about the expected return. The reader is by now familiar with the proposition that activities that carry the same expected return but a different amount of risk will not be equally attractive to all people, since people dif-

§25.5. 1. This model of criminal behavior was suggested by Gary S. Becker (see his article, Crime and Punishment: An Economic Approach, 76 J. Pol. Econ. 169 (1968)), and developed in the work of another economist, Isaac Ehrlich. See his article, The Deterrent Effect of Criminal Law Enforcement, 1 J. Leg. Studies 259 (1972).

2. If there is little wealth in the community, then even if it is highly concentrated the opportunities for lucrative criminal activity may be few. There may be few people worth robbing and they may be so wealthy that they find it profitable to devote substantial sums to self-protection.

fer in their taste for risk.[3] This has important implications for the choice between alternative methods of increasing punishment cost. An example will illustrate. Let the average expected punishment cost of robbery be $2000, a figure arrived at by multiplying the probability of apprehension and punishment (assumed to be 20 per cent) by the monetary equivalent, properly discounted to present value, of all of the costs to the bank robber of the average incarceration for robbery (assumed to be $10,000). Disturbed by the incidence of robbery, the state decides to double the punishment cost. It has two alternatives (we ignore the intermediate possibilities). One is to double the probability of apprehension and punishment, to 40 percent. The other is to double the severity of the sanction, to the equivalent of $20,000. Either method yields the same expected punishment cost, $4000. Superficially the only difference is that the first method is likely to be cheaper. True, the cost to society of incarcerating the convicted bank robber will now be higher, but the total incarceration costs for robbery may well be lower, depending on how sharply the incidence of robbery declines as a result of the higher expected punishment cost. In contrast, to increase the rate of apprehension and punishment from 50 to 100 percent, the state would have to increase the level of its spending on police and other crime-prevention tools substantially and to maintain the higher level of expenditures indefinitely.[4] The apparent disparity in costs between increasing the severity of the sanction and increasing the probability of imposing the sanction in a particular case would be even greater if the sanction were a fine rather than imprisonment (why?).

But the comparison ignores the existence of different tastes for risk. If robbers are risk preferrers, the same increase in expected punishment cost brought about by changing the severity of the sanction will have less deterrent effect than an increase brought about by a change in the probability of apprehension and punishment. Let the receipts from a robbery be $5000, subject either to a 20 percent chance of a $20,000 punishment or to a 40 percent chance of a $10,000 punishment. The expected net returns are the same ($1000). But the expected utility to a risk preferrer is greater in the first case because, as between identical expected returns, he prefers the one with the greater risk, or vari-

---

3. See, e.g., §4.5 *supra*.
4. As soon as it slackened in its efforts to keep the probability of apprehension and punishment high, that probability would fall and the crime rate rise.

ance about the expected return. (The range of possible returns varies from $5000 to −$15,000 in the first case and from $5000 to only −$5000 in the second.)

Another problem with increasing the severity of the sanction in order to reduce the incidence of a crime is that since the criminal's opportunities include other illegal, as well as legal, occupations, the effect of making the expected punishment cost of a particular crime very high may be to induce him to commit another, and more serious, crime.[5] This provides a rationale, independent of retributive considerations, for graduating punishment according to the gravity of the crime. The same consideration limits increasing the expenditure of resources on apprehension and prosecution of perpetrators of a particular crime. The principal effect of a "crash" program to wipe out burglary may be an increase in robbery (generally a more serious crime), since these are relatively close substitutes. To complete the symmetry, observe that increasing the severity of the sanction produces greater deterrence of risk-averse criminals than would increasing the probability of their apprehension and punishment.[6]

Although we have emphasized methods of altering the incentives of the prospective criminal, it is also possible to reduce the crime rate by increasing the incentives of prospective victims to take self-protective measures and by increasing the costs of the tools of crime, such as handguns. That many crimes can be prevented more effectively by the victims than by the police is implicitly recognized in the fact that the police do *not* provide armored car service. Thefts of large amounts of cash or negotiable securities can probably be reduced most economically by increased security precautions on the part of banks and other prospective victims rather than by increased expenditures on the public police force or more severe penalties for such thefts. Much more could be done along these lines with respect to crimes against private individuals. For example, fines could be imposed on people who left their cars unlocked or who failed to install minimum protective devices against burglary.[7]

5. This point is emphasized in George J. Stigler, The Optimum Enforcement of Laws, 78 J. Pol. Econ. 526 (1970).

6. Some evidence supporting this and other predictions of the economic theory of criminal behavior is presented in Isaac Ehrlich, *supra* note 1.

7. Do you recognize the analogy here to the problem of creating appropriate incentives for victims of costly interactions in common law settings to take precautionary measures? See, e.g., §2.6 *supra*. Is burglary insurance relevant here? Can insurance companies be expected to insist that their policyholders adopt preventive measures?

People are most concerned with crimes in which death or personal injury is inflicted, and handguns, because of their lethal and concealable character, are the weapons most commonly and dangerously employed in such crimes.[8] Proposals to control access to handguns have been made and to some extent enacted. Some proponents of gun control would like to disarm the entire population (except the police), and while the history of Prohibition suggests that this is probably an unwise measure, due to enforcement costs, more moderate measures might be both feasible and effective. Since many handguns used in crime are stolen guns, one possibility might be to fine anyone from whom a gun was stolen and later used in a crime unless he could prove that he had used due care to prevent its theft. This would create an incentive for gun owners to take cost-justified precautions to prevent the theft of their weapons. Another possibility might be to tax the sale of handguns more heavily than is done now, so as to increase their cost and make alternative instruments of crime more attractive to criminal offenders. The advertising of handguns might be forbidden; this would make their distribution less efficient and hence, again, more costly. And crimes in which a handgun was involved could be punished more severely than if another weapon were used: the felony-murder rule provides a precedent for this general approach.

As opponents of gun control like to point out, making it harder or more costly for people to obtain or use guns would not eliminate crimes of violence. The determined criminal could substitute a knife or other weapon. However, since other weapons tend to be less effective than handguns in killing or intimidating people,[9] effective gun control would both reduce directly the amount of personal injury inflicted by criminals and make crimes of violence less attractive to the criminal offender than other and less costly crimes.

§25.6.   *Criminal procedure.*   There are a number of distinctive features of criminal procedure which economic analysis can help to illuminate. One is the requirement that the prosecutor prove the defendant's guilt beyond a reasonable doubt. The premise of this requirement is that a mistake in favor of the prosecution (conviction of an innocent person) is more costly to society than a mistake in favor of the defendant (acquittal of a

---

8. See Franklin E. Zimring, The Medium Is the Message: Firearm Caliber as a Determinant of Death from Assault, 1 J. Leg. Studies 97 (1972).
9. See ibid.

guilty person). In a civil case the relative costs of mistake to the parties tend to be the same,[1] and a rule that increased the probability that a mistake would favor the defendant would simply transfer wealth from plaintiffs as a group to defendants as a group. But the typical criminal case is asymmetrical. The loss to the defendant, when his punishment consists of incarceration, loss of employment, public humiliation, or other nonpecuniary costs, does not take the form of an equivalent transfer to the community, represented by the prosecutor. The only gain to the state is the reduction in the crime rate due to the deterrent effect of punishment. The reduction in deterrence from acquitting a guilty person may well be less costly than the punishment cost sustained by the erroneously convicted person, especially since such a conviction *reduces* the deterrent effect of punishment.[2] The last point can best be grasped by imagining that people were selected completely at random to be punished (say) for theft. Then the expected punishment cost for theft would be identical for everybody (different attitudes toward risk aside), but the expected benefits would be higher for those who actually stole, so the prospect of punishment would not deter theft at all.

The economic analysis of sanctions is especially helpful in clarifying an important issue in current discussions of reform of criminal procedure: the likely effect of proposed reforms on the crime rate. There is a "liberal" reform platform that proposes (1) expanding the number of judges in order to enable speedier trials and an end to or reduction in the amount of plea bargaining, and (2) setting bail at a level that permits all people accused of crime to be at liberty until conviction. There is a "conservative" platform that proposes (1) denial of bail to accused people who are expected to commit further crimes if they are at liberty pending trial, and (2) curtailment of procedural rights, such as the right to exclude from trial illegally obtained evidence where the illegality is unrelated to the defendant's guilt or innocence.[3]

Speedier trials would increase the expected punishment cost for accused criminals who are now admitted to bail. The present value of a dollar received in the future is less than that of a dollar to be received immediately, the difference being the interest

§25.6. 1. See §24.2 *supra*.

2. See Richard A. Posner, An Economic Approach to Legal Procedure and Judicial Administration, forthcoming in 2 J. Leg. Studies (1973).

3. The analysis that follows draws in part on William M. Landes, The Bail System: An Economic Approach, 2 J. Leg. Studies 79 (1973).

that can be earned in the second case.[4] The analysis of future costs is symmetrical: the present cost of a dollar to be paid in the future is less than a dollar, since interest is earned until the obligation to pay materializes. The higher an individual's personal discount (interest) rate, the larger the difference between the cost of a dollar to be paid today and a dollar to be paid a year from now. If, as is widely assumed, criminals typically have high discount rates, a reduction in the interval between arrest and incarceration could increase substantially the expected cost and hence deterrent effect of criminal punishment.

With respect to those accused of crime who are now denied bail, the effect of speedier trial would be the opposite. Especially if the convicted defendant receives no credit against his sentence for the period of pretrial incarceration, any reduction in the interval between arrest and trial will reduce the total punishment cost. But even if full credit is granted, the cost will be reduced. For people who are guilty of crime but are either acquitted at trial or receive a sentence shorter than the period of their pretrial incarceration, that incarceration *is* their punishment and any measure that reduces the length of the incarceration reduces the effective punishment cost.

A more liberal bail policy, by postponing the commencement of punishment, would reduce the expected punishment cost to people accused of crime who are now denied bail; but this effect would be at least partially offset by the provision of speedier trials, which would accelerate the imposition of punishment for those admitted to bail. The net effect of combining bail liberalization with speedier trials on the average expected punishment cost is thus ambiguous. The fraction of the criminal accused admitted to bail today, the frequency with which guilty people are acquitted, the average length of pretrial incarceration, and the frequency with which convicted defendants are given credit for time already served are relevant variables. In contrast, an increase in pretrial incarceration, as advocated by proponents of preventive detention, would unambiguously increase the expected punishment cost of criminal activity. But those who advocate preventive detention also advocate speedier trials, which would reduce the effect of preventive detention in increasing punishment costs.

Merely increasing the number of judges might not affect the incidence of plea bargaining. As we have already seen, plea bar-

4. On discounting to present value, see, e.g., §4.10 *supra*.

gaining takes place because negotiation is a cheaper way of resolving controversies than litigation, and its incidence is mainly
determined by the relative costs of negotiation and of litigation
and by the amount of uncertainty over the outcome of litigation
— factors not greatly affected by the number of judges.[5] More
judges might enable speedier trials — although even this is not
certain[6] — and speedier trials might affect the stakes to the defendant (and prosecutor?) and thereby the terms of the bargain.
But not the *amount* of bargaining.

If plea bargaining were forbidden and there were no increase
in the number of judges — if, in other words, the demand for
judicial time increased several-fold with no increase in the supply — the result would be an enormous increase in the waiting
period for criminal trials. The expected punishment cost of people free on bail would fall precipitously and that of people incarcerated until trial would increase (unless they could successfully argue that their constitutional right to a speedy trial was
infringed by the delay). Since litigation is more costly than plea
bargaining, there would be some increase in the legal expenses of
criminal activity, but most of these expenses are now borne by
the government and by private lawyers (which means, in part at
least, by their paying clients) rather than by the accused criminals themselves. Although the average sentence should not be
affected by whether it is negotiated or imposed after trial, the
variance in sentencing would increase since a trial is likely to
result in either acquittal or a stiff sentence (why?). This would
introduce additional risk into the expected cost of punishment,
with consequences that we have already discussed.

Finally, a reduction in the criminal defendant's procedural
rights would, by increasing the probability of punishment, increase the expected punishment cost — and reduce the amount
of risk associated with the cost.

In sum, the "conservative" proposals seem likely, if adopted,
to increase the deterrent effect of criminal punishment. The
"liberal" proposals would probably reduce it but the magnitude
of the reduction might be a good deal less than opponents imply.
The liberal proposals are somewhat lacking in internal coherence,
however, especially in the attempted linkage of more judges–
speedier trials–less plea bargaining. Another objection to the

5. See §24.3 *supra*. But an increase in their number might reduce the relative
costs of litigation some (why?).
6. Cf. §24.8 *supra*.

liberal position relates to its piecemeal implementation. Bail reform has progressed rapidly; expansion in the number of criminal court judges has lagged far behind. Our analysis suggests that the admission of more people to bail, without any other change in the system, unambiguously reduces the deterrent effect of criminal punishment.

§25.7. *The economics of organized crime.* Much of the emphasis of law enforcement in recent years has been placed on the control of "organized crime." The term is used to describe criminals organized into illegal firms linked up in national or even international cartels, operating in such criminal fields as loan-sharking, prostitution, gambling, and narcotics, but also, and increasingly, in legitimate fields as well, and employing violence and the corruption of police as key business methods.

From the standpoint of economic analysis some of these attributes seem realistic, others fanciful. The activities associated with organized crime primarily involve willing buyer-seller relationships rather than forced exchanges. Since such relationships ordinarily entail some degree of organization and specialization, we are not surprised to find firms, rather than individuals, active in these activities. The creation and maintenance of organizations is facilitated by the difficulty of apprehension. Were apprehension easy, the relative conspicuousness of an organization in comparison to an individual would make it highly vulnerable. But because the activities of organized crime involve willing victims, the organization is in relatively little danger of apprehension, at least by the usual method of victim complaint. Moreover, the large sums generated in the businesses in which organized crime is active (such as prostitution, gambling, and loan-sharking), together with the absence of a complaining victim, who might be suspicious of police or prosecutorial inaction, facilitate the corruption of the law enforcement authorities.

It is not surprising that organized crime should employ violence, since it is forbidden to enforce its contracts by lawful means. Nor is it surprising that it should attempt to enter legitimate businesses, since they provide attractive investment opportunities for people with money to invest and with entrepreneurial skills. Should such entry be encouraged or discouraged? On the one hand, a method of reducing the incidence of organized crime is to increase the expected return of alternative, legitimate activity. On the other hand, to the extent that profits earned in organized crime can be safely invested in legitimate activities to yield additional profits, the expected return to organized crime is higher than it would otherwise be.

The features in our composite description of organized crime that seem least compelling from an economic standpoint are the alleged national and even international scale of operations and the alleged monopoly profits. Large-scale operations in the usual organized crime fields would encounter substantial diseconomies for two reasons. First, all of these fields are forms of retailing, which is generally a highly decentralized business, indicating that there are probably substantial diseconomies of scale. Second, the covert form that organized crime enterprises are constrained to assume probably prevents them from establishing the elaborate control machinery, involving voluminous communication, that is associated with very large firms in other fields.

It has been suggested that legal sanctions for typical organized crime businesses such as prostitution and gambling have the effect of creating a "tariff" that enables people willing to assume the risk of criminal punishment to obtain monopoly profits by entering those businesses.[1] This analysis is incorrect. Expected punishment cost is a cost of doing illegal business and must, like other costs, be covered. A price for an illegal service that includes this cost is not a monopoly price; it is a competitive price, albeit a higher one than would prevail if the activity were legal and involved no punishment costs. Whether or not the activities of organized crime are cartelized and hence yield monopoly profits is a question that is not answered by observing that they are illegal.

From an economic standpoint, the primary effect of making illegal the activities in which organized crime engages is to increase the costs, and hence prices, of certain market transactions.[2] To the economist, lending money at high rates, charging money for sexual favors, and operating gambling casinos are no less appropriate market transactions than the sale of potatoes. But if society wants to discourage them the use of the criminal sanction is (depending on enforcement costs) a rational method of doing so, since even if imperfectly enforced it increases the cost and hence price of the service and so reduces the amount consumed.

§25.7. 1. Herbert L. Packer, The Limits of the Criminal Sanction 277–282 (1968).

2. But an offsetting factor should be noted: the criminal enterprise may avoid having to pay excise and other taxes.

SUGGESTED READINGS

1. Gary S. Becker, Crime and Punishment: An Economic Approach, 76 J. Pol. Econ. 169 (1968).

2. Isaac Ehrlich, The Deterrent Effect of Criminal Law Enforcement, 1 J. Leg. Studies 259 (1972).

3. William M. Landes, The Bail System: An Economic Approach, 2 J. Leg. Studies 79 (1973).

4. George J. Stigler, The Optimum Enforcement of Laws, 78 J. Pol. Econ. 526 (1970).

PROBLEMS

1. Should fines for the same offense be graduated according to the wealth of the offender? Why would this be incorrect from an economic standpoint?

2. It is commonly said that people who occupy positions of trust should be well paid in order to reduce the temptation to betray their trust. Can you think of an economic basis for this view?

3. What would be the consequences if, instead of requiring the defendant to post bail, the state were required to pay the defendant the costs he incurred by remaining in jail pending trial?

4. Would it be a good idea, from an economic standpoint, to compensate the defendant who is acquitted of a criminal charge? What would be the appropriate measure of compensation? What implications, if any, would compensation have for the appropriate standard of proof in a criminal case?

5. In a suit for treble damages under the antitrust laws, should the plaintiff be required to establish the defendant's liability beyond a reasonable doubt?

6. Would flogging or other forms of corporal punishment be efficient methods of criminal punishment?

CHAPTER 26

LAW ENFORCEMENT

We have been discussing legal remedies as if they were self-executing, which of course they are not. In the common law fields and in many statutory areas the enforcement of law — the process by which violations are investigated and a legal sanction applied to the violator — is, like its formulation, entrusted mainly to private persons: the litigants, their lawyers, and various specialists in proof or investigation whom they hire. We examined this process in Chapter 23. However, a good deal of the responsibility for law enforcement has been entrusted, either concurrently with private enforcement or exclusively, to public agencies. The present chapter inquires into some of the properties of public enforcement. The first section considers the merits of a public monopoly of some types of law enforcement.

§26.1. *Public vs. private law enforcement.*   The law enforcement responsibility of public agencies is frequently exclusive: a private citizen cannot prosecute for murder. However, there is a large area of private enforcement and a good deal of overlap between the public and private law enforcement domains. The private treble-damage action to enforce the antitrust laws is an example, and so, in principle at least, is a tort action for intentional killing where punitive damages are sought. But private enforcement is circumscribed in three major respects. First, the characteristic criminal remedies, such as imprisonment, cannot be obtained in private actions. Second, a private citizen ordinarily may not initiate a lawsuit unless he can show that he was a victim of the unlawful act: he cannot sue merely to obtain a penalty, or damages sustained by someone else. The natural "entrepreneurs" of private enforcement to obtain penalties would be lawyers; but they are further barred by the rule against "fomenting" litigation. Third, public agencies frequently enjoy a monopoly of the enforcement of the rules committed to their authority: a private individual injured by a violation of the Federal Trade Commission Act or of a rule interpreting it cannot bring a private action against the violator.

These restrictions could be abrogated and free entry into the law enforcement business permitted.[1] Entry would occur first in areas where the costs imposed by a single violation of law, and hence the potential damages, are substantial but so widely diffused that no individual has an incentive to sue merely for the damages he has sustained or for a penalty that is a small multiple of those damages. This is the area, illustrated by the antitrust laws and laws regulating pollution and consumer transactions, in which existing restrictions on private enforcement are most harmful to the community interest in effective enforcement. With free entry, entrepreneurs would search for violations, bring suit against the violators, and recover their investigation and litigation expenses — as well as compensation for entrepreneurial risk and initiative — out of the judgments awarded. The rate of apprehension of wrongdoers would rise as resources were drawn by large expected returns into the activity of trying to apprehend violators. As the apprehension rate rose, the penalty components of the judgments would be reduced (assuming it was not desired to increase the level of deterrence), the flow of additional resources into the particular branch of law enforcement thereby checked, and an equilibrium produced in which the marginal cost of private law enforcement was equal to its marginal benefits, as measured by the desired level of costs imposed on violators.

The present system may well be less conducive to optimum investment in law enforcement. The resources of the law enforcement agencies are determined not only by the expected returns to those resources in various alternative uses but also by political considerations entering into the appropriations process. Competition in law enforcement might also create stronger incentives to prosecute violations vigorously; the publicly employed prosecutor does not have a direct pecuniary stake in the outcome of the cases that he handles.

Private entry need not be limited to cases in which the sanction is monetary. The family of a murderer's victim might be

§26.1. 1. As proposed in Gary S. Becker & George J. Stigler, Law Enforcement, Corruption, and Compensation of Enforcers (unpublished manuscript, U. of Chi. Grad. Sch. of Bus. & Dept. of Econ.)

permitted to hire a private prosecutor if it believed that he would be more effective than the public prosecutor.

The world of free entry into law enforcement may seem a purely academic construct, and in fact it has, as we shall see in a moment, practical drawbacks. Yet it would represent an extension of, rather than a revolution in, existing policies. The importance of private enforcement of public law has long been recognized not only in statutes such as the antitrust laws that explicitly provide for private enforcement but in the judicial principle that even where a criminal statute is silent with respect to private enforcement, anyone within the class of those intended to be protected by the statute who is injured as a result of its violation may bring a private damage action. Perhaps the most important harbinger of the free entry principle is the evolving consumer class action.[2] The initiative in these actions is not supplied by any of the victims — they are typically unaware that they are victims — but by venturesome lawyers who look to a judicial award of attorneys' fees as the source of compensation for their services. The fiction of an attorney-client relationship is maintained; in fact the lawyer is acting as an entrepreneur of law enforcement.

A major constraint on legal entrepreneurship is that the lawyer for the class may not retain the damages awarded. This reduces his incentive to press for the maximum damages award and may, as mentioned, result in settlements that are inordinately favorable to defendants but include a large attorney's fee. Moreover, the legal fee awarded by a court is computed on the basis of services rendered and does not include compensation for entrepreneurial risk. This problem could be overcome by allowing the lawyer-entrepreneur to retain the damages (including any penalties) and his attorney's fee. To be sure, the actual victims of the violation would go uncompensated, but this is not crucial from an economic standpoint, since in a consumer class action it is the lawyer rather than the member of the class whom we want to encourage to assume prosecutorial initiative. Moreover, the costs of distributing damages to a multitude of individual victims would often exceed the amount of damages. Observe that the costly notice to members of the class could also be dispensed with under the suggested approach.

2. See §24.5 *supra*. We use "consumer" loosely here, to refer to the type of violation in which the victim suffers only a small harm although the aggregate costs of the violation may be substantial. Pollution provides many examples of this type of violation.

In cases where the injury is not so widely diffused, it may be appropriate to continue the control over the initiation of a private action in the hands of the injured. A person who has a large stake should have adequate incentive to initiate legal action where it is likely to succeed, and contingent-fee arrangements enable him to finance the action. These are the cases where today the private enforcement of the law is a recognized and encouraged alternative to public enforcement. The case for free entry into law enforcement relates primarily to those cases where the absence of substantial injury to any single individual, coupled with the restrictions on legal entrepreneurship, preclude private enforcement under the existing rules. In these cases it can be argued not only that private suits should be freely permitted but also that the plaintiff, regardless of *his* actual damages, if any, should be entitled to retain in full any damages awarded.

A serious objection to free entry into law enforcement is that it might produce a great deal of frivolous prosecution and litigation: private entrepreneurs would eagerly thumb the statute books for forgotten laws carrying heavy penalties. Limitations of prosecutorial resources, combined with the public monopoly of law enforcement, result in the nonenforcement of many trivial, ill-considered, or obsolete laws. Legislation is frequently, and perhaps deliberately, a process of incomplete enactment. The legislature relies on the enforcement agency to revise and selectively apply the legislative product. Free entry into law enforcement might require changes, perhaps quite costly ones, in the operations of legislatures. It might require courts to adopt new standards relating to the interpretation and validity of statutes. It might require a new stratum of administrative agencies.

A second possible objection to free entry into law enforcement is more technical in nature and relates to the necessity of creating a new type of property right in order to give private enforcers correct incentives. Suppose, for example, that enforcer A laboriously compiles a case against malefactor X but that before he is able to complete the preparation of his case enforcer B — who has done no investigating at all but has heard about A's preparations — files a lawsuit against X. B may wish to purchase A's investigative files, but clearly A will not be able to reap the full harvest of his investment. A's position is similar to that of the inventor in a situation where there are no patent rights.[3] Discovery, whether of a new product or of a violation of law, is

3. See §2.9 *supra*.

often a costly undertaking. The right amount of it will not be undertaken unless the discoverer can obtain some kind of property right in the fruits of his discovery.

It is also necessary to impart to potential enforcers appropriate incentives to avoid imposing undue costs on violators, and on completely innocent people as well, through baseless or excessive investigation and litigation. As a first step, the enforcer should be required to compensate the accused if the latter is exonerated. The absence of such a feature explains the Internal Revenue Service's lack of enthusiasm for its informer program, under which anyone who reports a tax violator is entitled to receive ten percent of the amount of additional taxes recovered. The service considers the program more trouble than it is worth because most of the information supplied is spiteful misinformation. Were the informer required to pay an appropriate penalty in the event that his information did not result in the collection of additional taxes, the quality of the information received would be much better and the program might be successful.[4]

Even the guilty defendant should not be required to defend against the same claim over and over again (why?), and this underscores the importance of recognizing some kind of property right in enforcement claims under any system of free entry. A mechanism, like property rights, is necessary by which the legal claim against the defendant can be shifted to the enforcer in whose hands it will be most valuable — the enforcer, in other words, with the best chance of success. Then we can be reasonably confident that if only one suit can be brought for the particular violation, the party most likely to prosecute it successfully will be the one to bring it.

§26.2. *Choice of cases by the public agency.*   The process by which a law enforcement agency decides where to concentrate its resources is of great interest in view of the monopoly position in law enforcement that public agencies so frequently occupy. We explore the process here on the assumption that the agency acts as a rational maximizer, comparing expected returns and expected costs with alternative uses of its resources. The use of this economic model may seem inconsistent with our frequent intimations, more fully developed in the next chapter, that public law enforcement bodies are a part of the political process, a domain

---

4. The program is such a headache that the service does not advertise, and most people are probably unaware of, its existence.

in which value maximization is not the ruling criterion. But there is no inconsistency. We may assume that political considerations affect the weights that the agency applies to determine the return from winning a particular type of case: it may assign a high weight to punishing defection from a cartel and no weight to punishing membership in one. But once these weights are assigned and goals thus determined, presumably the agency tries to use its resources as effectively as possible in achieving its goals.

Discussions of the allocation of resources within public agencies typically emphasize the importance of the agency's devoting its major resources to the most important cases. Agencies are commonly lambasted for devoting disproportionate resources to trivial cases. Economic analysis suggests that this type of criticism is superficial. The importance of the case — the stakes to the agency of a successful outcome — is only one criterion of the efficient allocation of agency resources and it is frequently dominated by others.

The expected utility of a case to the agency is the stakes, if it prevails, discounted (multiplied) by the probability that it will prevail.[1] To simplify the analysis, we will assume initially that the agency has just two cases it is interested in, A and B, and the decision it must make is how to allocate a fixed budget between them. A is the more important case. If the agency wins it, the agency's utility will increase by 100 units; a victory in B is worth only 50 units. A loss in either case is worth zero.

Since the probability of a successful outcome, and hence the expected utility, is in both cases a function in part of how much the agency spends on prosecution, it is tempting to suggest that the agency devote all or most of its resources to trying to win A. But this would be correct only if the agency's outlays were the *only* factor affecting the probability of the outcome in either case, and plainly they are not. The defendant's outlays are critical, as is the relative effectiveness of the agency's and the defendant's outlays in influencing the outcome. Let us examine these two factors more closely.

(1) If the case is very important to the defendant, then, other things being equal, he will spend a large amount on its defense. The more he spends, either the less effective the agency's outlays will be in influencing the outcome in its favor or the more the agency itself will spend in order to neutralize the defendant's expenditures. In either event the expected utility of the case to the

§26.2. 1. Cf. §24.4 *supra*.

agency, net of its costs of prosecution, will be smaller. Thus, other things being equal, the rational maximizing agency will prefer to invest resources in a case that is relatively unimportant to the defendant. To be sure, if the stakes to plaintiff and defendant were always the same in a case, the reduction in cost to the agency from bringing a case that was unimportant to the defendant would be offset by the reduction in the agency's expected utility due to the unimportance of the outcome to it. But the stakes of the parties often diverge. A case may be important to the agency but not to the defendant because, although the monetary stakes — which are all the defendant cares about — are small, the case, if won by the agency, will constitute a useful precedent that will increase the effectiveness of its litigation outlays in future cases and deter some future violations altogether.[2] Yet the case may seem trivial to observers who ignore its precedent-setting significance.

(2) If outcome were a function solely of the parties' litigation expenditures, whenever they spent the same amount on the case the probability of the agency's winning would be 50 percent. But we know that agencies win on average a good deal more often than 50 percent of the time and that defendants on average probably spend more per case than agencies. Plainly, outcome also depends on the relative skill and experience of counsel, the state of the precedents, and how the law allocates the burdens of production and persuasion between the parties. Other things being equal, the agency will prefer to bring cases in which its expenditures are relatively more effective than the defendant's, especially since the less effective the defendant's expenditures are the less he will spend on the litigation; this will increase the impact of the agency's outlays still further.

Once it is accepted that the probability of the agency's prevailing varies across cases, it becomes easy to show that the agency may prefer the easier case to the harder even if the easier case is substantially less important to it. Suppose that, starting from an initial allocation of equal resources to cases A and B, the agency can increase the probability of prevailing in A from 60 to 65 percent by spending $1000 more on A and $1000 less on B and that this reduces the probability of its prevailing in B from, say, 80 percent to 70 percent. Suppose further that the agency can increase the probability of prevailing in B from 80 percent to

---

2. What if a loss by the agency would create a bad precedent? How does this consideration affect the analysis?

95 percent by spending $1000 more on B and $1000 less on A and that this reduces the probability of its prevailing in A from 60 to 55 percent. The expected utility generated by its initial allocation was $100 \times .60 + 50 \times .80$, or 100. Its expected utility from reallocating $1000 from B to A would be $100 \times .65 + 50 \times .70$, or 100. But its expected utility from reallocating $1000 from A to B — the big case to the small one — would be $100 \times .55 + 50 \times .95$, or 102.5, which is greater than under the alternative allocations.

If we enrich our simple model, the result is to confirm that the rational maximizing agency will often exhibit a strong, and perfectly sensible, preference for small cases. We assumed that the number of cases brought by the agency was a given; but number of cases brought, like expenditure per case, is one of the agency's choice variables. As an agency brings more and more cases of a particular type, its total expected utility will rise, but probably at a diminishing rate.[3] It becomes more difficult to find cases that are easy to win. The probability of success therefore declines. The higher the rate at which the probability of success declines with the number of cases brought, the fewer cases will be brought, other things being equal. Probably the rate will be higher in classes of relatively important cases than in classes of relatively unimportant cases. The universe of minor violations is ordinarily larger than the universe of major ones: one does not "run out" of cases that are easy to win so soon.

We also assumed that the budget of the agency was independent of its performance. This is clearly wrong: the agency that won no cases one year could expect a reduction in its appropriation the next. The legislature will withhold appropriations when it thinks the agency is failing to use its resources efficiently and we have seen that an exclusive concentration on large cases could be an inefficient use of resources.

Finally, we ignored settlements, although most criminal and administrative as well as most ordinary civil cases are settled rather than litigated. This fact is likely to make small cases even more attractive to the agency. A defendant will not contest a case if the cost of his defense would exceed his stakes in the case. Such cases are therefore easy for the plaintiff to win unless the plaintiff's stakes are also no greater than his costs, in which event

3. This is illustrated in Figure 21, which plots probability of winning on the vertical axis and number of cases on the horizontal axis. The area under the curve to the left of n (the number of cases brought) would, if multiplied by the utility of winning n cases, equal the total expected utility of bringing n cases.

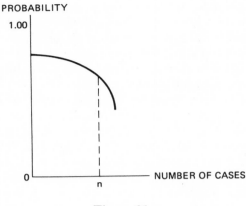

Figure 21

the plaintiff's threat to sue (and thereby compel the defendant to incur litigation costs) will not be credible. If the stakes of the parties are not equal, and the stakes to the plaintiff are greater than his litigation expenses but the defendant's stakes are less than the defendant's litigation expenses, the plaintiff should be able, at trivial cost, to induce the defendant to capitulate. This will be a class of small cases since the defendant's stakes must be smaller than his litigation costs. (The plaintiff's stakes must be larger but presumably the disparity is normally confined within a fairly narrow range.) Here then is another reason why we would expect to find the rational maximizing agency concentrating a seemingly disproportionate amount of resources on small cases. In sum, the agency that took its critics' advice to "reorder its priorities" by allocating a larger part of its resources to big cases would often experience diminished effectiveness.

§26.3. *The right to counsel.*   We suggested earlier one possible justification for requiring the state to provide counsel to indigent criminal defendants;[1] here we suggest another. The model developed in the preceding section teaches that a prosecuting agency's success depends on winning as many cases (weighted by their importance) as possible, as cheaply as possible. Since it will often be cheaper to convict a defendant who is not represented by counsel than one who is, even if the former is innocent and the latter guilty, prosecutors might have an incentive to

§26.3. 1. See §19.2 *supra.*

prosecute innocent indigents.[2] Such an incentive is socially undesirable since it imposes socially unproductive punishment costs, reduces the deterrent effect of criminal punishment,[3] and deflects prosecutorial resources from areas where they could be employed more productively from the standpoint of society. The right to counsel can thus be defended as a method of imparting correct incentives to prosecutors.

§26.4.   *Exclusionary rules of evidence.*   Since an enforcement agency's success depends in significant part on the probability of its winning cases, it will have an incentive to violate the defendant's procedural rights. Those rights ordinarily increase the cost to the agency of winning, or, what is the same thing, reduce the probability of the agency's success at any given level of expenditure compared to what it would be if the defendant did not have such rights. Since the profit to the agency from violating a procedural right is the successful prosecution that the violation makes possible, a logical sanction, if unconditional deterrence of such violations is desired, is to forbid the agency to use the fruits of the violation in its prosecution of the defendant. This is the effect of the rules that bar the direct or indirect use by the prosecution of illegally obtained evidence.

But is this an appropriate case for unconditional deterrence? The police cannot negotiate with potential criminal or noncriminal victims of unlawful searches or coercive interrogations the surrender of their rights for an appropriate price; the transaction costs would be prohibitive. Thus the appropriate rule would be to permit infringements subject to a duty to pay damages.

This has seemed an inappropriate course because it has been assumed that the principal victims of the violations, criminals convicted on the basis of the illegal evidence procured by the violation of their procedural rights, would not be entitled to substantial damages and so the deterrent effect of the approach would be nil. This may be a good prediction of how courts and juries will react; but in principle at least the costs to the convicted criminal of his punishment, assuming conviction would not have been possible without the illegal evidence, are the proper measure of his damages. There is, to be sure, a sense in which society is better off as a result of the criminal's having been convicted rather than set free, but if this were really believed to be true, the protection of the Fourth and Fifth Amendments would

---

2. What does this statement imply about the social control of prosecution?
3. See §25.6 *supra*.

be confined to people who were innocent. Since criminals are accorded rights under these provisions, society must attach a positive value to a criminal's remaining at liberty as a result of the constraints that the Constitution places upon the criminal process.

It might appear that in the present context conditional deterrence would have the same effect as unconditional deterrence: to cancel the punishment. But this is incorrect. Even if the defendant is paid damages equal to the cost to him of the punishment attributable to the illegally seized evidence, it does not follow that the police and prosecutor have gained nothing by the use of that evidence. They may consider the punishment worthwhile.[1] The exclusionary rule may thus overdeter violations of the constitutional protection.

SUGGESTED READINGS

1. Gary S. Becker & George J. Stigler, Law Enforcement, Corruption, and Compensation of Enforcers (unpublished manuscript, U. of Chi. Grad. Sch. of Bus. & Dept. of Econ.).

2. Richard A. Posner, The Behavior of Administrative Agencies, 1 J. Leg. Studies 305 (1972).

PROBLEMS

1. How should Congress and the Internal Revenue Service determine the proper level of investment in the enforcement of the federal tax laws? Suppose it is estimated that, last year, taxpayers evaded the payment of $10 billion in taxes. Should the government spend up to $10 billion to collect these taxes? Suppose the IRS has no idea how much evasion there is in the aggregate, but knows that for every additional dollar it spends on enforcement it collects $300 in additional revenue. Is this sufficient reason for spending more money on enforcement? What if the IRS increases its expenditures until an additional dollar brings in only $.75 in additional revenue? Is this conclusive evidence that the service is now spending too much?

2. As mentioned in this chapter, the Internal Revenue Service offers informers a reward of 10 percent of the unpaid taxes collected. Is this too much or too little? Would 100 percent be an appropriate reward? Could a figure higher than 100 percent be defended?

---

§26.4. 1. If the defendant was extremely dangerous, the benefits to society from incarcerating him, and thereby preventing him from committing further crimes during the period of incarceration, might exceed the costs to him of incarceration.

CHAPTER 27

THE ADMINISTRATIVE PROCESS

§27.1. *Two views of the administrative process.* The independent regulatory agency is an interesting combination of legislative, litigative, and enforcement functions. A brief discussion of its salient characteristics will serve to wrap up some of the themes of this part of the book.

We begin with a discussion of two contrasting views of the nature and problems of the independent agency. The traditional view holds that the administrative process is well designed to increase the efficiency of legal regulation but that the administrative agencies are characteristically mismanaged, due primarily to bad appointments both of agency members and of staff; hence, with better personnel their performance could be expected to improve greatly. A newer view, which draws on economic analysis, argues that the structure of the administrative process is designed to increase political control over the process of legal regulation rather than to increase efficiency but that within the constraints imposed by the fundamentally political purpose of regulation the evidence is consistent with the hypothesis that the agencies, like most other organizations, are rational utility maximizers. Both branches of the newer analysis suggest that the performance of the agencies would not be changed markedly by a change in personnel policies. To test the competing hypotheses, we first examine the principal reasons that have been offered for the view that the structure of the administrative process is designed to increase the efficiency of legal regulation.

§27.2. *Delegation.* The original rationale for the creation of independent agencies such as the Interstate Commerce Commission was that they were necessary in order to relieve Congress of some of the burdens of legislation. The idea was that Congress could not deal efficiently with the technical, particularized, and rapidly changing problems of a complex modern industry such as railroading. Also it was hoped that by delegation to an appointive agency certain highly charged problems could be taken out of politics and resolved in accordance with neutral criteria, such as efficiency. All this seems a rather unconvincing explanation for the creation of the independent agencies. The regulation of railroads and of other industries that have been brought under the administrative process could just as well have been delegated to the courts, whose traditional province is precisely to formulate rules governing relatively technical economic activity using (as we have seen) neutral, apolitical criteria such as efficiency. One can argue that the case method constrains the legislative flexibility and effectiveness of courts, but since the agencies have with rare exceptions relied exclusively on the case method as their legislative technique the argument provides little basis for preferring agencies to courts. Certainly the agencies have proved more susceptible to political influence than courts. Their more specialized jurisdiction subjects them to closer scrutiny by congressional appropriation subcommittees, through which the political influences that play on Congress are transmitted to the agency, and to closer attention by the industries that they regulate.

Perhaps the real purpose of delegation is not to improve the technical functioning of the legislative process, but precisely to assure a more sympathetic enforcement of policies *not* motivated by efficiency goals than could be expected from the courts. There is a natural antagonism between judicial and legislative attitudes, although it has been muted since the courts stopped avowedly giving narrow, grudging interpretations to statutes "in derogation of" the common law. Judicial rule making tends toward efficiency maximizing while the legislature gives greater weight to the redistribution of wealth. If Congress enacts a statute designed to reduce efficiency, such as the first Interstate Commerce Act, which facilitated the cartelization of the railroad industry, or the later Reed-Bullwinkle Act, which placed an explicit congressional imprimatur on cartel pricing in the industry, naturally it will also vest enforcement of the statute in an agency more likely to be sympathetic to the statutory purposes than the courts because the agency is responsive to the same political pressures that brought about enactment.

§27.3. *Combination of functions.*   A heralded innovation in the administrative process was the administrative agency's looseness of structure. It would be able to issue rules, bring cases, decide cases, conduct studies, propose legislation, and so on. The combination of functions was thought a source of strength — a tribute to vertical integration bestowed by people who frequently condemned it in other contexts. In practice, the most significant combination has probably been that of prosecution and adjudication. The analogy to vertical integration here is worth pursuing. Vertical integration in business may enable cost savings due to the substitution of orders for contracts as the method of coordinating the different levels of production. In an agency where prosecution and adjudication are independent (the National Labor Relations Board and its independent General Counsel are an example), coordination is achieved formally, in the manner of contract. The prosecutor infers from the agency's decisions and opinions what kind of prosecutions will "sell," and the agency infers from the evidence, briefs and argument presented by the prosecutor (to the extent not offset by the defendant's presentation) where the need for remedial action is most acute. Where the functions are merged, a less formal, less documentary coordination is possible and this may have advantages. But the opportunity to reap these advantages has been greatly reduced by the rules, many now codified in the Administrative Procedure Act, requiring internal separation between prosecution and adjudication in order to protect the procedural rights of defendants.

Are these rules of separation necessary? They are. Otherwise the agency would have an incentive to follow procedures that frequently resulted in the imposition of sanctions on innocent parties. Such procedures are presumably cheaper than ones scrupulously designed to protect the rights of the innocent. The benefits of such procedures would accrue to the agency for they would enable it to increase the number of cases it won without exceeding its budget. The costs would be borne not by the agency but by those erroneously subjected to the administrative sanctions. Nor would the agency be too concerned about the reduction in deterrence that occurs when people who do not commit offenses still have a significant expected punishment cost, for most agency sanctions are preventive rather than deterrent in primary effect. The costs of being subjected to a Federal Trade Commission false-advertising order, for example, are not so great that the threat of such an order is likely to have a substantial deterrent effect;[1] but once an order is entered, it effectively prevents further violations by the party subject to the order because the law imposes heavy sanctions for violation of the order. Thus

§27.3. 1. See next section.

without some internal separation of functions, and probably a right of judicial review too, agencies could not be relied upon to establish an optimal rate of conviction of the innocent. Since, as in the case of criminal punishment,[2] administrative sanctions impose costs on defendants that are not simply transfers to someone else, the number of cases in which such a sanction is imposed on an innocent defendant is not a matter of indifference from the standpoint of efficiency.

§27.4.   *Administrative sanctions.*   The administrative agencies are oddly limited in the choice of sanctions to apply to violators of the laws that they administer. The normal remedy of the agency is the cease and desist order, in essence an injunction. The absence of other remedies is a frequent source of weakness and is inconsistent with the emphasis on flexibility that otherwise pervades the design of administrative agencies.

An example of the problems created by the absence of other remedies is provided by the Federal Trade Commission's (FTC) program of prosecuting sellers guilty of misrepresentation. If a seller is convicted in a commission proceeding, a cease and desist order is entered that forbids him to continue the misrepresentation and so prevents him from obtaining future profits from it. But his interim profits, obtained before the commission entered the order, are his to keep. Moreover, many misrepresentations are never discovered. Either the victim is unaware that he was deceived or, since he receives no bounty for turning in the seller to the FTC, does not deem it worth his while to lodge a complaint with the FTC. (Doubtless many people have no idea there is such an institution.) The appropriate sanction to achieve deterrence would be some multiple of the costs inflicted by the misrepresentation. The FTC has no power to apply such a sanction.

If it is unlikely that the commission's remedial machinery will be invoked by an injured consumer, it is quite likely that it will be invoked by a competitor of the alleged violator. Because the commission shoulders the litigation expenses that would otherwise be borne by the complainant in a private suit against the defendant, while the defendant is left to bear his own expenses in defending against the agency's suit, an incentive is created to invoke administrative processes to harass competitors. To illustrate, a firm that is losing sales to the new product of a competitor has an incentive to complain to the FTC that the advertising

2. See §25.6 *supra.*

for that product is deceptive, for if the commission files a complaint against the competitor the expenses of the prosecution will be borne entirely by the commission. The complainant has no incentive to avoid filing frivolous complaints; on the contrary, they increase the costs of his competitor relative to his own.

In an effort to overcome the weaknesses of its remedial powers, the FTC has recently taken to issuing orders that are punitive in intent and substance, although not in form. It has required advertisers found guilty of misrepresentation to include affirmative recantations in their subsequent advertising. The effect is to make that advertising extremely costly to the firm. The recantation requirement is defended as necessary to dispel the false impressions that the public may have received from the misrepresentations, but this justification, difficult to prove or to limit, may be a makeweight. The real point may be that the commission has discovered a method of imposing heavy costs, equivalent to a penal sanction, on violators of its rules.

The combination of prosecution and adjudication within the agencies and their lack of effective sanctions are related: the proponents of the administrative process were willing to trade severe sanctions for greater procedural flexibility, recognizing that the courts would not permit strong sanctions to be applied in a process that diverged appreciably from the conventional litigation system with its elaborate panoply of procedural rights. The trade has turned out to be a bad one from the standpoint of the agencies. The Administrative Procedure Act (and related legislation) has made administrative procedures very similar to judicial ones; however, the agencies' remedial powers have not been appreciably strengthened.

§27.5.   The behavior of administrative agencies.   If the analysis in the preceding sections is correct, and if the goal of the administrative process is efficient legal regulation, the structure of the process is a source of weakness rather than strength. The structure is rational, however, if its purpose is to support the politicization of regulation.[1] This interpretation meshes nicely with the evidence, discussed in an earlier chapter, that legislative regulation of the economy is guided by political rather than efficiency considerations, and with the analysis of the political process that explains why efficiency considerations so often take a back seat to distributive ones in legislative activity.

Nor is the evidence for the contrary view — that the failure of

§27.5. 1. See §23.5 *supra*.

the agencies to achieve efficient results is due to accidents of their behavior that could be remedied with superior personnel — persuasive. We have discussed one piece of such evidence already — that the agencies are preoccupied with trivial cases.[2] Another is that agency personnel are frequently paid lower salaries than their counterparts in the private sector and, a related point, that they frequently leave the agency for better paying jobs with the industry regulated by the agency. The inferences frequently drawn from this evidence are that agency personnel are inferior, that they are subtly corrupted in the performance of their duties for the agency by the prospect of employment by the regulated industry, and that the turnover of agency personnel is excessive. In fact the evidence is equally consistent with the inferences (1) that agency personnel are hired by the industry because the specialized training and experience acquired while working for the agency increase their productivity in that industry compared to alternative employments,[3] and (2) that agencies are able to attract competent people at salaries lower than private employers would have to pay precisely because the training and experience imparted by the agency enhance the lifetime earning power of the employee, a benefit for which he pays in the form of temporarily lower wages. Under this view, the hiring of the agency's employees by the regulated industry carries no implication of a reward for past favors, and the relatively low wages paid by the agency carries no implication that its employees are substandard.[4]

It remains to consider the mechanisms by which an agency and its staff are prevented from using resources wastefully. There is first the ambition of the agency members. Their aspirations for higher office or well-paying private employment are enhanced if they earn a reputation for efficiency. There is second the legislative appropriations process. The competition of agencies for appropriations corresponds to the competition of business firms for capital. The inefficient firm fares poorly in the capital markets; the inefficient agency presumably loses appropriations to its more efficient rival. Congressmen in general would appear to have nothing to gain from squandering taxpayers' money on feckless or extravagant bureaucrats.

Since the output of an agency is not sold in a market and is

2. See §26.2 *supra*.
3. See Ross D. Eckert, What Do Regulatory Commissions Maximize? (unpublished manuscript, Dept. of Econ., U. So. Calif. 1972).
4. Is it clear that the agency is harmed by the fact that former employees often represent litigants before the agency? Why not?

therefore difficult to evaluate, and since the incentives of Congressmen are complex, the discipline of the appropriations process is probably weaker than that of the capital markets.[5] And the absence of competition in any product market removes an important source of pressure to minimize costs. The average agency may therefore be somewhat more corrupt and less well managed than the average business firm; but the difference is probably less than conventionally supposed.

When we suggest that the typical administrative agency may be reasonably efficient we mean efficient in its use of its own resources. There is no presumption that the agency is trying to maximize the efficiency of the activity that it is regulating. But whatever the legislature's goal, it will be ill served by an agency that squanders its resources and so one predicts that such behavior will be rare. We may also predict that where an agency is involved in an activity that becomes politically untenable, the result will not be a reduction in the agency's activity at the same level of budgetary support — which would be wasteful. Rather, either the agency's budget will be cut or its activities redirected toward a goal approved by the dominant political authorities. The second direction will of course be preferred by the members of the agency and can be expected to be taken more often.

PROBLEM

The question of delay in administrative proceedings presents an interesting example of the conflict between the view that administrative agencies are created to serve the public interest but frequently fail to do so because of bad policies or personnel, and the view that the agencies are in fact designed to promote the interests of effective political groups — which they do more or less efficiently. Is delay always inefficient? And can you think of cases where delay helps or hurts particular interest groups affected by administrative action? Cf. §9.3 supra.

---

5. On the other hand, the agency, unlike the business firm, has to return to its capital market every year. An agency has no retained earnings.

CHAPTER 28

A NOTE ON JURISPRUDENCE

The basic theme of this book has been the profound relationship between legal and economic order. If there is such a relationship, it may be possible to deduce the basic formal characteristics of law itself from economic theory; that at least is the endeavor of this chapter.

Law is often defined simply as a command backed up by the coercive power of the state. By this definition, any order emanating from the sovereign power is law. But that strains the ordinary meaning of the term and it has been suggested that the definition, to be descriptive of the way in which the term is actually used, must include the following additional elements: (1) to count as law, a command must be capable of being complied with by those to whom it is addressed; (2) it must treat equally those who are similarly situated in all respects relevant to the command; (3) it must be public; (4) there must be a procedure by which the truth of any facts necessary to the application of the command according to its terms is ascertained.[1] These elements are part of the economic theory of law.

The basic function of law, in an economic perspective, is to alter incentives. This implies that law does not command the impossible, since a command impossible to fulfill does not alter the incentives of the person subject to it. If a person is told that he will be fined heavily unless he changes a radish into a strawberry, he will not change a radish into a strawberry. The impossible command is to be distinguished from the legal sanction that is unavoidable only because the cost of avoidance is greater than the cost of the sanction. There is no incongruity in making the party who breaches a contract liable in damages in a case where

---

1. See John Rawls, A Theory of Justice 237–239 (1971), and references cited there.

he had no real choice because the cost of performing the contract would have greatly exceeded the damages from nonperformance (or even because performance would have been literally impossible). The law has simply placed the risk of nonperformance on the party who fails to perform. The proper criticism of the various pockets of strict liability in the criminal law (e.g., reasonable mistake no defense in a prosecution for bigamy or statutory rape) is not that they are inconsistent with the idea of law but that the risk imposed is greater than the circumstances warrant.

The requirement that law must treat equals equally is another way of saying that the law must have a rational structure, for to treat differently things that are the same is irrational. Economic theory is a system of deductive logic: when correctly applied, it yields results that are consistent with one another. Insofar as the law has an implicit economic structure, it must be rational; it must treat like cases alike.

Law, viewed in the economic perspective as a system for altering incentives and thus regulating behavior, must also be public. If the content of a law became known only after the events to which it was applicable occurred, the existence of the law could have no effect on the conduct of the parties subject to it. Stated otherwise, the economic theory of law is a theory of law as deterrence, and a threat that is not communicated cannot deter.

Finally, the economic theory of law presupposes machinery for ascertaining the existence of the facts necessary to the correct application of a law. As mentioned previously,[2] the deterrent effect of law is weakened (and in the limit would disappear) if enforced without regard to whether the circumstances are those to which the law was intended to apply. Suppose there is a law against price fixers but no effort is made to ascertain who is fixing prices; instead, one in 10,000 people is selected at random and punished as a price fixer. Then there will be no incentive to avoid price fixing. The only difference between the price fixer and the person who does not fix prices is that the former has profits from price fixing; the expected liability of the two is the same.

It would appear, therefore, that economic theory, although commonly viewed as an unmoral principle of social order, has ethical implications. It provides unexpected support to those who believe that not all commands backed by state force are entitled to claim obedience as law.

2. See, e.g., §25.6 *supra.*

PROBLEM

Can the idea of "justice," as it is used in discussions of law and legal rules and institutions, be deduced from the economist's idea of efficiency? If not, are justice and efficiency incompatible?

INDEX

(*cont.*)